THE ATHENÆUM PRESS SERIES

G. L. KITTREDGE AND **C. T. WINCHESTER**

GENERAL EDITORS

WILLIAM WORDSWORTH.

Athenæum Press Series

POEMS

BY

WILLIAM WORDSWORTH

A SELECTION EDITED BY

EDWARD DOWDEN

PROFESSOR OF ENGLISH LITERATURE IN THE UNIVERSITY OF DUBLIN

GINN AND COMPANY

BOSTON · NEW YORK · CHICAGO · LONDON
ATLANTA · DALLAS · COLUMBUS · SAN FRANCISCO

12-40441

The Athenæum Press

GINN AND COMPANY · PRO-
PRIETORS · BOSTON · U.S.A.

In Memoriam

M. D.

PREFACE.

————◆◆◆————

THIS volume gives, as far as the space permits, what I
believe to be Wordsworth's best poems in the best text.
With a very few exceptions all the pieces chosen by Matthew
Arnold are included; but considerable additions to these
have been made. Doubtless every lover of Wordsworth's
poetry will regret the absence of something which he highly
esteems. This is inevitable; but I trust that nothing is
admitted which a lover of Wordsworth will consider unde-
serving of a place. The Selection is not designed as a substitute for the complete Poetical Works ; it is rather hoped that
readers as they use this volume will keep by them the Poetical Works, in any edition which preserves Wordsworth's own
arrangement. The best text in one volume is that edited
by the most learned and accurate of Wordsworth scholars
— Mr. Thomas Hutchinson. A chronological table, such as
may be seen in the seventh volume of the Aldine edition,
will be found useful.

Matthew Arnold's choice of poems was excellent ; his
choice of a text was not judicious ; probably his own early
associations of pleasure were with that inferior text. In
some instances he did what was illegitimate, — he silently
manufactured a text of his own, such as Wordsworth had
never sanctioned or seen, by piecing together readings from
more editions than one. The text here given is that which

Wordsworth finally approved; and, besides being the author-
itative, it is, on the whole, the best text.

Wordsworth's general design in arranging his poems necessarily disappears from a volume which does not include
" The Excursion " as a whole. The chronological arrangement has been adopted as the most instructive to a student.
In the Political Sonnets, although they are only a selection
from the series, the sequence, as determined by Wordsworth,
has been followed.

I hope that some readers will not trouble themselves with
the notes, and that all readers will sink into the beauty of
the poems before they concern themselves with questions as
to dates, occasions, sources, or text. But if notes on Wordsworth's poems are to be read, it will be found profitable to
pay careful attention to the variations of text. From no
other poet can so much be learnt as to the craftsmanship of
the poetic art. In the Aldine edition I recorded the more
interesting various readings. The same facts, with reference
to most of the poems included, are here set down; but in
many instances I have added what I suppose to have been
Wordsworth's reason for the changes which he made, and in
the Introduction I encourage the student to think out for
himself, in other instances, the motives of the poet. If a
distinction may be made between textual and literary criticism, I think I may claim that these textual notes are also
in the truest sense literary.

Errors in matters involving a multitude of details are, I
know, sure to occur; but I hope that the mistakes in my
attempted record of facts do not largely exceed the inevitable margin of error.

E. D.

ADDENDA.

Two books of importance to students of Wordsworth have appeared since the Introduction to the present volume was written : " A Description of the Wordsworth and Coleridge Manuscripts in the Possession of Mr. T. Norton Longman," edited, with notes, by W. Hale White (Longmans, Green & Co., 1897), and " Poems in Two Volumes by William Wordsworth, reprinted from the original edition of 1807 ; edited, with a note on the Wordsworthian Sonnet," by Thomas Hutchinson (London, David Nutt, 1807).

Mr. Hutchinson has called my attention to evidence furnished by Dorothy Wordsworth's " Recollections of a Tour made in Scotland " (ed. Knight, vol. I, pp. 187, 202), proving that Wordsworth was in Scotland in 1801. He believes that " To a Skylark " (p. 204) was probably written on this occasion.

" The Affliction of Margaret —— " (p. 186) is preceded in the Longman MS. copy by twelve lines " written for the ' Lyrical Ballads.' " The poem may be earlier than 1804.

P. 376. The alterations in " Ruth," effected in 1805 and 1815 (described in the paragraph following the two stanzas printed), were made in deference to Coleridge's misgivings on the point of " ventriloquism " in poetry : *i.e.*, throwing the writer's sentiments into the body of the characters of the poem. See Coleridge's letter to Southey, July, 1802 (S. T. C.'s Letters, vol. I, p. 387), and Crabb Robinson's Journal, Aug. 13, 1812.

P. 415, note on ll. 77, 78. The stanza in MS. referred to is as follows:

> He wore a Cloak, the same as women wear,
> As one whose blood did needful comfort lack :
> His face look'd pale as if it had grown fair :
> And, furthermore, he had upon his back,
> Beneath his cloak, a round and bulky Pack ;
> A load of wool or raiment, as might seem ;
> That on his shoulders lay as if it clave to him.

P. 422 (date of "When to the Attractions"). Lines 80–83 of this poem were probably written before July, 1802, for they seem to have suggested words of Coleridge in a letter to Southey of that date (S. T. C.'s Letters, vol. I, p. 372).

P. 428 ("The Highland Girl," ll. 49–52). Note from Virgil's tenth Eclogue as parallel, perhaps as Wordsworth's original:

> Atque utinam ex vobis unus, vestrique fuissem
> Aut custos gregis, aut maturae vinitor uvae!

From this Eclogue Wordsworth afterwards borrowed the name Lycoris.

P. 433. The measure of "Yarrow Unvisited" is that of "Leader Haughs and Yarrow," by Nicol Burne, found in the "Roxburghe Ballads."

P. 457. Lines 9–11 of the "Song at the Feast of Brougham Castle" perhaps owe something to Hudibras, bk. ii, canto i, ll. 567, 568:

> That shall infuse eternal spring
> And everlasting flourishing.

For several of the above notes I am indebted to Mr. Hutchinson's private communication and to his admirable edition of the "Poems" of 1807.

CONTENTS.

The figures in parenthesis refer to the pages of the Notes.

SONNETS.

POLITICAL SONNETS.

MISCELLANEOUS SONNETS.

INTRODUCTION.

I. FACTS OF WORDSWORTH'S LIFE.

WILLIAM WORDSWORTH, the second child of John Words-worth, an attorney, was born at Cockermouth in Cumberland, on April 7, 1770. His mother, whose maiden name was Anne Cookson, was the daughter of a mercer at Penrith. The Wordsworths were an old and respectable Yorkshire family; but if we are to trace an inheritance of genius, it must rather be sought in the poet's maternal ancestry. The boy, physically vigorous and active, was of a moody and violent temper. In 1778 his mother died, and in the same year he was sent to the grammar school at Hawkshead, close to Esthwaite Lake, where he remained, boarding in the cottage of a village dame, for about six years. A record, deeply interesting, of the growth of his mind during those years may be read in the opening books of his autobiographical poem, "The Prelude." Under William Taylor (idealized as the "Matthew" of his poems) and other masters Wordsworth became a good Latin scholar; he read for his amusement in Fielding, Swift, Cervantes, and Le Sage; but the chief influences of the time were those of woodland and fell, lake and mountain; in these he had more than the common delight of boyhood — his animal gladness was often spiritualized, or startled and awed by imaginative perceptions and feelings. Already as a schoolboy he had begun to write in verse; and among these early compositions, he tells us, was "a long poem running upon my own adventures, and the scenery of the country in which I was brought up."

Before his fourteenth year was complete Wordsworth had lost his father. He passed with his brothers — Richard, afterwards a solicitor, Christopher, the future Master of Trinity College, Cambridge, and John, who was to become a sailor — under the guardianship of uncles, and in 1787 was entered as a student at St. John's College, Cambridge. In consequence of having a considerable start of his fellow-students in mathematics, he had abundance of leisure time. He did not aim at university distinctions, but read classical authors for his pleasure, studied Italian under an acquaintance of the poet Gray, Agostino Isola, learned some French and a little Spanish, and enjoyed, without excess, the social pleasures of the place. The periods most stimulating to his mind were the long vacations; the summer of 1788 was spent among the English lakes; in 1789 he wandered amid the beautiful scenery of Derbyshire and Yorkshire with his sister Dorothy and her friend Mary Hutchinson, both dear companions; in the following year — during the early days of the French Revolutionary movement — he accomplished, with his college friend Robert Jones, a pedestrian tour, unusual at that time, through France, Switzerland, and the Italian lake country, returning by the Rhine. His first studies of English landscape are embodied in his early poem "An Evening Walk"; his continental travel furnished the material for "Descriptive Sketches." These poems were separately published in 1793.

Having taken his degree, Wordsworth spent the spring months of 1791 in London, entering with much imaginative interest into the life of the great city. During the summer he was with his friend Jones in North Wales; they toured on foot through valley and by stream, and climbed Snowdon by moonlight to witness from its summit the break of day (see

"The Prelude," B, xiv). Wordsworth's views as to a future career were unsettled; and desiring to acquire the French language more thoroughly, not uninfluenced also by the new hopes and aspirations of France, he left England in November of the same year to reside for a time at Orleans. As he passed through Paris he chose for his souvenir a pebble from the ruins of the Bastille. Somewhat austere of character and trained to simplicity of living, he accepted almost instinctively a republican faith; but this did not advance into distinct consciousness as a social and political creed until at Blois he came under the influence of a remarkable and admirable man, Michel Beaupuy, who afterwards highly distinguished himself as an officer in the Republican army. Wordsworth's interest in external nature now became subordinate to his interest in man; he looked for the speedy advent of a better age, when the inequalities of society should be redressed, when empty pomp should be abolished, when the injustice of power should cease, and when the people should be the framers of the laws under which they lived. In October, 1792, he was in Paris, and was deeply agitated by the events of the time; he would gladly have thrown himself into the political struggles of France, believing that one pure and energetic will might effect much. But his circumstances recalled him to England, and in December, after a year of memorable experiences, he was once more in London. For a time he was doubtless occupied with the superintendence of his "Evening Walk" and "Descriptive Sketches" as they passed through the press.

Although in 1793 Wordsworth defended the French Revolution in a letter to Watson, Bishop of Llandaff (posthumously published), the course of events gradually alienated his sympathies; he lost faith in the leaders of the movement and exulted when tidings reached him of the death of Robespierre; he found it difficult to retain faith in the people of France ; he still clung to the doctrine of the Revolution, but this support, too, gave way ; his entire view of moral and social questions became confused, and for a while he fell into a state of profound discouragement. The declaration of war against the Republic shocked his feelings ; and yet his heart could not be wholly given to France. Gradually, and by obscure processes, his mental health was restored ; his belief in the Revolutionary theories was gone ; but he gained even a deeper sense of the dignity of man, a deeper interest in human joys and sorrows ; he felt the sanative touch of nature ; hope returned to him in a purified form. And during the dark hours his sister's influence was one of healing ; her sense of beauty was as quick and sure as his own ; she had not perplexed her soul with tangled speculations ; her temper was gentler than his ; her sympathies were, not deeper indeed, but more delicate ; she lived less in ideas than he, but came nearer to a thousand little, yet precious, realities.

In the summer of 1793 Wordsworth, in company with his friend William Calvert of Windybrow, Keswick, visited the Isle of Wight. The sight of the fleet off Portsmouth, preparing for war, filled him with gloomy anticipations ; and as he wandered, a little later, for two days over Salisbury Plain, the thought of the calamities of the poor, consequent upon war, weighed upon him. From such reflections originated that powerful narrative of suffering and crime named, when first published in full in 1842, " Guilt and Sorrow." Having seen Stonehenge, Salisbury, and Bath, he journeyed by the Wye to the home of his friend Jones in Denbighshire. On the way he visited Tintern Abbey, and at Goodrich Castle met the little cottage girl of his " We are Seven." The remainder of the year was spent with his friend in Wales. But the North of England and his desire for his sister's presence drew him away. With her—an indefatigable pedestrian — he explored parts of the lake country in the days of spring, and again, alone or in her company, when the woods and hills showed their autumn colors. From the Calverts' house near Keswick he consulted a friend as to the possibility of his obtaining work as a journalist, and he even conceived the notion of starting a monthly miscellany under the title of "The Philanthropist." Such schemes were little suited to the genius of the poet; and, happily for literature, the generosity of a dying friend, whose confidence in Wordsworth's powers must have supported his own declining life, delivered him from the necessity of alien task-work. Early in 1795 young Raisley Calvert died, and it was found that he had made Wordsworth possessor of the sum of £900. We are all debtors to that young man, whose good deed, inspired by insight and faith, enabled a great poet to devote himself to his high calling.

How and where the summer of 1795 passed is uncertain; probably for part of the time Wordsworth was in the North of England, for part of the time in London. It is likely that he first met Coleridge in this year at Bristol, but the meeting did not yet lead to close intercourse or friendship. The loan of a house at Racedown, Dorsetshire, by the son of Mr. Pinney, a Bristol merchant, and the proposal of Basil Montague that he should take charge of his little boy, made Wordsworth's way clear; and now the possessors of an income of £70 or £80 a year, he and his sister entered into occupation of the Racedown farmhouse in the days of autumn. For a time he was engaged upon imitations, never published, of the satires of Juvenal, but for satire he had no real vocation. The more ambitious enterprise of a tragedy occupied him until the summer of the following year; but "The Borderers" was not published until 1842. It is deficient in action and wholly unsuited to the stage; yet the characterization

of Marmaduke, the ardent youth who leads the band of
borderers, and of his tempter Oswald, is not without power;
remarkable acquaintance is shown with what may be called
the psychology of the passions ; moral problems are skill-
fully probed; and certain passages deserve to be remembered as poetic interpretations of deep things of the heart
and conscience. The rejection of the drama when offered
to Covent Garden Theatre was, however, natural and was
right.

During the summer and autumn of 1796 there may have
been meetings with Coleridge, and when on the last day of
that year Coleridge took up his abode in the cottage at
Nether Stowey, the acquaintance ripened with a diminished
distance between the two homes. In June, 1797, Coleridge
was a guest at Racedown, and felt himself "a little man"
by Wordsworth's side. The story of "Margaret," incorporated in "The Excursion," but then known as "The Ruined
Cottage" and "The Borderers," were read aloud ; and Coleridge in return repeated a part of his tragedy "Osorio."
In July the Wordsworths accompanied their new friend
to Nether Stowey, and Coleridge felt not only the power
of Wordsworth's genius, but also the charm of his "exquisite sister" — "her information various ; her eye watchful in minutest observation of nature ; her taste a perfect
electrometer. It bends, protrudes, and draws in at subtlest
beauties and most recondite faults." During the visit Charles
Lamb also made a brief sojourn at Nether Stowey.

The presence of Coleridge and the beauty of the Nether
Stowey district were strong inducements to a change of
residence ; and it fortunately happened that a spacious
house at three miles' distance, surrounded by beautiful
grounds, Alfoxden, was to be obtained at a trifling rent.
Hither in mid July came Wordsworth with his sister, and
for a time Coleridge and the Wordsworths were "three

people, but one soul." A delightful record of their daily life remains in the journal of Dorothy Wordsworth ; but the spirit of the season is best of all discovered in the poems of her brother which were written at Alfoxden ; in those which are narrative there 's a deep inquisition into the permanent passions of humanity ; in those which are personal there is the wisdom of a calm but radiant joy. To this period belong *Simon Lee*, *The Last of the Flock*, *The Thorn*, *Her Eyes are Wild*, and also *Expostulation and Reply*, *The Tables Turned*, *Lines Written in Early Spring*, *To My Sister*. On an autumn excursion on foot to the Valley of Stones, with Wordsworth and his sister, Coleridge's *Ancient Mariner* was planned, and as poems multiplied in manuscript, the joint volume of " Lyrical Ballads " was designed. Coleridge's contributions were meant to ennoble romance by allying it to truth of human feeling ; Wordsworth's, to shed an ideal light over reality. The volume, which opened with " The Ancient Mariner " and closed with " Lines Written a few Miles above Tintern Abbey," was issued late in the year 1798 by Cottle, a friendly publisher at Bristol. Before the " Lyrical Ballads " appeared, the two poets, accompanied by Dorothy Wordsworth, had left England (September 16) to spend the winter in Germany.

At Hamburg they parted, Coleridge proceeding to Ratzeburg, Wordsworth and his sister to Goslar, close to the Hartz forest. It was a lifeless town, in which the English visitors saw little or no society, and the winter was one of extreme severity. Wordsworth's heart and imagination turned fondly to his native country ; he walked daily on the ramparts, or in the public grounds, having for his sole companion a glancing kingfisher ; but in thought he was among the English woodlands and meadows. During these months of ice and snow he composed the " Lucy " group of poems, " Ruth," " Lucy Gray," " Nutting " and " The Poet's Epi-

taph." "The Prelude," a poetical record of the growth of
his own mind, was conceived in outline, and some fragments were written. On Jan. 4, 1799, Coleridge informs a
friend that "Wordsworth has left Goslar and is on his road
into higher Saxony to cruise for a pleasanter place." He
seems to have quitted the old town permanently some weeks
later (February 10); his precise movements we cannot follow, but we know that on April 20 or 21, in passing through
Göttingen, he saw Coleridge; that he made speed to arrive
at Yarmouth, and proceeded thence to visit the Hutchinsons at Sockburn-on-Tees on the borders of Durham and
Yorkshire.

On October 26 he was still at Sockburn when Coleridge
returned from Germany, and, having Cottle for his companion, came to see their friend. Almost immediately the
three started for a tour to the English Lakes; at Greta
Bridge Cottle parted from the others, and the travellers were
joined by Wordsworth's brother John. Desirous to find a
place of abode, Wordsworth was much attracted to Grasmere, and noticed a small house, at the part of the village
known as Townend, which was vacant. A little later the
small house was taken; and in midwinter, with his sister,
Wordsworth proceeded chiefly on foot from Sockburn to
Grasmere, a wild journey, but full of enjoyment; they entered their cottage on the evening of December 20.[1] On
the way, near a spring about three miles from Richmond,
a peasant had related to them the tradition which forms the
subject of "Hart-leap Well."

With Dove Cottage, Grasmere, much of Wordsworth's
noblest poetry is associated. It was chiefly composed in
the open air, while he sat in his cottage garden or roamed
among the hills; and strong as was his frame of body, he
was often exhausted when evening came, by the intensity

[1] St. Thomas' Eve, not as commonly stated St. Thomas' evening.

of his imaginative excitement. His manner of life was in the utmost degree simple and frugal, but he and his sister were rich in the best pleasures of the mind; and small as was their dwelling, they found space in it for hospitality. Their brother John, their beloved friend Mary Hutchinson, Coleridge and his wife, were visitors at Dove Cottage in the year 1800. By the close of that year a new edition of " Lyrical Ballads," with an added second volume, was ready for publication. Among the poems which now appeared were " Michael," " The Brothers," " Ruth," and " Poems on the Naming of Places." To the first volume was prefixed a remarkable preface, setting forth certain principles which guided the poet in his art, and expounding his views on the subject of poetic diction. Later editions of " Lyrical Ballads " were published in 1802 and 1805.

The year 1801 was one of pause in Wordsworth's creative activity; he modernized the old poem "The Cuckoo and the Nightingale," Chaucer's " Prioresse Tale," and a passage from Chaucer's " Troilus and Cressida," but produced little original work. In the spring of 1802 his imaginative energy reawakened; almost every day some new lyric came into existence or was carried towards completion, and now for the first time he studiously cultivated the sonnet. At the close of July, taking advantage of the short peace with the French, he crossed the channel with his sister and spent a month at Calais. Wordsworth's sympathies were now detached from France and were wholly given to the land of his birth; his views of the French people and their ruler, his fears and hopes for England, are expressed in a series of admirable sonnets written on the seacoast of France or in London after his return. But public interests did not entirely occupy his heart; he had obtained the promise of Mary Hutchinson that she would be his wife, and on Oct. 4, 1802, the marriage was cele-

brated at Brompton in Yorkshire. It was a marriage founded
on deep affection and one full of blessings for his entire
life. Mary Wordsworth was not beautiful in person, except
as goodness creates a beauty of its own; her temper of
happy tranquillity and love, her steadfast household energy,
her wisdom of good sense, her womanly strength, her sure
instinct for literary beauty made her a fitting wife for
Wordsworth. How deep were his joy, his tenderness, and
his unwavering love may be read in the last book of "The
Prelude," in the stanzas "She was a Phantom of Delight";
in the poem, among those on the "Naming of Places," "To
M. H.," in the lines beginning "Oh, dearer far than life or
light are dear"; and in the touching sonnet "To a Painter,"
written after thirty-eight years of wedded life :

> Morn into noon did pass, noon into eve,
> And the old day was welcome as the young,
> As welcome and as beautiful — in sooth
> More beautiful as being a thing more holy :
> Thanks to thy virtues, to the eternal youth
> Of all thy goodness, never melancholy ;
> To thy large heart and humble mind, that cast
> Into one vision future, present, past.

Mary Wordsworth survived her husband some years, dying
on Jan. 17, 1859 ; she was buried by his side in Grasmere
churchyard.

In June, 1803, Wordsworth's first child — a son — was
born, and two months later, accompanied by Dorothy, and
for part of the way by Coleridge (who since 1800 had resided at Greta Hall, Keswick), he visited some of the most
interesting scenes in Scotland. A detailed account of the
tour is given in the journal of Dorothy Wordsworth, a record
inspired by the delight of wandering, and showing everywhere the writer's exquisite sensibility to natural beauty.
Some of her brother's most radiant and spiritual poems

belong to this Scottish tour. In the first week Wordsworth looked upon the grave of Burns; in the last at Lasswade he made the acquaintance of his great contemporary, Walter Scott. Scott partly read for the travelers and partly recited, in an enthusiastic style of chant, the first four cantos of "The Lay of the Last Minstrel"; he accompanied them to Rosslyn, met them again at Melrose, and was their guide up the Teviot to Hawick, with a legend or ballad, says Lockhart, on his lips associated with every tower or rock they passed.

During the year 1804 Wordsworth was at work upon "The Prelude," which, before December closed, had reached the eleventh book. Early in the following year came the first great sorrow since his boyhood. His brother John, captain of an East Indiaman, perished in the wreck of his ship (February 5) two miles from Weymouth Beach; to the last his bearing had been calm and in every way exemplary. John Wordsworth was a man of high character, a lover of literature, a lover of nature, and the sympathy between the brothers had been complete; they had not met since their parting at Grisdale Tarn on Michaelmas day, 1800. Wordsworth conveyed something of his brother's spirit into his poem "The Happy Warrior," which presents a lofty ideal of heroic manhood; his sense of the discipline of pain is expressed in the "Elegiac Stanzas, suggested by a Picture of Peele Castle." His grief was deep and abiding; his joy in life was, indeed, not quenched, but the happiness that continued to be his took upon itself a sober coloring. He threw himself upon poetical work, partly as a refuge from pain, and by the middle of May, 1805, had brought "The Prelude" to a close.

The sorrow which matured Wordsworth's mind was turned to wise uses, and there were new sources of gladness to set over against the sorrow. Voices of children cheered his home ; Dorothy was born in 1804, Thomas in 1806 ; and the cottage growing narrow for his household, he accepted for the winter of 1806–1807 the offer made by his friend Sir George Beaumont, a landscape painter of some distinction, of a farmhouse at Coleorton in Leicestershire. Here he was visited by Coleridge, lately returned from Italy, and his son Hartley. The old friendship was renewed under sadder circumstances, for Coleridge's abiding mood was one of dejection only veiled by transitory cheerfulness. He had taken with him to Malta five books of " The Prelude" in manuscript ; and now the remainder of that poem, which belonged in a special sense to him, was read aloud. His homage to Wordsworth's spiritual power and strength of purpose, and the pathetic sense of his own infirmities, were poured forth on the night of the recital of " The Prelude " in memorable verse.

During his residence at the Coleorton farmhouse, Wordsworth composed the " Song at the Feast of Brougham Castle," in which the spirit of chivalry is expressed, and at the same time is controlled by the spirit of a finer and deeper wisdom. Here, too, he saw in proof the last pages of two small but inestimable volumes, the " Poems " of 1807.[1] They contain a series of noble sonnets, the poems of the Scottish tour, many lyrics of external nature, the record of fortitude in " Resolution and Independence," and the Ode afterwards named "Intimations of Immortality from Recollections of Early Childhood." The reception of these volumes by the reviewers was far from favourable; but Wordsworth's "faith in the whispers of the lonely Muse " was not dependent on the public journals. " Trouble not yourself," he wrote to Lady Beaumont, " upon their present reception ; of what moment is that compared with what I trust is their destiny? — to console the afflicted ; to add

---

[1] The earlier proofs were sent to the printer from Grasmere.

sunshine to daylight by making the happy happier ; to teach the young and the gracious of every age to see, to think and feel, and, therefore, to become more actively and securely virtuous ; this is their office, which I trust they will faithfully perform, long after we (that is, all that is mortal of us) are mouldered in our graves." The political sonnets in the volume of 1807 show how ardently Words- worth entered into the struggle maintained by England against the dominance of Napoleon Bonaparte. He looked upon his native country as now the champion at once of freedom and of order ; and his reliance was not on her material strength, but on the awakened moral energy of the people and the righteousness of a great cause. Two years after the appearance of the " Poems," he published an elab- orate pamphlet on " The Relations of Great Britain, Spain, and Portugal," criticising, with great severity, as dishonour- able, and therefore in the highest sense impolitic, the Con- vention of Cintra. He looked at events not from the point of view of a military expert, not even from the politician's point of view ; but as one who saw that all present good and all hope for the future resided in the spiritual virtue of a nation. The people of the peninsula had risen against an intolerable tyranny ; no temporary advantage in warfare, even supposing such an advantage were gained, could com- pensate the evil caused by an arrangement which thwarted or checked the noblest passions of an outraged race. No political prose so ardent and so weighty with solemn thought had been written since the days of Burke ; but events had moved rapidly ; when Wordsworth's pamphlet appeared the Convention was an accomplished fact of the past. His pas- sionate meditation fell upon unheeding ears, yet it remains as a lofty interpretation of moral truths which exist inde- pendently of the occasion that called it forth. Another remarkable piece of Wordsworth's prose belongs in its earliest form to the year 1810 — his "Guide to the Lakes," originally prefixed to a volume of "Views" drawn by the Rev. J. Wilkinson. In it the poet exhibits his mind working in an analytic way; he appears as a profound and searching student of the characteristics of landscape; he handles with complete intellectual mastery the matter which in his verse is rendered for the emotions and the imagination.

After a visit to London in the spring of 1807, Wordsworth returned, in company with Scott, to Coleorton. Later in the year he saw, for the first time, the beautiful country that surrounds Bolton Priory in Yorkshire, and gathered from its history and tradition material for "The White Doe of Rylstone," half of which was composed at Stockton-on-Tees, in November and December. When he reëntered his Grasmere cottage the poem was continued, but it remained unpublished until 1815. It is less a narrative of material events and outward action than of a process of the soul; yet with the purification through suffering of the spirit of his heroine, Wordsworth finely connects something of the decaying feudal temper and manners, something also of the beauty and the pathos of external nature; while in the doe, which is partly a gentle woodland creature and partly a spirit of fidelity and love, he finds, as it were, a visible presentment of the sanctity of Emily's moral being. The poem is one that grew from a sorrow chastened and subdued; it tells of the higher wisdom which came to Wordsworth himself through the discipline of affliction.

Dove Cottage was now hardly habitable by the Wordsworth household. On returning from London, whither he had been drawn by alarming accounts of Coleridge's health, Wordsworth, with his family, moved in the summer of 1808 to Allan Bank, a newly built house, situated upon a small height on the way from Grasmere to Easedale; and during the winter and for upwards of a year that followed, Coleridge, then engaged upon his periodical "The Friend," was their guest. For some time De Quincey was also received as a member of the household. A second daughter — Catherine — was added to Wordsworth's family, and in May, 1810, a son — William — his last-born child. Not many of his shorter poems belong to the period of residence at Allan Bank; he was for a time occupied with his Convention of Cintra pamphlet, and for a time with his essay on the district of the Lakes; but he also worked much upon "The Excursion." When it was published in 1814 the public, then and during subsequent years engaged with Byron's poems and the Waverley novels, cared little for it. "The Excursion" indeed made a large demand upon the reader's thought and sympathy ; it embodied a philosophy of life, which could interpret itself to the public only by degrees ; it spoke of things which could be but slowly realized. Five hundred copies sufficed for the sales of six years ; but Wordsworth bore neglect with equanimity. "I shall continue to write," he says to Southey, "with, I trust, the light of Heaven upon me."

Allan Bank, with smoky chimneys and damp walls, did not prove a very comfortable place of residence ; the proprietor required it for his own use ; and in the spring of 1811 Wordsworth took up a temporary abode at the parsonage close to the church at Grasmere. It became next year a home of sorrow. On June 4, 1812, little Catherine, a child of most engaging disposition, died after a short illness; on December 1, Thomas, the best-beloved of the household, was lost. The father and mother could not endure to remain where every object oppressed their hearts with mournful remembrance ; they felt it dutiful to seek the means of recovering tranquility. About two miles distant from Grasmere a beautifully situated dwelling-place — Rydal Mount —

was about to become vacant ; and in the spring of 1813 Wordsworth entered into possession of that house in which his remaining years were spent.

He had been fortunate in obtaining the post of distributor of stamps in the county of Westmoreland ; the salary was £400 a year and the duties were not oppressive ; his means, though not large, were yet sufficient. It was decided that John the elder of his two surviving sons, should receive an University education ; and while instructing the boy, Wordsworth revived his own interest in classical literature. His " Laodamia" and " Dion " are among the fruits of these studies in the classics ; they have a dignity of expression, a poise of feeling, which contrast with some of his earlier poems. In 1814 Wordsworth again saw Scotland, was guided by Hogg, the Ettrick Shepherd, to Yarrow, and recorded in song his visit to that romantic stream. Yarrow was revisited many years later, in 1831, but the occasion had much of sadness, for at that moment Scott, broken in strength and spirits, was about to leave his home, seeking in vain for health in Italy. The year 1815 is memorable chiefly as that in which Wordsworth first collected his poetical works, and rearranged certain of them in groups corresponding to the faculty with which the grouped pieces are most clearly connected, — Poems of the Imagination, Poems of the Fancy, Poems of Sentiment and Reflection. A preface set forth Wordsworth's views respecting the powers requisite for the production of poetry, its various kinds, and the distinction between fancy and imagination ; the earlier preface to " Lyrical Ballads " was reprinted as an appendix. The poetry written in the year which followed the appearance of these volumes was chiefly suggested by political events. With the battle of Waterloo a great period of national struggle had closed ; what the poet had prayed for and hoped was now accomplished ; and he poured forth his gratitude and joy in the "Thanksgiving Ode" and other kindred pieces which were published in 1816. That England should keep what now had been won seemed to Wordsworth more important than to seek for new things ; his temper naturally grew more conservative ; the danger from a foreign tyranny was at an end, but he feared internal dangers from a rash spirit of reform ; he regarded the feudal power still surviving in England as a needful counterpoise to the popular power, already, as he believed, far in excess of the degree of knowledge and the standard of morals attained by the masses. In 1818 Wordsworth opposed with energy the candidature of Brougham for the representation in Parliament of the county of Westmoreland, and published two "Addresses to the Freeholders," in which he pleaded against overweening reformers as "the vanguard of a ferocious revolution." Little verse was written in that year ; but to it belongs one poem of high spiritual import, that "Composed upon an Evening of Extraordinary Splendour and Beauty." His interest in earlier unpublished work, if it had declined, now revived; "Peter Bell," written long before, in the Alfoxden days, and "The Waggoner," a poem of 1805, were published separately in 1819 ; they were ridiculed, — and "Peter Bell," admirable as are many passages, lent itself to ridicule, — but they were read, and when, in 1820, a new edition of Wordsworth's miscellaneous poems was called for, these were included as a part of the collection. In the same year appeared the beautiful sequence of sonnets in which is traced the course of the river Duddon.

It was long since Wordsworth had travelled on the continent. In the autumn of 1820, accompanied by his wife and sister and a few friends, he journeyed by the Rhine to Switzerland and the Italian lakes, returning by Paris. Journals kept by Mrs. Wordsworth, by Dorothy Wordsworth, and by Crabb Robinson, who joined the tourists at Lucerne, record the course and incidents of travel. A series of verse

memorials of the tour was published by Wordsworth two
years later. After a visit to his brother at Cambridge and
to Sir George Beaumont at Coleorton, he was again at Rydal
Mount by the close of 1820. He had assisted Sir George
Beaumont to choose the site of a church about to be erected,
and not long afterwards he sent his friend certain sonnets in
remembrance of the occasion. The question of Catholic
emancipation, now occupying the attention of Parliament,
kept his thoughts directed to matters connected with the
Church, and it occurred to him that certain points in the
religious history of the country might be advantageously
presented to view in verse. Hence originated the "Ecclesiastical Sonnets," published with the title "Ecclesiastical
Sketches" in 1822, and as he proceeded the first design
expanded in his hands beyond the bounds of England. In
later reprints additions were made, nor did the series reach
its final completion until 1845. In early life Wordsworth
had found spiritual promptings, guidance, and support chiefly,
in his own soul and in the influence of external nature; with
advancing years he came to value highly the organization of
religion, the communities of worship, the worth of authority
and tradition, the infusion of a spirit of piety through rites
and ceremonies. He had not lost the gains of his youth,
but he added to them others which came with a closer in-
corporation in the society of his fellows.

There is little of external incident to record in Wordsworth's elder years. The happy monotony of life at Rydal
Mount was varied by occasional moods of creative impulse,
and by more frequent wanderings from home in summer or
autumn. In 1823 he travelled with his wife in Belgium and
Holland; the next year their holiday was in Wales. When
Sir George Beaumont died, in 1827, an annuity of £100 was
left by him to be spent by Wordsworth in a yearly tour. In
1828 Coleridge was his companion on an excursion to Bel-

gium and the Rhine ; a year later he visited Ireland ; was again in Scotland in 1831 and in 1833 ; and in 1837, when approaching the age of seventy, he saw for the first time Rome and Florence. Many of his later verses are connected with these summer wanderings. Only two new volumes of poetry appeared after the publications of 1822 ; one of these was " Yarrow Revisited and Other Poems " (1835) ; the other, " Poems, Chiefly of Early and Late Years " (1842), in which was included the tragedy of " The Borderers." But as successive editions of his collected writings appeared, he added now and again to their contents ; and he occupied himself much in the revisal of previous work.

Many alterations were effected in the texts of 1827 and of 1832. For the stereotyped edition of 1836–1837 a thorough revisal was undertaken, which, though the improvements are many, was certainly carried too far ; in 1840 and in 1845 further improvements were introduced, but in not a few instances he wisely restored the earlier readings. When in March, 1843, Southey died, Wordsworth became his successor to the laureateship ; in 1844 Sir Robert Peel placed his name on the civil list, with a pension of £300 a year. He had received from Oxford in 1839 the honorary degree of D.C.L., and when Keble, as Professor of Poetry, presented him to the Vice-Chancellor, the Sheldonian Theatre rang with applause.

Two matters of public interest called him into activity in these declining years ; he took strong views as to the rights of authors with respect to copyright ; and he was a vigorous opponent in 1844–1845 of the proposed Kendal and Windermere Railway. He did not undervalue the benefits to be expected from railways in their legitimate application ; but the particular scheme in question seemed to him inappropriate and ill judged ; " the staple," as he expressed it, of the Lake district " is its beauty and its character of seclusion and retirement"; and he held that the gains likely to result from the contemplated intrusion would not compensate the sacrifice.

Wordsworth at length had attained to honor and to widespread influence. But one who reaches his years must needs endure sorrow. His sister had for long been an invalid, weakened in intellect. His sister-in-law, Sarah Hutchinson, to whom he was much attached, died in 1836. Scott, Coleridge, Lamb, Crabbe, Hogg, Felicia Hemans, had all passed away. In 1847 his beloved daughter Dora, who had become the wife of Edward Quillinan, died, and Wordsworth, at the age of seventy-seven, had not strength to recover from the blow ; all that he could attain was resignation underlying the passion of grief. But his time of sorrow was not long drawn out. On Sunday, March 10, 1850, he received a chill, which resulted in pleuritic inflammation. During his illness his thoughts were often with his lost Dora. At noon on April 23 he peacefully breathed his last. Westminster Abbey, though his marble figure is seated there, is not his resting-place. His body lies, with the bodies of those dearest to him, in Grasmere church-yard, below the hills that his feet had so often trodden, and among the rural folk whose joys and sorrows he had interpreted to the world.

Several portraits of Wordsworth exist ; that by Haydon, the subject of a fine sonnet by Elizabeth Barrett Browning, best renders the strength and brooding passion of his countenance. The forehead was ample ; the eyes not large, but capable of deep spiritual illumination; the nose slightly arched ; the mouth expressive of force ; the cheeks furrowed. In figure Wordsworth was tall, and neither slight nor massive. His over-fervid temperament caused him at an early age to look older than he actually was. A portrait by Pickersgill, which the poet himself approved, hangs in the hall of St. John's College, Cambridge ; but its expression of weak amiability is the reverse of characteristic. A bust by Chautrey's pupil, Angus Fletcher, is faithful in outline and has caught the meaning of his face.

In social converse he was grave, but animated, ready to receive and ready to communicate. He took a deep and kindly interest in the concerns of his humbler neighbors. On his visits to London during his later years he entered freely into society, and could be genial in the company of younger men, even when their opinions on moral and social questions differed widely from his own. He read what pleased him and what he considered best, but he had not the wide-ranging passion for books of a literary student.

II. CHARACTERISTICS OF WORDSWORTH'S GENIUS.

WITH many men of genius high powers conflict one with another, or operate singly and fail in mutual help. Nothing is more characteristic of Wordsworth than the harmony existing between the several faculties of his nature ; his various powers not only act in unison, they seem, as it were, to interpenetrate one another, each living and moving in its fellow. Byron's genius impresses us as a magnificent but warring chaos ; his nobler impulses were met and baffled by his baser passions ; and the cynicism of "Don Juan" is the result. With Keats, sensation sometimes tyrannizes over reflection. In Coleridge the will failed to sustain imagination and thought, and so his works became fragmentary. There was a practical side to Shelley's mind, but he reserved it for his prose ; in verse, if not a visionary, he is almost a pure idealist. It is seldom indeed that complete intellectual and moral conciliation is effected in any one of us. The spirit wars against the senses, and the senses against the spirit ; the intellect distrusts the imagination, and the imagination shrinks back from the intellect ; the real and the ideal seem to be opposed or to stand wide apart ; now the outward gains upon us, and again we take refuge in the citadel of the soul ; passion and conscience are at odds ; excitements mar our tranquillity or some dulness hangs weights of lead upon our nobler excitements ; our desire for freedom rebels against obedience to law, or we give ourselves up to the ease and bondage of customs, conventions, unrealized creeds ; we observe, accumulate, analyse, and lose the unifying and vivifying power of the mind ; our manhood scorns or laments our youth, our old age wearies of the interests of our manhood. In Wordsworth's nature and in Wordsworth's work a harmony is effected between faculties and moods, which with most men are rivals for possession of supreme or exclusive power. The special character of what he achieved is happily defined by Mr. Aubrey de Vere, as consisting " First, in the unusually large number of qualities, often not only remote from each other, but apparently opposed to each other, which are represented by his higher poetry ; secondly, in the absolute unity in which these various qualities are blended ; and thirdly, in the masterful moral strength which results from their united expression. . . . In his best poetry the diverse elements of the human intellect and of the human heart are found, not only in greater variety, but in a closer and more spiritual union than in any other poetry of his time."

Two of his senses, and those the senses most needful for a poet's uses — eye and ear — were susceptible of the finest impressions ; a third sense, from which poetry derives some contributions, as readers of Herrick and of Keats must be well aware, — that of smell, — was with Wordsworth absolutely lacking. Noticing when a boy of fourteen the strongly accentuated outlines of the branches and leaves of an oak which stood out against the evening sky, it struck him that an infinite variety of natural appearances remained still unrecorded in poetry, and he resolved to supply in some degree the deficiency. His feeling for colour and his feeling for form were alike fine and strong. The tones of his colouring are not exaggerated ; they are those of nature. Take, for example, his description of the four yew trees of Borrowdale :

> a pillared shade
> Upon whose grassless floor of red-brown hue,
> By sheddings from the pining umbrage tinged
> Perennially — beneath whose sable roof
> Of boughs, as if for festal purpose decked
> With unrejoicing berries — ghostly Shapes
> May meet at noontide.

The solemn phantasy in this poem is supported by the most exact observation. Wordsworth's report of phenomena has a fidelity which gives it some of the unfathomable suggestiveness of nature. The following from " A Night Piece," describing the sudden apparition of the moon, from amid sundered clouds, may serve as one other example out of a thousand :

> He looks up, — the clouds are split
> Asunder, — and above his head he sees
> The clear Moon, and the glory of the heavens.
> There, in a black-blue vault she sails along,
> Followed by multitudes of stars, that, small,
> And sharp, and bright, along the dark abyss
> Drive as she drives. How fast they wheel away,
> Yet vanish not ! The wind is in the trees
> But they are silent ; still they roll along,
> Immeasurably distant ; and the vault,
> Built round by those white clouds, enormous clouds,
> Still deepens its unfathomable depth.

Wordsworth's ear was sensitive in the highest degree to all the wandering voices and homeless sounds of nature ; but, while the processes of his mind had the logic of music, his appreciation of music as an art was slight, and he never applied himself, as Browning did, to its study. The song of the solitary reaper in its simplicity and suggestiveness is almost like the voice of the nightingale or the cuckoo. It is such words as

> The stationary blasts of waterfalls,

or

> Winds thwarting winds, bewildered and forlorn,

or

> Then sometimes in that silence, while he hung,
> Listening, a gentle shock of mild surprise
> Has carried far into his heart the voice
> Of mountain torrents,

that are most characteristic of Wordsworth as a student of sound.

But while his observations with eye and ear were close and exact, he was seldom a mere observer. He spoke somewhat slightingly of Scott's method of noting down the objects upon which his eye rested, and so securing in his descriptions a literal fidelity to fact. Wordsworth's special gift was rather to interpret than to describe. He gazed or listened in a "wise passiveness," contemplating, brooding, until the soul in things seemed to be drawn forth to meet his own spirit and to confer with it. There was a time, as he tells us, when the mere eye tyrannized over the other powers, when the sense of sight became an irresistible appetite; but it was a time of moral disturbance and dissonance, when his faculties were dislocated and refused to work together. The state of feeling which was normal with Wordsworth is expressed in the opening lines of his ode on "The Power of Sound" ·

> Thy functions are ethereal,
> As if within thee dwelt a glancing mind,
> Organ of vision ! And a Spirit aërial

> Informs the cell of Hearing, dark and blind ;
> Intricate labyrinth, more dread for thought
> To enter than oracular cave.

The spirit with him lives in the sense ; through eye and ear he comes into communion with the inmost life of things, and that life is felt as a spiritual activity. Accordingly, though there is a high austerity in Wordsworth's poetry, no writings tend less than his to asceticism, in the narrower meaning of that word. He cannot suspect his senses, for his senses are the inlets for influences of the soul.

Wordsworth's strength of intellect was as remarkable as the fineness of his senses. A large body of original thought could be brought together from his writings. It is not of every eminent poet that this can be said. Byron's power of reflection was not extraordinary. Shelley accepted *en bloc* from Godwin the body of intellectual doctrine which lies behind his poetry, doctrine vivified by his ardent feeling, and over which he threw the coloured web of his imaginings. But if we could conceive of Wordsworth as other than a great poet, we might still honour him as an original thinker. His mind did not indeed ordinarily proceed in the way of analysis and ratiocination (though of these he was capable) ; and he is at times somewhat less than just to scientific thinkers who, as he puts it, "murder to dissect." He was less interested in truth as a series of propositions than in truth as a vital power ; truth impregnated with feeling, and expressing itself in spiritual energy. He viewed nature, the individual man, and human society, not as consisting of a series of mechanical arrangements, but each as a living unity. And in the discovery of truth he brought to the aid of the analytic understanding on the one hand imagination, and on the other a faith which, as he conceived, could justify itself to the reason.

To suppose that Wordsworth's was a mild, gentle, tranquil nature, moved by no deep and strong passions, is a
vulgar error. He felt ardently and profoundly. But mere
passion did not dominate him and carry him away. His
emotions were illuminated by thought and were brought
into harmony with conscience ; they did not whirl him out
of his course, but bore him onward with a continuous impulse in his true orbit. No poet attains to clearer altitudes
of illuminated joy than Wordsworth, and, because he is
borne thither by no unworthy desire, he finds repose upon
the heights ; yet at the heart of his calm there is a quickening passion. Few poets have more truly represented an
arid anguish of the heart ; but as his genius and moral
nature matured he chose rather to exhibit sorrow in its
strengthening and purifying power. He has not often rendered into verse the passion of lovers ; but the group of
poems connected with "Lucy" give expression to profound
and tender feeling; and Wordsworth himself declared that
he deliberately turned away from this common theme of
poets because he feared, so deeply did it move him, that he
could not keep the treatment within due bounds. The
dramatic power which enables a poet to enter, as Shakespeare did, into a world of what we may call abnormal or
perverted passions, — hatred, revenge, jealousy, pride, the
lust of power, the rage for pleasure, — Wordsworth did not
possess. But he could interpret unerringly and in all their
fulness some of the strongest emotions belonging to the
best parts of our humanity : the parental passion, as in
"Michael," and "The Affliction of Margaret —— "; fraternal affection, as in "The Brothers"; wedded love, as in
the verses beginning "O dearer far than life and light are
dear"; the loyalty of friendship, as in the sonnet, "The Pine
of Monte Mario"; the ardour of religion, as in the sonnets
suggested by King's College, Cambridge. And in the

breadth and energy of his political feeling, as the "Poems Dedicated to National Independence and Liberty" amply prove, he may be placed by the side of Milton. It is, indeed, Wordsworth's strength in his total being which masks the power of passion in him. If his capacity for reflection had been less, if his conscience had not been ever in command, if his will had not been so steadfast, and if all of these had not been brought into harmonious and consentaneous operation, the force of the impulses that moved his heart would be more immediately felt.

Wordsworth distinguished between the Fancy and the Imagination — the one a faculty chiefly occupied in aggregating and associating, the other in modifying and creating. The inferior faculty he possessed, but in no extraordinary degree ; his highest self appears in work of the imagination. With some poets the imagination deserts reality ; they create an ideal world from slight hints and suggestions of the actual world which suffice to quicken into activity their genius for invention. Wordsworth's imagination rather discovers the ideal within the real. It modifies the appearance of things so as to bring out more adequately their inward life and being. It illuminates the world with "a light that never was, on sea or land" ; but this light is a truth of the human spirit, which reveals, as nothing else can, the meaning of the phenomena around us. It creates a region of beauty, wonder, joy for those who can enter there ; but this is not a region of illusion ; on entering it, we only come into possession of our rightful heritage. For him no opposition can exist between imagination and reason ; they operate together in the search for the truth of things. A poet whose genius is simply lyrical sings upon the impulse of the moment. The actual occasion of many of Wordsworth's poems was separated by a considerable interval of time from the hour of creation. What had been begotten of joy was afterwards brought forth by meditation. He recollected emotion in tranquillity, and revived it in a purer form. The dross of circumstances had been refined, and thought had nourished feeling before the poet's work came to the light. The ideal had gradually evolved itself from reality.

Memory and hope are fellow-workers in Wordsworth's poetry. At the basis of what he has written lay the cheerful faith, the optimism, of his age, but modified by individual reflection. He looked forward, though in no violent revolutionary spirit, to a great destiny for mankind ; he viewed the world as a high-school for the education of the individual mind ; much of his poetry is occupied with the subject of the loss and the recovery of faith, hope, imaginative power, wisdom, joy; he believed, moreover, in the immortality of the human soul. But some whose temper is optimistic think scornfully of the past, and some aspirants towards a higher future life belittle the present. Wordsworth did neither. He reverenced the past ; he had a sense of the continuity of human existence, both social and individual. He regarded the days of his own life, with all the modifications which sorrow and experience and deepening reflection brought, as " bound each to each by natural piety." And, in like manner, he felt that the life of a nation is a growing unity ; that the old order is not to be lightly cast aside ; that tradition and prescription are a precious heritage ; that new institutions must grow out of those received from our fathers. The man of genius whose gaze is wholly turned to the future runs the risk of advocating freedom at the expense of order ; he who lives wholly in the past may forget the expanding life of society, and become the champion of a traditional order which is incompatible with the growth of freedom. Examples of both dangers may be found in some of Wordsworth's contemporaries. Among them he appears as a reconciler. He knows the worth of freedom both for the individual life and for nations ; but he finds the truest freedom in willing obedience to the highest law.

It cannot be said that Wordsworth, like the poets who can project themselves out of themselves in epic and dramatic work, is a poet for all readers. What is characteristic of him is the synthesis between external things and his own mind and his own mood. He draws things towards himself and meets them half way ; what he writes is never purely objective. And hence he selects his audience ; to enter into his work we must have something of the Wordsworthian mind and temper. We could hardly say of any one whom Shakespeare or Homer left untouched that he had a true feeling for poetry. But many genuine lovers of the poetry of Shakespeare and Homer are unmoved by that of Wordsworth ; they cannot remain at the Wordsworthian standpoint, or they cannot advance towards things along the line by which he advances, and fail to reach that midway resting-place where the Wordsworthian synthesis is effected. They speak of him as an egoist ; and if it be egoism never wholly to escape from one's own personality and one's own peculiar manner of regarding objects, they are right.

In disinterested intellectual curiosity Wordsworth was deficient. He could not yield himself to what did not somehow bear upon his moral nature. He was not a discursive reader ; he was not deeply interested in the study of minds of a type wholly different from his own. Within a certain range he was a great critic, but as a critic he was profound rather than broad. He had little care for the scientific movement of his time ; he was repelled by Goethe ; he undervalued Byron ; he loved and honored Scott personally, but it may be questioned whether he ever felt aright Scott's power as an interpreter of human life. The

limitation of Wordsworth's intellectual interests was to a
certain extent a source of strength ; it saved him from
many distractions ; but one who is an exclusive disciple of
Wordsworth incurs some risk of narrowness. It is wise at
times to descend from the mountain-height, to quit the
pastoral valley, and to fare forth into the world and wave
of men.

He was deficient in one of the most liberalising gifts of
mind — a sense of humour. At rare times in his poetry, as
in some passages of " Peter Bell " and some passages of
" The Idiot Boy," Wordsworth shows an inclination for
frolic ; it is the frolic of good spirits in one habitually
grave, and he cannot caper lightly and gracefully. His
writings in all their extent hardly show more of humour than
this. He did not observe, or did not think fit to record,
the details of the social comedy so freely provided for our
entertainment ; and having attained to his own solution of
the problems of our existence, he had no feeling for those
ironies and incongruities of human life which give rise to
the finest kind of humour, those which are presented, for
instance, so genially and so pathetically by Cervantes. He
reverenced our nature, and could have no sympathy with
such cruel and bitter laughter as that of Swift. At one
time he attempted translations from Juvenal ; but the
laughter of indignation against vice and folly was not
Wordsworth's mode of expressing ethical feeling. He
teaches us many things ; but he does not teach us how to
laugh wisely and kindly. We cannot find a place for Falstaff in the scenes of " The Excursion " ; and a world
which excludes Falstaff is not the whole wide world ; but
we have excellent companions in the Pastor, the Solitary
and the philosophic Pedlar ; they teach us to think and to
love ; and thought and love should help us to laugh. If
Wordsworth's seriousness of moral temper needs to be

relieved, we find such a relief in his poetry through his delight in beauty. He speaks in one of his sonnets of "the mighty ravishment of spring," and some of that vernal rapture lives in his own verse.

III. WORDSWORTH IN RELATION TO HIS AGE.

WORDSWORTH'S originality as a poet does not consist in detachment from his age ; his poetry embodies some of the leading tendencies of his time, but in passing through his mind these were purified and ennobled. The years of his early manhood were those of the great Revolutionary upheaval in France, and Wordsworth was for a time an ardent partisan on the side of the Revolution. What remained to him of that early faith after the historical development of the movement in France had alienated his sympathies? The answer to this question has been so well given by Dr Edward Caird that little need be added to his statement. Of the so-called "return to nature" in the second half of the eighteenth century, a new feeling for the wilder and grander aspects of natural beauty in the visible world was a part. Rousseau, a prophet of the Revolution, had given eloquent utterance to this feeling. Wordsworth, endowed as he was with the finest sensibility of eye and ear and possessing a poet's imagination, was peculiarly well fitted to express this sentiment. He dealt with it not in a vague rhetorical way, but with all the advantages derived from exact observation, and a close, imaginative study of the facts of the external world. And because his temper was one of sanity, he did not, in the manner of some other writers inspired by the Revolution, set up — at least in his maturer work — any opposition between nature and human society. Half of

Byron's feeling for external nature lies in his recoil, sometimes rather rhetorical than real, from man and the conditions of humanity. Wordsworth, on the contrary, sees man
in connection with external nature, and interprets in his
poetry their spiritual interaction and coöperation.

A second note of the Revolutionary epoch is expressed by
the word " simplification."   This also had its exponent in
Rousseau, while in English literature it found a voice through
Cowper, Day (the author of " Sandford and Merton ") and
other writers.   It was a " return to nature " from luxury,
convention, ceremonial, the artificial life of courts and cities.
"God made the country," said Cowper, "and man made the
town."   The life of the peasant was supposed to be more
favorable for the true development of manhood than the life
of the courtier.   The Revolution did homage to man as man,
and professed to strip off and despise the accidental trappings of our humanity.   Dangers, however, accompanied
this cry for " simplification " — the danger of sentimentality,
the danger of extravagance, the danger of one-sided bitterness.   Each of these is abundantly illustrated by the literature of the time.   Wordsworth began, not with declama-
tions against luxury, but by simplifying his own life with a
view to accomplishing his proper work; " plain living and
high thinking " became his rule ; and therefore he could not
be a sentimentalist.   His strong good sense preserved him
from such extravagances and crude experiments as make certain passages in the life of Thomas Day read like scenes
from a comedy.   He did not plead for a recovery of bar-
barism ; simple as was his manner of living in Dove Cottage,
he and his sister enjoyed the cultured delights of the mind ;
Spenser and Ariosto, Dante and Shakespeare were their companions ; they desired to build up, not to pull down ; and so
they were free from bitterness.   When Wordsworth's early
faith in the French Revolution was lost, he did not lose his

sense of the dignity of plain manhood ; rather he realized this more fully, as it passed from the form of an abstract doctrine to that of a concrete experience.   He could discern all that makes our human nature venerable in a leech gatherer or a pedlar ; but neither of these appears in his verse as an indignant champion of the rights of man.   " Humble and rustic life," he tells us, " was generally chosen " for the matter of his poetry, " because in that condition the essential passions of the heart find a better soil in which they can attain their maturity, are under less restraint, and speak a plainer and more emphatic language ; because in that condition of life our elementary feelings exist in a state of greater simplicity, and consequently may be more accurately contemplated and more forcibly communicated ; because the manners of rural life germinate from those elementary feelings, and, from the necessary character of rural occupations, are more easily comprehended, and are more durable ; and, lastly, because in that condition the passions of men are incorporated with the beautiful and permanent forms of nature."

Wordsworth's deep sense of the worth of native manhood carries with it, almost of necessity, a faith and hope in the future destiny of man.   But the over-sanguine optimism of the Revolutionary period, which looked forward to a terrestrial Paradise, to be attained as soon as the last throne should be cast down and the last church demolished, was not Wordsworth's creed, or was not his creed for long.   He did not expect, or he soon ceased to expect, that the millenium was about to arrive as the result of any new political form or political combination ; but a conviction grew upon him that the whole frame of things is essentially good, and that there is a power in nature to breathe grandeur, even if not happiness, as he says, "upon the very humblest face of human life."   It was not that he shut his eyes to the evil or sorrow of the world; he saw these, and looked at them unflinchingly; but he seemed also to see through and beyond them, and to discover light as the cause of the shadow; and as he advanced in years his philosophic faith was strengthened by a faith distinctively Christian. "He can stand in the shadow of death and pain, ruin and failure, with a sympathy that is almost painful in its quiet intensity; yet the sense of 'something far more deeply interfused' which makes 'our noisy years seem moments in the being of the eternal silence'; the faith in the omnipotence 'of love and man's unconquerable mind' is never destroyed or even weakened in him. The contemplation of evil and pain always ends with him, by an inevitable recoil, in an inspired expression of his faith in the good which transmutes and transfigures it, as clouds are changed into manifestations of the sunlight they strive to hide."[1] And such convictions as these, while they necessarily tended to check extravagant hopes of any sudden advent of an age of gold, did not lessen his interest in whatever he believed might really tend to ameliorate the condition of society, influences for good with which he trusted that his own work as a poet might in its degree coöperate.

The war of England against the French Republic for a time caused a painful division in Woodsworth's feelings, and checked his sympathies with his native land. The defence of European liberty against the Napoleonic tyranny converted him into an English patriot. The struggle in Spain, which seemed to Wordsworth to be the uprising of a wronged and indignant people against their oppressors, not a war of monarchs or of dynasties, aroused his most passionate interest; his thoughts and feelings can be read in the political sonnets and in the pamphlet on the Convention of Cintra. The true strength of a nation, as he believed, resides not in

[1] E. Caird.

material resources, not in mechanical arrangements, not in the power of armies, not in natural advantages of frontier or mountain and flood, but in its moral temper, in the soul. And when at length Napoleon was overthrown, Wordsworth looked upon the victory not primarily as a military achievement, bnt as the triumph of moral forces.

The English people, he thought, had been tried and had stood the test. English institutions had undergone a prolonged strain, and they had borne it well. His attachment to the constitution, to the church, to all that is inherited and traditional, had grown strong, and he had come to regard with distrust some of those tendencies of his own day that made for change. Living among a peasantry who, compared with the shifting population of great cities, might be named aristocratic, and whose best feelings were bound up with permanent objects and interests, he feared the inroad of new forces which might disturb and confuse their hearts and lives. He rejoiced in the advance of modern science in so far as science served the cause of order in things intellectual ; in so far as it furnished guidance and support to the power of the mind when faring forth on its explorations ; in so far as the knowledge which it attained could be made subservient to moral or spiritual purposes. He distrusted science when it chained the spirit of man to merely material things, when it converted a human being into a mere lens for microscopic observation, when it resulted in mere accumulation of external details, or when its conjectures and hypotheses seemed to give the lie to truths of the conscience and the heart. Great mechanical and industrial progress was a feature of the time. Wordsworth could exult in every proof of intellectual mastery exercised over the blind elements, in the imparting of something almost like a soul to brute matter, in the growing dominion of man over the powers of nature. But he feared that man might be dazzled, not strengthened, by this newly acquired sovereignty ; that man might come to trust more in material resources than in moral power ; that mechanical progress might be pursued in a degree out of proportion to the real needs of society ; that the rage for wealth might convert wealth into the source of a new slavery ; that arts and inventions might forget human virtue; that the old domestic morals of the land and its simple manners might suffer an irreparable loss. Our century has shown that there were grounds for both his hopes and his fears.

The advocates of great political changes in England during the earlier years of the century were in the main spokesmen of the mechanical and industrial movement. A middle-class plutocracy did not excite Wordsworth's highest admiration. He loved the people ; he entered into their private joys and sorrows ; but he did not believe that either they or the lower middle class were qualified for political power, nor did he think that the possession of political power would add to the worth and happiness of their lives. And so he strenuously opposed the Reform Bill of 1832. He looked upon the Church as a great national institution for the spiritual education and spiritual sustenance of the people. He believed that the extension of the franchise to Roman Catholics would inevitably lead to the disestablishment of the Church, first in Ireland, afterwards in England. And therefore he resisted Catholic Emancipation. He did so, not in a spirit of intolerant bigotry, but, as he held, in the interests of the people, and in accordance with the logic of the English constitution. At a later time he was guilty of what to some persons will appear even a more flagrant act of hostility to the modern spirit : he set himself against the introduction of railways into the district of the English Lakes. But Wordsworth was not a belated prophet hurling anathemas against the steam-engine. Weighing the mischief against the promised gains, he concluded that the particular project of the Kendal and Windermere Railway would, if carried out, damage one of the most precious possessions of beauty still remaining to the British people, and he refused to be deluded by what he terms a false utilitarian lure.

The mechanical and materialistic tendencies of the time were to some extent met and held in check, at least with minds of a certain type, by what has been called the transcendental movement in thought, and at a subsequent date by the movement in the Church of England which had Oxford for its centre. With both of these Wordsworth was in sympathy — with the transcendental movement in his youth, with the High Church movement in his more advanced years. The former was in part a recoil from the turbid atheism, the abstract deism, and the dry orthodoxy of the eighteenth century. An emotional fervour had been infused into religion and philosophy ; God and nature and man seemed to draw near and to confer one with the other. In his highest imaginative moments Wordsworth became aware of a Presence in external nature and in the mind of man which he could not call other than divine :

> A motion and a spirit that impels
> All thinking things, all objects of all thought,
> And rolls through all things.

The forms and motions of external things, tumult and peace, the darkness and the light, were for him "characters of the great Apocalypse." In the law of conscience he recognized " God's most intimate presence in the soul." When with growing years he became better acquainted with suffering, trial, and human infirmity, he came to value more than he did at first all those aids to the spiritual in man which are afforded by institutions, customs, ceremonies, places, rites, ordinances, about which our best feelings have gathered and which are associated with our most sacred experiences. He found higher uses than he had formerly conceived in what is historical, in what is traditional. And if the Divine Spirit communicates with man through symbols in external nature, why also should not God speak to man through the symbols of the Church? In both phases of thought and feeling there is this in common — a sense that the soul can never rest satisfied with material things; that it is sought by God, and must seek after God if haply it may find Him. But at no time would Wordsworth have given his approval to a religion of mechanical pomp, to a system of spurious symbolism, or to gross rites, which, as he says, "trample upon soul and sense." His sympathy with the Oxford movement went as far as what we may call a transposed transcendentalism can go; but it went no farther. To the structure of Wordsworth's faith buttresses, and arches, pillar and traceried window were added; the basis remained as it had been from the first.

We have considered Wordsworth in relation to the political, the philosophical, and religious movements of his time; it remains to say a word of his relation to tendencies of a purely literary kind. Before "Lyrical Ballads" appeared, the reaction from the school of Pope and the poets of Queen Anne's reign was already in full operation. The new romance and the new sentiment had appeared in prose and verse. Walpole's "Castle of Otranto" had stimulated the imagination of the public with its crude revival of mediævalism, its gross horrors, mysteries, and marvels. Mrs. Radcliffe and Matthew Gregory Lewis followed, working in a somewhat similar manner upon a larger canvas. Percy's "Reliques," Chatterton's "Rowley Poems," Macpherson's "Ossian" aided in what has been termed the "renaissance of wonder" in English poetry. On the other hand, a realism, somewhat hard and dry, was powerfully exhibited in the poems of Crabbe. Wordsworth could not and would not desert reality for romance ; before all else he would be true to nature and to human life. But his genius did not lead him to a literal transcription of details ; he could not present facts in Crabbe's manner. What if reality could be shown in the light of the ideal, a light which reveals those truths that ennoble reality ? Would not this also effect something in the "renaissance of wonder," and in a better way than could be effected by the extravagances of romance? This was what Wordsworth attempted, and what he achieved. He was a great naturalist in literature, but he was also a great idealist ; and between the naturalist and the idealist in Wordsworth no opposition existed; each worked with the other, each served the other. While Scott, by allying romance with reality, saved romantic fiction from the extravagances and follies into which it had fallen, Wordsworth's special work was to open a higher way for naturalism in art by its union with ideal truth.

For such poetry a plain style was more appropriate than an ornate style. Wordsworth's theory of a poetic diction arose partly from the demands of his subjects, partly from his instinctive tendencies as an artist ; it was partly the result of a reaction from the artificial language, the gaudiness and inane phraseology of many eighteenth century writers; and it had also a certain connection with his democratic convictions and democratic feeling. He did not allege that poetry was written as men ordinarily speak, or that prose and poetry are identical. It was obvious that rhyme and metrical arrangement constituted an essential distinction of poetry. What Wordsworth maintained was that if to this distinction were added a second, — that the language employed by the poet should be a selected and purified diction derived from that really used by men, and especially by men in a state of vivid emotion, — the style of the poet was sufficiently distinguished. He desired freedom in expression ; he desired that language should vary with the theme, should rise and fall with the emotion expressed ; and he saw that an artificial poetic diction, common to all the poets of a period and applied alike to every subject, is fatal to poetic truth and freedom. He sought a language which should be rather the body than the robe of thought and feeling. In his practice there is no dignity of poetic language which he rejects when that dignity naturally arises out of his subject ; but he could not endure the system of plastering on verbal ornaments to suit a prevailing fashion. " I have," he says, " at all times endeavored to look steadily at my subject"; the right word, he believed, would arise from such a faithful intuition rather than from reference to a vocabulary accepted by other poets. It is true that in setting forth his theory he expressed himself less guardedly than could be wished, and so laid himself open to Coleridge's rejoinder in "Biographia Literaria." But, understood aright, Wordsworth's theory was essentially sound, and meant little more than this, — that the entire language of men is at the service of the poet, and that his selection from that language should be determined not by arbitrary rule or custom, but by the demands of the subject and the truth of the writer's vision and feeling. It was indeed an assertion of freedom in consonance with the spirit of his age ; it was part of a legitimate return to nature.

IV. DEVELOPMENT OF WORDSWORTH'S GENIUS.

SOME of the changes or modifications which came to Wordsworth's mind and temper have been already indicated. His earliest imaginative interests were those connected with external nature ; during his second residence in France an interest in man became predominant. Of his feeling for nature in boyhood the special characteristic was the union of an ardent physical joy with occasional moods of spiritual awe or spiritual rapture. His first published poems, "An Evening Walk" and "Descriptive Sketches," written in the favourite form of the eighteenth century, the rhymed couplet, and employing much of the eighteenth-century poetic diction, read like exercises or studies preparatory to his maturer work. The observation of nature is exact, but it is laboured; the details of landscape are skilfully composed, but the Wordsworthian interpretation of landscape is not in any high degree present. In the earlier poem the sights and sounds of evening, sunset, and moonrise in the Lake country are recorded almost with historical exactitude ; each noun has its studied epithet ; the cock, the swan, the wandering mother with her desolate children are each portrayed in a careful vignette; but the descriptions are little more than descriptions. If there be natural magic in any lines, it is in those which tell of the sound of streams unheard by day :

> While in sweet cadence, rising small and still,
> The far-off minstrels of the haunted hill,
> As the last bleating of the fold expires,
> Tune in the mountain dells their water lyres.

But here, instead of the Wordsworthian ideality, we have a touch of romance. "Descriptive Sketches" is more ambitious in its design than "An Evening Walk"; it paints scenes of greater variety upon a larger canvas ; and with its studious portrayal of Swiss and Italian landscape there mingles some of Wordsworth's revolutionary sentiment and doctrine. Now and again occurs a line or a phrase which is more than descriptive. "The unwearied sweep of wood," "The ringing woods of morn," "Dilated hang the misty pines," "A mighty waste of mist the valley fills, A solemn sea," — these are

words which do more than depict; they interpret for the
imagination; but such words are rare. In the wonderful
lines describing the Simplon Pass, written for " The Prelude,"
Wordsworth recovered an expression from " Descriptive
Sketches " — *black drizzling crags;* but observe how the
later lines are vital with imaginative energy, and the earlier
lines are little more than a record of observations:

> The immeasurable height
> Of woods decaying never to be decayed,
> The stationary blasts of waterfalls,
> And in the narrow rent, at every turn
> Winds thwarting winds bewildered and forlorn,
> The torrents shooting from the clear blue sky,[1]
> The rocks that muttered close upon our ears,
> Black drizzling crags that spake by the wayside
> As if a voice were in them.

Here is Wordsworth's mature manner; the life of the human spirit interprets the life of nature. In " Descriptive
Sketches " the text, as it were, of nature is studied, but the
meaning is caught only in fragments:

> By floods, that, thundering from their dizzy height,
> Swell more gigantic on the steadfast sight;
> Black drizzling crags, that, beaten by the din,
> Vibrate, as if a voice complained within;
> Bare steeps, where Desolation stalks, afraid,
> Unsteadfast, by a blasted yew upstayed.

Instead of effecting a complete fusion between the fact and
the imaginative feeling, the poet interposed his personified
figure of " Desolation."

Wordsworth's first narrative poem of importance was
" Guilt and Sorrow " (1791–1794), of which a fragment ap-
peared in " Lyrical Ballads " with the title " The Female
Vagrant." It is inspired by that sentiment for the wrongs

---

[1] This line also comes from " Descriptive Sketches."

suffered by the poor at the hands of society which was part of the Revolutionary temper. A soldier's widow, now desolate and impoverished, and a sailor, victim of the press-gang, who in his wild distress had murdered a man, meet in the ruins of the "Dead-House" on Salisbury Plain; the sailor next morning chances to discover his dying wife, surrenders himself to justice and is executed. In its earlier form the spirit of the poem was more stern and severe than we find it in "Guilt and Sorrow" as published in 1842. Here Wordsworth studies the workings of the human spirit in pain with unfaltering fidelity, and in the landscape of the poem there are a grandeur and a gloom which seem to correspond with and to dignify the human passions. But in "Guilt and Sorrow" there is little of that quality, found in later tales of suffering, which entitles Wordsworth to the name of a "son of consolation." The study of the passions here might almost be characterized as anatomical; indeed, it partakes too much of spiritual vivisection. And the same remark is in some degree applicable to the elaborate poem which followed, — the tragedy of "The Borderers." It is the custom with critics to speak slightingly, if not contemptuously, of Wordsworth's drama; no serious student of his poetry can afford to neglect it. "The Borderers" should be read not as a stage drama, to produce which Wordsworth was disqualified by his imperfect sympathy with action, but as the exhibition in dramatic form of imaginative inquest into moral problems; and read thus it will be found to be a work of no slight significance. When his faith in the principles of the French Revolution was strained and at length gave way, Wordsworth was driven back to an arduous research into the first principles of morals; this research conducted by the intellect alone, with such a mind as that of Wordsworth could not attain to a solid basis of belief; before assurance could be reached, all his higher faculties must coöperate, and then by a deep mysterious process — yet one which could be justified to reason, heart, and conscience — faith might be recovered, or re-created. In "The Borderers" he shows how a youth of generous spirit and lofty aspirations may be perverted from the truth by the influence of one who has blinded the moral instincts within him, and applied a powerful understanding to the disintegration of the truths of our spiritual nature. The lure of the tempter, Oswald, is that by the criticism of the understanding freedom from moral obligation may be attained, or a new and higher morality substituted for the old, and the bounds of man's intellectual empire may be so enlarged. His doctrines have something in common with those of a book which influenced many young minds in the Revolution days, as if it were a veritable scientific gospel, — Godwin's "Political Justice." The young leader of Wordsworth's borderers, Marmaduke, falls into the snare ; is guilty, though with no base intentions, of an irreparable crime, and discovering his error, devotes all his future life to penitential expiation. This could hardly be made the material of an acting play ; but it was fit matter for a searching moral exploration. "The Borderers " is Wordsworth's earliest study, of large dimensions, in human nature ; and the first sustained work of a great poet — whether a failure or a success — is always of importance in the development of his genius ; it sometimes serves as a key to much that follows.

The poems which appeared in "Lyrical Ballads " — and to these we may add, as belonging to the same period, "The Story of Margaret " ("The Excursion," Book i) and "Peter Bell " — exhibit a remarkable advance. Wordsworth had recovered faith, he had recovered joy, and his charity, less connected with abstract principles of universal fraternity and more with humble realities, had grown finer and more deep. Still there remained with him something of the Revolution ary contrast between nature, simple, beneficent, glad, and society, which so often does wrong to the life of the natural man. In the main the poems of this date fall into two groups, — those which tell of happy communing with nature, and those which present the passions of men and women who suffer through their affections. To the first of these groups belong such pieces as " Lines Written in Early Spring," "Expostulation and Reply," "The Tables Turned," "Lines Written a few miles above Tintern Abbey"; to the second group belong "The Thorn," "The Mad Mother," "The Complaint of a Forsaken Indian Woman," "The Last of the Flock," and "The Tale of Margaret." A motto for both groups might be found in a stanza from "Lines Written in Early Spring":

> To her fair works did nature link
> The human soul that through me ran;
> And much it griev'd my heart to think
> What man has made of man.

The poems of nature are not poems of observation and description; they are rather poems of contemplative passion. Wordsworth's mind submits itself to the object, but, while seeming to be passive, it reacts upon the appearances of nature; it infuses its own mood; each poem is the outcome of a synthesis between the "fair works" of the external world and the "human soul." The eye, as we are told, in the "Lines Written a few miles above Tintern Abbey," is "made quiet by the power of harmony," and by virtue of the "deep power of joy" the spirit sees "into the life of things." The poems which deal with the passions of humanity aim at following — as Wordsworth himself expresses it — "the fluxes and refluxes of the mind when agitated by the great and simple affections of our nature." His own statement of his design is worth more than the words of critics: "The

principal object proposed in these poems," he wrote in the
preface to the second edition of "Lyrical Ballads," " was to
choose incidents and situations from common life, and to
relate or describe them, throughout, as far as was possible,
in a selection of language really used by men, and, at the
same time, to throw over them a certain colouring of imagination, whereby ordinary things should be presented to the
mind in an unusual aspect ; and further, and above all, to
make these incidents and situations interesting by tracing
in them truly, though not ostentatiously, the primary laws of
our nature, — chiefly as far as regards the manner in which
we associate ideas in a state of excitement.   Humble and
rustic life was generally chosen. . . .   The language, too,
of these men has been adopted (purified, indeed, from what
appears to be its real defects, from all lasting and rational
causes of dislike or disgust), because such men hourly
communicate with the best objects from which the best
part of language is originally derived ; and because from
their rank in society and the sameness and narrow circle
of their intercourse, being less under the influence of social
vanity, they convey their feelings and notions in simple
and unelaborated expressions." [1]   It matters comparatively
little whether Wordsworth's statement of a theory of poetical
diction can be sustained in all its parts ; his practice was
an effort to express the truth of human passion, and even

[1] Since this Introduction was written, M. Legouis' admirable study,
"La Jeunesse de William Wordsworth," has appeared. He exhibits
the recoil from Godwin's teaching in several of the poems of "Lyrical
Ballads"; Godwin's homage to the reason is replaced by a reverence
for the deep instincts and primitive passions of man. See his remarks
on "The Mad Mother," "The Idiot Boy," "Simon Lee," "The Old
Cumberland Beggar." Of the earlier poem, "The Borderers," M.
Legouis writes : "It is the work of a Godwinian who, having at first
seen only the nobler aspect of the master's system, is suddenly conscious
of alarm and shock at its consequences."

his failures were on the side of truth. Partly as the result of his peculiar genius, partly as the outcome of what he had acquired through the Revolutionary sentiment, he valued the primary, universal, and permanent passions of man as man more than those which belong to a special class of society or a particular epoch of human history. Thus — to follow his own analysis in a passage of the preface, afterwards suppressed as too intellectual an exposition of work which should expound itself to the feelings and imagination — he endeavours in the " Mad Mother " and the " Idiot Boy " to trace the maternal passion through some of its subtle windings; in the "Forsaken Indian" to accompany the last struggles of a human being, cleaving in solitude to life and society, while death approaches fast; in " We are Seven " to show the inability of childhood to admit the notion of death; in " The Brothers " to exhibit the strength of moral attachment when early associated with the great and beautiful objects of nature ; in " Simon Lee " to deepen and purify the feeling with which we contemplate the infirmity of old age. In all these and like poems, the action and situation are subordinate to the passion or sentiment. The incident of " Simon Lee " is no tale except to a sensitive and meditative heart, and then " Perhaps a tale you 'll make it." Poor Susan only hears the song of a caged thrush ; but the visions of green pastures, the milk-pail, and one dear cottage rise before her, and for a moment her heart is in heaven. Old Timothy does no more than turn the key in the door of his hut, as he departs to the chase, but the action is significant of desolation and its silent grief. When some of Wordsworth's contemporaries attempted to deal with themes like these, they fell into the sentimental vice of the time ; or they put forth a Radical manifesto ; or, from an aristocratic standpoint, they patronized the poor. Wordsworth's adherence to the

truth of things carried him past sentimentalism to the realities of passion ; his veneration for human nature saved him
alike from the spirit of angry revolt and the spirit of patron-
age.   In style some of the " Lyrical Ballads " suffer from
Wordsworth's aggressive revolt against the poetical ideas of
the eighteenth century ; and it is to be regretted that " The
Idiot Boy," a poem of no high excellence, occupies so large
a part of the volume of 1798.   " Peter Bell " might with
advantage have taken its place, for if the tale of that wild
rover is equally exposed to the ridicule of the critics, there
is much in it which is vigorous in the exposition of character, and much which renders with true imagination the psychology of the passions.   Wordsworth chooses for the hero
of his poem a man hard and wild, insensible to all the gentle
influencings of nature and of social life, and he shows how,
through fear and awe and the avenging " spirits of the mind,"
such a temper as Peter's may be smitten and subdued, until
the buried waters of human sympathy flow even from the
rock.

The second volume of " Lyrical Ballads," which appeared
in 1800, includes some of the poems written in Germany
and the earliest of the poems of Grasmere.   Neither the
literature nor the life of Germany contributed much to Wordsworth's mind.   If any piece of his reminds us of the ballad
poetry of the German revival, it is the unfinished fragment
of " The Danish Boy," which, however, had no foreign
original and was entirely of the writer's invention.   During
the bitter winter at Goslar, Wordsworth's spirit created its
own environment ; the only Teutonic acquaintance celebrated
by the poet in song was a forlorn fly that crawled for warmth
on the edge of his stove ; his heart and his imagination remained at home.   The poems of this period are significant
as proving Wordsworth's power of detachment from his
actual surroundings, and the deep imaginative passion with

which he could revive or create what was invisible to the bodily eye.   He brooded also with a fervent introspection on the history of his own mind, on all that had evoked the power of poetry within him, on the influences that warred against the poetic power, and on the processes by which healing and restoration returned to his spirit.

Of the early Grasmere poems several were designed to form a group of pastorals.   And the character of Wordsworth's pastorals is that they are at once real and ideal. The amorous shepherds of an imaginary Arcady had bewailed the cruelty of Arcadian shepherdesses, with all the graces of literary decoration, in countless songs and madrigals of the Elizabethan days.   The pastorals of Pope were not a direct study of nature, but an adaptation of classical ideas to eighteenth-century sentiment and modes.   Crabbe, who had known the hardships and the vices of rural life, indignant against the pseudo-ideality of nymphs and swains, had resolved to set down in verse the literal facts :

> No ; cast by Fortune on a frowning coast,
> Which neither groves nor happy valleys boast ;
> Where other cares than those the Muse relates,
> And other shepherds dwell with other mates ;
> By such examples taught, I paint the cot,
> As Truth will paint it, and as Bards will not.

But truth, as Crabbe conceived it, was not the whole truth ; he sometimes failed to penetrate beyond the harsh and bitter rind of reality to the sweet fruit of life.   Wordsworth was as faithful as Crabbe in his presentation of fact, and he discovered deeper truths of human nature.   His " Michael " verifies itself in every line, and all that is pathetic, all that is sublime in the paternal passion of the old shepherd is verified to the imagination as effectively as are the humblest details.   The peasant folk of the Lake district were indeed of a higher order than the "wild amphibious race" of Crabbe's "Village." "The class of statesmen, or estatesmen, so-called because owners of the ground they occupy," — writes one who for long ministered to their spiritual needs, — "have many of the qualities of an aristocracy. Tall in general and of finely formed features, which have a certain hardness of expression, derived from constant conflict with an ungenial climate, they are independent in their feelings and bearing ; but this independence is usually free from rudeness, and is oftener allied to a proud and sensitive shyness. Completely devoid of hypocrisy, they are honest and truthful, save, it may be, for a certain slackness in the exercise of judicial condemnation, arising, in large part at least, from the kindness of heart which makes them unwilling permanently to depress a neighbour's character or fortunes. . . . They are apt to be keen and tenacious in regard to their rights of property, so that litigation has been with some 'statesmen a favourite pastime ; but in times of sickness or trial they are excellent neighbours, helping freely with personal tendence as well as with the contents of their household stores. They are calm in judgment, and their affections are slowly kindled, but when once kindled, though sparing of outward expression, they burn with a steady, enduring warmth ; and when their blood is up, they will, with as unflinching a spirit and as decisive energy as any men in England, do yeoman's service in behalf of person or cause that is dear to them."[1] It was among such men as these that Wordsworth found his subjects for imaginative study. How he felt towards them may be read in the "First Book of The Recluse," written, perhaps, in the spring of 1800, in which he pours forth his joy and gratitude on finding a settled home in the delightful vale of Grasmere :

[1] Rev. R. P. Graves, "Recollections of Wordsworth," in "Lectures on Literature and Art."

> From crowded streets remote,
> Far from the living and dead Wilderness
> Of the thronged world, Society is here
> A true community — a genuine frame
> Of many into one incorporate.
> *That* must be looked for here ; paternal sway,
> One household, under God, for high and low,
> One family and one mansion ; to themselves
> Appropriate, and divided from the world,
> As if it were a cave, a multitude
> Human and brute, possessors undisturbed
> Of this Recess — their legislative Hall,
> Their Temple, and their glorious Dwelling-place.

The ardour and agitations of Wordsworth's youth were not lost, but were transformed and exalted. The voice of Nature and that of Reason both said to him " Be mild and cleave to gentle things." The aspirings, the undaunted quest of his earlier years survived ; there were still victories to be won, " bounds to be leapt, darkness to be explored "; but thought, passion and imagination were not divided from one another, and hand in hand they went forward to their high emprise.[1]

After the publication of the second volume of " Lyrical Ballads " came a season of comparative rest. Perhaps it is not a mere fancy to suppose that the quickening of Wordsworth's poetic fervour in 1802 was not unconnected with the feelings which led to his marriage in the autumn of that year. He was not indeed the conventional lover who lives in raptures and despair, but he loved deeply and well. Except in a few instances, of which the most remarkable is " Resolution and Independence," he did not, during the spring of 1802, set himself to deal with subjects in which he perceived poetical promise ; he did not move towards objective themes; but

---

[1] For Wordsworth's feeling towards the people among whom he lived, see " The Prelude," Book VIII.

his heart lay open to impulses of the moment or the hour, and poem followed poem with more than common spontaneity. It was not the habit of his mind, as he has said, to make " a present joy " the matter of a song. He was accustomed to recollect and revive emotion in tranquillity; a moment of exquisite excitement dropped a seed, as it were, into his mind, but sometimes months or years passed before the seed began to germinate. In 1802 he often wrote upon the impulse of the moment, and often exhausted himself with the ardour of composition. But even if it be true that in this there was something of a lover's mood, Wordsworth's poems had rarely direct reference to the new joy and hope of his life, and in the work of this creative year the impulses that came to him in solitude are counterpoised by impulses that had their origin in public events. In 1802 he wrote his earliest and some of his greatest political sonnets. The first suggestion was derived from Milton's sonnets, and in the political poetry of England no note so deep, so pure and full, had been heard since Milton sang.

The year 1803 is memorable as that which gave its origin to the first series of Wordsworth's Itinerary Poems. These form a considerable body of his poetical work, and in reading some of the later series, we feel as if Wordsworth did not always write under a genuine inspiration ; he sometimes applied his mind to topics which might yield poetry ; he sometimes seems to have been engaged in performing a poet's duty towards the conspicuous objects of travel. But in the " Memorials of the Scotch Tour of 1803 " almost everything is a surprise of beauty, of passion, or of thought. He sees a Highland girl beside her cabin, within hearing of the waterfall, and, while forfeiting nothing of her reality, — her home-bred sense, her maidenly shyness, her human kindness, — she becomes of a sudden the spirit of the lake and bay. He hears the greeting of a woman who passes along the road : " What, are you stepping westward ? " and the words sound, as it were, oracular, telling of that bright region towards which in this season of joy his soul advanced by natural right in endless progress.

The spring and autumn of 1804 were devoted to carrying forward that history of a soul, " The Prelude," which, by virtue of its insight into the processes by which genius is developed and matured, stands unique among imaginative autobiographies. Before it reached its close Wordsworth had lost his brother John, and that loss which occurred early in 1805, may be taken as marking a real epoch in the growth of his mind and of his work. The radiance of his joy was henceforth tempered ; he felt more than hitherto the need of whatever might strengthen and support his heart ; there is a more distinctively ethical vein in what he wrote ; the experiences by which he transformed his sorrow into gain colour his verse. The " Ode to Duty " tells of his desire to bring all his powers into willing subjection to a law of right ; abandonment to the pure impulses of our nature is good, but the joy of obedience to a great and benignant taskmaster is better and more secure. In the " Character of the Happy Warrior " he dwells upon those moral powers which reinforce and ennoble our highest instincts, which help us to face great moments of trial with brightness like that of a man inspired, and which can control, subdue, transmute the worst calamities of life. In the " Elegiac Stanzas, suggested by a Picture of Peele Castle," he speaks of that deeper humanizing of the soul which comes through sorrow wisely borne, and he greets with welcome the fortitude and patient cheer which render grief endurable. In the ode " Intimations of Immortality," while confessing the loss of the " celestial light," the " visionary gleam " that clothed all objects in former days, he does not yield to despondency, but rather finds strength " in what remains behind " :

> In the soothing thoughts that spring
> Out of human suffering; —
> In the faith that looks through death
> In years that bring the philosophic mind.

Even his love of nature is purified and deepened by the sense of man's mortality :

> Thanks to the human heart by which we live
> Thanks to its tenderness, its joys and fears,
> To me the meanest flower that blows can give
> Thoughts that do often lie too deep for tears.

The great problem of life, as Wordsworth conceived it, says Mr. Leslie Stephen, is " to secure a continuity between the period at which we are guided by half-conscious instincts and that in which a man is able to supply the place of these primitive impulses by reasoned convictions." Until he had himself been tested by harsh experience, and had found that pain and loss made no fatal breach in the progress of the soul towards good, Wordsworth's nature had not reached its full maturity.

Such thoughts as these, which now became ruling ideas with Wordsworth, preside over his narrative poem, " The White Doe of Rylstone," and his poem of lofty meditation, "The Excursion." The former of these is a tragic story of the "Rising of the North" against the government of Queen Elizabeth. The father and brothers of the Norton family perish in the rash strife ; only the afflicted daughter of the house survives. The poem tells of the death of hope and joy, but also of their new and purer birth :

> Dire overthrow, and yet how high
> The re-ascent in sanctity !
> From fair to fairer ; day by day
> A more divine and loftier way.

And the Doe, Emily's companion in joy and sorrow, serves as a beautiful symbol and embodiment of those sympathies "aloft ascending and descending deep," which bind us to the entire life of nature, sympathies which sorrow should not break, but rather strengthen. Wordsworth's own words, addressed to Isabella Fenwick, form the best commentary on the poem: "The subject being taken from feudal times, has led to its being compared to some of Walter Scott's poems that belong to the same age and state of society. The comparison is inconsiderate. Sir Walter pursued the customary and very natural course of conducting an action, presenting various turns of fortune, to some outstanding point on which the mind might rest as a termination or catastrophe. The course I attempted to pursue is entirely different. Everything that is attempted by the principal personages in "The White Doe" fails, so far as its object is external and substantial. So far as it is moral and spiritual it succeeds. The heroine of the poem knows that her duty is not to interfere with the current of events, either to forward or delay them, but

> To abide
> The shock and finally secure
> O'er pain and grief a triumph pure.

. . . How insignificant a thing does personal prowess appear compared with the fortitude of patience and heroic martyrdom."

"The Excursion" — forming the second part of the unfinished "Recluse" — sets forth more fully than any other poem of Wordsworth his views of Man, Nature, and Society. If we may speak of any one idea as presiding over the entire work, it is that of the joy and duty of preserving the continuity of our moral life, or, if this be lost, of recovering what may be recovered from the ruins, and effecting a restoration of our inward being. The Wanderer and the Solitary, the two chief personages of the poem, are a contrasted pair. Wordsworth's philosophic pedlar, after a boyhood of ardent

delight in nature and in books and a manhood of beneficent
activity, has now reached the illuminated heights of old age ;
he has seen much of human life, and entered with sympathy
into the anxieties that wear and the sorrows that too often
corrode the heart ; yet his happiness is still maintained, his
benevolence is warm, his faith is serene in its assurance ;
he still possesses love and hope and joy. The Solitary,
born in a higher station but endowed with less of wisdom
and stability of spirit, has endured two shattering strokes of
fate — first, the loss of his wife and children, a private grief ;
and secondly, the ruin of those bright visions of social
reform which rose like an exhalation from the political
upheaval in France. His fortitude and his faith have given
way under the stress of suffering and disappointment ; he
has retired from the world into a retreat among the mountains, a self-indulgent but not a happy privacy ; and the
whole of human life he regards with a certain sceptical bitterness ; yet flashes of his old vivacity return to him for
moments, and though his view of human nature is clouded
with distrust, he has not lost his natural kindliness of disposition. To raise his downcast spirit, to infuse faith and
hope and moral wisdom into his heart, is the effort of the
Wanderer. And to assist him in this effort the old man
engages the pastor of the mountain parish to narrate the
stories of some of those who lie at rest in the church-yard
graves — pathetic records told in

> words of heartfelt truth,
> Tending to patience when affliction strikes ;
> To hope and love ; to confident repose
> In God ; and reverence for the dust of Man.

Wordsworth does not profess that by discourse or tale moral
restoration can be procured ; but he believed that these
might quicken what was best in a despondent spirit, and
that they might coöperate with other tendencies towards

good. His Wanderer has carried on into the decline of life all that was most precious in his exultant youth, and he has added the deeper sympathy aud higher wisdom of maturer years. The Solitary may perhaps recover something of what he has lost, or attain to something saner and more enduring. It was Wordsworth's intention in the third part of " The Recluse " to tell his readers more concerning this not impossible renovation ; but the design which he cherished was never accomplished.

The publication of " The Excursion " in 1814 may be taken as an important note of time in the progress of Wordsworth's art ; after that date he attempted no work of great dimensions. About the same time he again felt the influence of classical poetry ; his manner of expression became more dignified, but he adopted no conventional system of phraseology, and his style, uniting truth with something of majesty, remained characteristically his own. The manner was appropriate to the subjects ; for some time he had ceased to write on homely themes drawn from peasant life ; the narratives of the tenants of the church-yard among the mountains in " The Excursion " dealt with matter which at an earlier period might have been treated in the form of lyrical ballads. Now his imagination looked away from its immediate surroundings to records of the past ; but it was not the play and colour of ancient mythology that attracted him ; he was rather drawn towards subjects into which ethical wisdom might be infused. " Laodamia," enforces the duty of lifting up the passions to their highest level, above the mortal fluctuations of earthly sorrow and earthly desire. " Dion " sets forth, in an illustrious example, the truth that, even with worthy ends in view, man must not overleap the " eternal bars " of justice and law :

> Him, only him, the shield of Jove defends
> Whose means are fair and spotless as his ends.

" Artegal and Elidure," a tale drawn from British legend, shows how a brother is saved by a brother's magnanimity, how self-surrendering love conquers and reclaims base distrust and converts a wild rebel into a noble penitent. To call these poems didactic would be a mistake ; the ethical purport is taken up by the imagination and the passion of the poet ; they teach moral truth, but, as it were, inevitably ; and they do not preach ; it is the critics drawing out their meaning into weary doctrine who are the preachers.

In the year 1816 Wordsworth's noble series of political poems reached a close, and he was not again inspired to write on political themes in a great manner. From the first these poems had been of rare dignity of utterance ; under the exaltation of final and stupendous victory the form expands from the sonnet to the ode. Wordsworth's enthusiasm is boundless, but it is purified, and can find no satisfaction except in gratitude to the Almighty God of battles, the Lord of Hosts. Not by force of mortal arms had the triumph been achieved, but by the might of a righteous cause ; by the soul of a nation ; and by the divine wrath against the tyrant, the divine pity for the oppressed, which breathed through the spirit of a people who did not shrink from sacrifice or death. The temper of these poems is higher than ethical ; it is, in the truest sense, religious ; there is a breadth and majesty in the versification which corresponds with the sublimity of the occasion.

Before this date, if we set aside the poem on " Intimations of Immortality " and the " Stanzas to Duty," Wordsworth had not made the ode a chosen vehicle for his feelings. Now, from time to time, he applied it to other than political themes. The " Vernal Ode " of 1817, the " Ode to Lycoris " and the " Pass of Kirkstone " of the same year, the lines of 1818 " Composed upon an Evening of Extraordinary Splendour and Beauty," the " Ode on the Power of Sound " of ten years later, the "Devotional Incitements" of 1832 belong in essence, if not always exactly in form, to this class, and they may be reckoned among Wordsworth's most admirable achievements. A general topic, around which high thoughts and ardent emotions may gather, is selected by the imagination, and is viewed in various aspects, the lyrical movement of the poem varying if the point of view be changed. One example may suffice: the "Vernal Ode," composed when spring was leading forth her new and lovely communities of blossoms and of birds, finds a source of joy and thanksgiving in the immortality of succession granted to mortal things, even where immortality is denied, as far as we know, to the individual creature. The stars themselves shall pass away, but shall we therefore sink in dejection before the thought that all fair things are doomed to extinction ?

> What if those bright fires
> Shine subject to decay ;
> Sons haply of extinguished sires,
> Themselves to lose their light, or pass away
> Like clouds before the wind,
> Be thanks poured out to Him whose hand bestows
> Nightly, on human kind
> That vision of endurance and repose.
> — And though to every draught of vital breath,
> Renewed throughout the bounds of earth or ocean,
> The melancholy gates of Death
> Respond with sympathetic motion ;
> Though all that feeds on nether air,
> Howe'er magnificent or fair,
> Grows but to perish, and entrust
> Its ruins to their kindred dust ;
> Yet by the Almighty's ever-during care,
> Her procreant vigils Nature keeps
> Amid the unfathomable deeps ;
> And saves the peopled fields of earth
> From dread of emptiness or dearth.

> Thus, in their stations, lifting tow'rd the sky
> The foliaged head in cloud-like majesty,
> The shadow-casting race of trees survive :
> Thus, in the train of Spring, arrive
> Sweet flowers ; — what living eye hath viewed
> Their myriads ? — endlessly renewed,
> Wherever strikes the sun's glad ray ;
> Where'er the subtle waters stray ;
> Wherever sportive breezes bend
> Their course, or genial showers descend!
> Mortals rejoice ! the very Angels quit
> Their mansions, unsusceptible of change,
> Amid your pleasant bowers to sit,
> And through your sweet vicissitudes to range.

Wordsworth at no time wrote lines of higher intention or more admirable execution than these of 1817 ; indeed, between Milton and Wordsworth it would not be easy to find a nobler strain of imagination.

Here the lines have been quoted with a purpose. Although several of his most memorable poems were written after 1820, we may perhaps say that by that date the vitality of his genius had declined ; the stream of his verse did not quickly dwindle, but it ran less swiftly ; it did not always force its own way, but was conducted through prepared channels. His best work comes less frequently and less surely ; he could set himself subjects (the series of " Ecclesiastical Sonnets " is an example), and apply his mind to them with good results, but he was less often than in earlier years irresistibly compelled to declare a vision or to utter a rapture in song. He sought more for the external suggestions of poetry, and many of his verses were written on the occasion of foreign travel. He had indeed given full and perfect expression to his most characteristic thoughts and feelings. But now and again the old inspiration returns, as in the sonnet on " The Pine Tree of Monte Mario," and not a few other pieces, and returns with its original force.

Up to about 1820, however, there was development, if there was also something of decline. A reader who lives long with Wordsworth's poetry comes gradually to set a high value upon a considerable body of his later writings. And this is as it should be ; nothing is more characteristic of his genius than the calm and clear illumination which followed its hours of morning and of noon. We do not know him aright until our spirits can join with his in an evening voluntary. That almost all his best work was produced between 1798 and 1808, as Mathew Arnold alleged and Mr. John Morley repeats, is far from being the fact. The lines quoted from the " Vernal Ode " are an example of his later manner. Principal Shairp, who was a close student of Wordsworth's poetry and entered deeply into his spirit, takes the year 1808, when the poet quitted his Grasmere cottage, as the close of the springtime of his genius; but he extends the second epoch, or " full midsummer," as far as 1818 or 1820. It was the period of " The Excursion," " Laodamia," " Dion," the " Vernal Ode," the " Ode to Lycoris," the " Longest Day," the " Pass of Kirkstone," the " Evening of Extraordinary Splendour and Beauty," many passionate political poems, and the Duddon sonnets. Whoever fails to recognize Wordsworth's mature genius in such poems as these is really but ill acquainted with Wordsworth. The third epoch, the " sober autumn," reaching from 1820 to 1846, when Wordsworth ceased to write, has a peculiar beauty and value of its own. We may not accept Mr. Aubrey de Vere's statement that the poems of this autumnal season have more " latent imagination " than those of earlier years, or that they " exhibit faculties more perfectly equipoised," but we feel that Wordsworth's work would lack something of great worth if we were not shown how the radiance of his youth passes into the light — solemn and serene — of his old age. He himself speaks in his " Guide to the Lakes " of the peculiar, spiritual beauty of the most fortunate days of September, when the vivifying heats of summer have declined, and the air is lighter and more pellucid; some of this September grace and spiritual clearness may be perceived and felt in the best verse of the poet's declining years. Its strength is attuned to gentleness; it is rich in the wisdom of the heart; its tranquillity covers a deep experience of joy and sorrow; it is touched with Christian humility; its vision is that of a seer who beholds the things not very far off.

Mr. R. Holt Hutton, a penetrating critic, read before the Wordsworth Society a paper which he entitled "On Wordsworth's Two Styles." It contrasts the manner of Wordsworth's poems of youth with that of the poems of his maturer and later years — "the classic style of fresh energy, born of his long devotion to Nature's own rhythms," with the style "of gracious and stately feeling, born of his benignity, of his deep-set, calm sympathy with human feeling"; the style of the "Solitary Reaper" with the style of "Devotional Incitements." In the earlier style, according to the critic's analysis, objective fact, especially when appealing to the sense of vision, plays a much larger part than in the later; there is in it a pure elasticity, a buoyancy almost unique in poetry; and in the greater of the early pieces "emotion is uniformly suggested rather than expressed, or, if I may be allowed the paradox, expressed by reticence, by the jealous parsimony of a half-voluntary, half-involuntary reserve." In the later style "the keenness of objective vision is still felt, but is less dominant; the buoyancy is much diminished"; while on the other hand, "emotion is much more freely, frankly and tenderly expressed, so that there is often in it a richness and mellowness of effect quite foreign to Wordsworth's earlier mood"; feeling "flows naturally, and with a sweet and tender lustre shining upon it, into musical expression." In illustration of his analysis Mr. Hutton contrasts

" The Daffodils " (" I wandered lonely as a cloud ") with " The Primrose of the Rock," and the earliest with the latest of the three Yarrow poems. The later style, says Mr. Hutton, " has this advantage over the earlier, that when its subject is equally fine — which, as I admit, it often is not — the workmanship is far more complete, often almost of crystal beauty, and without the blots, the baldness, the dead-wood, which almost all Wordsworth's earlier works exhibit."

The truth is, not that Wordsworth in his later years failed to produce work of high value, but that the proportion which such work bore to the total mass is far smaller than it had been in his more fervid days. The power of sustained inspiration ebbed away, but in shorter poems, and especially in the sonnet, he was sometimes as fortunate as ever. Even so late as 1846, the last year of his authorship, he wrote lines which no lover of Wordsworth's poetry could willingly forget, lines which tell of the healing influence of the sound of waters heard by night :

> The unremitting voice of nightly streams
> Wants not a healing influence that can creep
> Into the human breast, and mix with sleep
> To regulate the motions of our dreams
> For kindly issues.

Such an influence the stream of Wordsworth's own song possesses, though a dwindled stream, while the shadows of old age lay around him.

V. CLASSIFICATION OF WORDSWORTH'S POEMS.

In a volume of selections, such as the present, it is not possible to preserve Wordsworth's arrangement of his poems, and the chronological arrangement (except in the case of a

few political sonnets, where the original order is preserved)
has been adopted as on the whole the most instructive for a
student. The chronological study is important and fruitful,
but Wordsworth himself had the strongest objection to such
a mode of presenting his complete poetical works, and in a
complete text for general readers more would be lost than
gained by such a departure from his carefully considered
scheme. Indeed the chronology is only in part ascertained;
for many poems we have no nearer date than that of publication; not a few of those to which the author, trusting to
his memory, affixed the supposed year of composition, were
incorrectly dated. His own arrangement was first made for
the edition of 1815; and in all later editions which had his
authority it was maintained. His guiding wish was that the
shorter pieces should be regarded, first, as composing an
entire work within themselves, and secondly, as adjuncts to
the great philosophical poem "The Recluse," of which "The
Prelude" and "The Excursion" form parts. He compared "The Excursion" to the body of a Gothic church, and
"The Prelude" to its ante-chapel; his minor pieces, he says,
if properly arranged, may be likened "to the little cells, ora-
tories, and sepulchral recesses ordinarily included" in such
an edifice. While it is highly desirable that the reader of
the complete works should be provided with a chronological
table as nearly exact as the state of our knowledge admits,
he should also make himself acquainted with Wordsworth's
plan as a master builder, and should consider the poems as
they were placed by the author with a view to their mutual
illustration. Wordsworth desired that his entire work should
be regarded as a great unity, having a beginning, a middle,
and an end. He also desired that it should, as far as
possible, correspond with that which formed the subject of
the whole — the life of man, commencing with Childhood,
and progressing to Old Age, Death, and Immortality.

When he came to consider the poems more in detail, he perceived three principles under which they might be grouped : they might be arranged according to the themes of which they treat ; or secondly, according to the moulds or forms in which they are cast; or, thirdly, according to the powers of mind predominant in their production ; finally, these three principles might be made to work together, and preside in harmonious confederacy over the whole.

Wordsworth decided in favour of the last of these methods. The whole body of his work was arranged so as to have a beginning, middle, and end on the model of its theme of human life.　First, as belonging to his own early years he placed the " Poems written in Youth," next the poems referring generally to the Period of Childhood.　The collection closed with " Poems referring to Old Age," " Epitaphs and Elegiac Pieces," suggested by Death, and the " Ode — Intimations of Immortality."　The first poem of those of Childhood, that which tells of the binding together of all our days in " natural piety," furnishes a motto for the " Ode " which takes up the same thought and develops it, and which forms the headstone of the entire edifice, or — shall we say ? — the high-altar of the church.　Having passed the poems of Childhood, we find the principle of arrangement according to the predominant faculty introduced ; and under this principle the first group is that of " Poems founded on the Affections." The attentive reader will notice that the pieces under this heading do not follow one another at hap-hazard.　While the method is not one of absolute rigidity, in general the poems observe the sequence in which our affections are naturally developed, — first the love of brothers and sisters ; next the passions of friends and of lovers ; then the affection of husband and wife, and finally the loves and griefs of parents. So we pass from "The Brothers " and "Artegal and Elidure " to the stanzas which tell of Wordsworth's companionship with Coleridge and the " Lucy " group, from these to poems connected with Mary Wordsworth, and again to " The Childless Father," " The Emigrant Mother," and " Michael." The " Poems on the Naming of Places " introduces a new principle of classification, that in which the mould or form determines the group. The moulds of poetry are enumerated by Wordsworth as the Narrative, the Dramatic, the Lyrical (including Hymn, Elegy, Ode, Song, Ballad), the Idyllium, Didactic poetry, and lastly Philosophical Satire. Under the Idyllium he places not only the Idyl proper, but the Epitaph, the Inscription, the Sonnet, and such loco-descriptive poems as those on the Naming of Places. But the names given to rock and grove, to woodland pool and mountain peak, are derived from beloved persons — John's Grove, Emma's Dell, Joanna's Rock, Mary's and Sarah's rocks ; the poems are thus connected with the affections, and they appropri-- ately follow the " Poems founded on the Affections."

The psychological classification based on the predominant faculties is continued in the " Poems of the Fancy," " Poems of the Imagination " and " Poems of Sentiment and Reflec- tion." But under the second of these headings are many subordinate groups, some formed, as the several series of Itinerary Poems, by virtue of a community of subject, others, as the Miscellaneous Sonnets, by virtue of identity of form. In arranging the individual pieces which make up these groups Wordsworth was guided by a desire to exhibit their mutual illustration, while at the same time he aimed at preserving due proportion and introducing an agreeable variety. How carefully all this was considered and carried out may be seen by any one who will turn to the " Miscel- laneous Sonnets " in any complete edition which preserves Wordsworth's arrangement. These sonnets were written at various times and seasons, and if chronologically placed many that stand side by side would be severed from one another; as arranged by their author they form not a linked chain of sonnets, but a sequence, so far as a sequence can be made from disconnected poems by happy ordering. I may be permitted to refer the reader to a note in the Aldine edition of Wordsworth (vol. iii, pp. 327, 328), where I have exhibited in detail the sequence of the Miscellaneous Sonnets, Part I. Here it may suffice to call attention to the mutual illustration afforded by Sonnets iii–xvi of Part II; written at various intervals from 1815 to 1827, these poems are so disposed as to constitute a continuous pleading against despondency and in favour of heroic effort, courage, tranquillity, and cheerful hope. But no one can have read the "Poems of the Imagination," which are placed first in that group, and have failed to perceive the importance of Wordsworth's arrangement. "Beggars," for example and "Gipsies," which stand side by side, may be said to belong to each other; so again with "Laodamia" and "Dion"; so with "Star-Gazers" and the "Power of Music"; so with "The Pass of Kirkstone" and "To Enterprise." In fact, Wordsworth had not overstated the matter when he says that for him who reads with reflection the arrangement will "serve as a commentary," unostentatiously directing him to the poet's purposes both particular and general. He admits that there is necessarily a certain amount of cross division between the groups; the poems of the Fancy and those of the Imagination might without impropriety, he says, have been enlarged from the "Poems founded on the Affections," as these might be enlarged from the former classes and from the group "proceeding from Sentiment and Reflection." Still, in assigning their positions to the several poems he exercised his best judgment, and it is worth something to us to stand at the writer's point of view. If we obliterate his arrangement, we efface no insignificant part of the expression of his mind.

The several groups founded on the predominant faculties may in the general arrangement, presenting the course of human life, be said to represent the maturity of manhood, when the faculties have attained their full development, and are still untouched by decline. To complete the large design, it only remains to add to these the poems referring to Old Age, to Death, and to Immortality. Whether Wordsworth's scheme justifies itself or not to a reader's intelligence, there, at all events, it is: something which Wordsworth himself considered of high importance; something which he pondered long; and something therefore deserving of careful study, which an editor of the complete poetical works is bound to preserve as an essential and a characteristic feature of the whole.

———

VI.   THE TEXT OF WORDSWORTH'S POEMS.[1]

No English poet was a more careful and conscientious craftsman than Wordsworth; he could not be content if he had done less than his best. His judgment was excellent, and his sensibility and skill in all matters of detail increased as he continued to practise his art. But of course to rehandle in a critical mood work which was produced in the fervour of creation is a process attended with risks. When the emotions are aroused and the mind is all vital, remote relations are apprehended, occult connections are felt, which it is hardly possible to keep before the mental vision while the eye moves critically from point to point. Wordsworth began the revision of his poems at the earliest possible moment, in 1800; in each new edition — in 1803, 1805, 1815, 1820, 1827, 1832 — omissions, additions, and altera-

———

[1] In this section I have made use of some passages already printed in the article on the same subject in my " Transcripts and Studies."

tions were made. For the first stereotyped edition, that of 1836–1837, a very searching revisal was carried out; in 1840 the work was begun anew; further changes were made in the text of 1845, and many earlier readings were then restored. Even the edition completed in 1850, the year of Wordsworth's death, shows that to the last he had his eye upon perfection.

Among readers who have not carefully studied Wordsworth's text, an impression is common that he did his work much wrong. The impression, if we have regard to the final result, is certainly erroneous. A few poems suffered loss, but, on the whole, the gain was great. The latest text is the best text. It was a most happy circumstance that Wordsworth lived long enough to consider from a sufficient distance in time the alterations of 1836–1837. Many of them were improvements; but the poet, having taken in hand a thorough revisal of his works for that edition, seems to have acquired a certain pleasure in the process of effecting alterations; what should have been the task of his best moments became a daily business; he was sometimes entangled in new thoughts; his insight was often perplexed; his discretion occasionally failed; and the rehandling was carried a great deal too far. In 1845 Wordsworth retained what was best from the revision of 1836–1837, and perceiving the error of his ways, he cancelled most of the changes that were injudicious, and in these passages recovered the text of earlier years. Substantially his labours of nearly half a century were completed by the year 1845.

From no other English poet can lessons in the poetic craft so full, so detailed, and so instructive be obtained as those to be had by one who follows Wordsworth through the successive editions, and puts to himself the repeated question " For what reason was this change, for what reason was that, introduced? " A reason there always was, though now and again it may have been an insufficient reason.

Sometimes the suggestion which led to an alteration came from an external quarter; from friends, such as Lamb or Coleridge ; or from hostile critics ; and in certain instances, though Wordsworth at first resisted, his better judgment went over to the side of his critics; but in general the changes express the independent thoughts and feelings of the poet himself, and we can read in them something of the growth of his mind. To classify all the alterations of text with reference to the ground of each would be an endless task; in each instance the student must endeavour to think out for himself the motive of the variation ; but it may be helpful to indicate here a few of the more obvious grounds of change.

1. *Words Incorrectly used.* — An example will be found in the poem " There was a Boy," where the word "scene " was used of audible, not visual, phenomena ; "a wild scene of jocund din " in later texts became "concourse wild of jocund din." In " Ruth," ll. 196, 198, Wordsworth originally wrote :

> And there exulting in her wrongs,
> Among the music of her songs,
> She fearfully carouz'd.

Lamb objected that " carouse " in this sense was not English, and the lines became :

> And there, with many a doleful song
> Made of wild words, her cup of wrong
> She fearfully caroused.

Out of forty-two passages in which the word " frame " occurred, as substantive or verb, in the earliest texts, it remains after the final revision in only eight. (For the probable grounds of the changes, see " The Academy," Dec. 2, 1893, p. 486, in an article by Mr. Thomas Hutchinson.) Again, while in two passages the words " sombre " and " sombrous " are retained, where they mean shady or over-shadowing, they disappear from four passages, where they had been used in the sense of dark, dull, or dusky. (See the same article in "The Academy.")

2. *Words used too Frequently.*—Certain poets may almost be identified by an affection for some particular adjective ; with one it is "dim," with another "sterile," with another "wan." The word "visionary" is a favourite with Words-worth, but he uses it always with perfect propriety. One adjective, however, of facile application and somewhat vague suggestiveness — "sweet" — haunted his imagination in early years, and starred his verse all over as the daisy stars an English lawn. He determined to deal severely with this small offender ; it was hunted as a criminal, discovered in its nestling-places, dragged to the critical judgment-seat, and sentenced, in many instances, to perpetual banishment. Sweet smiles, sweet looks, sweet flowers, sweet bowers, sweet flocks, sweet mornings greet us no more where once they did, and bright looks, soft bowers, fine flocks take their place.

> No Nightingale did ever chaunt
> So sweetly to reposing bands

as the Solitary Reaper sang in her poet's inward ear.

> No sweeter voice was ever heard
> In spring-time from the cuckoo-bird

than that voice of hers. In later texts the lines become,

> No Nightingale did ever chaunt
> More welcome notes to weary bands.
>
> .   .   .   .
>
> A voice so thrilling ne'er was heard
> In spring-time from the cuckoo-bird,

and the changes at once justify themselves to the reader's imagination. Mr. T. Hutchinson has accumulated statistics : " In 1827 Wordsworth removed the word *sweet* from ten places in the poems ; in 1832 from one place ; in 1836 from ten ; in 1840 from one ; and in 1845 from three."

3. *Words mispronounced.* — Wordsworth's use of the word "towards" has been made the subject of a careful examination by Mr. Hutchinson, in "The Academy," Dec. 2, 1893. In many instances it was altered to "toward," where the final *s* marred the melody of a line ; this change was of course effected without difficulty. But Wordsworth's opinion as to the correct pronunciation of the word altered as time went on ; at first he regarded it as a dissyllable ; from 1836 onwards he uses it invariably as a monosyllable, but as early as 1827 he seems to have preferred the monosyllable pronunciation. The matter seems very trifling ; yet, trifling or not, it involved Wordsworth in a considerable series of alterations, and in some instances entire sentences were recast in order to avoid the dissyllabic "toward" or "towards." At least twenty-four passages were re-handled for this reason, and the process begun in 1827 was not completed until the final edition of 1849–1850.

4. *Metrical Errors.* — An example will be found in "Personal Talk, "l. 3 (ed. 1807),

> About friends who live within an easy walk,

which was easily set right ("Of friends," etc.) in the edition of 1815. In "The Sparrow's Nest" until 1845 "fear'd it" stood as the rhyme to "near it."

5. *Inharmonious Effects of Sound.* — In several instances the clashing of the "th" with "th" in the earlier texts was avoided by the alteration of a word. Thus, in "Strange Fits of Passion" the words "Benea*th th*e evening moon" became in 1836 "Beneath an evening moon." A more interesting example is noted by Mr Hutchinson : in "The Redbreast and the Butterfly," edd. 1807–1820, occur the lines :

> The Bird whom, by some name or other,
> All men who know thee call their Brother.

His objection to the hum of the labial-nasal in *whom, some, name* led Wordsworth into a grammatical error in edd. 1827–1845, which read :

> " The Bird, *who* by some name or other," etc.

But why did he not alter " whom " of 1807–1820 into "that" in accordance with his general practice in edd. 1827–1836? Doubtless it was because of the unusually large number of *th* sounds occurring in the opening lines of the poem. . . . However, the claims of grammar prevailed over considerations of euphony, and in his final revision of the poems (for ed. 1849), Wordsworth corrected thus :

> The Bird, *that* by some name or other. [1]

Again, in " Nutting," the inharmonious succession of the *en* sound in the line " Ev*en* th*en* wh*en* from the bower I turned away " was got rid of by the new reading of 1836, — " Ere from the mutilated bower I turned." In the same year the line " Th*at at* no season fade " in the poem " To a Young Lady who had been reproached for taking long walks in the country " became " Which at," etc. In line 51 of " Laodamia," originally " That then, when tens of thousands were deprest," a *th* sound was removed in 1820 by the substitution of " Which " for " That," but it seems as if " th*en*, wh*en* t*en*s " escaped Wordsworth's notice. Yet his ear was peculiarly sensitive to the disagreeable recurrence of identical sounds ; in " Beggars " he altered the admirable line " Pouring out sorrows like a sea " because (as he told a friend) " *sea* " clashes with " was beautiful to *see*," which occurs, (not as rhyme) at the distance of four lines.

6. *Errors in Observation or Statement of Fact.* — In " The Brothers " the "broad *green* wave " that flashed images round Leonard as he sailed under a cloudless sky, becomes a " broad

---

[1] " The Academy," Dec. 2, 1893.

blue wave. The "cowslip-gathering at May's dewy prime" remembered by the "Female Vagrant," becomes in ed. 1820 a cowslip-gathering of June. The poem was written in the South of England, and the scene is laid in the South; perhaps Wordsworth at first overlooked the fact that the Vagrant's early days were spent "by Derwent's side," where spring flowers would be tardy in arrival. Again, in more than one passage of the early texts the female bird is made the chief songster; in later editions the sex of the bird is changed. In the "Complaint of a Forsaken Indian Woman," in the earlier texts occur the lines :

> In sleep did I behold the skies,
> I saw the crackling flashes drive.

The author perceived that the word "crackling" required a verb of hearing, and the final reading is the following :

> In rustling conflict through the skies
> I heard, I saw the flashes drive.

Sir Walter, in "Hart-Leap Well," "chid and cheered" his hounds weary with the chase; a good master would first cheer and afterwards chide, and so the words were altered. The old Leech-gatherer, when questioned as to his occupation, in edd. 1807–1815, answered, "with pleasure and surprise :

> And there was, while he spake, a fire about his eyes."

But the sudden response of his eyes would have anticipated the slow and solemn words on his lips, and the text accordingly became :

> Ere he replied, a flash of mild surprise
> Broke from the sable orbs of his yet-vivid eyes.

7. *Errors of Exaggeration.* — At first the hunted hart of "Hart-Leap Well" covered in his three leaps "nine roods"; the extravagance was more than even a willing imagination

could credit, and the nine roods became four.   In the same poem the over-strained horse stood "foaming like a mountain cataract "; the foam of a cataract is a continuous moving mass of white; the horse could not be more than thickly flecked; and the words in 1820 were altered to "white with foam as if with cleaving sleet."   In the lines "To my Sister," Wordsworth wrote, in 1798 :

> One moment now may give us more
>   Than fifty years of reason.

The assertion was too extreme and too definite in its excess, and the closing words became, in 1837 " Than years of toiling reason."

8. *Errors of Triviality and Needless Grotesqueness.* — The instances are many.   Simon Lee, during two and twenty years, stood before the reader in that "long blue livery coat"

> That's fair behind and fair before,

and which is only faintly referred to after 1815; during several years more he remained bereft of his right eye; finally the eye was restored to Simon, but the lustre of his livery was dimmed.   It did not assist the pathos of the poem to make the old huntsman too piteously grotesque a figure.   In 1819 the opening stanza of " Peter Bell," Part I, ran as follows :

> All by the moonlight river-side
>   It gave three miserable groans;
> " 'T is come then to a pretty pass,"
> Said Peter to the groaning Ass,
>   " But I will *bang* your bones."

And, again, in a later stanza there is a second bone-banging. Already in the following year this had been erased.   A verse of the poem which Shelley prefixed as a motto to his satirical " Peter Bell the Third " — that verse descriptive of a pos-

sible vision of prosaic horror below the water into which
the Potter is staring :

> Is it a party in a parlour
> Crammed just as they on earth were crammed,
> Some sipping punch — some sipping tea,
> But, as you by their faces see,
> 　All silent and all — damned ?

that verse, which is no invention of Shelley's — disappeared
hastily, and disappeared so effectually that its existence at
any time in Wordsworth's poems has been denied. "The
Idiot Boy," written with speed and in a gleeful mood, was
always a favourite with its author. Yet he made a sacrifice
of some passages, which seemed to approach too near the
ludicrous :

> Beneath the moon which shines so bright,
> 　Till she is tired, let Betty Foy
> With girt and stirrup *fiddle-faddle ;*
> But wherefore set upon a saddle
> Him whom she loves, her Idiot Boy ?

Betty fiddle-faddled from 1798 to 1820; and then she or
her poet tired, and she fiddle-faddled no more. In that
tragic poem "The Thorn" the infant's grave was at first
described as if it had been studied by an undertaker :

> I 've measured it from side to side,
> 'T is three feet long, and two feet wide.

Wordsworth declared to Crabb Robinson that these lines
" ought to be liked "; and perhaps he was right, for it is
only conjectured that Martha Ray buried her baby there,
and we are interested in receiving the exact evidence of a
prosaic witness. Nevertheless, the lines were dignified as
follows :

> Though but of compass small, and bare
> To thirsty suns and parching air.

The fire which burned in Martha's bones, when Stephen deserted her, in the earlier record,

> Dried her body to a cinder,
> And almost turned her brain to tinder.

For which lines we read from 1815 onwards —

> A fire was kindled in her breast,
> Which might not burn itself to rest.

"Old Farmer Simpson," who knew the sorrows of Martha, disappeared from the poem in 1820, and "grey-haired Wilfred of the glen" enters *vice* Farmer Simpson removed. The processes by which dignity and eloquence were added to the fine poem "Beggars" can be traced in the notes of the present volume. In 1807 the "Blind Highland Boy" embarked on his perilous voyage in a humble craft :

> A household tub, like one of those
> Which women use to wash their clothes.

In 1815, on Coleridge's suggestion, a turtle-shell replaced the honest, if prosaic, tub ; and by and by the turtle-shell came to resemble the pearly car of Amphitrite. Many readers will prefer — and perhaps justly — the original version of the voyage.

9. *Intrusion of the Personal.* — Wordsworth's poems, even when on objective themes, are impressed with the characteristics of his mind ; they are distinctively Wordsworthean ; but as he advanced in the poetic art he desired to avoid the intrusion of all that belonged to him accidentally as an individual, and also the intrusion of self-consciousness in poems where it was needless or out of place. On this point he was sensitive. In "Beggars" the line "In all my walks through field or town" was altered, as he himself declared, because it was "obtrusively personal" ; the subject of the poem was the majestic vagrant and her wanton boys ; it

neither concerns them nor us to know where the historical William Wordsworth chose to direct his walks. Probably for a like reason he altered a line in " Personal Talk " —

> By my half-kitchen and half-parlour fire.

At one time he regretted the loss of these words, which reminded him of the modest cottage at Grasmere and its happy interior; but the fact that Dorothy cooked in the sitting-room does not really concern the reader of the poem. In the " Poems " of 1807 appeared a group with the general title " Moods of My Own Mind "; the title disappeared from later editions. So also from a "A Whirl-blast," the concluding lines —

> Oh ! grant me, Heaven, a heart at ease,
> That I may never cease to find,
> Even in appearances like these,
> Enough to nourish and to stir my mind —

were omitted as a self-conscious return of the poet upon himself. It was that reserve of the personal which is an element of artistic idealization that led Wordsworth to substitute imaginary names, Emma, Emmeline, Laura, for the actual Dorothy and Dora; but in two instances, after the loss of his daughter (in "The Kitten and the Falling Leaves" and "The Longest Day "), when she entered into the ideality of death, Wordsworth indulged his desire to connect her memory with his poems, and displaced "Laura" for the name "Dora."

10. *Extravagance or Violence of Feeling.* — In the "Tribute to the Memory of a Dog," feelings were expressed and language was employed which at a later time seemed to Wordsworth of a kind that should be reserved for human creatures. The two opening lines —

> Lie here sequester'd : — be this little mound
> For ever thine, and be it holy ground —

were omitted in 1827. The line "I pray'd for thee, and that thy end were past" became in 1820 "We grieved for thee, and wished thy end were past." In 1837 the reading

> For love that comes wherever life and sense
> Are given by God, in thee was most intense.

replaced the earlier

> For love, that comes to all ; the holy sense,
> Best gift of God, in thee was most intense.

Little "Music" gallantly tried to save her drowning companion. Wordsworth did not love the generous dog less ; but he was unwilling to associate the idea of "holiness" with a brute ; and perhaps in the hierarchy of our emotions more is lost than gained by an unreasonable levelling-up. Excess of an opposite kind was tempered in the later texts of "A Poet's Epitaph." The lawyer is forbidden to approach the poet's resting place. In 1800 the lines ran —

> Go, carry to some other place
> The hardness of thy coward eye,
> The falsehood of thy sallow face.

Lamb, in a letter to Wordsworth, censured the common satire upon parsons and lawyers, and also the words addressed to the philosopher, "thy pin point of a soul." Wordsworth yielded ; the pin-point became first "that abject thing, thy soul," and finally "thy ever-dwindling soul" ; the indictment of the lawyer was reduced to —

> The keenness of that practised eye,
> The hardness of that sallow face.

The "Ode, 1815," was written in a mood of high and stern enthusiasm ; Wordsworth triumphed over the defeat of the enemies of England and of freedom ; the divine purpose had been terribly accomplished; and addressing the Almighty disposer of events, he dared to put forth the lines:

> But thy most dreaded instrument
> In working out a pure intent
> Is Man — arrayed for mutual slaughter —
> Yea, Carnage is thy daughter !

Weak brethren were offended; and the poet himself lapsed from his mood of fierce exultation; he omitted the last two lines, and transformed the first two as follows:

> But Man is Thy most awful instrument
> In working out a pure intent.

It was enough, and the conflict in a reader's mind between the enthusiasm of justice and the sense of human pity, which is only a finer form of justice, was averted. But we gladly remember that Wordsworth was capable of writing the omitted lines.

11. *Imagery or Sentiment Inconsistent with the Unity of a Poem.* — An excellent example of Wordsworth's severity in dealing with his own work is seen in the omission of the fine stanza with which " Dion " originally opened. The brightness, purity, and grace of Dion's soul in his happier hours were typified by the image of the majestic swan oaring his way by moonlight on the lake of Locarno; few things more admirable are to be found in Wordsworth's poetry; but the stanza did not assist the poem as a whole; it detained the reader too long from the subject; and, as Wordsworth says, it rather precluded than prepared for the due effect of the allusion to the genius of Plato. It was degraded to a place in the notes. Some of Wordsworth's friends protested; but he remained inexorable, or would yield only so far as to suggest that it might be placed as a separate fragment of the descriptive poetry immediately after " Dion." The

pathetic poem "Poor Susan," in the earliest form, closed
with a stanza which dangerously approached the sentimental :

> Poor Outcast ! return — to receive thee once more
> The house of thy Father will open its door,
> And thou once again in thy plain russet gown,
> May'st hear the thrush sing from a tree of its own.

We are as thankful as Charles Lamb was for the excision of
this stanza.   We are not called on to speculate with respect
to poor Susan's future ; the whole virtue of the poem
resides in the sudden moment of reverie of a country maiden
in the heart of a great city, reverie summoned up by the
song of a caged bird ; when the mist and the river, the hill
and the stream fade from Susan's eyes, and all the colours
have passed away, the incident has closed, and there the
poem must end.

12. *The Vague and Inexact made Vivid or Precise.* — Many
changes are of this character, and the gain is often considerable.   Thus in " Michael," the old shepherd, engaged in
shearing, sits, in the original text, " with sheep before him "
under " the large old oak " near his door ; in the edition of
1836 he sits " with a fettered sheep before him stretched "
under the large old oak that " stood single " near his door.
In " Nutting," the boy, before arriving at the hazel nook, in
the text of 1800, forces his way " among the woods, and
o'er the pathless rocks "; in 1836 —

> O'er pathless rocks,
> Through beds of matted fern, and tangled thicket.

In " Stanzas written in my pocket copy of Thomson's
' Castle of Indolence ' " the beetle was described in 1815
" with his radiance manifold "; in 1827 " The beetle panoplied in gems and gold."   The Leech-gatherer in 1807 props
upon the staff his " body, limbs, and face"; in 1836 the eye

travels up from the ground, seeing first the limbs, then the body, and then dwells upon the old man's pale face :

> Himself he propped, limbs, body, and pale face,

— the idea of a pallid face being recollected from a stanza never printed (but which is found in a manuscript letter from Coleridge to Sir George Beaumont); in which Wordsworth had written " His face look'd pale as if it had grown fair." One more example out of many may suffice : in the sonnet " September 1, 180? " which describes the dejected white-robed Negro, seen on the deck of a ship that bore Wordsworth from Calais to Dover, the closing lines of the earliest version (in "The Morning Post," Feb. 11, 1803) were as follows :

> She was a Negro woman out of France
> Rejected like all others of that race,
> Not one of whom may now find footing there ;
> What is the meaning of this Ordinance ?
> Dishonoured Despots, tell us if ye dare.

After a series of alterations, the lines — contrasting the woman's languor of despair with the native brilliance of her eyes — became the following :

> Yet still her eyes retained their tropic fire,
> That, burning independent of her mind,
> Joined with the lustre of her rich attire
> To mock the Outcast — O ye Heavens, be kind !
> And feel thou, Earth, for this afflicted Race !

The later version of the sonnet is indeed a new creation.

13, 14. *New Ideas introduced; Emended Sequence of Ideas.* — The " Song for the Wandering Jew " at first consisted of five stanzas; the perpetual Wanderer, the Jew, thinks of other wanderers of earth, of air, of sea, to each of whom the rest is at some time granted which to him is forever denied; the wandering streams, the chamois, the raven, the sea-horse recur to his mind. The streams are unconscious wanderers of the earth ; but there are also unconscious wanderers of air — the clouds ; and to include this illustration a stanza was added. Earth, air, and sea have also their animate wanderers — the chamois, the sea-horse, and the raven ; but the surroundings of these creatures are little like the wilderness of a world trodden by the afflicted Jew. What creature roams a barren waste like his ? Wordsworth adds another illustration and places the new stanza immediately before that in which the mind of the Jew returns upon itself ; the ostrich is vagrant over the desert sands, yet even the ostrich has a place of rest, when at night she broods upon her eggs. It may be noted that the sequence of stanzas in this poem was changed in 1827 and again in 1836, a kind of alteration of which there are several examples, the most remarkable, perhaps, occurring in " Ruth " and " Simon Lee "; it may be entitled *Emended sequence of ideas.* Again, in the poem " To the Cuckoo," beginning " O blithe Newcomer ! " the original idea of the second stanza was that the voice of the bird wanders restlessly :

> I hear thy restless shout :
> From hill to hill it seems to pass,
> About, and all about !

The reader of the notes in the present volume can trace the interesting series of changes, extending over nearly forty years, by which the stanza attained its final perfection. It may be sufficient here to call attention to the text of 1827. Wordsworth had noticed one day that the cuckoo's voice heard from a distant tree did not seem louder as he approached the tree; he unfortunately drifted after the new observation, and from 1827 to 1843 the text stood :

> While I am lying on the grass,
> Thy twofold shout I hear,
> That seems to fill the whole air's space,
> As loud far off as near.

Happily he rejected a line which might not verify itself at once to the reader's imagination, and the final text of these four lines is gained by a combination of the readings of 1807 (ll. 1 and 3), 1827 (l. 2), and 1815 (l. 4).

15. *Ideas reversed.* — This is of rare occurrence; but two examples, one of slight importance, one of great and central significance, may be noted. In the " Danish Boy," a fragment written in Germany in 1799, it was intended to give in ballad form the story of a Danish Prince, who had fled from battle, and was murdered by the inhabitant of a cottage in which he had taken refuge. The Spirit of the youth haunts the valley in which the crime had been committed :

> A piping Shepherd he might be,
> A Herd-boy of the wood.

But the Apparition was that of a prince, and it is seen arrayed in " a regal vest of fur " in colour " like a raven's wing." How then could it be mistaken for a shepherd or a herd-boy ? Perceiving the inconsistency, Wordsworth in 1802 altered the lines that have been quoted into their exact opposite :

> Nor piping shepherd shall he be,
> Nor herd-boy of the wood.

This is a comparatively trivial emendation. But in "Laodamia" the very motive of the poem is affected by the well-known change at the close. In the earlier versions the " impassioned queen" was forgiven, if forgiveness was needed, because she had loved much ; her death was almost an euthanasia ; and she was dismissed from earth,

> to gather flowers
> Of blissful quiet 'mid unfading bowers.

In 1827 her passion was accounted a crime against reason, and her punishment was severe and perpetual ; in 1832 she was still punished, but her sufferings were purgatorial ;

finally the indictment against her was made less severe, and we are left with a hope that after her appointed time of pain is passed, she may be restored to sacred communion with her husband. This is not the place to discuss questions of justice or of mercy; the reader will find among the notes to the poem Wordsworth's statement with respect to his change of view.

16. *Personification.* — In his earliest poems, "An Evening Walk" and "Descriptive Sketches," Wordsworth does not shrink from personifications in the manner of his poetical predecessors of the eighteenth century, though perhaps less facile than some of them. A reaction followed, and the poet often preferred to speak of inanimate objects as inanimate. But gradually he came to feel that it is natural for the passions to transfer their own life to objects by which they are moved, and that the rule which imposes the literalness of the understanding upon the feelings is an arbitrary and artificial rule. Accordingly in many instances in the later text " he " or " she " replaces " it," and " his " or " her " replaces " its." One or two examples sufficiently illustrate this class of alterations. In " Michael," l. 233, in 1827,

> the sun himself
> Has scarcely been more diligent than I.

replaces the earlier reading " the sun itself." In " The Excursion," Book iii, 522, we find previous to 1827 :

> See, rooted in the earth, its kindly bed,
> The unendangered myrtle.

In 1827 and onwards, " her kindly bed." The soul, the heart, the voice in earlier editions are frequently neuter ; in later editions, feminine. A remarkable example is in the sonnet addressed to Milton (" London, 1802 "):

> and yet thy heart
> The lowliest duties on herself did lay. (1820).

Previously "itself"; and the change was made although if any heart was masculine Milton's might be so described. Similarly in "The Excursion," Book ii, ll. 411, 412 (the Solitary speaking):

> my voice
> Delivering her decisions. (1827.)

Previously "its decisions." The voice, an emanation from the soul, is feminine; but the touch, a passive function of the body, is neuter. An interesting example occurs in "The Excursion," Book viii, ll. 325–327:

> And even the touch, so exquisitely poured
> Through the whole body, with a languid will
> Performs its functions.

So stood the text in the first, and so it stands in the final edition. But in edd. 1827–1832, probably observing that he had attributed "will" to the touch, Wordsworth introduced the reading "her functions." In 1837 he returned to the original text, and this notwithstanding the attribution to the touch of a will.

17. *Deepening Religious Feeling.* — The change which took place in Wordsworth's feelings may be understood in one of its aspects if we set side by side the words from the Tintern Abbey poem of 1798:

> Knowing that Nature never did betray
> The heart that loved her

and words from an "Evening Voluntary" of 1834:

> But who *is* innocent? By grace divine,
> Not otherwise, O Nature! we are thine.

In Wordsworth's earlier temper there was something of stoicism, which as years went by was replaced or tempered by Christian faith. Perhaps the most striking example of this class of alterations will be found at the close of the story of Margaret in the first book of "The Excursion." The auditor of the story is touched with sorrow; the Wanderer, who has related the tale, exhorts him to check all excess of vain despondency or regret:

> Be wise and cheerful; and no longer read
> The forms of things with an unworthy eye.

So stood the passage from 1814 to 1845; in the latter of these years the lines became the following:

> Nor more [*i.e.* of sorrow] would she have craved as due to One
> Who, in her worst distress, had ofttimes felt
> The unbounded might of prayer; and learned, with soul
> Fixed on the Cross, that consolation springs,
> From sources deeper far than deepest pain,
> For the meek Sufferer. Why then should we read
> The forms of things with an unworthy eye?

The Wanderer proceeds to tell how, reading aright the forms of things, he recognized in all the emblems of desolation about the ruined cottage so still an image of tranquillity that transitory sorrow and despair

> Appeared an idle dream, that could not live
> Where meditation was.

So from 1814 to 1845. In the latter year:

> Appeared an idle dream, that could maintain,
> Nowhere, dominion o'er the enlightened spirit
> Whose meditative sympathies repose
> Upon the breast of faith.

This list could be much extended; but enough has been said to quicken the attention of the student of Wordsworth. He should consider for himself the reason of each emendation; the reason is seldom very obscure, and much will be learnt from such research.

VII. WORDSWORTH'S PROSE WORKS AS ILLUSTRATING HIS POEMS.

WORDSWORTH'S prose writings (which Dr. Grosart has collected into three volumes) well deserve to be read for their own sake ; but they are also of importance as a commentary on his poetical work. They fall into four chief divisions : First, those which are literary, including Wordsworth's Prefaces, his essays upon Epitaphs, the " Letter to a Friend of Robert Burns," the notes on his own poems dictated in 1843 to Isabella Fenwick, and certain letters to various correspondents; secondly, letters and other writings dealing with education, with which may be connected the admirable advice to the young, published in " The Friend " as a reply to " Mathetes " (John Wilson), who had sought for counsel in the mental and moral difficulties of ardent and aspiring youth ; thirdly, writings which may be called by a word of Wordsworth's employment " loco-descriptive," in particular his " Guide through the District of the Lakes," and the two letters on the Kendal and Windermere Railway ; last, political and social writings, — the " Apology for the French Revolution," the pamphlet suggested by the Convention of Cintra, the " Two Addresses to the Freeholders of Westmoreland," 1818, a posthumous paper on the Catholic Relief Bill, 1829, and the long note on Legislation for the Poor, the Working Classes, and the Church Establishment, which appeared in 1835 as a Postscript to " Yarrow Revisited and Other Poems."

Wordsworth's general views on the nature of poetry, on truth of language, and on the functions of metre will be found in the " Preface to the Lyrical Ballads " and the appendix on " Poetic Diction," which first appeared in 1802. If we are to define the end or object of poetry, it may be stated as

" the production of excitement in co-existence with an over-balance of pleasure " ; that is to say, its end is rather emotional than intellectual ; the truths of science, if once taken into the general consciousness of humanity, and dwelling there as the possession of enjoying and suffering men, may become genuine material or sources of song : " Poetry is the breath and finer spirit of all knowledge, it is the impassioned expression which is in the countenance of all science . . . the poet binds together by passion and knowledge the vast empire of human society, as it is spread over the whole earth, and over all time." But the poet does not create with the deliberate end in view of moving his fellows ; he creates because he is prompted to utterance by his own feelings ; not, however, by feelings in their crude form, when they tend to action, or to some realization of themselves in the real world. Poetry is " the spontaneous overflow of powerful feelings," but its origin is from those feelings " recollected in tranquillity ; the emotion is contemplated till, by a species of reaction, the tranquillity gradually disappears, and an emotion, kindred to that which was before the subject of contemplation, is gradually produced, and does itself actually exist in the mind." No description of Wordsworth's own method of composition could be more accurate. Passion is idealized before it is expressed ; and if the passion be of a tragic or pathetic kind the pain is subdued and an overbalance of pleasure is secured partly through the influence of metre, which tends to restrain as well as excite emotion, which divests language, in a certain degree, of its reality, and which communicates a series of small but continual and regular impulses of pleasurable surprise.

The first collected edition of Wordsworth's poems — that of 1815 — contained two essays on his art ; the Preface, which deals with the classification of his poems, and especially attempts to determine the difference between Fancy

and Imagination ; and the Essay supplementary to the Preface, which treats of poetry as a study, points out the quali-
fications which must exist before the decisions of a critic
can be of absolute value, rapidly surveys the poetical literature of England during the seventeenth and eighteenth cen-
turies, and from that survey draws the conclusion that every
author, as far as he is great and at the same time original,
has had the task of creating the taste by which he is to be
enjoyed.   The Preface, while discussing general principles,
is also in the strictest sense a comment by Wordsworth upon
his own work as a poet.   Fancy, according to Wordsworth, is
an aggregative and associative power, but the materials which
it brings together and connects may be insusceptible of
change ; and where they admit of modification it is enough,
for the purposes of Fancy, if the modification be slight,
limited, and evanescent.   Imagination also aggregates and
associates ; but the materials which it demands are plastic,
pliant, indefinite.   It impresses, according to fixed laws, the
results of processes of the mind upon external objects ; Milton's fleet far off at sea "*hangs* in the clouds "; the voice of
Wordsworth's stock-dove is "*buried* among trees."   Properties are conferred upon the object by Imagination, or acutal
properties are abstracted, until the object can react upon
the mind, which has performed the process, like a new existence.   The old Leech-gatherer is compared to a huge stone
" couched upon the bald top of an eminence " ; but the
stone resembles a sea-beast sunning itself on a shelf of rock ;
the stone is endowed with something of the power of life to
approximate it to the sea-beast, and the sea-beast stripped
of its vital qualities to assimilate it to the stone ; which intermediate image is thus treated for the purpose of bringing
the original image, that of the stone, to a nearer resemblance
to the figure and condition of the aged Man, who is divested
of so much of the indications of life and motion as to bring

him to the point where the two objects unite and coalesce in just comparison. Thus Imagination modifies, confers, abstracts; but it also *creates*. It creates by innumerable processes, as, for example, by consolidating numbers into unity, and again by dissolving and separating unity into number. Milton's Messiah goes forth to expel the rebel angels " attended by ten thousand thousand Saints "; but the retinue of Saints, and the Person of the Messiah himself, are lost almost and merged in the splendour of an indefinite abstraction — " Far off *his coming* shone."

Wordsworth's " Guide through the District of the Lakes " was designed less as a series of directions for the tourist (though these are not neglected) than as a companion for the *minds* of persons interested in landscape. The series of books on English landscape by Gilpin have something in common with Wordsworth's " Guide," but Gilpin viewed the features of natural beauty in special connection with the pictorial art, and considered landscape as lending itself to, or as capable of modification for, the purposes of the painter. Wordsworth's study may be described as an analysis of the several elements which make up the scenery of Westmoreland and Cumberland, and, as such, it is in fact an analysis of the material which inspired much of his poetry. Wordsworth's poetry, however, is seldom merely descriptive ; it is never literal in its descriptions. Scott, said Wordsworth, " went out with his pencil and note-book and jotted down whatever struck him most — a river rippling over the sands, a ruined tower on a rock above it, a promontory, and a mountain ash waving its red berries. He went home and wove the whole together into a poetical description." " After a pause," writes Mr. Aubrey de Vere, " Wordsworth resumed with a flashing eye and impassioned voice, ' But Nature does not permit an inventory to be made of her charms ! He should have left his pencil and note-book at home ; fixed his

eye, as he walked, with a reverent attention on all that surrounded him, and taken all into a heart that can understand
and enjoy.'" The topographical study of Wordsworth's
poetry, the identification of precise localities, is a matter of
curiosity, which has an interest of its own, and especially as
enhancing the worth of certain places through their associa-
tion with the poet's work; but it adds little to our sense
of the truth of what he has written, except as showing that
such truth is not literal but ideal. In the literal details of
landscape much is accidental; Wordsworth discovers truth,
which is general and abiding. No poet is more veracious
than he; but the body of landscape is chiefly important to
him as expressing its spirit. His yew-trees of Borrowdale
are drawn with his eye upon the object:

> Huge trunks! and each particular trunk a growth
> Of intertwisted fibres serpentine
> Up-coiling, and inveterately convolved.

We see their grassless floor of red-brown hue, the sable roof
of boughs, the unrejoicing berries; but it is the genius of
the yew-tree, its spiritual power, that chiefly interests Wordsworth's imagination; the dark grove is

> Not uninformed with Phantasy, and looks
> That threaten the profane;

and, except to one who visits the spot, it matters little what
position on the globe was occupied until the great storm of
1883 by these solemn denizens of the world of imagination.

But the elements which make up the characteristic landscape of the Lakes deserve, like the character of the people
of the district, the closest study by a lover of Wordsworth's
poetry; and his own analysis of its beauty is the best possible aid to that study. The aspect of the country as formed
by nature is first investigated; secondly, that aspect as
affected by the inhabitants; and thirdly, Wordsworth notices

the changes that had recently taken place in the district, and suggests certain " rules of taste for" preventing their bad effects." Having given a general topographical view of the locality, — a number of valleys diverging from a point midway between Great Gavel and Scawfell, like spokes from the nave of a wheel, the ridges that enclose these valleys rising towards the centre, and the mountains climbing in stages above one another, — Wordsworth proceeds with his survey in detail. The forms, the surface, the colours of the mountains are investigated ; the forms endlessly diversified, abrupt and precipitous, or soft and elegant, the surface, turf rendered rich and green by the moisture of the climate, or, in the rocky parts, schist, encrusted with lichens, bluish or hoary gray; ferns turning lemon-coloured in October, or passing from orange to russet-brown ; the apparent forms of all things often magically changed by the clouds and vapours that float around them ; in winter hoar-frost and snow, with all the varieties they create. A study follows of the valleys, the lakes, their islands, their winged inhabitants or visitors, the tarns, the woods, the atmospheric effects ; nothing essential is omitted ; nothing without some significance is included. The little volume is indeed a masterpiece in its kind ; a great scholar's primer for the study of natural beauty. And now and again will be found a passage which not merely indirectly interprets certain general characteristics of Wordsworth's poetry, but serves as the writer's comment on some particular poem. Thus, the idea of the "Address to Kilchurn Castle " is rendered into prose as follows : " It is, I grant, easy to conceive that an ancient castellated building, hanging over a precipice or raised upon an island or the peninsula of a lake, like that of Kilchurn Castle, upon Loch Awe, may not want, whether deserted or inhabited, sufficient majesty to preside for a moment in the spectator's thoughts over the high mountains among which it is embosomed ; but its titles are from antiquity — a power readily submitted to upon occasion as the vicegerent of Nature : it is respected as having owed its existence to the necessities of things, as a monument of security in times of disturbance and danger long passed away, — as a record of the pomp and violence of passion, and a symbol of the wisdom of law ; it bears a countenance of authority, which is not impaired by decay." Or compare the sonnet beginning with the words " Well may'st thou halt," in which the " lovely Cottage, in its guardian nook" is spoken of as a " precious leaf " in the book of Nature, with the following from Wordsworth's " Guide " : " These humble dwellings remind the contemplative spectator of a production of Nature, and may (using a strong expression) rather be said to have grown than to have been erected ; to have risen, by an instinct of their own, out of the native rock, so little is there in them of formality, such is their wildness and beauty." Or, again, compare the lines from " Fidelity " —

> The crags repeat the raven's croak
> In symphony austere.

with words from the "Guide " : " The waters were agitated; and the iron tone of the raven's voice, which strikes upon the ear at all times as the more dolorous from its regularity, was in fine keeping with the wild scene before our eyes." [1]

Wordsworth's political writings may be said to represent three periods in the history of his mind. The " Apology for the French Revolution " expresses his youthful ardour for what seemed the cause of liberty in France. The same temper of mind and the same opinions are reflected in certain passages of " Descriptive Sketches." His mature con-

[1] Note also the passage of the " Guide " which speaks of Carver's description of floating in his boat in the middle of Lake Erie or Ontario, and compare the poem " To H. C."

victions with respect to national well-being, and the true
spirit in which a war of freedom should be conducted, are
uttered in the pamphlet on " The Convention of Cintra."
It constitutes by far the most instructive comment in existence upon the political sonnets. His other prose writings
on public matters represent his later temper of conservatism,
allied with what may be described as the spirit of conservative reform, and they correspond with the mood of mind and
the regulative thoughts expressed in many poems of his elder
years. From first to last his veneration for man as man
and his deep interest in the joys and sorrows of the people
were predominant. Their interests never ceased to be dear
to his heart ; he only changed his beliefs as to the best mode
of doing them service. In the Postscript of 1835 to " Yarrow Revisited " he pleads against the *laissez faire* policy of
utilitarian doctrinaires; he maintains that all persons, whether
feeble and old or able-bodied, who cannot find employment
or procure wages sufficient to support the body in health
and strength, are entitled to state support; he even dares to
urge a right of nature; he maintains that a Christian government should stand *in loco parentis* towards all its subjects,
and that the claim of the state to allegiance involves the
duty of parental protection ; and he was among the early
advocates of coöperative industries, in which the workers
possess a share of the capital.

The most spirit-stirring of his political writings is undoubtedly the Convention of Cintra pamphlet. Wordsworth's
point of view is identical with that maintained in the sonnets which treat of the affairs of Spain and Portugal ; the
same thoughts are here expressed in prose, animated by the
same enthusiasm and bearing as its burden the same moral
wisdom. Removed from petty and conflicting self-interests,
and from factions which force men astray against their wills,
placed among the enduring, free, and passionate presences

of nature, Wordsworth could look into the life of things ; could submit himself to the vast impalpable motives of justice, and of the deep fraternity of nations ; could pursue those trains of reasoning and meditation which originate from and are addressed to the universal spirit of man. His purpose was not merely, with the energy of a wide-ranging intellect, to use truth as a powerful tool in the hand, but to " infuse truth as a vital fluid in the heart." It was not knowledge merely which he wished to convey; but knowledge animated by the breath and life of appropriate feeling ; it was not wisdom alone as a possession, but wisdom as a power.[1]

Two or three examples of parallels between the sonnets and the pamphlet may suffice. The majestic sonnet beginning " The power of Armies is a visible thing " asserts that the power of a brave and indignant People is superior to the mechanism of armies, as being untameable and incapable of circumscription ; it is like the wind upon the wing or like the wind sleeping " within its awful caves " ; it springs indigenous, like the subtle element of waters rising from the soil. In the pamphlet we read : "A military spirit there should be, and a military action, not confined like an ordinary river in one channel, but spreading like the Nile over the whole face of the land. . . . In the moral virtues and qualities of passion which belong to a people must the ultimate salvation of a people be sought for. . . . The Spaniards must now be taught that their strength *chiefly* lies in moral qualities, more silent in their operation, more permanent in their nature; in the virtues of perseverance, constancy, fortitude, and watchfulness, in a long memory and a quick feeling, to rise upon a favourable summons, a texture of life

[1] I have here made use of a few sentences from my article on " Wordsworth's Prose Works " in " Studies on Literature, 1789–1877."

which, though cut through (as hath been feigned of the bodies of the Angels), unites again." The sonnet "Indignation of a High-minded Spaniard" expresses the wrath and horror caused, not by the injuries of the French, but by the tyrant's specious promises of future benefit. Such "blasphemies" are described by the pamphlet as a "warfare against the conscience and the reason" — "The Spaniards groan less over the blood which has been shed than over the arrogant assumptions of beneficence made by him from whose order that blood had flowed. . . . Through the terrors of the Supreme Ruler of things, as set forth by works of destruction and ruin, we see but darkly ; we may reverence the chastisement, may fear it with awe, but it is not natural to incline towards it in love ; moreover, devastation passes away — a perishing power among things that perish ; whereas, to found and to build, to create and to institute, to bless through blessing, this has to do with objects where we trust we can see clearly, — it reminds us of what we love,— it aims at permanence." The "blasphemies" of the French lay in the assumption of this divine power of "blessing." "Say, what is Honour ? " asks Wordsworth in the sonnet; and he answers :

> 'T is the finest sense
> Of *justice* which the human mind can frame,
> Intent each lurking frailty to disclaim,
> And guard the way of life from all offence
> Suffered or done.

And the pamphlet : " For national independence and liberty, and *that* honour by which these and other blessings are to be preserved, honour — which is no other than the most elevated and pure conception of justice which can be formed — these are more precious than life."

The subject would admit of much fuller treatment, but enough has been said to indicate the importance of the study of Wordsworth's prose works as subsidiary to what he has written in verse.

The reader who desires to study Wordsworth's life in detail may be directed to the Memoirs by Christopher Wordsworth and the Life by Professor Knight. Of short biographies the best is that by Mr. Myers in the English Men of Letters series. Of the earlier criticisms the most important are that of Coleridge in " Biographia Literaria," the articles of Henry Taylor and those of De Quincey; the most valuable of recent date are those of Principal Shairp (" Studies in Poetry and Philosophy," " Aspects of Poetry," and "Poetic Interpretation of Nature "), Matthew Arnold (Introduction to Golden Treasury Selections), R. H. Hutton (" Essays Theological and Literary "), Aubrey de Vere (" Essays, Chiefly on Poetry "), Leslie Stephen (" Hours in a Library," No. XIII), Walter Pater ("Appreciations"), Dean Church (Ward's English Poets, vol. iv), Edward Caird (Essays on Literature and Philosophy). The Wordsworth Society issued in its Transactions some papers of considerable value. A bibliography of Wordsworth's writings is given in the Aldine edition of his poetical works, vol. vii.

A BIBLIOGRAPHICAL NOTE.

[For further details see the Aldine edition of Wordsworth, Vol. VII.]

1. An Evening Walk. An Epistle in Verse. 4to. 1793.
2. Descriptive Sketches in Verse. 4to. 1793.
3. Lyrical Ballads, with a few other Poems. 8vo. 1798.
4. Lyrical Ballads, with other Poems, in two volumes. 8vo. 1800.
5. Lyrical Ballads, with Pastoral and other Poems, in two volumes. 8vo. 1802.
6. Lyrical Ballads, with Pastoral and other Poems, in two volumes. 8vo. 1805.
7. Poems, in two volumes. 12mo. 1807.
8. Concerning the Relations of Great Britain, Spain, and Portugal to each other and to the common Enemy, at this crisis; and specifically as affected by the Convention of Cintra. 8vo. 1809.
9. The Excursion. 4to. 1814.
10. Poems [first collected edition], two volumes. 8vo. 1815.
11. The White Doe of Rylstone; or, the Fate of the Nortons. 4to. 1815.
12. A Letter to a Friend of Robert Burns. 8vo. 1816.
13. Thanksgiving Ode, January 18, 1816, with other short pieces. 8vo. 1816.
14. Two Addresses to the Freeholders of Westmoreland. 8vo. 1818.
15. Peter Bell, a Tale in Verse. 8vo. 1819. 2d ed., 1819.
16. The Waggoner, a Poem, to which are added Sonnets. 8vo. 1819.
17. The River Duddon, a series of Sonnets; Vandracour and Julia; and other Poems, to which is annexed a topographical description of the Country of the Lakes. 8vo. 1820. [The Topographical Description is here enlarged from Wordsworth's anonymous Introduction to Wilkinson's "Select Views," 1810.]
18. The Miscellaneous Poems of William Wordsworth, in four volumes. 12mo. 1820.
19. The Excursion [2d ed.]. 8vo. 1820.
20. Memorials of a Tour on the Continent. 8vo. 1822.

21. Ecclesiastical Sketches.   8vo.   1822.

22. A Description of the Scenery of the Lakes [first separate edition].
    12mo.   1822.   4th ed., 1823.   5th ed., 1835.

23. The Poetical Works of William Wordsworth, in five volumes.
    12mo.   1827.   ["The Excursion" now first included in a col-
    lected edition.]

24. The Poetical Works of William Wordsworth.   Paris, Galignani.
    8vo.   1828.

25. Selections from the Poems of William Wordsworth, Esq.   Chiefly
    for the use of schools and young persons.   12mo.   1831.   2d ed.,
    1834.

26. The Poetical Works of William Wordsworth, in four volumes.
    8vo.   1832.

27. Lines written after the death of Charles Lamb.   8vo.   [No title or
    date; privately printed 1835 or 1836.]

28. Yarrow Revisited, and other Poems.   12mo.   1835.   2d ed., 1836.
    3d ed., 1839.

29. The Excursion.   8vo.   1836.

30. The Poetical Works of William Wordsworth, in six volumes.   8vo.
    1836–1837.   [First stereotyped edition; reprinted 1840, 1841,
    1842, 1843, 1846, 1849.]

31. The Sonnets of William Wordsworth.   8vo.   1838.

32. Poems, Chiefly of Early and Late Years.   8vo.   1842.   [Added
    also as a seventh volume to the collected edition of Poetical
    Works.]

33. Select Pieces from the Poems of William Wordsworth.   12mo.
    1843.

34. Lines on Grace Darling.   12mo.   [No date, privately printed,
    1843.]

35. Kendal and Windermere Railway.   Two letters.   12mo.   1844 or
    early in 1845.

36. The Poems of William Wordsworth [one volume edition].   Royal
    8vo.   1845.

37. Ode, performed in the Senate-House, Cambridge.   4to.   Cambridge,
    1847.   [Also published as " Ode.   On the Installation of His
    Royal Highness Prince Albert as Chancellor of the University
    of Cambridge."   London, no date, but doubtless 1847.]

38. The Poetical Works of William Wordsworth, in six volumes.
    12mo.   1849–1850.

39. The Prelude.   8vo.   1850.   [Posthumous publication.]

40. The Recluse.   Part First, Book First.   8vo.   1888.

Of recent editions that by Professor Knight and my own edition in
　　Bell's "Aldine Edition of the British Poets" are the most
　　important.

Wordsworth's Prose Works were collected in three volumes by Dr.
　　Grosart in 1876.

The standard biographies of Wordsworth are (1) that by his nephew
　　Christopher Wordsworth, (2) that by Professor Knight. Of
　　short lives the best is that of Mr. Myers in the "English Men
　　of Letters" series.

There are several volumes of Selections, including those by Henry
　　Reed, Matthew Arnold, F. T. Palgrave, Professor Knight, and
　　other members of the Wordsworth Society, C. K. Shorter, W. J.
　　Rolfe, A. J. George. Mr. George has also edited "The Prelude"
　　and "Wordsworth's Prefaces and Essays on Poetry."

For criticism see Coleridge's "Biographia Literaria," Henry Taylor's
　　"Notes from Books," John Wilson's "Essays, Critical, etc.,"
　　De Quincey's "Recollections of Wordsworth" and "Words-
　　worth's Poetry," G. Brimley's "Essays," Lowell's "Among my
　　Books," David Masson's "Wordsworth, Shelley, Keats, etc.,"
　　J. C. Shairp's "Studies in Poetry and Philosophy" and "Aspects
　　of Poetry," Leslie Stephen's "Hours in a Library, Third Series,"
　　R. H. Hutton's "Essays, Theological and Literary," Stopford
　　Brooke's "Theology in the English Poets," E. Dowden's
　　"Studies in Literature" and "Transcripts and Studies," Matthew
　　Arnold's Preface to his volume of Selections, W. Bagehot's
　　"Literary Studies," Dean Church's "Dante and Other Essays,"
　　H. N. Hudson's "Studies in Wordsworth," A. de Vere's "Essays,
　　Chiefly on Poetry," "La Jeunesse de William Wordsworth," by
　　Émile Legouis. Of these the most useful as an introduction to
　　Wordsworth is the essay in Shairp's "Studies in Poetry and
　　Philosophy." I may mention here my own reprint of the first
　　edition of "Lyrical Ballads," which has appeared in two editions.

WORDSWORTH'S POEMS.

If thou indeed derive thy light from Heaven,
Then, to the measure of that heaven-born light,
Shine, Poet! in thy place, and be content : —
The stars preëminent in magnitude,
And they that from the zenith dart their beams,
(Visible though they be to half the earth,
Though half a sphere be conscious of their brightness)
Are yet of no diviner origin,
No purer essence, than the one that burns,
Like an untended watch-fire on the ridge
Of some dark mountain ; or than those which seem
Humbly to hang, like twinkling winter lamps,
Among the branches of the leafless trees.
All are the undying offspring of one Sire :
Then, to the measure of the light vouchsafed,
Shine, Poet! in thy place, and be content.

WORDSWORTH'S POEMS.

—••ŧ�֍ŧ•◦—

LINES

Left upon a Seat in a Yew-tree, which stands near the lake of Esthwaite, on a
desolate part of the shore, commanding a beautiful prospect.

NAY, Traveller! rest. This lonely Yew-tree stands
Far from all human dwelling: what if here
No sparkling rivulet spread the verdant herb?
What if the bee love not these barren boughs?
Yet, if the wind breathe soft, the curling waves,   5
That break against the shore, shall lull thy mind
By one soft impulse saved from vacancy.
————————————Who he was
That piled these stones and with the mossy sod
First covered, and here taught this aged Tree   10
With its dark arms to form a circling bower,
I well remember. — He was one who owned
No common soul. In youth by science nursed,
And led by nature into a wild scene
Of lofty hopes, he to the world went forth   15
A favoured Being, knowing no desire
Which genius did not hallow ; 'gainst the taint
Of dissolute tongues, and jealousy, and hate,
And scorn, — against all enemies prepared,
All but neglect. The world, for so it thought,   20
Owed him no service ; wherefore he at once
With indignation turned himself away,
And with the food of pride sustained his soul

LINES.

In solitude. — Stranger ! these gloomy boughs
Had charms for him ; and here he loved to sit,   25
His only visitants a straggling sheep,
The stone-chat, or the glancing sand-piper :
And on these barren rocks, with fern and heath,
And juniper and thistle, sprinkled o'er,
Fixing his downcast eye, he many an hour   30
A morbid pleasure nourished, tracing here
An emblem of his own unfruitful life :
And, lifting up his head, he then would gaze
On the more distant scene, — how lovely 't is
Thou seest, — and he would gaze till it became   35
Far lovelier, and his heart could not sustain
The beauty, still more beauteous !   Nor, that time,
When nature had subdued him to herself,
Would he forget those Beings to whose minds,
Warm from the labours of benevolence,   40
The world, and human life, appeared a scene
Of kindred loveliness : then he would sigh,
Inly disturbed, to think that others felt
What he must never feel : and so, lost Man !
On visionary views would fancy feed,   45
Till his eye streamed with tears.   In this deep vale
He died, — this seat his only monument.
If Thou be one whose heart the holy forms
Of young imagination have kept pure,
Stranger ! henceforth be warned ; and know that pride,   50
Howe'er disguised in its own majesty,
Is littleness ; that he, who feels contempt
For any living thing, hath faculties
Which he has never used ; that thought with him
Is in its infancy.   The man whose eye   55
Is ever on himself doth look on one,
The least of Nature's works, one who might move

The wise man to that scorn which wisdom holds
Unlawful, ever.   O be wiser, Thou!
Instructed that true knowledge leads to love ;   60
True dignity abides with him alone
Who, in the silent hour of inward thought,
Can still suspect, and still revere himself,
In lowliness of heart.   1795.

MARGARET ; OR THE RUINED COTTAGE.

'T WAS summer, and the sun had mounted high :
Southward the landscape indistinctly glared
Through a pale steam ; but all the northern downs,
In clearest air ascending, showed far off
A surface dappled o'er with shadows flung   5
From brooding clouds ; shadows that lay in spots
Determined and unmoved, with steady beams
Of bright and pleasant sunshine interposed ;
To him most pleasant who on soft cool moss
Extends his careless limbs along the front   10
Of some huge cave, whose rocky ceiling casts
A twilight of its own, an ample shade,
Where the wren warbles, while the dreaming man,
Half conscious of the soothing melody,
With side-long eye looks out upon the scene,   15
By power of that impending covert, thrown
To finer distance.   Mine was at that hour
Far other lot, yet with good hope that soon
Under a shade as grateful I should find
Rest, and be welcomed there to livelier joy.   20
Across a bare wide Common I was toiling
With languid steps that by the slippery turf

Were baffled ; nor could my weak arm disperse
The host of insects gathering round my face,
And ever with me as I paced along.   25

    Upon that open moorland stood a grove,
The wished-for port to which my course was bound.
Thither I came, and there, amid the gloom
Spread by a brotherhood of lofty elms,
Appeared a roofless Hut ; four naked walls   30
That stared upon each other ! — I looked round,
And to my wish and to my hope espied
The Friend I sought ; a Man of reverend age,
But stout and hale, for travel unimpaired.
There was he seen upon the cottage-bench,   35
Recumbent in the shade, as if asleep ;
An iron-pointed staff lay at his side.

.   .   .   .

. . . Supine the Wanderer lay,
His eyes as if in drowsiness half shut,
The shadows of the breezy elms above   40
Dappling his face. He had not heard the sound
Of my approaching steps, and in the shade
Unnoticed did I stand some minutes' space.
At length I hailed him, seeing that his hat
Was moist with water-drops, as if the brim   45
Had newly scooped a running stream. He rose,
And ere our lively greeting into peace
Had settled, " 'T is," said I, " a burning day :
My lips are parched with thirst, but you, it seems
Have somewhere found relief." He, at the word,   50
Pointing towards a sweet-briar, bade me climb
The fence where that aspiring shrub looked out
Upon the public way. It was a plot
Of garden ground run wild, its matted weeds

Marked with the steps of those, whom, as they passed,   55
The gooseberry trees that shot in long lank slips,
Or currants, hanging from their leafless stems,
In scanty strings, had tempted to o'erleap
The broken wall.   I looked around, and there,
Where two tall hedge-rows of thick alder boughs   60
Joined in a cold damp nook, espied a well
Shrouded with willow-flowers and plumy fern.
My thirst I slaked, and, from the cheerless spot
Withdrawing, straightway to the shade returned
Where sate the old Man on the cottage-bench ;   65
And, while, beside him, with uncovered head,
I yet was standing, freely to respire,
And cool my temples in the fanning air,
Thus did he speak.   " I see around me here
Things which you cannot see : we die, my Friend,   70
Nor we alone, but that which each man loved
And prized in his peculiar nook of earth
Dies with him, or is changed ; and very soon
Even of the good is no memorial left.
— The Poets, in their elegies and songs   75
Lamenting the departed, call the groves,
They call upon the hills and streams, to mourn,
And senseless rocks ; nor idly ; for they speak,
In these their invocations, with a voice
Obedient to the strong creative power   80
Of human passion.   Sympathies there are
More tranquil, yet perhaps of kindred birth,
That steal upon the meditative mind,
And grow with thought.   Beside yon spring I stood,
And eyed its waters till we seemed to feel   85
One sadness, they and I.   For them a bond
Of brotherhood is broken : time has been
When, every day, the touch of human hand

Dislodged the natural sleep that binds them up
In mortal stillness ; and they ministered   90
To human comfort.   Stooping down to drink,
Upon the slimy foot-stone I espied
The useless fragment of a wooden bowl,
Green with the moss of years, and subject only
To the soft handling of the elements :   95
There let it lie — how foolish are such thoughts !
Forgive them ; — never — never did my steps
Approach this door but she who dwelt within
A daughter's welcome gave me, and I loved her
As my own child.   Oh, Sir ! the good die first,   100
And they whose hearts are dry as summer dust
Burn to the socket.   Many a passenger
Hath blessed poor Margaret for her gentle looks,
When she upheld the cool refreshment drawn
From that forsaken spring ; and no one came   105
But he was welcome ; no one went away
But that it seemed she loved him.   She is dead,
The light extinguished of her lonely hut,
The hut itself abandoned to decay,
And she forgotten in the quiet grave.   110

   " I speak," continued he, " of One whose stock
Of virtues bloomed beneath this lonely roof.
She was a Woman of a steady mind,
Tender and deep in her excess of love ;
Not speaking much, pleased rather with the joy   115
Of her own thoughts : by some especial care
Her temper had been framed, as if to make
A Being, who by adding love to peace
Might live on earth a life of happiness.
Her wedded Partner lacked not on his side   120
The humble worth that satisfied her heart :

Frugal, affectionate, sober, and withal
Keenly industrious.   She with pride would tell
That he was often seated at his loom,
In summer, ere the mower was abroad   125
Among the dewy grass, — in early spring,
Ere the last star had vanished. — They who passed
At evening, from behind the garden fence
Might hear his busy spade, which he would ply,
After his daily work, until the light   130
Had failed, and every leaf and flower were lost
In the dark hedges.   So their days were spent
In peace and comfort; and a pretty boy
Was their best hope, next to the God in heaven.

"Not twenty years ago, but you I think   135
Can scarcely bear it now in mind, there came
Two blighting seasons, when the fields were left
With half a harvest.   It pleased Heaven to add
A worse affliction in the plague of war:
This happy Land was stricken to the heart!   140
A Wanderer then among the cottages,
I, with my freight of winter raiment, saw
The hardships of that season : many rich
Sank down, as in a dream, among the poor;
And of the poor did many cease to be,   145
And their place knew them not.   Meanwhile, abridged
Of daily comforts, gladly reconciled
To numerous self-denials, Margaret
Went struggling on through those calamitous years
With cheerful hope, until the second autumn,   150
When her life's Helpmate on a sick-bed lay,
Smitten with perilous fever.   In disease
He lingered long ; and, when his strength returned,
He found the little he had stored, to meet

The hour of accident or crippling age,   155
Was all consumed.   A second infant now
Was added to the troubles of a time
Laden, for them and all of their degree,
With care and sorrow ; shoals of artisans
From ill-requited labour turned adrift   160
Sought daily bread from public charity,
They, and their wives and children — happier far
Could they have lived as do the little birds
That peck along the hedge-rows, or the kite
That makes her dwelling on the mountain rocks !   165

  " A sad reverse it was for him who long
Had filled with plenty, and possessed in peace,
This lonely Cottage.   At the door he stood,
And whistled many a snatch of merry tunes
That had no mirth in them ; or with his knife   170
Carved uncouth figures on the heads of sticks —
Then, not less idly, sought, through every nook
In house or garden, any casual work
Of use or ornament ; and with a strange,
Amusing, yet uneasy, novelty,   175
He mingled, where he might, the various tasks
Of summer, autumn, winter, and of spring.
But this endured not ; his good humour soon
Became a weight in which no pleasure was :
And poverty brought on a petted mood   180
And a sore temper : day by day he drooped,
And he would leave his work — and to the town
Would turn without an errand his slack steps ;
Or wander here and there among the fields.
One while he would speak lightly of his babes,   185
And with a cruel tongue : at other times
He tossed them with a false unnatural joy :

And 't was a rueful thing to see the looks
Of the poor innocent children. ' Every smile,'
Said Margaret to me, here beneath these trees,   190
' Made my heart bleed.' "

      At this the Wanderer paused;
And, looking up to those enormous elms,
He said, " 'T is now the hour of deepest noon.
At this still season of repose and peace,
This hour when all things which are not at rest   195
Are cheerful; while this multitude of flies
With tuneful hum is filling all the air;
Why should a tear be on an old Man's cheek?
Why should we thus, with an untoward mind,
And in the weakness of humanity,   200
From natural wisdom turn our hearts away;
To natural comfort shut our eyes and ears;
And, feeding on disquiet, thus disturb
The calm of nature with our restless thoughts? "

HE spake with somewhat of a solemn tone: 205
But, when he ended, there was in his face
Such easy cheerfulness, a look so mild,
That for a little time it stole away
All recollection; and that simple tale
Passed from my mind like a forgotten sound.   210
A while on trivial things we held discourse,
To me soon tasteless. In my own despite,
I thought of that poor Woman as of one
Whom I had known and loved. He had rehearsed
Her homely tale with such familiar power,   215
With such an active countenance, an eye
So busy, that the things of which he spake
Seemed present; and, attention now relaxed,

A heart-felt chillness crept along my veins.
I rose ; and, having left the breezy shade,   220
Stood drinking comfort from the warmer sun,
That had not cheered me long — ere, looking round
Upon that tranquil Ruin, I returned,
And begged of the old Man that, for my sake,
He would resume his story.

                              He replied,   225
" It were a wantonness, and would demand
Severe reproof, if we were men whose hearts
Could hold vain dalliance with the misery
Even of the dead ; contented thence to draw
A momentary pleasure, never marked   230
By reason, barren of all future good.
But we have known that there is often found
In mournful thoughts, and always might be found,
A power to virtue friendly ; were 't not so,
I am a dreamer among men, indeed   235
An idle dreamer !   'T is a common tale,
An ordinary sorrow of man's life,
A tale of silent suffering, hardly clothed
In bodily form. — But without further bidding
I will proceed.

                      While thus it fared with them,   240
To whom this cottage, till those hapless years,
Had been a blessèd home, it was my chance
To travel in a country far remote ;
And when these lofty elms once more appeared
What pleasant expectations lured me on   245
O'er the flat Common ! — With quick step I reached
The threshold, lifted with light hand the latch ;
But, when I entered, Margaret looked at me
A little while ; then turned her head away

Speechless, — and, sitting down upon a chair,   250
Wept bitterly.   I wist not what to do,
Nor how to speak to her.   Poor Wretch! at last
She rose from off her seat, and then, — O Sir!
I cannot *tell* how she pronounced my name : —
With fervent love, and with a face of grief   255
Unutterably helpless, and a look
That seemed to cling upon me, she enquired
If I had seen her husband.   As she spake
A strange surprise and fear came to my heart,
Nor had I power to answer ere she told   260
That he had disappeared — not two months gone.
He left his house : two wretched days had past,
And on the third, as wistfully she raised
Her head from off her pillow, to look forth,
Like one in trouble, for returning light,   265
Within her chamber-casement she espied
A folded paper, lying as if placed
To meet her waking eyes.   This tremblingly
She opened — found no writing, but beheld
Pieces of money carefully enclosed,   270
Silver and gold.   'I shuddered at the sight,'
Said Margaret, 'for I knew it was his hand
That must have placed it there ; and ere that day
Was ended, that long anxious day, I learned,
From one who by my husband had been sent   275
With the sad news, that he had joined a troop
Of soldiers, going to a distant land.
— He left me thus — he could not gather heart
To take a farewell of me ; for he feared
That I should follow with my babes, and sink   280
Beneath the misery of that wandering life.'

    " This tale did Margaret tell with many tears :
And, when she ended, I had little power

To give her comfort, and was glad to take
Such words of hope from her own mouth as served   285
To cheer us both.   But long we had not talked
Ere we built up a pile of better thoughts,
And with a brighter eye she looked around
As if she had been shedding tears of joy.
We parted. — 'T was the time of early spring ;   290
I left her busy with her garden tools ;
And well remember, o'er that fence she looked,
And, while I paced along the foot-way path,
Called out, and sent a blessing after me,
With tender cheerfulness, and with a voice   295
That seemed the very sound of happy thoughts.

" I roved o'er many a hill and many a dale,
With my accustomed load ; in heat and cold,
Through many a wood and many an open ground,
In sunshine and in shade, in wet and fair,   300
Drooping or blithe of heart, as might befall ;
My best companions now the driving winds,
And now the ' trotting brooks ' and whispering trees,
And now the music of my own sad steps,
With many a short-lived thought that passed between,   305
And disappeared.
              I journeyed back this way,
When, in the warmth of midsummer, the wheat
Was yellow ; and the soft and bladed grass,
Springing afresh, had o'er the hay-field spread
Its tender verdure.   At the door arrived,   310
I found that she was absent.   In the shade,
Where now we sit, I waited her return.
Her cottage, then a cheerful object, wore
Its customary look, — only, it seemed,
The honeysuckle, crowding round the porch,   315

Hung down in heavier tufts ; and that bright weed.
The yellow stone-crop, suffered to take root
Along the window's edge, profusely grew,
Blinding the lower panes.   I turned aside,
And strolled into her garden.   It appeared   320
To lag behind the season, and had lost
Its pride of neatness.   Daisy-flowers and thrift
Had broken their trim border-lines, and straggled
O'er paths they used to deck: carnations, once
Prized for surpassing beauty, and no less   325
For the peculiar pains they had required,
Declined their languid heads, wanting support.
The cumbrous bind-weed, with its wreaths and bells,
Had twined about her two small rows of peas,
And dragged them to the earth.
               Ere this an hour   330
Was wasted. — Back I turned my restless steps;
A stranger passed ; and, guessing whom I sought,
He said that she was used to ramble far. —
The sun was sinking in the west ; and now
I sate with sad impatience.   From within   335
Her solitary infant cried aloud;
Then, like a blast that dies away self-stilled,
The voice was silent.   From the bench I rose ;
But neither could divert nor soothe my thoughts.
The spot, though fair, was very desolate —   340
The longer I remained, more desolate :
And, looking round me, now I first observed
The corner stones, on either side the porch,
With dull red stains discoloured, and stuck o'er
With tufts and hairs of wool, as if the sheep,   345
That fed upon the Common, thither came
Familiarly, and found a couching-place
Even at her threshold.   Deeper shadows fell

From these tall elms; the cottage-clock struck eight; —
I turned, and saw her distant a few steps.   350
Her face was pale and thin — her figure, too,
Was changed.   As she unlocked the door, she said,
'It grieves me you have waited here so long,
But, in good truth, I 've wandered much of late,
And sometimes — to my shame I speak — have need   355
Of my best prayers to bring me back again.
While on the board she spread our evening meal,
She told me — interrupting not the work
Which gave employment to her listless hands —
That she had parted with her elder child;   360
To a kind master on a distant farm
Now happily apprenticed. — 'I perceive
You look at me, and you have cause; to-day
I have been travelling far; and many days
About the fields I wander, knowing this   365
Only, that what I seek I cannot find;
And so I waste my time: for I am changed;
And to myself,' said she, 'have done much wrong
And to this helpless infant.   I have slept
Weeping, and weeping have I waked; my tears   370
Have flowed as if my body were not such
As others are; and I could never die.
But I am now in mind and in my heart
More easy; and I hope,' said she, 'that God
Will give me patience to endure the things   375
Which I behold at home.'

               It would have grieved
Your very soul to see her.   Sir, I feel
The story linger in my heart; I fear
'T is long and tedious; but my spirit clings
To that poor Woman : — so familiarly   380
Do I perceive her manner, and her look,

And presence ; and so deeply do I feel
Her goodness, that, not seldom, in my walks
A momentary trance comes over me ;
And to myself I seem to muse on One 385
By sorrow laid asleep; or borne away,
A human being destined to awake
To human life, or something very near
To human life, when he shall come again
For whom she suffered.   Yes, it would have grieved 390
Your very soul to see her: evermore
Her eyelids drooped, her eyes downward were cast;
And, when she at her table gave me food,
She did not look at me.   Her voice was low,
Her body was subdued.   In every act 395
Pertaining to her house-affairs, appeared
The careless stillness of a thinking mind
Self-occupied; to which all outward things
Are like an idle matter.   Still she sighed,
But yet no motion of the breast was seen, 400
No heaving of the heart.   While by the fire
We sate together, sighs came on my ear,
I knew not how, and hardly whence they came.

"Ere my departure, to her care I gave,
For her son's use, some tokens of regard, 405
Which with a look of welcome she received ;
And I exhorted her to place her trust
In God's good love, and seek his help by prayer.
I took my staff, and, when I kissed her babe,
The tears stood in her eyes.   I left her then 410
With the best hope and comfort I could give :
She thanked me for my wish ; — but for my hope
It seemed she did not thank me.
                                        I returned,
And took my rounds along this road again

When on its sunny bank the primrose flower   415
Peeped forth, to give an earnest of the Spring.
I found her sad and drooping : she had learned
No tidings of her husband ; if he lived,
She knew not that he lived ; if he were dead,
She knew not he was dead.   She seemed the same   420
In person and appearance; but her house
Bespake a sleepy hand of negligence ;
The floor was neither dry nor neat, the hearth
Was comfortless, and her small lot of books,
Which, in the cottage-window, heretofore   425
Had been piled up against the corner panes
In seemly order, now, with straggling leaves
Lay scattered here and there, open or shut,
As they had chanced to fall.   Her infant Babe
Had from his Mother caught the trick of grief,   430
And sighed among its playthings.   I withdrew,
And once again entering the garden saw,
More plainly still, that poverty and grief
Were now come nearer to her : weeds defaced
The hardened soil, and knots of withered grass :   435
No ridges there appeared of clear black mould,
No winter greenness ; of her herbs and flowers,
It seemed the better part was gnawed away
Or trampled into earth; a chain of straw,
Which had been twined about the slender stem   440
Of a young apple-tree, lay at its root ;
The bark was nibbled round by truant sheep.
— Margaret stood near, her infant in her arms,
And, noting that my eye was on the tree,
She said, 'I fear it will be dead and gone   445
Ere Robert come again.'   When to the House
We had returned together, she enquired
If I had any hope : — but for her babe

And for her little orphan boy, she said,
She had no wish to live, that she must die   450
Of sorrow.   Yet I saw the idle loom
Still in its place ; his Sunday garments hung
Upon the self-same nail; his very staff
Stood undisturbed behind the door.
                   And when,
In bleak December, I retraced this way,   455
She told me that her little babe was dead,
And she was left alone.   She now, released
From her maternal cares, had taken up
The employment common through these wilds, and gained,
By spinning hemp, a pittance for herself ;   460
And for this end had hired a neighbour's boy
To give her needful help.   That very time
Most willingly she put her work aside,
And walked with me along the miry road,
Heedless how far ; and, in such piteous sort   465
That any heart had ached to hear her, begged
That, wheresoe'er I went, I still would ask
For him whom she had lost.   We parted then —
Our final parting ; for from that time forth
Did many seasons pass ere I returned   470
Into this tract again.
                 Nine tedious years ;
From their first separation, nine long years,
She lingered in unquiet widowhood ;
A Wife and Widow.   Needs must it have been
A sore heart-wasting !   I have heard, my Friend,   475
That in yon arbour oftentimes she sate
Alone, through half the vacant sabbath day ;
And, if a dog passed by, she still would quit
The shade, and look abroad.   On this old bench
For hours she sate ; and evermore her eye   480

Was busy in the distance, shaping things
That made her heart beat quick.   You see that path,
Now faint, — the grass has crept o'er its grey line;
There, to and fro, she paced through many a day
Of the warm summer, from a belt of hemp   485
That girt her waist, spinning the long-drawn thread
With backward steps.   Yet ever as there passed
A man whose garments showed the soldier's red,
Or crippled mendicant in sailor's garb,
The little child who sate to turn the wheel   490
Ceased from his task; and she with faltering voice
Made many a fond enquiry; and when they,
Whose presence gave no comfort, were gone by,
Her heart was still more sad.   And by yon gate,
That bars the traveller's road, she often stood,   495
And when a stranger horseman came, the latch
Would lift, and in his face look wistfully;
Most happy, if, from aught discovered there
Of tender feeling, she might dare repeat
The same sad question.   Meanwhile her poor Hut   500
Sank to decay; for he was gone, whose hand,
At the first nipping of October frost,
Closed up each chink, and with fresh bands of straw
Chequered the green-grown thatch.   And so she lived
Through the long winter, reckless and alone;   505
Until her house by frost, and thaw, and rain,
Was sapped; and while she slept, the nightly damps
Did chill her breast; and in the stormy day
Her tattered clothes were ruffled by the wind,
Even at the side of her own fire.   Yet still   510
She loved this wretched spot, nor would for worlds
Have parted hence; and still that length of road,
And this rude bench, one torturing hope endeared,
Fast rooted at her heart: and here, my Friend, —

In sickness she remained; and here she died; 515
Last human tenant of these ruined walls!"

The old Man ceased: he saw that I was moved;
From that low bench, rising instinctively,
I turned aside in weakness, nor had power
To thank him for the tale which he had told. 520
I stood, and leaning o'er the garden wall
Reviewed that Woman's sufferings; and it seemed
To comfort me while with a brother's love
I blessed her in the impotence of grief.
Then towards the cottage I returned; and traced 525
Fondly, though with an interest more mild,
That secret spirit of humanity
Which, 'mid the calm, oblivious tendencies
Of nature, 'mid her plants, and weeds, and flowers,
And silent overgrowings, still survived. 530
The old Man, noting this, resumed, and said,
"My Friend! enough to sorrow you have given,
The purposes of wisdom ask no more:
Nor more would she have craved as due to One
Who, in her worst distress, had ofttimes felt 535
The unbounded might of prayer; and learned, with soul
Fixed on the Cross, that consolation springs,
From sources deeper far than deepest pain,
For the meek Sufferer. Why then should we read
The forms of things with an unworthy eye? 540
She sleeps in the calm earth, and peace is here.
I well remember that those very plumes,
Those weeds, and the high spear-grass on that wall,
By mist and silent rain-drops silvered o'er,
As once I passed, into my heart conveyed 545
So still an image of tranquillity,
So calm and still, and looked so beautiful

Amid the uneasy thoughts which filled my mind,
That what we feel of sorrow and despair
From ruin and from change, and all the grief 550
That passing shows of Being leave behind,
Appeared an idle dream, that could maintain,
Nowhere, dominion o'er the enlightened spirit
Whose meditative sympathies repose
Upon the breast of Faith.   I turned away, 555
And walked along my road in happiness."

   He ceased.   Ere long the sun declining shot
A slant and mellow radiance, which began
To fall upon us, while, beneath the trees,
We sate on that low bench: and now we felt, 560
Admonished thus, the sweet hour coming on.
A linnet warbled from those lofty elms,
A thrush sang loud, and other melodies,
At distance heard, peopled the milder air.
The old Man rose, and, with a sprightly mien 565
Of hopeful preparation, grasped his staff;
Together casting then a farewell look
Upon those silent walls, we left the shade;
And, ere the stars were visible, had reached
A village-inn, — our evening resting-place.

                              1795–1798.

THE REVERIE OF POOR SUSAN.

AT the corner of Wood Street, when daylight appears,
Hangs a Thrush that sings loud, it has sung for three
      years:
Poor Susan has passed by the spot, and has heard
In the silence of morning the song of the Bird.

'T is a note of enchantment; what ails her ?   She sees   5
A mountain ascending, a vision of trees ;
Bright volumes of vapour through Lothbury glide,
And a river flows on through the vale of Cheapside.

Green pastures she views in the midst of the dale,
Down which she so often has tripped with her pail ;   10
And a single small cottage, a nest like a dove's,
The one only dwelling on earth that she loves.

She looks, and her heart is in heaven : but they fade,
The mist and the river, the hill and the shade :
The stream will not flow, and the hill will not rise,   15
And the colours have all passed away from her eyes !

1797.

A NIGHT-PIECE.

———— THE sky is overcast,
With a continuous cloud of texture close,
Heavy and wan, all whitened by the Moon,
Which through that veil is indistinctly seen,
A dull, contracted circle, yielding light   5
So feebly spread, that not a shadow falls,
Chequering the ground—from rock, plant, tree, or tower.
At length a pleasant instantaneous gleam
Startles the pensive traveller while he treads
His lonesome path, with unobserving eye   10
Bent earthwards ; he looks up — the clouds are split
Asunder, — and above his head he sees
The clear Moon, and the glory of the heavens.
There, in a black-blue vault she sails along,
Followed by multitudes of stars, that, small   15

And sharp, and bright, along the dark abyss
Drive as she drives : how fast they wheel away,
Yet vanish not ! — the wind is in the tree,
But they are silent ; — still they roll along
Immeasurably distant ; and the vault,   20
Built round by those white clouds, enormous clouds,
Still deepens its unfathomable depth.
At length the Vision closes ; and the mind,
Not undisturbed by the delight it feels,
Which slowly settles into peaceful calm,   25
Is left to muse upon the solemn scene.

                                                  1798.

WE ARE SEVEN.

———— A SIMPLE Child,
That lightly draws its breath,
And feels its life in every limb,
What should it know of death ?

I met a little cottage Girl :   5
She was eight years old, she said ;
Her hair was thick with many a curl
That clustered round her head.

She had a rustic, woodland air,
And she was wildly clad :   10
Her eyes were fair, and very fair ;
— Her beauty made me glad.

" Sisters and brothers, little Maid,
How many may you be ? "
" How many ?   Seven in all," she said   15
And wondering looked at me.

"And where are they? I pray you tell."
She answered, "Seven are we;
And two of us at Conway dwell,
And two are gone to sea.   20

"Two of us in the church-yard lie,
My sister and my brother;
And, in the church-yard cottage, I
Dwell near them with my mother."

"You say that two at Conway dwell,   25
And two are gone to sea,
Yet ye are seven! — I pray you tell,
Sweet Maid, how this may be."

Then did the little Maid reply,
"Seven boys and girls are we;   30
Two of us in the church-yard lie,
Beneath the church-yard tree."

"You run about, my little Maid,
Your limbs they are alive;
If two are in the church-yard laid,   35
Then ye are only five."

"Their graves are green, they may be seen,"
The little maid replied,
"Twelve steps or more from my mother's door,
And they are side by side   40

"My stockings there I often knit,
My kerchief there I hem;
And there upon the ground I sit,
And sing a song to them.

"And often after sunset, Sir,   45
When it is light and fair,
I take my little porringer,
And eat my supper there.

LITTLE

"The first that died was sister Jane ;
In bed she moaning lay,   50
Till God released her of her pain ;
And then she went away.

"So in the church-yard she was laid ;
And, when the grass was dry,   *And all the Summer dry*
Together round her grave we played,   55
My brother John and I.

"And when the ground was white with snow,
And I could run and slide,
My brother John was forced to go,
And he lies by her side."   60

"How many are you, then," said I,
"If they two are in heaven?"
Quick was the little Maid's reply,   *THE LITTLE MAIDEN*
"O Master! we are seven."   *DID REPLY*

"But they are dead; those two are dead!   65
Their spirits are in heaven!"
'T was throwing words away; for still
The little Maid would have her will,
And said, "Nay, we are seven!"

1798.

SIMON LEE

THE OLD HUNTSMAN; WITH AN INCIDENT IN WHICH
HE WAS CONCERNED.

In the sweet shire of Cardigan,
Not far from pleasant Ivor-hall,
An old Man dwells, a little man,
'T is said he once was tall.
Full five-and-thirty years he lived   5
A running huntsman merry;
And still the centre of his cheek
Is red as a ripe cherry.

No man like him the horn could sound,
And hill and valley rang with glee   10
When Echo bandied, round and round,
The halloo of Simon Lee.
In those proud days, he little cared
For husbandry or tillage;
To blither tasks did Simon rouse   15
The sleepers of the village.

He all the country could outrun,
Could leave both man and horse behind;
And often, ere the chase was done,
He reeled, and was stone-blind.   20
And still there 's something in the world
At which his heart rejoices;
For when the chiming hounds are out,
He dearly loves their voices !

But, oh the heavy change ! — bereft   25
Of health, strength, friends, and kindred, see!
Old Simon to the world is left
In liveried poverty.

His Master 's dead, — and no one now
Dwells in the Hall of Ivor;   30
Men, dogs, and horses, all are dead;
He is the sole survivor.

And he is lean and he is sick;
His body dwindled and awry,
Rests upon ankles swoln and thick;   35
His legs are thin and dry.
One prop he has, and only one,
His wife, an aged woman,
Lives with him, near the waterfall,
Upon the village Common.   40

Beside their moss-grown hut of clay,
Not twenty paces from the door,
A scrap of land they have, but they
Are poorest of the poor.
This scrap of land he from the heath   45
Enclosed when he was stronger;
But what to them avails the land
Which he can till no longer?

Oft, working by her Husband's side,
Ruth does what Simon cannot do;   50
For she, with scanty cause for pride,
Is stouter of the two.
And, though you with your utmost skill
From labour could not wean them,
'T is little, very little — all   55
That they can do between them.

Few months of life has he in store
As he to you will tell,
For still, the more he works, the more
Do his weak ankles swell.   60

My gentle Reader, I perceive
How patiently you 've waited,
And now I fear that you expect
Some tale will be related.

O Reader ! had you in your mind   65
Such stores as silent thought can bring,
O gentle Reader ! you would find
A tale in every thing.
What more I have to say is short,
And you must kindly take it :   70
It is no tale ; but, should you think,
Perhaps a tale you 'll make it.

One summer-day I chanced to see
This old Man doing all he could
To unearth the root of an old tree,   75
A stump of rotten wood.
The mattock tottered in his hand ;
So vain was his endeavour,
That at the root of the old tree
He might have worked for ever.   80

" You 're overtasked, good Simon Lee,
Give me your tool," to him I said ;
And at the word right gladly he
Received my proffered aid.
I struck, and with a single blow   85
The tangled root I severed,
At which the poor old Man so long
And vainly had endeavoured.

The tears into his eyes were brought,
And thanks and praises seemed to run   90
So fast out of his heart, I thought
They never would have done.

— I 've heard of hearts unkind, kind deeds
With coldness still returning ;
Alas ! the gratitude of men   95
Hath oftener left me mourning.

1798.

LINES WRITTEN IN EARLY SPRING.

I HEARD a thousand blended notes,
While in a grove I sate reclined,
In that sweet mood when pleasant thoughts
Bring sad thoughts to the mind.

To her fair works did Nature link   5
The human soul that through me ran ;
And much it grieved my heart to think
What man has made of man.

Through primrose tufts, in that green bower,
The periwinkle trailed its wreaths ;   10
And 't is my faith that every flower
Enjoys the air it breathes.

The birds around me hopped and played,
Their thoughts I cannot measure : —
But the least motion which they made   15
It seemed a thrill of pleasure.

The budding twigs spread out their fan,
To catch the breezy air ;
And I must think, do all I can,
That there was pleasure there.   20

If this belief from heaven be sent,
If such be Nature's holy plan,
Have I not reason to lament
What man has made of man?

1798.

TO MY SISTER.

It is the first mild day of March:
Each minute sweeter than before,
The redbreast sings from the tall larch
That stands beside our door.

There is a blessing in the air,   5
Which seems a sense of joy to yield
To the bare trees, and mountains bare,
And grass in the green field.

My sister! ('t is a wish of mine)
Now that our morning meal is done,   10
Make haste, your morning task resign;
Come forth and feel the sun.

Edward will come with you; — and, pray,
Put on with speed your woodland dress;
And bring no book: for this one day   15
We 'll give to idleness.

No joyless forms shall regulate
Our living calendar:
We from to-day, my Friend, will date
The opening of the year.   20

Love, now a universal birth,
From heart to heart is stealing,
From earth to man, from man to earth :
— It is the hour of feeling.

One moment now may give us more   25
Than years of toiling reason :
Our minds shall drink at every pore
The spirit of the season.

Some silent laws our hearts will make,
Which they shall long obey :   30
We for the year to come may take
Our temper from to-day.

And from the blessed power that rolls
About, below, above,
We 'll frame the measure of our souls :   35
They shall be tuned to love.

Then come, my Sister ! come, I pray,
With speed put on your woodland dress ;
And bring no book : for this one day
We 'll give to idleness.   40

1798.

EXPOSTULATION AND REPLY.

"WHY, William, on that old grey stone,
Thus for the length of half a day,
Why, William, sit you thus alone,
And dream your time away?

" Where are your books ? — that light bequeathed   5
To Beings else forlorn and blind !
Up ! up ! and drink the spirit breathed
From dead men to their kind.

" You look round on your Mother Earth,
As if she for no purpose bore you ;   10
As if you were her first-born birth,
And none had lived before you ! "

One morning thus, by Esthwaite lake,
When life was sweet, I knew not why,
To me my good friend Matthew spake,   15
And thus I made reply :

" The eye — it cannot choose but see ;
We cannot bid the ear be still ;
Our bodies feel, where'er they be,
Against or with our will.   20

" Nor less I deem that there are Powers
Which of themselves our minds impress ;
That we can feed this mind of ours
In a wise passiveness.

" Think you, 'mid all this mighty sum   25
Of things for ever speaking,
That nothing of itself will come,
But we must still be seeking ?

" — Then ask not wherefore, here, alone,
Conversing as I may,   30
I sit upon this old grey stone,
And dream my time away."   1798.

THE TABLES TURNED.

AN EVENING SCENE ON THE SAME SUBJECT.

Up! up! my Friend, and quit your books;
Or surely you'll grow double:
Up! up! my Friend, and clear your looks;
Why all this toil and trouble?

The sun, above the mountain's head, 5
A freshening lustre mellow
Through all the long green fields has spread,
His first sweet evening yellow.

Books! 't is a dull and endless strife:
Come, hear the woodland linnet, 10
How sweet his music! on my life,
There 's more of wisdom in it.

And hark! how blithe the throstle sings!
He, too, is no mean preacher:
Come forth into the light of things, 15
Let Nature be your teacher.

She has a world of ready wealth,
Our minds and hearts to bless —
Spontaneous wisdom breathed by health,
Truth breathed by cheerfulness. 20

One impulse from a vernal wood
May teach you more of man,
Of moral evil and of good,
Than all the sages can.

Sweet is the lore which Nature brings; 25
Our meddling intellect
Mis-shapes the beauteous forms of things: —
We murder to dissect.

Enough of Science and of Art;
Close up those barren leaves;   30
Come forth, and bring with you a heart
That watches and receives.   1798.

THE COMPLAINT

OF A FORSAKEN INDIAN WOMAN.

Written at Alfoxden, where I read Hearne's Journey with deep interest. It was composed for the volume of Lyrical Ballads.

When a Northern Indian, from sickness, is unable to continue his journey with his companions, he is left behind, covered over with deer-skins, and is supplied with water, food, and fuel, if the situation of the place will afford it. He is informed of the track which his companions intend to pursue, and if he be unable to follow, or overtake them, he perishes alone in the desert; unless he should have the good fortune to fall in with some other tribes of Indians. The females are equally, or still more, exposed to the same fate. See that very interesting work, HEARNE's *Journey from Hudson's Bay to the Northern Ocean.* In the high northern latitudes, as the same writer informs us, when the northern lights vary their position in the air, they make a rustling and a crackling noise, as alluded to in the following poem.

I.

BEFORE I see another day,
Oh let my body die away!
In sleep I heard the northern gleams;
The stars, they were among my dreams;
In rustling conflict through the skies,   5
I heard, I saw the flashes drive,
And yet they are upon my eyes,
And yet I am alive;
Before I see another day,
Oh let my body die away!   10

II.

My fire is dead: it knew no pain;
Yet is it dead, and I remain:
All stiff with ice the ashes lie;
And they are dead, and I will die.
When I was well, I wished to live,   15
For clothes, for warmth, for food, and fire;
But they to me no joy can give,
No pleasure now, and no desire,
Then here contented will I lie!
Alone, I cannot fear to die.   20

III.

Alas! ye might have dragged me on
Another day, a single one!
Too soon I yielded to despair;
Why did ye listen to my prayer?
When ye were gone my limbs were stronger;   25
And oh, how grievously I rue,
That, afterwards, a little longer,
My friends, I did not follow you!
For strong and without pain I lay,
Dear friends, when ye were gone away.   30

IV.

My Child! they gave thee to another,
A woman who was not thy mother.
When from my arms my Babe they took,
On me how strangely did he look!
Through his whole body something ran,   35
A most strange working did I see;
— As if he strove to be a man,
That he might pull the sledge for me:

And then he stretched his arms, how wild !
Oh mercy ! like a helpless child !   40

v.

My little joy ! my little pride !
In two days more I must have died.
Then do not weep and grieve for me ;
I feel I must have died with thee.
O wind, that o'er my head art flying   45
The way my friends their course did bend,
I should not feel the pain of dying,
Could I with thee a message send ;
Too soon, my friends, ye went away ;
For I had many things to say.   50

vi.

I 'll follow you across the snow ;
Ye travel heavily and slow ;
In spite of all my weary pain,
I 'll look upon your tents again.
— My fire is dead, and snowy white   55
The water which beside it stood ;
The wolf has come to me to-night,
And he has stolen away my food.
For ever left alone am I ;
Then wherefore should I fear to die ?   60

vii.

Young as I am, my course is run,
I shall not see another sun ;
I cannot lift my limbs to know
If they have any life or no.
My poor forsaken Child, if I   65
For once could have thee close to me,

With happy heart I then would die,
And my last thought would happy be ;
But thou, dear Babe, art far away,
Nor shall I see another day.   70

1798.

THE OLD CUMBERLAND BEGGAR.

The class of Beggars, to which the Old Man here described belongs, will
probably soon be extinct. It consisted of poor, and, mostly, old and infirm
persons, who confined themselves to a stated round in their neighbourhood,
and had certain fixed days, on which, at different houses, they regularly
received alms, sometimes in money, but mostly in provisions.

I SAW an aged Beggar in my walk ;
And he was seated, by the highway side,
On a low structure of rude masonry
Built at the foot of a huge hill, that they
Who lead their horses down the steep rough road   5
May thence remount at ease.   The aged Man
Had placed his staff across the broad smooth stone
That overlays the pile ; and, from a bag
All white with flour, the dole of village dames,
He drew his scraps and fragments, one by one ;   10
And scanned them with a fixed and serious look
Of idle computation.   In the sun,
Upon the second step of that small pile,
Surrounded by those wild, unpeopled hills,
He sat, and ate his food in solitude :   15
And ever, scattered from his palsied hand,
That, still attempting to prevent the waste,
Was baffled still, the crumbs in little showers
Fell on the ground ; and the small mountain birds,
Not venturing yet to peck their destined meal,   20

Approached within the length of half his staff.
  Him from my childhood have I known ; and then
He was so old, he seems not older now;
He travels on, a solitary Man,
So helpless in appearance, that for him   25
The sauntering Horseman throws not with a slack
And careless hand his alms upon the ground,
But stops, — that he may safely lodge the coin
Within the old Man's hat ; nor quits him so,
But still, when he has given his horse the rein,   30
Watches the aged Beggar with a look
Sidelong, and half-reverted. She who tends
The toll-gate, when in summer at her door
She turns her wheel, if on the road she sees
The aged beggar coming, quits her work,   35
And lifts the latch for him that he may pass.
The post-boy, when his rattling wheels o'ertake
The aged Beggar in the woody lane,
Shouts to him from behind ; and if, thus warned,
The old man does not change his course, the boy   40
Turns with less noisy wheels to the roadside,
And passes gently by, without a curse
Upon his lips, or anger at his heart.
  He travels on, a solitary Man ;
His age has no companion. On the ground   45
His eyes are turned, and, as he moves along,
They move along the ground; and, evermore,
Instead of common and habitual sight
Of fields with rural works, of hill and dale,
And the blue sky, one little span of earth   50
Is all his prospect. Thus, from day to day,
Bow-bent, his eyes forever on the ground,
He plies his weary journey ; seeing still,
And seldom knowing that he sees, some straw,

Some scattered leaf, or marks which, in one track,   55
The nails of cart or chariot-wheel have left
Impressed on the white road, — in the same line,
At distance still the same.   Poor Traveller !
His staff trails with him ; scarcely do his feet
Disturb the summer dust ; he is so still   60
In look and motion, that the cottage curs,
Ere he has passed the door, will turn away,
Weary of barking at him.   Boys and girls,
The vacant and the busy, maids and youths,
And urchins newly breeched — all pass him by :   65
Him even the slow-paced waggon leaves behind.

But deem not this Man useless. — Statesmen ! ye
Who are so restless in your wisdom, ye
Who have a broom still ready in your hands
To rid the world of nuisances ; ye proud,   70
Heart-swoln, while in your pride ye contemplate
Your talents, power, or wisdom, deem him not
A burthen of the earth !   'T is Nature's law
That none, the meanest of created things,
Of forms created the most vile and brute,   75
The dullest or most noxious, should exist
Divorced from good — a spirit and pulse of good,
A life and soul, to every mode of being
Inseparably linked.   Then be assured
That least of all can aught — that ever owned   80
The heaven-regarding eye and front sublime
Which man is born to — sink, howe'er depressed,
So low as to be scorned without a sin ;
Without offence to God cast out of view ;
Like the dry remnant of a garden-flower   85
Whose seeds are shed, or as an implement
Worn out and worthless.   While from door to door,
This Old Man creeps, the villagers in him

Behold a record which together binds
Past deeds and offices of charity,   90
Else unremembered, and so keeps alive
The kindly mood in hearts which lapse of years,
And that half-wisdom half-experience gives,
Make slow to feel, and by sure steps resign
To selfishness and cold oblivious cares.   95
Among the farms and solitary huts,
Hamlets and thinly-scattered villages,
Where'er the aged Beggar takes his rounds,
The mild necessity of use compels
To acts of love; and habit does the work   100
Of reason; yet prepares that after-joy
Which reason cherishes. And thus the soul,
By that sweet taste of pleasure unpursued,
Doth find herself insensibly disposed
To virtue and true goodness.
      Some there are   105
By their good works exalted, lofty minds
And meditative, authors of delight
And happiness, which to the end of time
Will live, and spread, and kindle: even such minds
In childhood, from this solitary Being,   110
Or from like wanderer, haply have received
(A thing more precious far than all that books
Or the solicitudes of love can do!)
That first mild touch of sympathy and thought,
In which they found their kindred with a world   115
Where want and sorrow were. The easy man
Who sits at his own door, — and, like the pear
That overhangs his head from the green wall,
Feeds in the sunshine; the robust and young,
The prosperous and unthinking, they who live   120
Sheltered, and flourish in a little grove

Of their own kindred ; — all behold in him
A silent monitor, which on their minds
Must needs impress a transitory thought
Of self-congratulation, to the heart   125
Of each recalling his peculiar boons,
His charters and exemptions ; and, perchance,
Though he to no one give the fortitude
And circumspection needful to preserve
His present blessings, and to husband up   130
The respite of the season, he, at least,
And 't is no vulgar service, makes them felt.

Yet further. — Many, I believe, there are
Who live a life of virtuous decency,
Men who can hear the Decalogue and feel   135
No self-reproach ; who of the moral law
Established in the land where they abide
Are strict observers ; and not negligent
In acts of love to those with whom they dwell,
Their kindred, and the children of their blood.   140
Praise be to such, and to their slumbers peace !

But of the poor man ask, the abject poor ;
Go, and demand of him, if there be here
In this cold abstinence from evil deeds,
And these inevitable charities,   145
Wherewith to satisfy the human soul ?
No — man is dear to man ; the poorest poor
Long for some moments in a weary life
When they can know and feel that they have been,
Themselves, the fathers and the dealers-out   150
Of some small blessings ; have been kind to such
As needed kindness, for this single cause,
That we have all of us one human heart.
— Such pleasure is to one kind Being known,
My neighbour, when with punctual care, each week   155

Duly as Friday comes, though pressed herself
By her own wants, she from her store of meal
Takes one unsparing handful for the scrip
Of this old Mendicant, and, from her door
Returning with exhilarated heart,   160
Sits by her fire, and builds her hope in heaven.
    Then let him pass, a blessing on his head!
And while in that vast solitude to which
The tide of things has borne him, he appears
To breathe and live but for himself alone,   165
Unblamed, uninjured, let him bear about
The good which the benignant law of Heaven
Has hung around him: and, while life is his,
Still let him prompt the unlettered villagers
To tender offices and pensive thoughts.   170
— Then let him pass, a blessing on his head!
And, long as he can wander, let him breathe
The freshness of the valleys; let his blood
Struggle with frosty air and winter snows;
And let the chartered wind that sweeps the heath   175
Beat his grey locks against his withered face.
Reverence the hope whose vital anxiousness
Gives the last human interest to his heart.
May never HOUSE, misnamed of INDUSTRY,
Make him a captive! — for that pent-up din,   180
Those life-consuming sounds that clog the air,
Be his the natural silence of old age!
Let him be free of mountain solitudes;
And have around him, whether heard or not,
The pleasant melody of woodland birds.   185
Few are his pleasures: if his eyes have now
Been doomed so long to settle upon earth
That not without some effort they behold
The countenance of the horizontal sun,

Rising or setting, let the light at least   190
Find a free entrance to their languid orbs.
And let him, *where* and *when* he will, sit down
Beneath the trees, or on a grassy bank
Of highway side, and with the little birds
Share his chance-gathered meal; and, finally,   195
As in the eye of Nature he has lived,
So in the eye of Nature let him die!

1797–1798.

ANIMAL TRANQUILLITY AND DECAY.

THE little hedgerow birds,
That peck along the roads, regard him not.
He travels on, and in his face, his step,
His gait, is one expression: every limb,
His look and bending figure, all bespeak   5
A man who does not move with pain, but moves
With thought. — He is insensibly subdued
To settled quiet : he is one by whom
All effort seems forgotten ; one to whom
Long patience hath such mild composure given,   10
That patience now doth seem a thing of which
He hath no need.   He is by nature led
To peace so perfect that the young behold
With envy, what the Old Man hardly feels.

1798.

LINES

COMPOSED A FEW MILES ABOVE TINTERN ABBEY, ON REVISIT-
ING THE BANKS OF THE WYE DURING A TOUR. JULY 13,
1798.

FIVE years have past; five summers, with the length
Of five long winters ! and again I hear
These waters, rolling from their mountain-springs
With a soft inland murmur.[1] — Once again
Do I behold these steep and lofty cliffs,   5
That on a wild secluded scene impress
Thoughts of more deep seclusion; and connect
The landscape with the quiet of the sky.
The day is come when I again repose
Here, under this dark sycamore, and view   10
These plots of cottage-ground, these orchard-tufts,
Which at this season, with their unripe fruits,
Are clad in one green hue, and lose themselves
'Mid groves and copses.   Once again I see
These hedge-rows, hardly hedge-rows, little lines   15
Of sportive wood run wild : these pastoral farms,
Green to the very door; and wreaths of smoke
Sent up, in silence, from among the trees !
With some uncertain notice, as might seem
Of vagrant dwellers in the houseless woods,   20
Or of some Hermit's cave, where by his fire
The Hermit sits alone.
                          These beauteous forms,
Through a long absence, have not been to me
As is a landscape to a blind man's eye :
But oft, in lonely rooms, and 'mid the din   25
Of towns and cities, I have owed to them
In hours of weariness, sensations sweet,

[1] The river is not affected by the tides a few miles above Tintern.

Felt in the blood, and felt along the heart; *emotion*
And passing even into my purer mind,
With tranquil restoration: — feelings too   30
Of unremembered pleasure: such, perhaps,
As have no slight or trivial influence
On that best portion of a good man's life,
His little, nameless, unremembered, acts
Of kindness and of love.   Nor less, I trust,   35
To them I may have owed another gift,
Of aspect more sublime; that blessed mood,
In which the burthen of the mystery,
In which the heavy and the weary weight
Of all this unintelligible world,   40
Is lightened : — that serene and blessed mood
In which the affections gently lead us on, —
Until, the breath of this corporeal frame
And even the motion of our human blood
Almost suspended, we are laid asleep   *peace w/o body*   45
In body, and become a living soul:
While with an eye made quiet by the power
Of harmony, and the deep power of joy,
We see into the life of things.
                              If this
Be but a vain belief, yet, oh ! how oft —   50
In darkness and amid the many shapes
Of joyless daylight; when the fretful stir
Unprofitable, and the fever of the world,
Have hung upon the beatings of my heart —
How oft, in spirit, have I turned to thee,   55
O sylvan Wye ! thou wanderer thro' the woods,
How often has my spirit turned to thee !

   And now, with gleams of half-extinguished thought,
With many recognitions dim and faint,
And somewhat of a sad perplexity,   60

The picture of the mind revives again :
While here I stand, not only with the sense
Of present pleasure, but with pleasing thoughts
That in this moment there is life and food
For future years.   And so I dare to hope,   65
Though changed, no doubt, from what I was when first
I came among these hills ; when like a roe
I bounded o'er the mountains, by the sides
Of the deep rivers, and the lonely streams,
Wherever nature led : more like a man   70
Flying from something that he dreads, than one
Who sought the thing he loved.   For nature then
(The coarser pleasures of my boyish days,
And their glad animal movements all gone by)
To me was all in all. — I cannot paint   75
What then I was.   The sounding cataract
Haunted me like a passion ; the tall rock,
The mountain, and the deep and gloomy wood,
Their colours and their forms, were then to me
An appetite ; a feeling and a love,   80
That had no need of a remoter charm,
By thought supplied, nor any interest
Unborrowed from the eye. — That time is past,
And all its aching joys are now no more,
And all its dizzy raptures.   Not for this   85
Faint I, nor mourn, nor murmur ; other gifts
Have followed ; for such loss, I would believe,
Abundant recompence.   For I have learned
To look on nature, not as in the hour
Of thoughtless youth ; but hearing oftentimes   90
The still, sad music of humanity,
Nor harsh nor grating, though of ample power
To chasten and subdue.   And I have felt
A presence that disturbs me with the joy

Of elevated thoughts ; a sense sublime,
Of something far more deeply interfused,
Whose dwelling is the light of setting suns,
And the round ocean and the living air,
And the blue sky, and in the mind of man ;
A motion and a spirit, that impels   100
All thinking things, all objects of all thought,
And rolls through all things.   Therefore am I still
A lover of the meadows and the woods,
And mountains ; and of all that we behold
From this green earth ; of all the mighty world   105
Of eye, and ear, — both what they half create,[1]
And what perceive ; well pleased to recognise
In nature and the language of the sense,
The anchor of my purest thoughts, the nurse,
The guide, the guardian of my heart, and soul   110
Of all my moral being.

                    Nor perchance,
If I were not thus taught, should I the more
Suffer my genial spirits to decay :
For thou art with me here upon the banks
Of this fair river ; thou my dearest Friend,   115
My dear, dear Friend ; and in thy voice I catch
The language of my former heart, and read
My former pleasures in the shooting lights
Of thy wild eyes.   Oh ! yet a little while
May I behold in thee what I was once,   120
My dear, dear Sister ! and this prayer I make,
Knowing that Nature never did betray
The heart that loved her ; 't is her privilege,
Through all the years of this our life, to lead
From joy to joy : for she can so inform   125

[1] This line has a close resemblance to an admirable line of
Young's, the exact expression of which I do not recollect.

The mind that is within us, so impress
With quietness and beauty, and so feed
With lofty thoughts, that neither evil tongues,
Rash judgments, nor the sneers of selfish men,
Nor greetings where no kindness is, nor all   *nature*   130
The dreary intercourse of daily life,
Shall e'er prevail against us, or disturb
Our cheerful faith, that all which we behold
Is full of blessings.   Therefore let the moon
Shine on thee in thy solitary walk ;   135
And let the misty mountain-winds be free
To blow against thee : and, in after years,
When these wild ecstasies shall be matured
Into a sober pleasure ; when thy mind
Shall be a mansion for all lovely forms,   140
Thy memory be as a dwelling-place
For all sweet sounds and harmonies ; oh ! then,
If solitude, or fear, or pain, or grief,
Should be thy portion, with what healing thoughts
Of tender joy wilt thou remember me,   145
And these my exhortations ! Nor, perchance —
If I should be where I no more can hear
Thy voice, nor catch from thy wild eyes these gleams
Of past existence — wilt thou then forget
That on the banks of this delightful stream   150
We stood together ; and that I, so long
A worshipper of Nature, hither came
Unwearied in that service : rather say
With warmer love — oh ! with far deeper zeal
Of holier love.   Nor wilt thou then forget,   155
That after many wanderings, many years
Of absence, these steep woods and lofty cliffs,
And this green pastoral landscape, were to me
More dear, both for themselves and for thy sake !

1798.

THERE WAS A BOY.

THERE was a Boy; ye knew him well, ye cliffs
And islands of Winander! — many a time,
At evening, when the earliest stars began
To move along the edges of the hills,
Rising or setting, would he stand alone,   5
Beneath the trees, or by the glimmering lake;
And there, with fingers interwoven, both hands
Pressed closely palm to palm and to his mouth
Uplifted, he, as through an instrument,
Blew mimic hootings to the silent owls,   10
That they might answer him. — And they would shout
Across the watery vale, and shout again,
Responsive to his call, — with quivering peals,
And long halloos, and screams, and echoes loud
Redoubled and redoubled; concourse wild   15
Of jocund din!   And, when there came a pause
Of silence such as baffled his best skill:
Then, sometimes, in that silence, while he hung
Listening, a gentle shock of mild surprise
Has carried far into his heart the voice   20
Of mountain-torrents; or the visible scene
Would enter unawares into his mind
With all its solemn imagery, its rocks,
Its woods, and that uncertain heaven received
Into the bosom of the steady lake.   25
This boy was taken from his mates, and died
In childhood, ere he was full twelve years old.
Preëminent in beauty is the vale
Where he was born and bred: the church-yard hangs
Upon a slope above the village-school;   30
And, through that church-yard when my way has led
On summer-evenings, I believe, that there

A long half-hour together I have stood
Mute — looking at the grave in which he lies !

1798.

STRANGE fits of passion have I known :
   And I will dare to tell,
But in the Lover's ear alone,
   What once to me befell.

When she I loved looked every day   5
   Fresh as a rose in June,
I to her cottage bent my way,
   Beneath an evening-moon.

Upon the moon I fixed my eye,
   All over the wide lea ;   10
With quickening pace my horse drew nigh
   Those paths so dear to me.

And now we reached the orchard-plot ;
   And, as we climbed the hill,
The sinking moon to Lucy's cot   15
   Came near, and nearer still.

In one of those sweet dreams I slept,
   Kind Nature's gentlest boon !
And all the while my eyes I kept
   On the descending moon.   20

My horse moved on ; hoof after hoof
   He raised, and never stopped :
When down behind the cottage roof,
   At once, the bright moon dropped.

What fond and wayward thoughts will slide   25
  Into a Lover's head!
"O mercy!" to myself I cried,
  "If Lucy should be dead!"

1799.

SHE dwelt among the untrodden ways
  Beside the springs of Dove,
A maid whom there were none to praise
  And very few to love:

A violet by a mossy stone   5
  Half hidden from the eye!
— Fair as a star, when only one
  Is shining in the sky.

She lived unknown, and few could know
  When Lucy ceased to be;   10
But she is in her grave, and, oh,
  The difference to me!

1799.

I TRAVELLED among unknown men,
  In lands beyond the sea;
Nor, England! did I know till then
  What love I bore to thee.

'T is past, that melancholy dream!   5
  Nor will I quit thy shore
A second time; for still I seem
  To love thee more and more.

Among thy mountains did I feel
  The joy of my desire;   10
And she I cherished turned her wheel
  Beside an English fire.

Thy mornings showed, thy nights concealed
  The bowers where Lucy played ;
And thine, too, is the last green field   15
  That Lucy's eyes surveyed.

              1799.

THREE years she grew in sun and shower,
Then Nature said, "A lovelier flower
  On earth was never sown ;
This Child I to myself will take ;
She shall be mine, and I will make   5
  A Lady of my own.

" Myself will to my darling be
Both law and impulse : and with me
  The Girl, in rock and plain,
In earth and heaven, in glade and bower,   10
Shall feel an overseeing power
  To kindle or restrain.

" She shall be sportive as the fawn
That wild with glee across the lawn,
  Or up the mountain springs ;   15
And her's shall be the breathing balm,
And her's the silence and the calm
  Of mute insensate things.

" The floating clouds their state shall lend
To her ; for her the willow bend ;   20
  Nor shall she fail to see
Even in the motions of the Storm
Grace that shall mould the Maiden's form
  By silent sympathy.

" The stars of midnight shall be dear   25
To her ; and she shall lean her ear
   In many a secret place
Where rivulets dance their wayward round,
And beauty born of murmuring sound
   Shall pass into her face.   30

" And vital feelings of delight
Shall rear her form to stately height,
   Her virgin bosom swell ;
Such thoughts to Lucy I will give
While she and I together live   35
   Here in this happy dell."

Thus Nature spake — the work was done —
How soon my Lucy's race was run !
   She died, and left to me
This heath, this calm, and quiet scene ;   4c
The memory of what has been,
   And never more will be.

1799.

A SLUMBER did my spirit seal ;
   I had no human fears ;
She seemed a thing that could not feel
   The touch of earthly years.

No motion has she now, no force ;   5
   She neither hears nor sees ;
Rolled round in earth's diurnal course,
   With rocks, and stones, and trees.

1799.

A POET'S EPITAPH.

ART thou a Statist in the van
　　Of public conflicts trained and bred?
— First learn to love one living man;
　　Then may'st thou think upon the dead.

A Lawyer art thou? — draw not nigh!　　　　5
　　Go, carry to some fitter place
The keenness of that practised eye,
　　The hardness of that sallow face.

Art thou a Man of purple cheer?
　　A rosy Man, right plump to see?　　　　10
Approach; yet, Doctor, not too near,
　　This grave no cushion is for thee.

Or art thou one of gallant pride,
　　A Soldier, and no man of chaff?
Welcome! — but lay thy sword aside,　　　　15
　　And lean upon a peasant's staff.

Physician art thou? one, all eyes,
　　Philosopher! a fingering slave,
One that would peep and botanize
　　Upon his mother's grave?　　　　20

Wrapt closely in thy sensual fleece,
　　O turn aside, — and take, I pray,
That he below may rest in peace,
　　Thy ever-dwindling soul, away!

A Moralist perchance appears;　　　　25
　　Led, Heaven knows how! to this poor sod:
And he has neither eyes nor ears;
　　Himself his world, and his own God!

One to whose smooth-rubbed soul can cling
    Nor form, nor feeling, great or small;   30
A reasoning, self-sufficing thing,
    An intellectual All-in-all!

Shut close the door; press down the latch;
    Sleep in thy intellectual crust;
Nor lose ten tickings of thy watch   35
    Near this unprofitable dust.

But who is He, with modest looks,
    And clad in homely russet brown?
He murmurs near the running brooks
    A music sweeter than their own.   40

He is retired as noontide dew,
    Or fountain in a noon-day grove;
And you must love him, ere to you
    He will seem worthy of your love.

The outward shows of sky and earth,   45
    Of hill and valley, he has viewed;
And impulses of deeper birth
    Have come to him in solitude.

In common things that round us lie
    Some random truths he can impart, —   50
The harvest of a quiet eye
    That broods and sleeps on his own heart.

But he is weak; both Man and Boy,
    Hath been an idler in the land;
Contented if he might enjoy   55
    The things which others understand.

— Come hither in thy hour of strength;
  Come, weak as is a breaking wave!
Here stretch thy body at full length;
  Or build thy house upon this grave.   60

1799.

LUCY GRAY;

OR, SOLITUDE.

OFT I had heard of Lucy Gray:
And, when I crossed the wild,
I chanced to see at break of day
The solitary child.

No mate, no comrade Lucy knew;   5
She dwelt on a wide moor,
— The sweetest thing that ever grew
Beside a human door!

You yet may spy the fawn at play,
The hare upon the green;   10
But the sweet face of Lucy Gray
Will never more be seen.

" To-night will be a stormy night —
You to the town must go;
And take a lantern, Child, to light   15
Your mother through the snow."

" That, Father! will I gladly do:
'T is scarcely afternoon —
The minster-clock has just struck two,
And yonder is the moon!"   20

At this the father raised his hook,
And snapped a faggot-band;
He plied his work; — and Lucy took
The lantern in her hand.

Not blither is the mountain roe: 25
With many a wanton stroke
Her feet disperse the powdery snow,
That rises up like smoke.

The storm came on before its time:
She wandered up and down;   30
And many a hill did Lucy climb:
But never reached the town.

The wretched parents all that night
Went shouting far and wide;
But there was neither sound nor sight   35
To serve them for a guide.

At day-break on a hill they stood
That overlooked the moor;
And thence they saw the bridge of wood,
A furlong from their door.   40

They wept — and, turning homeward, cried,
" In heaven we all shall meet ";
— When in the snow the mother spied
The print of Lucy's feet.

Then downwards from the steep hill's edge   45
They tracked the footmarks small;
And through the broken hawthorn hedge,
And by the long stone-wall;

And then an open field they crossed:
The marks were still the same;   50
They tracked them on, nor ever lost;
And to the bridge they came.

They followed from the snowy bank
Those footmarks, one by one,
Into the middle of the plank;   55
And further there were none !

— Yet some maintain that to this day
She is a living child;
That you may see sweet Lucy Gray
Upon the lonesome wild.   60

O'er rough and smooth she trips along,
And never looks behind;
And sings a solitary song
That whistles in the wind.

1799.

RUTH.

WHEN Ruth was left half desolate,
Her father took another Mate;
And Ruth, not seven years old,
A slighted child, at her own will
Went wandering over dale and hill,   5
In thoughtless freedom, bold.

And she had made a pipe of straw,
And music from that pipe could draw
Like sounds of winds and floods;

Had built a bower upon the green,   10
As if she from her birth had been
An infant of the woods.

Beneath her father's roof, alone
She seemed to live ; her thoughts her own ;
Herself her own delight ;   15
Pleased with herself, nor sad, nor gay ;
And, passing thus the live-long day,
She grew to woman's height.

There came a Youth from Georgia's shore —
A military casque he wore,   20
With splendid feathers drest ;
He brought them from the Cherokees ;
The feathers nodded in the breeze,
And made a gallant crest.

From Indian blood you deem him sprung :   25
But no ! he spake the English tongue,
And bore a soldier's name ;
And, when America was free
From battle and from jeopardy,
He 'cross the ocean came.   30

With hues of genius on his cheek
In finest tones the Youth could speak :
— While he was yet a boy,
The moon, the glory of the sun,
And streams that murmur as they run,   35
Had been his dearest joy.

He was a lovely Youth ! I guess
The panther in the wilderness
Was not so fair as he ;

And, when he chose to sport and play, 40
No dolphin ever was so gay
Upon the tropic sea.

Among the Indians he had fought,
And with him many tales he brought
Of pleasure and of fear ; 45
Such tales as told to any maid
By such a Youth, in the green shade,
Were perilous to hear.

He told of girls — a happy rout !
Who quit their fold with dance and shout, 50
Their pleasant Indian town,
To gather strawberries all day long;
Returning with a choral song
When daylight is gone down.

He spake of plants that hourly change 55
Their blossoms, through a boundless range
Of intermingling hues ;
With budding, fading, faded flowers
They stand the wonder of the bowers
From morn to evening dews. 60

He told of the magnolia, spread
High as a cloud, high over head !
The cypress and her spire ;
— Of flowers that with one scarlet gleam
Cover a hundred leagues and seem 65
To set the hills on fire.

The Youth of green savannahs spake,
And many an endless, endless lake,
With all its fairy crowds

Of islands, that together lie   70
As quietly as spots of sky
Among the evening clouds.

" How pleasant," then he said, " it were
A fisher or a hunter there,
In sunshine or in shade   75
To wander with an easy mind ;
And build a household fire, and find
A home in every glade !

" What days and what bright years !   Ah me !
Our life were life indeed, with thee   80
So passed in quiet bliss,
And all the while," said he, " to know
That we were in a world of woe,
On such an earth as this ! "

And then he sometimes interwove   85
Fond thoughts about a father's love;
" For there," said he, " are spun
Around the heart such tender ties,
That our own children to our eyes
Are dearer than the sun.   90

" Sweet Ruth ! and could you go with me
My helpmate in the woods to be,
Our shed at night to rear ;
Or run, my own adopted bride,
A sylvan huntress at my side,   95
And drive the flying deer !

" Belovèd Ruth ! " — No more he said,
The wakeful Ruth at midnight shed
A solitary tear :

She thought again — and did agree 100
With him to sail across the sea,
And drive the flying deer.

" And now, as fitting is and right,
We in the church our faith will plight,
A husband and a wife." 105
Even so they did; and I may say
That to sweet Ruth that happy day
Was more than human life.

Through dream and vision did she sink,
Delighted all the while to think 110
That on those lonesome floods,
And green savannahs, she should share
His board with lawful joy, and bear
His name in the wild woods.

But, as you have before been told, 115
This Stripling, sportive, gay and bold,
And, with his dancing crest,
So beautiful, through savage lands
Had roamed about, with vagrant bands
Of Indians in the West. 120

The wind, the tempest roaring high,
The tumult of a tropic sky,
Might well be dangerous food
For him, a Youth to whom was given
So much of earth — so much of heaven, 125
And such impetuous blood.

Whatever in those climes he found
Irregular in sight or sound
Did to his mind impart

A kindred impulse, seemed allied   130
To his own powers, and justified
The workings of his heart.

Nor less, to feed voluptuous thought,
The beauteous forms of nature wrought,
Fair trees and gorgeous flowers;   135
The breezes their own languor lent;
The stars had feelings, which they sent
Into those favoured bowers.

Yet, in his worst pursuits, I ween
That sometimes there did intervene   140
Pure hopes of high intent:
For passions linked to forms so fair
And stately, needs must have their share
Of noble sentiment.

But ill he lived, much evil saw,   145
With men to whom no better law
Nor better life was known;
Deliberately, and undeceived,
Those wild men's vices he received,
And gave them back his own.   150

His genius and his moral frame
Were thus impaired, and he became
The slave of low desires:
A Man who without self-control
Would seek what the degraded soul   155
Unworthily admires.

And yet he with no feigned delight
Had wooed the Maiden, day and night
Had loved her, night and morn:

What could he less than love a Maid   160
Whose heart with so much nature played?
So kind and so forlorn !

Sometimes, most earnestly, he said,
" O Ruth ! I have been worse than dead ;
False thoughts, thoughts bold and vain,   165
Encompassed me on every side
When I, in confidence and pride,
Had crossed the Atlantic main.

" Before me shone a glorious world —
Fresh as a banner bright, unfurled   170
To music suddenly :
I looked upon those hills and plains,
And seemed as if let loose from chains,
To live at liberty.

" No more of this : for now, by thee   175
Dear Ruth ! more happily set free
With nobler zeal I burn ;
My soul from darkness is released,
Like the whole sky when to the east
The morning doth return."   180

Full soon that better mind was gone ;
No hope, no wish remained, not one, —
They stirred him now no more ;
New objects did new pleasure give,
And once again he wished to live   185
As lawless as before.

Meanwhile, as thus with him it fared,
They for the voyage were prepared,
And went to the sea-shore,

But, when they thither came the Youth   190
Deserted his poor Bride, and Ruth
Could never find him more.

God help thee Ruth !— Such pains she had,
That she in half a year was mad,
And in a prison housed ;   195
And there, with many a doleful song
Made of wild words, her cup of wrong
She fearfully caroused.

Yet sometimes milder hours she knew,
Nor wanted sun, nor rain, nor dew,   200
Nor pastimes of the May ;
— They all were with her in her cell ;
And a clear brook with cheerful knell
Did o'er the pebbles play.

When Ruth three seasons thus had lain,   205
There came a respite to her pain ;
She from her prison fled ;
But of the Vagrant none took thought ;
And where it liked her best she sought
Her shelter and her bread.   210

Among the fields she breathed again :
The master-current of her brain
Ran permanent and free ;
And, coming to the Banks of Tone,
There did she rest ; and dwell alone   215
Under the greenwood tree.

The engines of her brain, the tools
That shaped her sorrow, rocks and pools,
And airs that gently stir

The vernal leaves — she loved them still;   220
Nor ever taxed them with the ill
Which had been done to her.

A Barn her *winter* bed supplies;
But, till the warmth of summer skies
And summer days is gone,   225
(And all do in this tale agree)
She sleeps beneath the greenwood tree,
And other home hath none.

An innocent life, yet far astray!
And Ruth will, long before her day,   230
Be broken down and old :
Sore aches she needs must have! but less
Of mind, than body's wretchedness,
From damp, and rain, and cold.

If she is prest by want of food,   235
She from her dwelling in the wood
Repairs to a road-side;
And there she begs at one steep place
Where up and and down with easy pace
The horsemen travellers ride.   240

That oaten pipe of hers is mute,
Or thrown away; but with a flute
Her loneliness she cheers :
This flute, made of a hemlock stalk,
At evening in his homeward walk   245
The Quantock woodman hears.

I, too, have passed her on the hills
Setting her little water-mills
By spouts and fountains wild —

Such small machinery as she turned   250
Ere she had wept, ere she had mourned,
A young and happy Child !

Farewell, and when thy days are told,
Ill-fated Ruth, in hallowed mould
Thy corpse shall buried be,   255
For thee a funeral bell shall ring,
And all the congregation sing
A Christmas psalm for thee.

1799.

INFLUENCES OF BEAUTY AND FEAR IN BOYHOOD.

(FROM "THE PRELUDE," BOOK I.)

DUST as we are, the immortal spirit grows
Like harmony in music; there is a dark
Inscrutable workmanship that reconciles
Discordant elements, makes them cling together
In one society.   How strange, that all   5
The terrors, pains, and early miseries,
Regrets, vexations, lassitudes interfused
Within my mind, should e'er have borne a part,
And that a needful part, in making up
The calm existence that is mine when I   10
Am worthy of myself !   Praise to the end !
Thanks to the means which Nature deigned to employ ;
Whether her fearless visitings, or those
That came with soft alarm, like hurtless light
Opening the peaceful clouds ; or she would use   15
Severer interventions, ministry
More palpable, as best might suit her aim.

One summer evening (led by her) I found
A little boat tied to a willow tree
Within a rocky cave, its usual home. 20
Straight I unloosed her chain, and stepping in
Pushed from the shore.   It was an act of stealth
And troubled pleasure, nor without the voice
Of mountain-echoes did my boat move on;
Leaving behind her still, on either side, 25
Small circles glittering idly in the moon,
Until they melted all into one track
Of sparkling light.   But now, like one who **rows**,
Proud of his skill, to reach a chosen point
With an unswerving line, I fixed my view 30
Upon the summit of a craggy ridge,
The horizon's utmost boundary; far above
Was nothing but the stars and the grey sky.
She was an elfin pinnace ; lustily
I dipped my oars into the silent lake, 35
And, as I rose upon the stroke, my boat
Went heaving through the water like a swan ;
When, from behind that craggy steep till then
The horizon's bound, a huge peak, black and huge,
As if with voluntary power instinct 40
Upreared its head.   I struck and struck again,
And growing still in stature the grim shape
Towered up between me and the stars, and still,
For so it seemed, with purpose of its own
And measured motion like a living thing, 45
Strode after me.   With trembling oars I turned,
And through the silent water stole my way
Back to the covert of the willow tree ;
There in her mooring-place I left my bark, —
And through the meadows homeward went, in **grave** 50
And serious mood ; but after I had seen

That spectacle, for many days, my brain
Worked with a dim and undetermined sense
Of unknown modes of being; o'er my thoughts
There hung a darkness, call it solitude   55
Or blank desertion.   No familiar shapes
Remained, no pleasant images of trees,
Of sea or sky, no colours of green fields;
But huge and mighty forms, that do not live
Like living men, moved slowly through the mind   60
By day, and were a trouble to my dreams.

                                   1799–1800.

INFLUENCE OF NATURAL OBJECTS

IN CALLING FORTH AND STRENGTHENING THE IMAGINATION IN
BOYHOOD AND EARLY YOUTH.   WRITTEN IN GERMANY.

WISDOM and Spirit of the universe!
Thou Soul, that art the Eternity of thought!
And giv'st to forms and images a breath
And everlasting motion, not in vain,
By day or star-light, thus from my first dawn   5
Of childhood didst thou intertwine for me
The passions that build up our human soul;
Not with the mean and vulgar works of Man;
But with high objects, with enduring things,
With life and nature; purifying thus   10
The elements of feeling and of thought,
And sanctifying by such discipline
Both pain and fear, — until we recognize
A grandeur in the beatings of the heart.

Nor was this fellowship vouchsafed to me   15
With stinted kindness.   In November days,

When vapours rolling down the valleys made
A lonely scene more lonesome ; among woods
At noon ; and 'mid the calm of summer nights,
When, by the margin of the trembling lake,   20
Beneath the gloomy hills, homeward I went
In solitude, such intercourse was mine :
Mine was it in the fields both day and night,
And by the waters, all the summer long.
And in the frosty season, when the sun   25
Was set, and, visible for many a mile,
The cottage-windows through the twilight blazed,
I heeded not the summons : happy time
It was indeed for all of us ; for me
It was a time of rapture !   Clear and loud   30
The village-clock tolled six — I wheeled about,
Proud and exulting like an untired horse
That cares not for his home. — All shod with steel
We hissed along the polished ice, in games
Confederate, imitative of the chase   35
And woodland pleasures, — the resounding horn,
The pack loud-chiming, and the hunted hare.
So through the darkness and the cold we flew,
And not a voice was idle : with the din
Smitten, the precipices rang aloud ;   40
The leafless trees and every icy crag
Tinkled like iron ; while far-distant hills
Into the tumult sent an alien sound
Of melancholy, not unnoticed while the stars,
Eastward, were sparkling clear, and in the west   45
The orange sky of evening died away.

   Not seldom from the uproar I retired
Into a silent bay, or sportively
Glanced sideway, leaving the tumultuous throng,

To cut across the reflex of a star;　　　　　　50
Image, that, flying still before me, gleamed
Upon the glassy plain: and oftentimes,
When we had given our bodies to the wind,
And all the shadowy banks on either side
Came sweeping through the darkness, spinning still　　55
The rapid line of motion, then at once
Have I, reclining back upon my heels,
Stopped short; yet still the solitary cliffs
Wheeled by me — even as if the earth had rolled
With visible motion her diurnal round!　　　　　60
Behind me did they stretch in solemn train,
Feebler and feebler, and I stood and watched
Till all was tranquil as a summer sea.

　　　　　　　　　　　　　　　　1799.

——————

NUTTING.

————————————— It seems a day
(I speak of one from many singled out),
One of these heavenly days that cannot die;
When, in the eagerness of boyish hope,
I left our cottage-threshold, sallying forth　　　5
With a huge wallet o'er my shoulders slung.
A nutting-crook in hand; and turned my steps
Tow'rd some far-distant wood, a Figure quaint,
Tricked out in proud disguise of cast-off weeds
Which for that service had been husbanded,　　　10
By exhortation of my frugal Dame —
Motley accoutrement, of power to smile
At thorns, and brakes, and brambles, — and, in truth,
More ragged than need was! O'er pathless rocks,

Through beds of matted fern, and tangled thickets,   15
Forcing my way, I came to one dear nook
Unvisited, where not a broken bough
Drooped with its withered leaves, ungracious sign
Of devastation; but the hazels rose
Tall and erect, with tempting clusters hung,   20
A virgin scene! — A little while I stood,
Breathing with such suppression of the heart
As joy delights in; and, with wise restraint
Voluptuous, fearless of a rival, eyed
The banquet; — or beneath the trees I sate   25
Among the flowers, and with the flowers I played;
A temper known to those, who, after long
And weary expectation, have been blest
With sudden happiness beyond all hope.

Perhaps it was a bower beneath whose leaves   30
The violets of five seasons re-appear
And fade, unseen by any human eye;
Where fairy water-breaks do murmur on
For ever; and I saw the sparkling foam,
And — with my cheek on one of those green stones   35
That, fleeced with moss, under the shady trees,
Lay round me, scattered like a flock of sheep —
I heard the murmur and the murmuring sound,
In that sweet mood when pleasure loves to pay
Tribute to ease; and, of its joy secure,   40
The heart luxuriates with indifferent things,
Wasting its kindliness on stocks and stones,
And on the vacant air.   Then up I rose,
And dragged to earth both branch and bough, with crash
And merciless ravage: and the shady nook   45
Of hazels, and the green and mossy bower,
Deformed and sullied, patiently gave up
Their quiet being: and, unless I now

Confound my present feelings with the past,
Ere from the mutilated bower I turned　　　　　5c
Exulting, rich beyond the wealth of kings,
I felt a sense of pain when I beheld
The silent trees, and saw the intruding sky —
Then, dearest Maiden, move along these shades
In gentleness of heart; with gentle hand　　　55
Touch — for there is a spirit in the woods.

　　　　　　　　　　　　　1799.

MATTHEW.

In the School of Hawkshead is a tablet, on which are inscribed, in gilt
letters, the Names of the several persons who have been Schoolmasters there
since the foundation of the School, with the time at which they entered upon
and quitted their office. Opposite to one of those names the Author wrote the
following lines.

If Nature, for a favourite child,
In thee hath tempered so her clay,
That every hour thy heart runs wild,
Yet never once doth go astray.

Read o'er these lines ; and then review　　　5
This tablet, that thus humbly rears
In such diversity of hue
Its history of two hundred years.

—When through this little wreck of fame,
Cipher and syllable ! thine eye　　　　　10
Has travelled down to Matthew's name,
Pause with no common sympathy.

And, if a sleeping tear should wake,
Then be it neither checked nor stayed :

For Matthew a request I make   15
Which for himself he had not made.

Poor Matthew, all his frolics o'er,
Is silent as a standing pool ;
Far from the chimney's merry roar,
And murmur of the village school.   20

The sighs which Matthew heaved were sighs
Of one tired out with fun and madness ;
The tears which came to Matthew's eyes
Were tears of light, the dew of gladness.

Yet, sometimes, when the secret cup   25
Of still and serious thought went round,
It seemed as if he drank it up —
He felt with spirit so profound.

— Thou soul of God's best earthly mould !
Thou happy Soul ! and can it be   30
That these two words of glittering gold
Are all that must remain of thee ?

                      1799.

THE TWO APRIL MORNINGS.

WE walked along, while bright and red
Uprose the morning sun ;
And Matthew stopped, he looked, and said,
" The will of God be done ! "

A village schoolmaster was he,   5
With hair of glittering grey ;
As blithe a man as you could see
On a spring holiday.

And on that morning, through the grass,
And by the steaming rills,   10
We travelled merrily, to pass
A day among the hills.

" Our work," said I, " was well begun,
Then, from thy breast what thought,
Beneath so beautiful a sun,   15
So sad a sigh has brought ? "

A second time did Matthew stop ;
And fixing still his eye
Upon the eastern mountain-top,
To me he made reply :   20

" Yon cloud with that long purple cleft
Brings fresh into my mind
A day like this which I have left
Full thirty years behind.

" And just above yon slope of corn   25
Such colours, and no other,
Were in the sky, that April morn,
Of this the very brother.

" With rod and line I sued the sport
Which that sweet season gave,   30
And, to the church-yard come, stopped short
Beside my daughter's grave.

" Nine summers had she scarcely seen,
The pride of all the vale ;
And then she sang ; — she would have been   35
A very nightingale.

" Six feet in earth my Emma lay;
And yet I loved her more,
For so it seemed, than till that day
I e'er had loved before.   40

" And, turning from her grave, I met,
Beside the church-yard yew,
A blooming Girl, whose hair was wet
With points of morning dew.

" A basket on her head she bare;   45
Her brow was smooth and white :
To see a child so very fair,
It was a pure delight !

" No fountain from its rocky cave
E'er tripped with foot so free ;   50
She seemed as happy as a wave
That dances on the sea.

" There came from me a sigh of pain
Which I could ill confine ;
I looked at her, and looked again :   55
And did not wish her mine ! "

Matthew is in his grave, yet now,
Methinks, I see him stand,
As at that moment, with a bough
Of wilding in his hand.   60

                                    1799.

THE FOUNTAIN.

A CONVERSATION.

WE talked with open heart, and tongue
Affectionate and true,
A pair of friends, though I was young,
And Matthew seventy-two.

We lay beneath a spreading oak,　　　　　　　　5
Beside a mossy seat ;
And from the turf a fountain broke,
And gurgled at our feet.

" Now, Matthew ! " said I, " let us match
This water's pleasant tune　　　　　　　　　10
With some old border-song, or catch
That suits a summer's noon ;

" Or of the church-clock and the chimes
Sing here beneath the shade,
That half-mad thing of witty rhymes　　　　15
Which you last April made ! "

In silence Matthew lay, and eyed
The spring beneath the tree ;
And thus the dear old Man replied,
The grey-haired man of glee :　　　　　　　20

" No check, no stay, this Streamlet fears ;
How merrily it goes !
'T will murmur on a thousand years,
And flow as now it flows.

" And here, on this delightful day,　　　　　25
I cannot choose but think
How oft, a vigorous man, I lay
Beside this fountain's brink.

" My eyes are dim with childish tears,
My heart is idly stirred, 30
For the same sound is in my ears
Which in those days I heard.

" Thus fares it still in our decay :
And yet the wiser mind
Mourns less for what age takes away 35
Than what it leaves behind.

" The blackbird amid leafy trees,
The lark above the hill,
Let loose their carols when they please,
Are quiet when they will. 40

" With Nature never do *they* wage
A foolish strife ; they see
A happy youth, and their old age
Is beautiful and free :

" But we are pressed by heavy laws ; 45
And often, glad no more,
We wear a face of joy, because
We have been glad of yore.

" If there be one who need bemoan
His kindred laid in earth, 50
The household hearts that were his own ;
It is the man of mirth.

" My days, my Friend, are almost gone,
My life has been approved,
And many love me ; but by none 55
Am I enough beloved."

" Now both himself and me he wrongs,
The man who thus complains ;
I live and sing my idle songs
Upon these happy plains ;   60

" And, Matthew, for thy children dead
I 'll be a son to thee ! "
At this he grasped my hand, and said,
" Alas ! that cannot be."

We rose up from the fountain-side ;   65
And down the smooth descent
Of the green sheep-track did we glide ;
And through the wood we went ;

And, ere we came to Leonard's rock,
He sang those witty rhymes   70
About the crazy old church-clock,
And the bewildered chimes.

                                        1799.

HART-LEAP WELL.

Hart-Leap Well is a small spring of water, about five miles from Richmond
in Yorkshire, and near the side of the road that leads from Richmond to
Askrigg. Its name is derived from a remarkable Chase, the memory of which
is preserved by the monuments spoken of in the second Part of the following
Poem, which monuments do now exist as I have there described them.

THE Knight had ridden down from Wensley Moor
With the slow motion of a summer's cloud,
And now, as he approached a vassal's door,
" Bring forth another horse ! " he cried aloud.

"Another horse!" — That shout the vassal heard   5
And saddled his best Steed, a comely grey;
Sir Walter mounted him; he was the third
Which he had mounted on that glorious day.

Joy sparkled in the prancing courser's eyes;
The horse and horseman are a happy pair;   10
But, though Sir Walter like a falcon flies,
There is a doleful silence in the air.

A rout this morning left Sir Walter's Hall,
That as they galloped made the echoes roar;
But horse and man are vanished, one and all;   15
Such race, I think, was never seen before.

Sir Walter, restless as a veering wind,
Calls to the few tired dogs that yet remain:
Blanch, Swift, and Music, noblest of their kind,
Follow, and up the weary mountain strain.   20

The Knight hallooed, he cheered and chid them on
With suppliant gestures and upbraidings stern;
But breath and eyesight fail; and, one by one,
The dogs are stretched among the mountain fern.

Where is the throng, the tumult of the race?   25
The bugles that so joyfully were blown?
— This chase it looks not like an earthly chase;
Sir Walter and the Hart are left alone.

The poor Hart toils along the mountain-side;
I will not stop to tell how far he fled,   30
Nor will I mention by what death he died;
But now the Knight beholds him lying dead.

Dismounting, then, he leaned against a thorn ;
He had no follower, dog, nor man, nor boy :
He neither cracked his whip, nor blew his horn,   35
But gazed upon the spoil with silent joy.

Close to the thorn on which Sir Walter leaned,
Stood his dumb partner in this glorious feat ;
Weak as a lamb the hour that it is yeaned ;
And white with foam as if with cleaving sleet.   40

Upon his side the Hart was lying stretched :
His nostril touched a spring beneath a hill,
And with the last deep groan his breath had fetched
The waters of the spring were trembling still.

And now, too happy for repose or rest,   45
(Never had living man such joyful lot !)
Sir Walter walked all round, north, south, and west,
And gazed and gazed upon that darling spot.

And climbing up the hill — (it was at least
Four roods of sheer ascent) Sir Walter found   50
Three several hoof-marks which the hunted Beast
Had left imprinted on the grassy ground.

Sir Walter wiped his face, and cried, " Till now
Such sight was never seen by human eyes :
Three leaps have borne him from this lofty brow,   55
Down to the very fountain where he lies.

" I 'll build a pleasure-house upon this spot,
And a small arbour, made for rural joy ;
'T will be the traveller's shed, the pilgrim's cot,
A place of love for damsels that are coy.   60

" A cunning artist will I have to frame
A basin for that fountain in the dell !
And they who do make mention of the same,
From this day forth, shall call it HART-LEAP WELL.

" And, gallant Stag ! to make thy praises known,   65
Another monument shall here be raised ;
Three several pillars, each a rough-hewn stone,
And planted where thy hoofs the turf have grazed.

" And, in the summer-time when days are long,
I will come hither with my Paramour ;   70
And with the dancers and the minstrel's song
We will make merry in that pleasant bower.

" Till the foundations of the mountains fail
My mansion with its arbour shall endure ; —
The joy of them who till the fields of Swale,   75
And them who dwell among the woods of Ure !"

Then home he went, and left the Hart, stone-dead,
With breathless nostrils stretched above the spring.
— Soon did the Knight perform what he had said ;
And far and wide the fame thereof did ring.   80

Ere thrice the Moon into her port had steered,
A cup of stone received the living well ;
Three pillars of rude stone Sir Walter reared,
And built a house of pleasure in the dell.

And near the fountain, flowers of stature tall   85
With trailing plants and trees were intertwined, —
Which soon composed a little sylvan hall,
A leafy shelter from the sun and wind.

And thither, when the summer days were long,
Sir Walter led his wondering Paramour;　　　　　90
And with the dancers and the minstrel's song
Made merriment within that pleasant bower.

The Knight, Sir Walter, died in course of time,
And his bones lie in his paternal vale. —
But there is matter for a second rhyme,　　　　　95
And I to this would add another tale.

PART SECOND.

THE moving accident is not my trade;
To freeze the blood I have no ready arts:
'T is my delight, alone in summer shade,
To pipe a simple song for thinking hearts.　　　　　100

As I from Hawes to Richmond did repair,
It chanced that I saw standing in a dell
Three aspens at three corners of a square;
And one, not four yards distant, near a well.

What this imported I could ill divine:　　　　　105
And, pulling now the rein my horse to stop,
I saw three pillars standing in a line, —
The last stone-pillar on a dark hill-top.

The trees were grey, with neither arms nor head;
Half wasted the square mound of tawny green;　　　　　110
So that you just might say, as then I said,
" Here in old time the hand of man hath been."

I looked upon the hill both far and near,
More doleful place did never eye survey;
It seemed as if the spring-time came not here,　　　　　115
And Nature here were willing to decay.

I stood in various thoughts and fancies lost,
When one, who was in shepherd's garb attired,
Came up the hollow:—him did I accost,
And what this place might be I then inquired.　　120

The shepherd stopped, and that same story told
Which in my former rhyme I have rehearsed.
"A jolly place," said he, "in times of old!
But something ails it now: the spot is curst.

"You see these lifeless stumps of aspen wood—　　125
Some say that they are beeches, others elms—
These were the bower; and here a mansion stood,
The finest palace of a hundred realms!

"The arbour does its own condition tell;
You see the stones, the fountain, and the stream;　　130
But as to the great Lodge! you might as well
Hunt half a day for a forgotten dream.

"There's neither dog nor heifer, horse nor sheep,
Will wet his lips within that cup of stone;
And oftentimes, when all are fast asleep,　　135
This water doth send forth a dolorous groan.

"Some say that here a murder has been done,
And blood cries out for blood: but, for my part,
I've guessed, when I've been sitting in the sun,
That it was all for that unhappy Hart.　　140

"What thoughts must through the creature's brain
　　have passed!
Even from the topmost stone, upon the steep,
Are but three bounds—and look, Sir, at this last—
O Master! it has been a cruel leap.

"For thirteen hours he ran a desperate race;   145
And in my simple mind we cannot tell
What cause the Hart might have to love this place,
And come and make his deathbed near the well.

"Here on the grass perhaps asleep he sank,
Lulled by the fountain in the summer-tide;   150
This water was perhaps the first he drank
When he had wandered from his mother's side.

"In April here beneath the flowering thorn
He heard the birds their morning carols sing;
And he, perhaps, for aught we know, was born   155
Not half a furlong from that self-same spring.

"Now, here is neither grass nor pleasant shade;
The sun on drearier hollow never shone;
So will it be, as I have often said,
Till trees, and stones, and fountain, all are gone."   160

"Grey-headed Shepherd, thou hast spoken well;
Small difference lies between thy creed and mine:
This Beast not unobserved by Nature fell;
His death was mourned by sympathy divine.

"The Being, that is in the clouds and air,   165
That is in the green leaves among the groves,
Maintains a deep and reverential care
For the unoffending creatures whom he loves.

"The pleasure-house is dust:— behind, before,
This is no common waste, no common gloom;   170
But Nature, in due course of time, once more
Shall here put on her beauty and her bloom.

" She leaves these objects to a slow decay,
That what we are, and have been, may be known ;
But at the coming of the milder day,   175
These monuments shall all be overgrown.

" One lesson, Shepherd, let us two divide,
Taught both by what she shows, and what conceals ;
Never to blend our pleasure or our pride
With sorrow of the meanest thing that feels."   180

                                          1800.

THE BROTHERS.

" THESE Tourists, heaven preserve us ! needs must live
A profitable life : some glance along,
Rapid and gay, as if the earth were air,
And they were butterflies to wheel about
Long as the summer lasted ; some, as wise,   5
Perched on the forehead of a jutting crag,
Pencil in hand and book upon the knee,
Will look and scribble, scribble on and look,
Until a man might travel twelve stout miles,
Or reap an acre of his neighbour's corn.   10
But, for that moping Son of Idleness,
Why can he tarry *yonder?* — In our church-yard
Is neither epitaph nor monument,
Tombstone nor name — only the turf we tread
And a few natural graves."

                          To Jane, his wife,   15
Thus spake the homely priest of Ennerdale.
It was a July evening ; and he sate
Upon the long stone-seat beneath the eaves
Of his old cottage, — as it chanced, that day,

Employed in winter's work.　Upon the stone　　　20
His wife sate near him, teasing matted wool,
While, from the twin cards toothed with glittering wire,
He fed the spindle of his youngest child,
Who, in the open air, with due accord
Of busy hands and back-and-forward steps,　　　25
Her large round wheel was turning.　Towards the field
In which the Parish Chapel stood alone,
Girt round with a bare ring of mossy wall,
While half an hour went by, the Priest had sent
Many a long look of wonder: and at last,　　　30
Risen from his seat, beside the snow-white ridge
Of carded wool which the old man had piled
He laid his implements with gentle care,
Each in the other locked; and, down the path
That from his cottage to the church-yard led,　　　35
He took his way, impatient to accost
The Stranger, whom he saw still lingering there.

　'Twas one well known to him in former days,
A Shepherd-lad; who ere his sixteenth year
Had left that calling, tempted to entrust　　　40
His expectations to the fickle winds
And perilous waters; with the mariners
A fellow-mariner; — and so had fared
Through twenty seasons; but he had been reared
Among the mountains, and he in his heart　　　45
Was half a shepherd on the stormy seas.
Oft in the piping shrouds had Leonard heard
The tones of waterfalls, and inland sounds
Of caves and trees: — and, when the regular wind
Between the tropics filled the steady sail,　　　50
And blew with the same breath through days and weeks,
Lengthening invisibly its weary line
Along the cloudless Main, he, in those hours

Of tiresome indolence, would often hang
Over the vessel's side, and gaze and gaze ;   55
And, while the broad blue wave and sparkling foam
Flashed round him images and hues that wrought
In union with the employment of his heart,
He, thus by feverish passion overcome,
Even with the organs of his bodily eye,   60
Below him, in the bosom of the deep,
Saw mountains ; saw the forms of sheep that grazed
On verdant hills — with dwellings among trees,
And shepherds clad in the same country grey
Which he himself had worn.[1]

        And now, at last,   65
From perils manifold, with some small wealth
Acquired by traffic 'mid the Indian Isles,
To his paternal home he is returned,
With a determined purpose to resume
The life he had lived there ; both for the sake   70
Of many darling pleasures, and the love
Which to an only brother he has borne
In all his hardships, since that happy time
When, whether it blew foul or fair, they two
Were brother-shepherds on their native hills.   75
— They were the last of all their race : and now,
When Leonard had approached his home, his heart
Failed in him ; and, not venturing to enquire
Tidings of one so long and dearly loved,
He to the solitary church-yard turned ;   80
That, as he knew in what particular spot
His family were laid, he thence might learn
If still his Brother lived, or to the file

---

[1] This description of the Calenture is sketched from an imperfect recollection of an admirable one in prose, by Mr. Gilbert, author of the *Hurricane.*

Another grave was added. — He had found
Another grave, — near which a full half-hour   85
He had remained ; but, as he gazed, there grew
Such a confusion in his memory,
That he began to doubt ; and even to hope
That he had seen this heap of turf before, —
That it was not another grave, but one   90
He had forgotten.   He had lost his path,
As up the vale, that afternoon, he walked
Through fields which once had been well known to
          him :
And oh what joy this recollection now
Sent to his heart ! he lifted up his eyes,   95
And, looking round, imagined that he saw
Strange alteration wrought on every side
Among the woods and fields, and that the rocks,
And everlasting hills themselves were changed.

     By this the Priest, who down the field had come, 100
Unseen by Leonard, at the church-yard gate
Stopped short, — and thence, at leisure, limb by limb
Perused him with a gay complacency.
Ay, thought the Vicar, smiling to himself,
'T is one of those who needs must leave the path   105
Of the world's business to go wild alone :
His arms have a perpetual holiday ;
The happy man will creep about the fields,
Following his fancies by the hour, to bring
Tears down his cheek, or solitary smiles   110
Into his face, until the setting sun
Write fool upon his forehead. — Planted thus
Beneath a shed that over-arched the gate
Of this rude church-yard, till the stars appeared
The good Man might have communed with himself,   115
But that the Stranger, who had left the grave,

Approached; he recognized the Priest at once,
And, after greetings interchanged, and given
By Leonard to the Vicar as to one
Unknown to him, this dialogue ensued.   120
    Leonard.   You live, Sir, in these dales, a quiet life:
Your years make up one peaceful family;
And who would grieve and fret, if, welcome come
And welcome gone, they are so like each other,
They cannot be remembered?   Scarce a funeral   125
Comes to this church-yard once in eighteen months;
And yet, some changes must take place among you:
And you, who dwell here, even among these rocks,
Can trace the finger of mortality,
And see, that with our threescore years and ten   130
We are not all that perish. —— I remember,
(For many years ago I passed this road)
There was a foot-way all along the fields
By the brook-side — 't is gone — and that dark cleft!
To me it does not seem to wear the face   135
Which then it had!
    Priest.   Nay, Sir, for aught I know,
That chasm is much the same —
    Leonard.   But, surely, yonder —
    Priest.   Ay, there, indeed, your memory is a friend
That does not play you false. — On that tall pike
(It is the loneliest place of all these hills)   140
There were two springs which bubbled side by side,
As if they had been made that they might be
Companions for each other: the huge crag
Was rent with lightning — one hath disappeared;
The other, left behind, is flowing still.   145
For accidents and changes such as these,
We want not store of them; — a waterspout
Will bring down half a mountain; what a feast

For folks that wander up and down like you,
To see an acre's breadth of that wide cliff　　150
One roaring cataract ! a sharp May-storm
Will come with loads of January snow,
And in one night send twenty score of sheep
To feed the ravens ; or a shepherd dies
By some untoward death among the rocks :　　155
The ice breaks up and sweeps away a bridge ;
A wood is felled : — and then for our own homes !
A child is born or christened, a field ploughed,
A daughter sent to service, a web spun,
The old house-clock is decked with a new face ;　　160
And hence, so far from wanting facts or dates
To chronicle the time, we all have here
A pair of diaries, — one serving, Sir,
For the whole dale, and one for each fireside —
Yours was a stranger's judgment : for historians,　　165
Commend me to these valleys !
　　Leonard.　　　　　　　　Yet your Church-yard
Seems, if such freedom may be used with you,
To say that you are heedless of the past :
An orphan could not find his mother's grave :
Here 's neither head nor foot stone, plate of brass,　　170
Cross-bones nor skull, — type of our earthly state
Nor emblem of our hopes : the dead man's home
Is but a fellow to that pasture-field.
　　Priest.　Why, there, Sir, is a thought that 's new to me !
The stone-cutters, 't is true, might beg their bread　　175
If every English church-yard were like ours ;
Yet your conclusion wanders from the truth :
We have no need of names and epitaphs ;
We talk about the dead by our firesides.
And then, for our immortal part ! *we* want　　180
No symbols, Sir, to tell us that plain tale :

The thought of death sits easy on the man
Who has been born and dies among the mountains.
   Leonard.   Your Dalesmen, then, do in each other's
       thoughts
Possess a kind of second life : no doubt   185
You, Sir, could help me to the history
Of half these graves ?
   Priest.   For eight-score winters past,
With what I 've witnessed, and with what I 've heard,
Perhaps I might ; and, on a winter-evening,
If you were seated at my chimney's nook,   190
By turning o'er these hillocks one by one,
We two could travel, Sir, through a strange round ;
Yet all in the broad highway of the world.
Now there 's a grave — your foot is half upon it, —
It looks just like the rest ; and yet that man   195
Died broken-hearted.
   Leonard.   'T is a common case.
We 'll take another : who is he that lies
Beneath yon ridge, the last of those three graves ?
It touches on that piece of native rock
Left in the church-yard wall.
   Priest.   That 's Walter Ewbank. 200
He had as white a head and fresh a cheek
As ever were produced by youth and age
Engendering in the blood of hale fourscore.
Through five long generations had the heart
Of Walter's forefathers o'erflowed the bounds   205
Of their inheritance, that single cottage —
You see it yonder ! and those few green fields.
They toiled and wrought, and still, from sire to son,
Each struggled, and each yielded as before
A little — yet a little, — and old Walter,   210
They left to him the family heart, and land

With other burthens than the crop it bore.
Year after year the old man still kept up
A cheerful mind, — and buffeted with bond,
Interest, and mortgages ; at last he sank,   215
And went into his grave before his time.
Poor Walter ! whether it was care that spurred him
God only knows, but to the very last
He had the lightest foot in Ennerdale :
His pace was never that of an old man :   220
I almost see him tripping down the path
With his two grandsons after him : — but you,
Unless our Landlord be your host to-night,
Have far to travel, — and on these rough paths
Even in the longest day of midsummer —   225

    Leonard.   But those two Orphans !
    Priest.   Orphans ! — Such they were —
Yet not while Walter lived : for, though their parents
Lay buried side by side as now they lie,
The old man was a father to the boys,
Two fathers in one father : and if tears,   230
Shed when he talked of them where they were not,
And hauntings from the infirmity of love,
Are aught of what makes up a mother's heart,
This old Man, in the day of his old age,
Was half a mother to them. — If you weep, Sir,   235
To hear a stranger talking about strangers,
Heaven bless you when you are among your kindred !
Ay — you may turn that way — it is a grave
Which will bear looking at.

    Leonard.   These boys — I hope
They loved this good old Man ? —
    Priest.   They did — and truly: 240
But that was what we almost overlooked,
They were such darlings of each other. Yes,

Though from the cradle they had lived with Walter,
The only kinsman near them, and though he
Inclined to both by reason of his age,   245
With a more fond, familiar, tenderness ;
They, notwithstanding, had much love to spare,
And it all went into each other's hearts.
Leonard, the elder by just eighteen months,
Was two years taller : 't was a joy to see,   250
To hear, to meet them ! — From their house the school
Is distant three short miles, and in the time
Of storm and thaw, when every watercourse
And unbridged stream, such as you may have noticed
Crossing our roads at every hundred steps,   255
Was swoln into a noisy rivulet,
Would Leonard then, when elder boys remained
At home, go staggering through the slippery fords,
Bearing his brother on his back.   I have seen him,
On windy days, in one of those stray brooks,   260
Ay, more than once I have seen him, mid-leg deep,
Their two books lying both on a dry stone,
Upon the hither side : and once I said,
As I remember, looking round these rocks
And hills on which we all of us were born,   265
That God who made the great book of the world
Would bless such piety —
   Leonard.   It may be then —
   Priest.   Never did worthier lads break English bread :
The very brightest Sunday Autumn saw
With all its mealy clusters of ripe nuts,   270
Could never keep those boys away from church,
Or tempt them to an hour of sabbath breach.
Leonard and James !   I warrant, every corner
Among these rocks, and every hollow place
That venturous foot could reach, to one or both   275

Was known as well as to the flowers that grow there.
Like roe-bucks they went bounding o'er the hills;
They played like two young ravens on the crags :
Then they could write, ay and speak too, as well
As many of their betters — and for Leonard !　　　　　280
The very night before he went away,
In my own house I put into his hand
A Bible, and I 'd wager house and field
That, if he be alive, he has it yet.

　　Leonard.　It seems, these Brothers have not lived to be　285
A comfort to each other —

　　Priest.　　　　　　　That they might
Live to such end is what both old and young
In this our valley all of us have wished,
And what, for my part, I have often prayed :
But Leonard —

　　Leonard.　　Then James still is left among you !　　290

　　Priest.　'T is of the elder brother I am speaking :
They had an uncle ; — he was at that time
A thriving man, and trafficked on the seas :
And, but for that same uncle, to this hour
Leonard had never handled rope or shroud :　　　　　295
For the boy loved the life which we lead here ;
And though of unripe years, a stripling only,
His soul was knit to this his native soil.
But, as I said, old Walter was too weak
To strive with such a torrent ; when he died,　　　　　300
The estate and house were sold ; and all their sheep,
A pretty flock, and which, for aught I know,
Had clothed the Ewbanks for a thousand years : —
Well — all was gone, and they were destitute,
And Leonard, chiefly for his Brother's sake,　　　　　305
Resolved to try his fortune on the seas.
Twelve years are past since we had tidings from him.

If there were one among us who had heard
That Leonard Ewbank was come home again,
From the Great Gavel,[1] down by Leeza's banks, 310
And down the Enna, far as Egremont,
The day would be a joyous festival ;
And those two bells of ours, which there you see —
Hanging in the open air — but, O good Sir !
This is sad talk — they 'll never sound for him — 315
Living or dead. — When last we heard of him,
He was in slavery among the Moors
Upon the Barbary coast. — 'T was not a little
That would bring down his spirit ; and no doubt,
Before it ended in his death, the Youth 320
Was sadly crossed. — Poor Leonard ! when we parted,
He took me by the hand, and said to me,
If e'er he should grow rich, he would return,
To live in peace upon his father's land,
And lay his bones among us.
 Leonard.   If that day 325
Should come, 't would needs be a glad day for him ;
He would himself, no doubt, be happy then
As any that should meet him —
 Priest.   Happy ! Sir —
 Leonard. You said his kindred all were in their graves,
And that he had one Brother —
 Priest.   That is but · 330
A fellow-tale of sorrow. From his youth

---

[1] The Great Gavel, so called, I imagine, from its resemblance to
the gable end of a house, is one of the highest of the Cumberland
mountains. It stands at the head of the several vales of Ennerdale,
Wastdale, and Borrowdale.

The Leeza is a river which flows into the Lake of Ennerdale : on
issuing from the Lake, it changes its name, and is called the End,
Eyne, or Enna. It falls into the sea a little below Egremont.

James, though not sickly, yet was delicate;
And Leonard being always by his side
Had done so many offices about him,
That, though he was not of a timid nature, 335
Yet still the spirit of a mountain-boy
In him was somewhat checked ; and, when his Brother
Was gone to sea, and he was left alone,
The little colour that he had was soon
Stolen from his cheek ; he drooped, and pined, and
    pined — 340
  Leonard. But these are all the graves of full-grown
    men !
  Priest. Ay, Sir, that passed away : we took him to us ;
He was the child of all the dale — he lived
Three months with one, and six months with another,
And wanted neither food, nor clothes, nor love : 345
And many, many happy days were his.
But, whether blithe or sad, 't is my belief
His absent Brother still was at his heart.
And, when he dwelt beneath our roof, we found
(A practice till this time unknown to him) 350
That often, rising from his bed at night,
He in his sleep would walk about, and sleeping
He sought his brother Leonard. — You are moved !
Forgive me, Sir : before I spoke to you,
I judged you most unkindly.
  Leonard.   But this Youth, 355
How did he die at last?
  Priest.   One sweet May-morning
(It will be twelve years since when Spring returns),
He had gone forth among the new-dropped lambs,
With two or three companions, whom their course
Of occupation led from height to height 360
Under a cloudless sun — till he, at length,

Through weariness, or, haply, to indulge
The humour of the moment, lagged behind.
You see yon precipice ; — it wears the shape
Of a vast building made of many crags ; 365
And in the midst is one particular rock
That rises like a column from the vale,
Whence by our shepherds it is called, THE PILLAR.
Upon its aëry summit crowned with heath,
The loiterer, not unnoticed by his comrades, 370
Lay stretched at ease ; but, passing by the place
On their return, they found that he was gone.
No ill was feared ; till one of them by chance
Entering, when evening was far spent, the house
Which at that time was James's home, there learned 375
That nobody had seen him all that day :
The morning came, and still he was unheard of
The neighbours were alarmed, and to the brook
Some hastened ; some ran to the lake : ere noon
They found him at the foot of that same rock 380
Dead, and with mangled limbs.   The third day after
I buried him, poor Youth, and there he lies !
 Leonard.   And that then *is* his grave ! — Before his
  death
You say that he saw many happy years ?
 Priest.   Ay, that he did —
 Leonard.   And all went well with him ? — 385
 Priest.   If he had one, the Youth had twenty homes.
 Leonard.   And you believe, then, that his mind was
  easy ? —
 Priest.   Yes, long before he died, he found that time
Is a true friend to sorrow ; and unless
His thoughts were turned on Leonard's luckless fortune, 390
He talked about him with a cheerful love.
 Leonard.   He could not come to an unhallowed end !

Priest. Nay, God forbid!—You recollect I mentioned
A habit which disquietude and grief
Had brought upon him ; and we all conjectured   395
That, as the day was warm, he had lain down
On the soft heath, — and, waiting for his comrades,
He there had fallen asleep ; that in his sleep
He to the margin of the precipice
Had walked, and from the summit had fallen headlong : 400
And so no doubt he perished.   When the Youth
Fell, in his hand he must have grasped, we think,
His shepherd's staff ; for on that Pillar of rock
It had been caught mid-way ; and there for years
It hung ; — and mouldered there.

                      The Priest here ended — 405
The Stranger would have thanked him, but he felt
A gushing from his heart, that took away
The power of speech.   Both left the spot in silence ;
And Leonard, when they reached the church-yard gate,
As the Priest lifted up the latch, turned round, —   410
And, looking at the grave, he said, " My Brother ! "
The Vicar did not hear the words : and now,
He pointed towards his dwelling-place, entreating
That Leonard would partake his homely fare :
The other thanked him with an earnest voice ;   415
But added, that, the evening being calm,
He would pursue his journey.   So they parted.

   It was not long ere Leonard reached a grove
That overhung the road : he there stopped short,
And, sitting down beneath the trees, reviewed   420
All that the Priest had said : his early years
Were with him : — his long absence, cherished hopes,
And thoughts which had been his an hour before,
All pressed on him with such a weight, that now,
This vale, where he had been so happy, seemed   425

A place in which he could not bear to live :
So he relinquished all his purposes.
He travelled back to Egremont : and thence,
That night, he wrote a letter to the Priest,
Reminding him of what had passed between them ;   430
And adding, with a hope to be forgiven,
That it was from the weakness of his heart
He had not dared to tell him who he was.
This done, he went on shipboard, and is now
A Seaman, a grey-headed Mariner.   435

1800.

THE PET-LAMB.

A PASTORAL.

THE dew was falling fast, the stars began to blink ;
I heard a voice ; it said, " Drink, pretty creature, drink ! "
And, looking o'er the hedge, before me I espied
A snow-white mountain-lamb with a Maiden at its side.

Nor sheep nor kine were near ; the lamb was all alone,   5
And by a slender cord was tethered to a stone ;
With one knee on the grass did the little Maiden kneel,
While to that mountain-lamb she gave its evening meal.

The lamb, while from her hand he thus his supper took,
Seemed to feast with head and ears ; and his tail with
        pleasure shook.   10
" Drink, pretty creature, drink," she said in such a tone
That I almost received her heart into my own.

'T was little Barbara Lewthwaite, a child of beauty rare !
I watched them with delight, they were a lovely pair.
Now with her empty can the Maiden turned away :   15
But ere ten yards were gone her footsteps did she stay.

Right towards the lamb she looked ; and from a shady
        place
I unobserved could see the workings of her face :
If Nature to her tongue could measured numbers bring,
Thus, thought I, to her lamb that little Maid might sing :   20

" What ails thee, young One ? what ?   Why pull so at
        thy cord ?
Is it not well with thee ? well both for bed and board ?
Thy plot of grass is soft, and green as grass can be ;
Rest, little young One, rest ; what is 't that aileth thee ?

" What is it thou wouldst seek ?   What is wanting to
        thy heart ?   25
Thy limbs are they not strong ?   And beautiful thou art :
This grass is tender grass ; these flowers they have no
        peers ;
And that green corn all day is rustling in thy ears !

" If the sun be shining hot, do but stretch thy woollen
        chain,
This beech is standing by, its covert thou canst gain ;   30
For rain and mountain-storms ! the like thou need'st
        not fear,
The rain and storm are things that scarcely can come
        here.

" Rest, little young One, rest ; thou hast forgot the day
When my father found thee first in places far away ;

Many flocks were on the hills, but thou wert owned by
    none,   35
And thy mother from thy side for evermore was gone.

" He took thee in his arms, and in pity brought thee
    home :
A blessèd day for thee ! then whither wouldst thou roam?
A faithful nurse thou hast ; the dam that did thee yean
Upon the mountain-tops no kinder could have been.   40

" Thou know'st that twice a day I have brought thee in
    this can
Fresh water from the brook, as clear as ever ran ;
And twice in the day, when the ground is wet with dew,
I bring thee draughts of milk, warm milk it is and new.

" Thy limbs will shortly be twice as stout as they are now,   45
Then I 'll yoke thee to my cart like a pony in the plough ;
My playmate thou shalt be ; and when the wind is cold
Our hearth shall be thy bed, our house shall be thy fold.

" It will not, will not rest ! — Poor creature, can it be
That 't is thy mother's heart which is working so in thee?   50
Things that I know not of belike to thee are dear,
And dreams of things which thou canst neither see nor
    hear.

" Alas, the mountain-tops that look so green and fair !
I 've heard of fearful winds and darkness that come there ;
The little brooks that seem all pastime and all play,   55
When they are angry, roar like lions for their prey.

' Here thou need'st not dread the raven in the sky ;
Night and day thou art safe, — our cottage is hard by.

Why bleat so after me? Why pull so at thy chain?
Sleep — and at break of day I will come to thee again!" 60

— As homeward through the lane I went with lazy feet,
This song to myself did I oftentimes repeat;
And it seemed, as I retraced the ballad line by line,
That but half of it was hers, and one half of it was *mine.*

Again, and once again, did I repeat the song;   65
"Nay," said I, "more than half to the damsel must
        belong,
For she looked with such a look and she spake with
        such a tone,
That I almost received her heart into my own."
                                            1800.

POEMS ON THE NAMING OF PLACES.

By persons resident in the country and attached to rural objects, many
places will be found unnamed or of unknown names, where little Incidents
must have occurred, or feelings been experienced, which will have given to
such places a private and peculiar interest. From a wish to give some sort
of record to such Incidents, and renew the gratification of such feelings,
Names have been given to Places by the Author and some of his Friends,
and the following Poems written in consequence.

I.

IT was an April morning: fresh and clear
The Rivulet, delighting in its strength,
Ran with a young man's speed; and yet the voice
Of waters which the winter had supplied
Was softened down into a vernal tone.   5
The spirit of enjoyment and desire,
And hopes and wishes, from all living things

Went circling, like a multitude of sounds.
The budding groves seemed eager to urge on
The steps of June ; as if their various hues 10
Were only hindrances that stood between
Them and their object : but, meanwhile, prevailed
Such an entire contentment in the air
That every naked ash, and tardy tree
Yet leafless, showed as if the countenance 15
With which it looked on this delightful day
Were native to the summer. — Up the brook
I roamed in the confusion of my heart,
Alive to all things and forgetting all.
At length I to a sudden turning came 20
In this continuous glen, where down a rock
The Stream, so ardent in its course before,
Sent forth such sallies of glad sound, that all
Which I till then had heard, appeared the voice
Of common pleasure : beast and bird, the lamb, 25
The shepherd's dog, the linnet and the thrush
Vied with this waterfall, and made a song,
Which, while I listened, seemed like the wild growth
Or like some natural produce of the air,
That could not cease to be.   Green leaves were here ; 30
But 't was the foliage of the rocks — the birch,
The yew, the holly, and the bright green thorn,
With hanging islands of resplendent furze :
And, on a summit, distant a short space,
By any who should look beyond the dell, 35
A single mountain-cottage might be seen.
I gazed and gazed, and to myself I said,
" Our thoughts at least are ours ; and this wild nook,
My EMMA, I will dedicate to thee."
—— Soon did the spot become my other home, 40
My dwelling, and my out-of-doors abode.

And, of the Shepherds who have seen me there,
To whom I sometimes in our idle talk
Have told this fancy, two or three, perhaps,
Years after we are gone and in our graves,   45
When they have cause to speak of this wild place,
May call it by the name of EMMA'S DELL.

                                        1800.

                        II.

                    TO JOANNA.

AMID the smoke of cities did you pass
The time of early youth ; and there you learned,
From years of quiet industry, to love
The living Beings by your own fireside,
With such a strong devotion, that your heart   5
Is slow to meet the sympathies of them
Who look upon the hills with tenderness,
And make dear friendships with the streams and groves.
Yet we, who are transgressors in this kind,
Dwelling retired in our simplicity   10
Among the woods and fields, we love you well,
Joanna ! and I guess, since you have been
So distant from us now for two long years,
That you will gladly listen to discourse,
However trivial, if you thence be taught   15
That they, with whom you once were happy, talk
Familiarly of you and of old times.

    While I was seated, now some ten days past,
Beneath those lofty firs, that overtop
Their ancient neighbour, the old steeple-tower,   20
The Vicar from his gloomy house hard by
Came forth to greet me ; and when he had asked,
" How fares Joanna, that wild-hearted Maid !

And when will she return to us?" he paused;
And, after short exchange of village news,   25
He with grave looks demanded, for what cause,
Reviving obsolete idolatry,
I, like a Runic Priest, in characters
Of formidable size had chiselled out
Some uncouth name upon the native rock,   30
Above the Rotha, by the forest-side.
— Now, by those dear immunities of heart
Engendered between malice and true love,
I was not loth to be so catechised,
And this was my reply: — "As it befell,   35
One summer morning we had walked abroad
At break of day, Joanna and myself.
— 'T was that delightful season when the broom,
Full-flowered, and visible on every steep,
Along the copses runs in veins of gold.   40
Our pathway led us on to Rotha's banks;
And when we came in front of that tall rock
That eastward looks, I there stopped short — and stood
Tracing the lofty barrier with my eye
From base to summit; such delight I found   45
To note in shrub and tree, in stone and flower
That intermixture of delicious hues,
Along so vast a surface, all at once,
In one impression, by connecting force
Of their own beauty, imaged in the heart.   50
— When I had gazed perhaps two minutes' space,
Joanna, looking in my eyes, beheld
That ravishment of mine, and laughed aloud.
The Rock, like something starting from a sleep,
Took up the Lady's voice, and laughed again;   55
That ancient Woman seated on Helm-crag
Was ready with her cavern; Hammar-scar,

And the tall Steep of Silver-how, sent forth
A noise of laughter ; southern Loughrigg heard,
And Fairfield answered with a mountain tone ;   60
Helvellyn far into the clear blue sky
Carried the Lady's voice, — old Skiddaw blew
His speaking-trumpet ; — back out of the clouds
Of Glaramara southward came the voice ;
And Kirkstone tossed it from his misty head.   65
— Now whether (said I to our cordial Friend,
Who in the hey-day of astonishment
Smiled in my face) this were in simple truth
A work accomplished by the brotherhood
Of ancient mountains, or my ear was touched   70
With dreams and visionary impulses
To me alone imparted, sure I am
That there was a loud uproar in the hills.
And, while we both were listening, to my side
The fair Joanna drew, as if she wished   75
To shelter from some object of her fear.
— And hence, long afterwards, when eighteen moons
Were wasted, as I chanced to walk alone
Beneath this rock, at sunrise, on a calm
And silent morning, I sat down, and there,   80
In memory of affections old and true,
I chiselled out in those rude characters
Joanna's name deep in the living stone : —
And I, and all who dwell by my fireside,
Have called the lovely rock, JOANNA'S ROCK."   85

1800.

NOTE. — In Cumberland and Westmoreland are several Inscriptions, upon the native rock, which, from the wasting of time, and the rudeness of the workmanship, have been mistaken for Runic. They are without doubt Roman.

The Rotha, mentioned in this poem, is the River which, flowing through the lakes of Grasmere and Rydale, falls into Wynandermere.

On Helm-crag, that impressive single mountain at the head of the Vale of Grasmere, is a rock which from most points of view bears a striking resemblance to an old Woman cowering. Close by this rock is one of those fissures or caverns, which in the language of the country are called dungeons. Most of the mountains here mentioned immediately surround the Vale of Grasmere; of the others, some are at a considerable distance, but they belong to the same cluster.

III.

THERE is an Eminence, — of these our hills
The last that parleys with the setting sun;
We can behold it from our orchard-seat;
And, when at evening we pursue our walk
Along the public way, this Peak, so high   5
Above us, and so distant in its height,
Is visible; and often seems to send
Its own deep quiet to restore our hearts.
The meteors make of it a favourite haunt:
The star of Jove, so beautiful and large   10
In the mid heavens, is never half so fair
As when he shines above it.   'T is in truth
The loneliest place we have among the clouds.
And She who dwells with me, whom I have loved
With such communion, that no place on earth   15
Can ever be a solitude to me,
Hath to this lonely Summit given my Name.

1800.

THE CHILDLESS FATHER.

"UP, Timothy, up with your staff and away!
Not a soul in the village this morning will stay;
The hare has just started from Hamilton's grounds,
And Skiddaw is glad with the cry of the hounds."

— Of coats and of jackets grey, scarlet, and green,   5
On the slopes of the pastures all colours were seen ;
With their comely blue aprons, and caps white as snow,
The girls on the hills made a holiday show.

Fresh sprigs of green box-wood, not six months before,
Filled the funeral basin at Timothy's door ;   10
A coffin through Timothy's threshold had past ;
One Child did it bear, and that Child was his last.

Now fast up the dell came the noise and the fray,
The horse and the horn, and the hark ! hark away !
Old Timothy took up his staff, and he shut   15
With a leisurely motion the door of his hut.

Perhaps to himself at that moment he said :
" The key I must take, for my Ellen is dead."
But of this in my ears not a word did he speak ;
And he went to the chase with a tear on his cheek.   20

1800.

MICHAEL.

A PASTORAL POEM.

IF from the public way you turn your steps
Up the tumultuous brook of Greenhead Ghyll,
You will suppose that with an upright path
Your feet must struggle ; in such bold ascent
The pastoral mountains front you, face to face.   5
But, courage ! for around that boisterous brook
The mountains have all opened out themselves,
And made a hidden valley of their own.

No habitation can be seen ; but they
Who journey thither find themselves alone   10
With a few sheep, with rocks and stones, and kites
That overhead are sailing in the sky.
It is in truth an utter solitude ;
Nor should I have made mention of this Dell
But for one object which you might pass by,   15
Might see and notice not.   Beside the brook
Appears a straggling heap of unhewn stones !
And to that simple object appertains
A story — unenriched with strange events,
Yet not unfit, I deem, for the fireside,   20
Or for the summer shade.   It was the first
Of those domestic tales that spake to me
Of shepherds, dwellers in the valleys, men
Whom I already loved ; not verily
For their own sakes, but for the fields and hills   25
Where was their occupation and abode.
And hence this Tale, while I was yet a Boy
Careless of books, yet having felt the power
Of Nature, by the gentle agency
Of natural objects, led me on to feel   30
For passions that were not my own, and think
(At random and imperfectly indeed)
On man, the heart of man, and human life.
Therefore, although it be a history
Homely and rude, I will relate the same   35
For the delight of a few natural hearts ;
And, with yet fonder feeling, for the sake
Of youthful Poets, who among these hills
Will be my second self when I am gone.

   Upon the forest-side in Grasmere Vale   40
There dwelt a Shepherd, Michael was his name ;

An old man, stout of heart, and strong of limb.
His bodily frame had been from youth to age
Of an unusual strength : his mind was keen,
Intense, and frugal, apt for all affairs,   45
And in his shepherd's calling he was prompt
And watchful more than ordinary men.
Hence had he learned the meaning of all winds,
Of blasts of every tone ; and, oftentimes,
When others heeded not, He heard the South   50
Make subterraneous music, like the noise
Of bagpipers on distant Highland hills.
The Shepherd, at such warning, of his flock
Bethought him, and he to himself would say,
" The winds are now devising work for me ! "   55
And, truly, at all times, the storm, that drives
The traveller to a shelter, summoned him
Up to the mountains : he had been alone
Amid the heart of many thousand mists,
That came to him, and left him, on the heights.
So lived he till his eightieth year was past.
And grossly that man errs, who should suppose
That the green valleys, and the streams and rocks,
Were things indifferent to the Shepherd's thoughts.
Fields, where with cheerful spirits he had breathed   65
The common air ; hills, which with vigorous step
He had so often climbed ; which had impressed
So many incidents upon his mind
Of hardship, skill or courage, joy or fear ;
Which, like a book, preserved the memory   70
Of the dumb animals, whom he had saved,
Had fed or sheltered, linking to such acts
The certainty of honourable gain ;
Those fields, those hills — what could they less ? had laid
Strong hold on his affections, were to him   75

A pleasurable feeling of blind love,
The pleasure which there is in life itself.
　His days had not been passed in singleness.
His Helpmate was a comely matron, old —
Though younger than himself full twenty years.　　　80
She was a woman of a stirring life,
Whose heart was in her house : two wheels she had
Of antique form ; this large, for spinning wool ;
That small, for flax ; and if one wheel had rest
It was because the other was at work.　　　85
The Pair had but one inmate in their house,
An only Child, who had been born to them
When Michael, telling o'er his years, began
To deem that he was old, — in shepherd's phrase,
With one foot in the grave.　This only Son,　　　90
With two brave sheep-dogs tried in many a storm,
The one of an inestimable worth,
Made all their household.　I may truly say,
That they were as a proverb in the vale
For endless industry.　When day was gone,　　　95
And from their occupations out of doors
The Son and Father were come home, even then,
Their labour did not cease ; unless when all
Turned to the cleanly supper-board, and there,
Each with a mess of pottage and skimmed milk,　　　100
Sat round the basket piled with oaten cakes,
And their plain home-made cheese.　Yet when the meal
Was ended, Luke (for so the Son was named)
And his old Father both betook themselves
To such convenient work as might employ　　　105
Their hands by the fireside ; perhaps to card
Wool for the Housewife's spindle, or repair
Some injury done to sickle, flail, or scythe,
Or other implement of house or field.

Down from the ceiling, by the chimney's edge,   110
That in our ancient uncouth country style
With huge and black projection overbrowed
Large space beneath, as duly as the light
Of day grew dim the Housewife hung a lamp;
An aged utensil, which had performed   115
Service beyond all others of its kind.
Early at evening did it burn — and late,
Surviving comrade of uncounted hours,
Which, going by from year to year, had found,
And left, the couple neither gay perhaps   120
Nor cheerful, yet with objects and with hopes,
Living a life of eager industry.
And now, when Luke had reached his eighteenth year,
There by the light of this old lamp they sate,
Father and Son, while far into the night   125
The Housewife plied her own peculiar work,
Making the cottage through the silent hours
Murmur as with the sound of summer flies.
This light was famous in its neighbourhood,
And was a public symbol of the life   130
That thrifty Pair had lived.   For, as it chanced,
Their cottage on a plot of rising ground
Stood single, with large prospect, north and south,
High into Easedale, up to Dunmail-Raise,
And westward to the village near the lake;   135
And from this constant light, so regular
And so far seen, the House itself, by all
Who dwelt within the limits of the vale,
Both old and young, was named THE EVENING STAR.

Thus living on through such a length of years,   140
The Shepherd, if he loved himself, must needs
Have loved his Helpmate; but to Michael's heart
This son of his old age was yet more dear —

Less from instinctive tenderness, the same
Fond spirit that blindly works in the blood of all —   145
Than that a child, more than all other gifts
That earth can offer to declining man,
Brings hope with it, and forward-looking thoughts,
And stirrings of inquietude, when they
By tendency of nature needs must fail.   150
Exceeding was the love he bare to him,
His heart and his heart's joy!   For oftentimes
Old Michael, while he was a babe in arms,
Had done him female service, not alone
For pastime and delight, as is the use   155
Of fathers, but with patient mind enforced
To acts of tenderness; and he had rocked
His cradle, as with a woman's gentle hand.

    And, in a later time, ere yet the Boy
Had put on boy's attire, did Michael love,   160
Albeit of a stern unbending mind,
To have the Young-one in his sight, when he
Wrought in the field, or on his shepherd's stool
Sate with a fettered sheep before him stretched
Under the large old oak, that near his door   165
Stood single, and, from matchless depth of shade,
Chosen for the Shearer's covert from the sun,
Thence in our rustic dialect was called
The CLIPPING TREE,[1] a name which yet it bears.
There, while they two were sitting in the shade,   170
With others round them, earnest all and blithe,
Would Michael exercise his heart with looks
Of fond correction and reproof bestowed
Upon the Child, if he disturbed the sheep
By catching at their legs, or with his shouts   175
Scared them, while they lay still beneath the shears.

[1] Clipping is the word used in the North of England for shearing.

And when by Heaven's good grace the boy grew up
A healthy Lad, and carried in his cheek
Two steady roses that were five years old;
Then Michael from a winter coppice cut   180
With his own hand a sapling, which he hooped
With iron, making it throughout in all
Due requisites a perfect shepherd's staff,
And gave it to the Boy; wherewith equipt
He as a watchman oftentimes was placed   185
At gate or gap, to stem or turn the flock;
And, to his office prematurely called,
There stood the urchin, as you will divine,
Something between a hindrance and a help;
And for this cause not always, I believe,   190
Receiving from his Father hire of praise;
Though nought was left undone which staff, or voice,
Or looks, or threatening gestures, could perform.

But soon as Luke, full ten years old, could stand
Against the mountain blasts; and to the heights,   195
Not fearing toil, nor length of weary ways,
He with his Father daily went, and they
Were as companions, why should I relate
That objects which the Shepherd loved before
Were dearer now? that from the Boy there came   200
Feelings and emanations — things which were
Light to the sun and music to the wind;
And that the old Man's heart seemed born again?

Thus in his Father's sight the Boy grew up:
And now, when he had reached his eighteenth year,   205
He was his comfort and his daily hope.

While in this sort the simple household lived
From day to day, to Michael's ear there came
Distressful tidings.   Long before the time
Of which I speak, the Shepherd had been bound   210

In surety for his brother's son, a man
Of an industrious life, and ample means;
But unforeseen misfortunes suddenly
Had prest upon him; and old Michael now
Was summoned to discharge the forfeiture,   215
A grievous penalty, but little less
Than half his substance.   This unlooked-for claim,
At the first hearing, for a moment took
More hope out of his life than he supposed
That any old man ever could have lost.   220
As soon as he had armed himself with strength
To look his trouble in the face, it seemed
The Shepherd's sole resource to sell at once
A portion of his patrimonial fields.
Such was his first resolve; he thought again,   225
And his heart failed him.   "Isabel," said he,
Two evenings after he had heard the news,
" I have been toiling more than seventy years,
And in the open sunshine of God's love
Have we all lived; yet if these fields of ours   230
Should pass into a stranger's hand, I think
That I could not lie quiet in my grave.
Our lot is a hard lot; the sun himself
Has scarcely been more diligent than I;
And I have lived to be a fool at last   235
To my own family.   An evil man
That was, and made an evil choice, if he
Were false to us; and if he were not false,
There are ten thousand to whom loss like this
Had been no sorrow.   I forgive him; — but   240
'T were better to be dumb than to talk thus.

When I began, my purpose was to speak
Of remedies and of a cheerful hope.
Our Luke shall leave us, Isabel; the land

Shall not go from us, and it shall be free ;   245
He shall possess it, free as is the wind
That passes over it.   We have, thou know'st,
Another kinsman — he will be our friend
In this distress.   He is a prosperous man,
Thriving in trade — and Luke to him shall go,   250
And with his kinsman's help and his own thrift
He quickly will repair this loss, and then
He may return to us.   If here he stay,
What can be done?   Where every one is poor,
What can be gained ? "

              At this the old Man paused,   255
And Isabel sat silent, for her mind
Was busy, looking back into past times.
There 's Richard Bateman, thought she to herself,
He was a parish-boy — at the church-door
They made a gathering for him, shillings, pence   260
And halfpennies, wherewith the neighbours bought
A basket, which they filled with pedlar's wares ;
And, with this basket on his arm, the lad
Went up to London, found a master there,
Who, out of many, chose the trusty boy   265
To go and overlook his merchandise
Beyond the seas ; where he grew wondrous rich,
And left estates and monies to the poor,
And, at his birth-place, built a chapel, floored
With marble which he sent from foreign lands.   270
These thoughts, and many others of like sort,
Passed quickly through the mind of Isabel,
And her face brightened.   The old Man was glad,
And thus resumed : — " Well, Isabel ! this scheme
These two days, has been meat and drink to me.   275
Far more than we have lost is left us yet.
— We have enough — I wish indeed that I

Were younger; — but this hope is a good hope.
— Make ready Luke's best garments, of the best
Buy for him more, and let us send him forth   280
To-morrow, or the next day, or to-night:
— If he *could* go, the Boy should go to-night."
　　Here Michael ceased, and to the fields went forth
With a light heart.　The Housewife for five days
Was restless morn and night, and all day long   285
Wrought on with her best fingers to prepare
Things needful for the journey of her son.
But Isabel was glad when Sunday came
To stop her in her work: for, when she lay
By Michael's side, she through the last two nights   290
Heard him, how he was troubled in his sleep:
And when they rose at morning she could see
That all his hopes were gone.　That day at noon
She said to Luke, while they two by themselves
Were sitting at the door, " Thou must not go: 295
We have no other Child but thee to lose,
None to remember — do not go away,
For if thou leave thy Father he will die."
The Youth made answer with a jocund voice;
And Isabel, when she had told her fears,   300
Recovered heart.　That evening her best fare
Did she bring forth, and all together sat
Like happy people round a Christmas fire.
　　With daylight Isabel resumed her work;
And all the ensuing week the house appeared   305
As cheerful as a grove in Spring: at length
The expected letter from their kinsman came,
With kind assurances that he would do
His utmost for the welfare of the Boy;
To which, requests were added, that forthwith   310
He might be sent to him.　Ten times or more

The letter was read over ; Isabel
Went forth to show it to the neighbours round ;
Nor was there at that time on English land
A prouder heart than Luke's.   When Isabel   315
Had to her house returned, the old Man said,
" He shall depart to-morrow."   To this word
The Housewife answered, talking much of things
Which, if at such short notice he should go,
Would surely be forgotten.   But at length   320
She gave consent, and Michael was at ease.

   Near the tumultuous brook of Greenhead Ghyll,
In that deep valley, Michael had designed
To build a Sheepfold ; and, before he heard
The tidings of his melancholy loss,   325
For this same purpose he had gathered up
A heap of stones, which by the streamlet's edge
Lay thrown together, ready for the work.
With Luke that evening thitherward he walked :
And soon as they had reached the place he stopped,   330
And thus the old Man spake to him : — " My Son,
To-morrow thou wilt leave me : with full heart
I look upon thee, for thou art the same
That wert a promise to me ere thy birth,
And all thy life hast been my daily joy.   335
I will relate to thee some little part
Of our two histories ; 't will do thee good
When thou art from me, even if I should touch
On things thou canst not know of. —— After thou
First cam'st into the world — as oft befalls   340
To new-born infants — thou didst sleep away
Two days, and blessings from thy Father's tongue
Then fell upon thee.   Day by day passed on,
And still I loved thee with increasing love.
Never to living ear came sweeter sounds   345

Than when I heard thee by our own fireside
First uttering, without words, a natural tune ;
While thou, a feeding babe, didst in thy joy
Sing at thy Mother's breast.   Month followed month,
And in the open fields my life was passed   350
And on the mountains ; else I think that thou
Hadst been brought up upon thy Father's knees.
But we were playmates, Luke : among these hills,
As well thou knowest, in us the old and young
Have played together, nor with me didst thou   355
Lack any pleasure which a boy can know."
Luke had a manly heart; but at these words
He sobbed aloud.   The old Man grasped his hand,
And said, " Nay, do not take it so — I see
That these are things of which I need not speak. 360
— Even to the utmost I have been to thee
A kind and a good Father : and herein
I but repay a gift which I myself
Received at others' hands ; for, though now old
Beyond the common life of man, I still   365
Remember them who loved me in my youth.
Both of them sleep together : here they lived,
As all their Forefathers had done ; and when
At length their time was come, they were not loth
To give their bodies to the family mould.   370
I wished that thou should'st live the life they lived :
But, 't is a long time to look back, my Son,
And see so little gain from threescore years.
These fields were burthened when they came to me ;
Till I was forty years of age, not more   375
Than half of my inheritance was mine.
I toiled and toiled ; God blessed me in my work,
And till these three weeks past the land was free.
— It looks as if it never could endure

Another Master.   Heaven forgive me, Luke,   380
If I judge ill for thee, but it seems good
That thou should'st go."
                              At this the old Man paused ;
Then, pointing to the stones near which they stood,
Thus, after a short silence, he resumed :
" This was a work for us ; and now, my Son,   385
It is a work for me.   But, lay one stone —
Here, lay it for me, Luke, with thine own hands.
Nay, Boy, be of good hope ; — we both may live
To see a better day.   At eighty-four
I still am strong and hale ; — do thou thy part ;   390
I will do mine. — I will begin again
With many tasks that were resigned to thee :
Up to the heights, and in among the storms,
Will I without thee go again, and do
All works which I was wont to do alone,   395
Before I knew thy face. — Heaven bless thee, Boy !
Thy heart these two weeks has been beating fast
With many hopes ; it should be so — yes — yes —
I knew that thou could'st never have a wish
To leave me, Luke : thou hast been bound to me   400
Only by links of love : when thou art gone,
What will be left to us ! — But, I forget
My purposes.   Lay now the corner-stone,
As I requested ; and hereafter, Luke,
When thou art gone away, should evil men   405
Be thy companions, think of me, my Son,
And of this moment ; hither turn thy thoughts,
And God will strengthen thee : amid all fear
And all temptation, Luke, I pray that thou
May'st bear in mind the life thy Fathers lived,   410
Who, being innocent, did for that cause
Bestir them in good deeds.   Now, fare thee well —

When thou return'st, thou in this place wilt see
A work which is not here : a covenant
'T will be between us ; but, whatever fate   415
Befall thee, I shall love thee to the last,
And bear thy memory with me to the grave."
    The Shepherd ended here ; and Luke stooped down,
And, as his Father had requested, laid
The first stone of the Sheepfold.   At the sight   420
The old Man's grief broke from him ; to his heart
He pressed his Son, he kissèd him and wept ;
And to the house together they returned.
— Hushed was that House in peace, or seeming peace,
Ere the night fell : — with morrow's dawn the Boy   425
Began his journey, and when he had reached
The public way, he put on a bold face ;
And all the neighbours, as he passed their doors,
Came forth with wishes and with farewell prayers,
That followed him till he was out of sight.   430
    A good report did from their Kinsman come,
Of Luke and his well-doing : and the Boy
Wrote loving letters, full of wondrous news,
Which, as the Housewife phrased it, were throughout
" The prettiest letters that were ever seen."   435
Both parents read them with rejoicing hearts.
So, many months passed on : and once again
The Shepherd went about his daily work
With confident and cheerful thoughts ; and now
Sometimes when he could find a leisure hour   440
He to that valley took his way, and there
Wrought at the Sheepfold.   Meantime Luke began
To slacken in his duty ; and, at length,
He in the dissolute city gave himself
To evil courses : ignominy and shame   445
Fell on him, so that he was driven at last

To seek a hiding-place beyond the seas.
   There is a comfort in the strength of love ;
'T will make a thing endurable, which else
Would overset the brain, or break the heart :   450
I have conversed with more than one who well
Remember the old Man, and what he was
Years after he had heard this heavy news.
His bodily frame had been from youth to age
Of an unusual strength.   Among the rocks   455
He went, and still looked up to sun and cloud,
And listened to the wind ; and, as before,
Performed all kinds of labour for his sheep,
And for the land, his small inheritance.
And to that hollow dell from time to time   460
Did he repair, to build the Fold of which
His flock had need.   'T is not forgotten yet
The pity which was then in every heart
For the old Man — and 't is believed by all
That many and many a day he thither went,   465
And never lifted up a single stone.
   There, by the Sheepfold, sometimes was he seen
Sitting alone, or with his faithful Dog,
Then old, beside him, lying at his feet.
The length of full seven years, from time to time,   470
He at the building of this Sheepfold wrought,
And left the work unfinished when he died.
Three years, or little more, did Isabel
Survive her Husband : at her death the estate
Was sold, and went into a stranger's hand.   475
The Cottage which was named the Evening Star
Is gone — the ploughshare has been through the ground
On which it stood ; great changes have been wrought
In all the neighbourhood : — yet the oak is left
That grew beside their door ; and the remains   480

Of the unfinished Sheepfold may be seen
Beside the boisterous brook of Greenhead Ghyll.

1800.

FRAGMENT FROM THE RECLUSE.

BOOK I.

On Man, on Nature, and on Human Life,
Musing in solitude, I oft perceive
Fair trains of imagery before me rise,
Accompanied by feelings of delight
Pure, or with no unpleasing sadness mixed ;⠀⠀⠀⠀⠀5
And I am conscious of affecting thoughts
And dear remembrances, whose presence soothes
Or elevates the Mind, intent to weigh
The good and evil of our mortal state.
— To these emotions, whencesoe'er they come,⠀⠀10
Whether from breath of outward circumstance,
Or from the Soul — an impulse to herself —
I would give utterance in numerous verse.
Of Truth, of Grandeur, Beauty, Love, and Hope,
And melancholy Fear subdued by Faith ;⠀⠀⠀⠀15
Of blessèd consolations in distress ;
Of moral strength, and intellectual Power ;
Of joy in widest commonalty spread ;
Of the individual Mind that keeps her own
Inviolate retirement, subject there⠀⠀⠀⠀⠀⠀20
To Conscience only, and the law supreme
Of that Intelligence which governs all —
I sing : — " fit audience let me find though few ! "
⠀⠀So prayed, more gaining than he asked, the Bard —
In holiest mood.⠀⠀Urania, I shall need⠀⠀⠀⠀25

Thy guidance, or a greater Muse, if such
Descend to earth or dwell in highest heaven !
For I must tread on shadowy ground, must sink
Deep — and, aloft ascending, breathe in worlds
To which the heaven of heavens is but a veil.   30
All strength — all terror, single or in bands,
That ever was put forth in personal form —
Jehovah — with his thunder, and the choir
Of shouting Angels, and the empyreal thrones —
I pass them unalarmed.   Not Chaos, not   35
The darkest pit of lowest Erebus,
Nor aught of blinder vacancy, scooped out
By help of dreams — can breed such fear and awe
As falls upon us often when we look
Into our Minds, into the Mind of Man —   40
My haunt, and the main region of my song.
— Beauty — a living Presence of the earth,
Surpassing the most fair ideal Forms
Which craft of delicate Spirits hath composed
From earth's materials — waits upon my steps ;   45
Pitches her tents before me as I move,
An hourly neighbour.   Paradise, and groves
Elysian, Fortunate Fields — like those of old
Sought in the Atlantic Main — why should they be
A history only of departed things,   50
Or a mere fiction of what never was ?
For the discerning intellect of Man,
When wedded to this goodly universe
In love and holy passion, shall find these
A simple produce of the common day.   55
— I, long before the blissful hour arrives,
Would chant, in lonely peace, the spousal verse
Of this great consummation :— and, by words
Which speak of nothing more than what we are,

Would I arouse the sensual from their sleep   60
Of Death, and win the vacant and the vain
To noble raptures ; while my voice proclaims
How exquisitely the individual Mind
(And the progressive powers perhaps no less
Of the whole species) to the external World   65
Is fitted : — and how exquisitely, too —
Theme this but little heard of among men —
The external World is fitted to the Mind ;
And the creation (by no lower name
Can it be called) which they with blended might   70
Accomplish : — this is our high argument.
— Such grateful haunts foregoing, if I oft
Must turn elsewhere — to travel near the tribes
And fellowships of men, and see ill sights
Of madding passions mutually inflamed ;   75
Must hear Humanity in fields and groves
Pipe solitary anguish ; or must hang
Brooding above the fierce confederate storm
Of sorrow, barricadoed evermore
Within the walls of cities — may these sounds   80
Have their authentic comment ; that even these
Hearing, I be not downcast or forlorn ! —
Descend, prophetic Spirit ! that inspir'st
The human Soul of universal earth,
Dreaming on things to come ; and dost possess   85
A metropolitan temple in the hearts
Of mighty Poets ; upon me bestow
A gift of genuine insight ; that my Song
With star-like virtue in its place may shine,
Shedding benignant influence, and secure   90
Itself from all malevolent effect
Of those mutations that extend their sway
Throughout the nether sphere ! — And if with this

I mix more lowly matter; with the thing
Contemplated, describe the Mind and Man   95
Contemplating; and who, and what he was —
The transitory Being that beheld
This Vision; — when and where, and how he lived;
Be not this labour useless. If such theme
May sort with highest objects, then — dread Power!   100
Whose gracious favour is the primal source
Of all illumination — may my Life
Express the image of a better time,
More wise desires, and simpler manners; — nurse
My Heart in genuine freedom: — all pure thoughts   105
Be with me; — so shall thy unfailing love
Guide, and support, and cheer me to the end!

1800 (?).

THE SPARROW'S NEST.

BEHOLD, within the leafy shade,
Those bright blue eggs together laid!
On me the chance-discovered sight
Gleamed like a vision of delight.
I started — seeming to espy   5
The home and sheltered bed,
The Sparrow's dwelling, which, hard by
My Father's house, in wet or dry
My sister Emmeline and I
    Together visited.   10

She looked at it and seemed to fear it;
Dreading, tho' wishing, to be near it:
Such heart was in her, being then
A little Prattler among men.

The Blessing of my later years   15
Was with me when a boy :
She gave me eyes, she gave me ears ;
And humble cares, and delicate fears ;
A heart, the fountain of sweet tears ;
     And love, and thought, and joy.   20

          1801.

TO A YOUNG LADY

WHO HAD BEEN REPROACHED FOR TAKING LONG WALKS IN THE COUNTRY.

DEAR Child of Nature, let them rail !
— There is a nest in a green dale,
A harbour and a hold ;
Where thou, a Wife and Friend, shalt see
Thy own heart-stirring days, and be   5
A light to young and old.

There, healthy as a shepherd boy,
And treading among flowers of joy
Which at no season fade,
Thou, while thy babes around thee cling,   10
Shalt show us how divine a thing
A Woman may be made.

Thy thoughts and feelings shall not die,
Nor leave thee, when grey hairs are nigh,
A melancholy slave ;   15
But an old age serene and bright,
And lovely as a Lapland night,
Shall lead thee to thy grave.

          1801 or 1802.

ALICE FELL;

OR, POVERTY.

THE post-boy drove with fierce career,
For threatening clouds the moon had drowned ;
When, as we hurried on, my ear
Was smitten with a startling sound.

As if the wind blew many ways,   5
I heard the sound, — and more and more,
It seemed to follow with the chaise,
And still I heard it as before.

At length I to the boy called out ;
He stopped his horses at the word,   10
But neither cry, nor voice, nor shout,
Nor aught else like it, could be heard.

The boy then smacked his whip, and fast
The horses scampered through the rain ;
But, hearing soon upon the blast   15
The cry, I bade him halt again.

Forthwith alighting on the ground,
" Whence comes," said I, " this piteous moan ? "
And there a little Girl I found,
Sitting behind the chaise, alone.   20

" My cloak ! " no other word she spake,
But loud and bitterly she wept,
As if her innocent heart would break ;
And down from off her seat she leapt.

" What ails you, child ? " — she sobbed " Look here ! "   25
I saw it in the wheel entangled,
A weather-beaten rag as e'er
From any garden scare-crow dangled.

There, twisted between nave and spoke,
It hung, nor could at once be freed ;
But our joint pains unloosed the cloak,
A miserable rag indeed !

    30

" And whither are you going, child,
To-night along these lonesome ways ? "
" To Durham," answered she, half wild —
" Then come with me into the chaise."

    35

Insensible to all relief
Sat the poor girl, and forth did send
Sob after sob, as if her grief
Could never, never have an end.

    40

" My child, in Durham do you dwell ? "
She checked herself in her distress,
And said, " My name is Alice Fell ;
I 'm fatherless and motherless,

" And I to Durham, Sir, belong."
Again, as if the thought would choke
Her very heart, her grief grew strong;
And all was for her tattered cloak !

    45

The chaise drove on ; our journey's end
Was nigh ; and, sitting by my side,
As if she had lost her only friend
She wept, nor would be pacified.

    50

Up to the tavern-door we post ;
Of Alice and her grief I told ;
And I gave money to the host,
To buy a new cloak for the old.

    55

" And let it be of duffil grey,
    As warm a cloak as man can sell ! "
    Proud creature was she the next day,
    The little orphan, Alice Fell !   60

                                      1802.

BEGGARS.

SHE had a tall man's height or more ;
Her face from summer's noontide heat
No bonnet shaded, but she wore
A mantle, to her very feet
Descending with a graceful flow,   5
And on her head a cap as white as new-fallen snow.

Her skin was of Egyptian brown :
Haughty, as if her eye had seen
Its own light to a distance thrown,
She towered, fit person for a Queen   10
To lead those ancient Amazonian files ;
Or ruling Bandit's wife among the Grecian isles.

Advancing, forth she stretched her hand
And begged an alms with doleful plea
That ceased not ; on our English land   15
Such woes, I knew, could never be ;
And yet a boon I gave her, for the creature
Was beautiful to see — a weed of glorious feature.

I left her, and pursued my way ;
And soon before me did espy   20
A pair of little Boys at play,
Chasing a crimson butterfly ;

The taller followed with his hat in hand,
Wreathed round with yellow flowers the gayest of the
      land.

The other wore a rimless crown   25
With leaves of laurel stuck about;
And, while both followed up and down,
Each whooping with a merry shout,
In their fraternal features I could trace
Unquestionable lines of that wild Suppliant's face.   30

Yet *they*, so blithe of heart, seemed fit
For finest tasks of earth or air:
Wings let them have, and they might flit
Precursors to Aurora's car,
Scattering fresh flowers; though happier far, I ween,   35
To hunt their fluttering game o'er rock and level green.

They dart across my path — but lo,
Each ready with a plaintive whine!
Said I, "not half an hour ago
Your Mother has had alms of mine."   40
"That cannot be," one answered — "she is dead:" —
I looked reproof — they saw — but neither hung his
      head.

"She has been dead, Sir, many a day." —
"Hush, boys! you're telling me a lie;
It was your Mother, as I say!"   45
And, in the twinkling of an eye,
"Come! Come!" cried one, and without more ado,
Off to some other play the joyous Vagrants flew!
           1802.

SEQUEL TO THE FOREGOING.

COMPOSED MANY YEARS AFTER.

WHERE are they now, those wanton Boys?
For whose free range the dædal earth
Was filled with animated toys,
And implements of frolic mirth ;
With tools for ready wit to guide ;   5
And ornaments of seemlier pride,
More fresh, more bright, than princes wear ;
For what one moment flung aside,
Another could repair ;
What good or evil have they seen   10
Since I their pastime witnessed here,
Their daring wiles, their sportive cheer?
I ask — but all is dark between !
    They met me in a genial hour,
When universal nature breathed   15
As with the breath of one sweet flower, —
A time to overrule the power
Of discontent, and check the birth
Of thoughts with better thoughts at strife,
The most familiar bane of life   20
Since parting Innocence bequeathed
Mortality to Earth !
Soft clouds, the whitest of the year,
Sailed through the sky — the brooks ran clear ;
The lambs from rock to rock were bounding ;   25
With songs the budded groves resounding ;
And to my heart are still endeared
The thoughts with which it then was cheered ;
The faith which saw that gladsome pair
Walk through the fire with unsinged hair.   30

Or, if such faith must needs deceive —
Then, Spirits of beauty and of grace,
Associates in that eager chase ;
Ye, who within the blameless mind
Your favourite seat of empire find — 35
Kind Spirits ! may we not believe
That they, so happy and so fair
Through your sweet influence, and the care
Of pitying Heaven, at least were free
From touch of *deadly* injury ? 40
Destined whate'er their earthly doom,
For mercy and immortal bloom !

1817.

TO A BUTTERFLY.

STAY near me — do not take thy flight !
A little longer stay in sight !
Much converse do I find in thee,
Historian of my infancy !
Float near me ; do not yet depart ! 5
Dead times revive in thee :
Thou bring'st, gay creature as thou art !
A solemn image to my heart,
My father's family !

Oh ! pleasant, pleasant were the days, 10
The time, when, in our childish plays,
My sister Emmeline and I
Together chased the butterfly !
A very hunter did I rush
Upon the prey : — with leaps and springs 15

I followed on from brake to bush ;
But she, God love her, feared to brush
The dust from off its wings.　　1802.

TO THE CUCKOO.

O BLITHE New-comer !　I have heard,
I hear thee and rejoice.
O Cuckoo ! shall I call thee Bird,
Or but a wandering Voice ?

While I am lying on the grass　　　　　　5
Thy twofold shout I hear,
From hill to hill it seems to pass,
At once far off, and near.

Though babbling only to the Vale,
Of sunshine and of flowers,　　　　　　10
Thou bringest unto me a tale
Of visionary hours.

Thrice welcome, darling of the Spring !
Even yet thou art to me
No bird, but an invisible thing,　　　　　15
A voice, a mystery ;

The same whom in my school-boy days
I listened to ; that Cry
Which made me look a thousand ways
In bush, and tree, and sky.　　　　　　20

To seek thee did I often rove
Through woods and on the green ;
And thou wert still a hope, a love ;
Still longed for, never seen.

And I can listen to thee yet ;   25
Can lie upon the plain
And listen, till I do beget
That golden time again.

O blessèd Bird ! the earth we pace
Again appears to be   30
An unsubstantial faery place,
That is fit home for Thee !

                                            1802.

———

"MY HEART LEAPS UP WHEN I BEHOLD."

MY heart leaps up when I behold
    A rainbow in the sky :
So was it when my life began ;
So is it now I am a man ;
So be it when I shall grow old,   5
    Or let me die !
The Child is father of the Man ;
And I could wish my days to be
Bound each to each by natural piety.

                                            1802.

———

WRITTEN IN MARCH,

WHILE RESTING ON THE BRIDGE AT THE FOOT OF BROTHER'S WATER.

THE Cock is crowing,
The stream is flowing,
The small birds twitter,
The lake doth glitter,

The green field sleeps in the sun ;   5
  The oldest and youngest
  Are at work with the strongest;
  The cattle are grazing,
  Their heads never raising ;
There are forty feeding like one !   10

  Like an army defeated
  The snow hath retreated,
  And now doth fare ill
  On the top of the bare hill ;
The ploughboy is whooping — anon — anon :   15
  There 's joy in the mountains ;
  There 's life in the fountains ;
  Small clouds are sailing,
  Blue sky prevailing ;
The rain is over and gone !   20

           1802.

THE REDBREAST CHASING THE BUTTERFLY.

ART thou the bird whom Man loves best,
The pious bird with the scarlet breast,
  Our little English Robin ;
The bird that comes about our doors
When Autumn-winds are sobbing ?   5
Art thou the Peter of Norway Boors ?
  Their Thomas in Finland,
  And Russia far inland ?
The bird, that by some name or other
All men who know thee call their brother,   10
The darling of children and men ?

Could Father Adam[1] open his eyes
And see this sight beneath the skies,
He 'd wish to close them again.
— If the Butterfly knew but his friend,   15
Hither his flight he would bend ;
And find his way to me,
Under the branches of the tree :
In and out, he darts about ;
Can this be the bird, to man so good,   20
That, after their bewildering,
Covered with leaves the little children,
    So painfully in the wood ?
What ailed thee, Robin, that thou could'st pursue
    A beautiful creature,   25
That is gentle by nature ?
Beneath the summer sky
From flower to flower let him fly ;
'T is all that he wishes to do.
The cheerer Thou of our in-door sadness,   30
He is the friend of our summer gladness :
What hinders, then, that ye should be
Playmates in the sunny weather,
And fly about in the air together !
His beautiful wings in crimson are drest,   35
A crimson as bright as thine own :
Would'st thou be happy in thy nest,
O pious Bird ! whom man loves best,
Love him, or leave him alone !   1802.

[1] See *Paradise Lost*, Book XI, where Adam points out to Eve the ominous sign of the Eagle chasing " two birds of gayest plume," and the gentle Hart and Hind pursued by their enemy.

TO A BUTTERFLY.

I 've watched you now a full half-hour,
Self-poised upon that yellow flower ;
And, little Butterfly ! indeed
I know not if you sleep or feed.
How motionless ! — not frozen seas   5
More motionless ! and then
What joy awaits you, when the breeze
Hath found you out among the trees,
And calls you forth again !

This plot of orchard-ground is ours ;   10
My trees they are, my Sister's flowers ;
Here rest your wings when they are weary ;
Here lodge as in a sanctuary !
Come often to us, fear no wrong ;
Sit near us on the bough !   15
We 'll talk of sunshine and of song,
And summer days, when we were young ;
Sweet childish days, that were as long
As twenty days are now.

                                                1802.

TO THE SMALL CELANDINE.[1]

PANSIES, lilies, kingcups, daisies,
Let them live upon their praises ;
Long as there 's a sun that sets,
Primroses will have their glory ;
Long as there are violets,   5
They will have a place in story :

[1] Common Pilewort.

There 's a flower that shall be mine,
'T is the little Celandine.

Eyes of some men travel far
For the finding of a star ;   10
Up and down the heavens they go,
Men that keep a mighty rout !
I 'm as great as they, I trow,
Since the day I found thee out,
Little Flower ! — I 'll make a stir,   15
Like a sage astronomer.

Modest, yet withal an Elf
Bold, and lavish of thyself ;
Since we needs must first have met
I have seen thee, high and low,   20
Thirty years or more, and yet
'T was a face I did not know ;
Thou hast now, go where I may,
Fifty greetings in a day.

Ere a leaf is on a bush,   25
In the time before the thrush
Has a thought about her nest,
Thou wilt come with half a call,
Spreading out thy glossy breast
Like a careless Prodigal ;   30
Telling tales about the sun,
When we 've little warmth, or none.

Poets, vain men in their mood !
Travel with the multitude :
Never heed them ; I aver   35
That they all are wanton wooers ;

But the thrifty cottager,
Who stirs little out of doors,
Joys to spy thee near her home ;
Spring is coming, Thou art come !　　40

Comfort have thou of thy merit,
Kindly, unassuming Spirit !
Careless of thy neighbourhood,
Thou dost show thy pleasant face
On the moor, and in the wood,　　45
In the lane ; — there 's not a place,
Howsoever mean it be,
But 't is good enough for thee.

Ill befall the yellow flowers,
Children of the flaring hours !　　50
Buttercups, that will be seen,
Whether we will see or no ;
Others, too, of lofty mien ;
They have done as worldlings do,
Taken praise that should be thine,　　55
Little, humble Celandine !

Prophet of delight and mirth,
Ill-requited upon earth ;
Herald of a mighty band,
Of a joyous train ensuing,　　60
Serving at my heart's command,
Tasks that are no tasks renewing,
I will sing, as doth behoove,
Hymns in praise of what I love !

1802.

TO THE SAME FLOWER.

PLEASURES newly found are sweet
When they lie about our feet:
February last, my heart
First at sight of thee was glad;
All unheard of as thou art,   5
Thou must needs, I think, have had,
Celandine! and long ago,
Praise of which I nothing know.

I have not a doubt but he,
Whosoe'er the man might be,   10
Who the first with pointed rays
(Workman worthy to be sainted)
Set the sign-board in a blaze,
When the rising sun he painted,
Took the fancy from a glance   15
At thy glittering countenance.

Soon as gentle breezes bring
News of winter's vanishing,
And the children build their bowers,
Sticking 'kerchief-plots of mould   20
All about with full-blown flowers,
Thick as sheep in shepherd's fold!
With the proudest thou art there,
Mantling in the tiny square.

Often have I sighed to measure   25
By myself a lonely pleasure,
Sighed to think, I read a book
Only read, perhaps, by me;
Yet I long could overlook
Thy bright coronet and Thee,   30

And thy arch and wily ways,
And thy store of other praise.

Blithe of heart, from week to week
Thou dost play at hide-and-seek ;
While the patient primrose sits   35
Like a beggar in the cold,
Thou, a flower of wiser wits,
Slipp'st into thy sheltering hold ;
Liveliest of the vernal train
When ye all are out again.   40

Drawn by what peculiar spell,
By what charm of sight or smell,
Does the dim-eyed curious Bee,
Labouring for her waxen cells,
Fondly settle upon Thee   45
Prized above all buds and bells
Opening daily at thy side,
By the season multiplied?

Thou art not beyond the moon,
But a thing " beneath our shoon : "   50
Let the bold Discoverer thrid
In his bark the polar sea ;
Rear who will a pyramid ;
Praise it is enough for me,
If there be but three or four   55
Who will love my little Flower.

1802

RESOLUTION AND INDEPENDENCE.

I.

THERE was a roaring in the wind all night ;
The rain came heavily and fell in floods ;
But now the sun is rising calm and bright ;
The birds are singing in the distant woods ;
Over his own sweet voice the Stock-dove broods ;   5
The Jay makes answer as the Magpie chatters ;
And all the air is filled with pleasant noise of waters.

II.

All things that love the sun are out of doors ;
The sky rejoices in the morning's birth ;
The grass is bright with rain-drops ; — on the moors   10
The hare is running races in her mirth ;
And with her feet she from the plashy earth
Raises a mist, that, glittering in the sun,
Runs with her all the way, wherever she doth run.

III.

I was a Traveller then upon the moor,   15
I saw the hare that raced about with joy ;
I heard the woods and distant waters roar ;
Or heard them not, as happy as a boy :
The pleasant season did my heart employ :
My old remembrances went from me wholly ;   20
And all the ways of men, so vain and melancholy.

IV.

But, as it sometimes chanceth, from the might
Of joy in minds that can no further go,

As high as we have mounted in delight
In our dejection do we sink as low;   25
To me that morning did it happen so;
And fears and fancies thick upon me came;
Dim sadness — and blind thoughts, I knew not, nor could
      name.

v.

I heard the sky-lark warbling in the sky;
And I bethought me of the playful hare: 30
Even such a happy Child of earth am I;
Even as these blissful creatures do I fare;
Far from the world I walk, and from all care;
But there may come another day to me —
Solitude, pain of heart, distress, and poverty.   35

vi.

My whole life I have lived in pleasant thought,
As if life's business were a summer mood;
As if all needful things would come unsought
To genial faith, still rich in genial good;
But how can He expect that others should   40
Build for him, sow for him, and at his call
Love him, who for himself will take no heed at all?

vii.

I thought of Chatterton, the marvellous Boy,
The sleepless Soul that perished in his pride;
Of Him who walked in glory and in joy   45
Following his plough, along the mountain-side:
By our own spirits are we deified:
We Poets in our youth begin in gladness;
But thereof come in the end despondency and madness.

VIII.

Now, whether it were by peculiar grace,   50
A leading from above, a something given,
Yet it befell, that, in this lonely place,
When I with these untoward thoughts had striven,
Beside a pool bare to the eye of heaven
I saw a Man before me unawares: 55
The oldest man he seemed that ever wore grey hairs.

IX.

As a huge stone is sometimes seen to lie
Couched on the bald top of an eminence;
Wonder to all who do the same espy,
By what means it could thither come, and whence;   60
So that it seems a thing endued with sense:
Like a sea-beast crawled forth, that on a shelf
Of rock or sand reposeth, there to sun itself;

X.

Such seemed this Man, not all alive nor dead,
Nor all asleep — in his extreme old age: 65
His body was bent double, feet and head
Coming together in life's pilgrimage;
As if some dire constraint of pain, or rage
Of sickness felt by him in times long past,
A more than human weight upon his frame had cast.   70

XI.

Himself he propped, limbs, body, and pale face,
Upon a long grey staff of shaven wood:
And, still as I drew near with gentle pace,
Upon the margin of that moorish flood
Motionless as a cloud the old Man stood,   75

That heareth not the loud winds when they call
And moveth all together, if it move at all.

XII.

At length, himself unsettling, he the pond
Stirred with his staff, and fixedly did look
Upon the muddy water, which he conned,   80
As if he had been reading in a book :
And now a stranger's privilege I took ;
And, drawing to his side, to him did say,
" This morning gives us promise of a glorious day."

XIII.

A gentle answer did the old Man make,   85
In courteous speech which forth he slowly drew :
And him with further words I thus bespake,
" What occupation do you there pursue ?
This is a lonesome place for one like you."
Ere he replied, a flash of mild surprise   90
Broke from the sable orbs of his yet-vivid eyes,

XIV.

His words came feebly, from a feeble chest,
But each in solemn order followed each,
With something of a lofty utterance drest —
Choice word and measured phrase, above the reach   95
Of ordinary men ; a stately speech ;
Such as grave Livers do in Scotland use,
Religious men, who give to God and man their dues.

XV.

He told, that to these waters he had come
To gather leeches, being old and poor :   100

Employment hazardous and wearisome !
And he had many hardships to endure :
From pond to pond he roamed, from moor to moor ;
Housing, with God's good help, by choice or chance,
And in this way he gained an honest maintenance.   105

XVI.

The old Man still stood talking by my side ;
But now his voice to me was like a stream
Scarce heard ; nor word from word could I divide ;
And the whole body of the Man did seem
Like one whom I had met with in a dream ;   110
Or like a man from some far region sent,
To give me human strength, by apt admonishment.

XVII.

My former thoughts returned : the fear that kills ;
And hope that is unwilling to be fed ;
Cold, pain, and labour, and all fleshly ills ;   115
And mighty Poets in their misery dead.
— Perplexed, and longing to be comforted,
My question eagerly did I renew,
" How is it that you live, and what is it you do ? "

XVIII.

He with a smile did then his words repeat ;   120
And said, that, gathering leeches, far and wide
He travelled ; stirring thus about his feet
The waters of the pools where they abide.
" Once I could meet with them on every side ;
But they have dwindled long by slow decay ;   125
Yet still I persevere, and find them where I may."

XIX.

While he was talking thus, the lonely place,
The old Man's shape, and speech — all troubled **me** :
In my mind's eye I seemed to see him pace
About the weary moors continually,   130
Wandering about alone and silently.
While I these thoughts within myself pursued,
He, having made a pause, the same discourse **renewed.**

XX.

And soon with this he other matter blended,
Cheerfully uttered, with demeanour kind,   135
But stately in the main ; and when he ended,
I could have laughed myself to scorn to find
In that decrepit Man so firm a mind.
"God," said I, "be my help and stay secure ;
I 'll think of the Leech-gatherer on the lonely moor ! "   140

1802.

STANZAS

Written in my Pocket-Copy of Thomson's " CASTLE OF INDOLENCE."

WITHIN our happy Castle there dwelt One
Whom without blame I may not overlook ;
For never sun on living creature shone
Who more devout enjoyment with us took :
Here on his hours he hung as on a book,   5
On his own time here would he float away,
As doth a fly upon a summer brook ;
But go to-morrow, or belike to-day,
Seek for him, — he is fled ; and whither none can say.

Thus often would he leave our peaceful home,   10
And find elsewhere his business or delight ;
Out of our Valley's limits did he roam :
Full many a time, upon a stormy night,
His voice came to us from the neighbouring height :
Oft could we see him driving full in view   15
At mid-day when the sun was shining bright ;
What ill was on him, what he had to do,
A mighty wonder bred among our quiet crew.

Ah ! piteous sight it was to see this Man
When he came back to us, a withered flower, —   20
Or like a sinful creature, pale and wan.
Down would he sit ; and without strength or power
Look at the common grass from hour to hour :
And oftentimes, how long I fear to say,
Where apple-trees in blossom made a bower,   25
Retired in that sunshiny shade he lay ;
And, like a naked Indian, slept himself away.

Great wonder to our gentle tribe it was
Whenever from our Valley he withdrew ;
For happier soul no living creature has   30
Than he had, being here the long day through.
Some thought he was a lover, and did woo :
Some thought far worse of him, and judged him wrong ;
But verse was what he had been wedded to ;
And his own mind did like a tempest strong   35
Come to him thus, and drove the weary Wight along.

With him there often walked in friendly guise,
Or lay upon the moss by brook or tree,
A noticeable Man with large gray eyes,
And a pale face that seemed undoubtedly   40
As if a blooming face it ought to be ;

Heavy his low-hung lip did oft appear,
Deprest by weight of musing Phantasy;
Profound his forehead was, though not severe;
Yet some did think that he had little business here:　　45

Sweet heaven forfend! his was a lawful right;
Noisy he was, and gamesome as a boy;
His limbs would toss about him with delight
Like branches when strong winds the trees annoy.
Nor lacked his calmer hours device or toy　　50
To banish listlessness and irksome care;
He would have taught you how you might employ
Yourself; and many did to him repair, —
And certes not in vain; he had inventions rare.

Expedients, too, of simplest sort he tried:　　55
Long blades of grass, plucked round him as he lay,
Made, to his ear attentively applied,
A pipe on which the wind would deftly play;
Glasses he had, that little things display,
The beetle panoplied in gems and gold,　　60
A mailèd angel on a battle-day;
The mysteries that cups of flowers enfold,
And all the gorgeous sights which fairies do behold.

He would entice that other Man to hear
His music, and to view his imagery:　　65
And, sooth, these two were each to the other dear:
No livelier love in such a place could be:
There did they dwell — from earthly labour free,
As happy spirits as were ever seen;
If but a bird, to keep them company,　　70
Or butterfly sate down, they were, I ween,
As pleased as if the same had been a Maiden-queen.

1802.

A FAREWELL.

FAREWELL, thou little Nook of mountain-ground,
Thou rocky corner in the lowest stair
Of that magnificent temple which doth bound
One side of our whole vale with grandeur rare ;
Sweet garden-orchard, eminently fair,   5
The loveliest spot that man hath ever found,
Farewell ! — we leave thee to Heaven's peaceful care,
Thee, and the Cottage which thou dost surround.

Our boat is safely anchored by the shore,
And there will safely ride when we are gone ;   10
The flowering shrubs that deck our humble door
Will prosper, though untended and alone :
Fields, goods, and far-off chattels we have none :
These narrow bounds contain our private store
Of things earth makes, and sun doth shine upon ;   15
Here are they in our sight — we have no more.

Sunshine and shower be with you, bud and bell !
For two months now in vain we shall be sought :
We leave you here in solitude to dwell
With these our latest gifts of tender thought ;   20
Thou, like the morning, in thy saffron coat,
Bright gowan, and marsh-marigold, farewell !
Whom from the borders of the Lake we brought,
And placed together near our rocky Well.

We go for One to whom ye will be dear ;   25
And she will prize this Bower, this Indian shed,
Our own contrivance, Building without peer !
— A gentle Maid, whose heart is lowly bred,
Whose pleasures are in wild fields gatherèd,
With joyousness, and with a thoughtful cheer,   30

Will come to you ; to you herself will wed ;
And love the blessed life that we lead here.

Dear Spot ! which we have watched with tender heed,
Bringing thee chosen plants and blossoms blown
Among the distant mountains, flower and weed,   35
Which thou hast taken to thee as thy own,
Making all kindness registered and known ;
Thou for our sakes, though Nature's child indeed,
Fair in thyself and beautiful alone,
Hast taken gifts which thou dost little need.   40

And O most constant, yet most fickle Place,
Thou hast thy wayward moods, as thou dost show
To them who look not daily on thy face ;
Who, being loved, in love no bounds dost know,
And say'st, when we forsake thee, " Let them go ! "   45
Thou easy-hearted Thing, with thy wild race
Of weeds and flowers, till we return be slow,
And travel with the year at a soft pace.

Help us to tell Her tales of years gone by,
And this sweet spring, the best beloved and best ;   50
Joy will be flown in its mortality ;
Something must stay to tell us of the rest.
Here, thronged with primroses, the steep rock's breast
Glittered at evening like a starry sky ;
And in this bush our sparrow built her nest,   55
Of which I sang one song that will not die.

O happy Garden ! whose seclusion deep
Hath been so friendly to industrious hours ;
And to soft slumbers, that did gently steep
Our spirits, carrying with them dreams of flowers,   60
And wild notes warbled among leafy bowers ;

Two burning months let summer overleap,
And, coming back with Her who will be ours,
Into thy bosom we again shall creep.

                                        1802.

TO H. C.

SIX YEARS OLD.

O THOU ! whose fancies from afar are brought ;
Who of thy words dost make a mock apparel,
And fittest to unutterable thought
The breeze-like motion and the self-born carol ;
Thou faery voyager ! that dost float   5
In such clear water, that thy boat
May rather seem
To brood on air than on an earthly stream ;
Suspended in a stream as clear as sky,
Where earth and heaven do make one imagery ;   10
O blessed vision ! happy child !
Thou art so exquisitely wild,
I think of thee with many fears
For what may be thy lot in future years.
    I thought of times when Pain might be thy guest,   15
Lord of thy house and hospitality ;
And Grief, uneasy lover ! never rest
But when she sate within the touch of thee.
O too industrious folly !
O vain and causeless melancholy !   20
Nature will either end thee quite ;
Or, lengthening out thy season of delight,
Preserve for thee, by individual right,
A young lamb's heart among the full-grown flocks.

What hast thou to do with sorrow, 25
Or the injuries of to-morrow?
Thou art a dew-drop, which the morn brings forth,
Ill fitted to sustain unkindly shocks,
Or to be trailed along the soiling earth ;
A gem that glitters while it lives, 30
And no forewarning gives ;
But, at the touch of wrong, without a strife
Slips in a moment out of life.

1802.

TO THE DAISY.

" Her [1] divine skill taught me this,
   That from every thing I saw
   I could some instruction draw,
   And raise pleasure to the height
   Through the meanest object's sight.
   By the murmur of a spring,
   Or the least bough's rustelling ;
   By a Daisy whose leaves spread
   Shut when Titan goes to bed ;
   Or a shady bush or tree ;
   She could more infuse in me
   Than all Nature's beauties can
   In some other wiser man."

G. WITHER.

IN youth from rock to rock I went,
From hill to hill in discontent
Of pleasure high and turbulent,
   Most pleased when most uneasy;
But now my own delights I make, — 5
My thirst at every rill can slake,
And gladly Nature's love partake,
   Of Thee, sweet Daisy !

[1] His muse.

Thee Winter in the garland wears
That thinly decks his few grey hairs; 10
Spring parts the clouds with softest airs,
    That she may sun thee;
Whole Summer-fields are thine by right;
And Autumn, melancholy Wight!
Doth in thy crimson head delight 15
    When rains are on thee.

In shoals and bands, a morrice train,
Thou greet'st the traveller in the lane;
Pleased at his greeting thee again;
    Yet nothing daunted, 20
Nor grieved if thou be set at nought:
And oft alone in nooks remote
We meet thee, like a pleasant thought,
    When such are wanted.

Be violets in their secret mews 25
The flowers the wanton Zephyrs choose;
Proud be the rose, with rains and dews
    Her head impearling,
Thou liv'st with less ambitious aim,
Yet hast not gone without thy fame; 30
Thou art indeed by many a claim
    The Poet's darling.

If to a rock from rains he fly,
Or, some bright day of April sky,
Imprisoned by hot sunshine lie 35
    Near the green holly,
And wearily at length should fare;
He needs but look about, and there
Thou art!—a friend at hand, to scare
    His melancholy. 40

A hundred times, by rock or bower,
Ere thus I have lain couched an hour,
Have I derived from thy sweet power
    Some apprehension ;
Some steady love ; some brief delight ;   45
Some memory that had taken flight ;
Some chime of fancy wrong or right ;
    Or stray invention.

If stately passions in me burn,
And one chance look to Thee should turn,   50
I drink out of an humbler urn
    A lowlier pleasure ;
The homely sympathy that heeds
The common life, our nature breeds ;
A wisdom fitted to the needs   55
    Of hearts at leisure.

Fresh-smitten by the morning ray,
When thou art up, alert and gay,
Then, cheerful Flower ! my spirits play
    With kindred gladness :   60
And when, at dusk, by dews opprest
Thou sink'st, the image of thy rest
Hath often eased my pensive breast
    Of careful sadness.

And all day long I number yet,   65
All seasons through, another debt,
Which I, wherever thou art met,
    To thee am owing ;
An instinct call it, a blind sense ;
A happy, genial influence,   70
Coming one knows not how, nor whence,
    Nor whither going.

Child of the Year! that round dost run
Thy pleasant course, — when day 's begun
As ready to salute the sun   75
    As lark or leveret,
Thy long-lost praise thou shalt regain;
Nor be less dear to future men
Than in old time; — thou not in vain
    Art Nature's favourite.[1]   80

           1802.

TO THE SAME FLOWER.

WITH little here to do or see
Of things that in the great world be,
Daisy! again I talk to thee,
    For thou art worthy,
Thou unassuming Common-place   5
Of Nature, with that homely face,
And yet with something of a grace,
    Which Love makes for thee!

Oft on the dappled turf at ease
I sit, and play with similes,   10
Loose types of things through all degrees,
    Thoughts of thy raising:
And many a fond and idle name
I give to thee, for praise or blame,
As is the humour of the game,   15
    While I am gazing.

A nun demure of lowly port;
Or sprightly maiden, of Love's court,

[1] See, in Chaucer and the elder Poets, the honours formerly paid
to this flower.

In thy simplicity the sport
    Of all temptations ;   20
A queen in crown of rubies drest ;
A starveling in a scanty vest ;
Are all, as seems to suit thee best,
    Thy appellations.

A little cyclops, with one eye   25
Staring to threaten and defy,
That thought comes next — and instantly
    The freak is over,
The shape will vanish — and behold
A silver shield with boss of gold,   30
That spreads itself, some faery bold
    In fight to cover !

I see thee glittering from afar —
And then thou art a pretty star ;
Not quite so fair as many are   35
    In heaven above thee !
Yet like a star, with glittering crest,
Self-poised in air thou seem'st to rest ; —
May peace come never to his nest,
    Who shall reprove thee !   40

Bright *Flower !* for by that name at last,
When all my reveries are past,
I call thee, and to that cleave fast,
    Sweet silent creature !
That breath'st with me in sun and air,   45
Do thou, as thou art wont, repair
My heart with gladness, and a share
    Of thy meek nature !

                              1802.

TO THE DAISY.

BRIGHT Flower ! whose home is everywhere,
Bold in maternal Nature's care,
And all the long year through the heir
    Of joy or sorrow ;
Methinks that there abides in thee   5
Some concord with humanity,
Given to no other flower I see
    The forest thorough !

Is it that Man is soon deprest ?
A thoughtless Thing ! who, once unblest,   10
Does little on his memory rest,
    Or on his reason,
And Thou would'st teach him how to find
A shelter under every wind,
A hope for times that are unkind   15
    And every season ?

Thou wander'st the wide world about,
Unchecked by pride or scrupulous doubt,
With friends to greet thee, or without,
    Yet pleased and willing ;   20
Meek, yielding to the occasion's call,
And all things suffering from all,
Thy function apostolical
    In peace fulfilling.

                    1802.

WHEN TO THE ATTRACTIONS OF THE BUSY WORLD.

WHEN, to the attractions of the busy world,
Preferring studious leisure, I had chosen
A habitation in this peaceful Vale,
Sharp season followed of continual storm
In deepest winter; and, from week to week, 5
Pathway, and lane, and public road, were clogged
With frequent showers of snow. Upon a hill
At a short distance from my cottage, stands
A stately Fir-grove, whither I was wont
To hasten, for I found, beneath the roof 10
Of that perennial shade, a cloistral place
Of refuge, with an unincumbered floor.
Here, in safe covert, on the shallow snow,
And, sometimes, on a speck of visible earth,
The redbreast near me hopped; nor was I loth 15
To sympathise with vulgar coppice birds
That, for protection from the nipping blast,
Hither repaired. — A single beech-tree grew
Within this grove of firs! and, on the fork
Of that one beech, appeared a thrush's nest; 20
A last year's nest, conspicuously built
At such small elevation from the ground
As gave sure sign that they, who in that house
Of nature and of love had made their home
Amid the fir-trees, all the summer long 25
Dwelt in a tranquil spot. And oftentimes,
A few sheep, stragglers from some mountain-flock,
Would watch my motions with suspicious stare,
From the remotest outskirts of the grove, —
Some nook where they had made their final stand, 30

Huddling together from two fears — the fear
Of me and of the storm.   Full many an hour
Here did I lose.   But in this grove the trees
Had been so thickly planted, and had thriven
In such perplexed and intricate array,   35
That vainly did I seek, beneath their stems
A length of open space, where to and fro
My feet might move without concern or care;
And, baffled thus, though earth from day to day
Was fettered, and the air by storm disturbed,   40
I ceased the shelter to frequent, — and prized,
Less than I wished to prize, that calm recess.

   The snows dissolved, and genial Spring returned
To clothe the fields with verdure.   Other haunts
Meanwhile were mine; till, one bright April day,   45
By chance retiring from the glare of noon
To this forsaken covert, there I found
A hoary pathway traced between the trees,
And winding on with such an easy line
Along a natural opening, that I stood   50
Much wondering how I could have sought in vain
For what was now so obvious.   To abide,
For an allotted interval of ease,
Under my cottage-roof, had gladly come
From the wild sea a cherished Visitant;   55
And with the sight of this same path — begun,
Begun and ended, in the shady grove,
Pleasant conviction flashed upon my mind
That, to this opportune recess allured,
He had surveyed it with a finer eye,   60
A heart more wakeful; and had worn the track
By pacing here, unwearied and alone,
In that habitual restlessness of foot
That haunts the Sailor measuring o'er and o'er

His short domain upon the vessel's deck,   65
While she pursues her course through the dreary sea.
   When thou hadst quitted Esthwaite's pleasant shore,
And taken thy first leave of those green hills
And rocks that were the play-ground of thy youth,
Year followed year, my Brother ! and we two,   70
Conversing not, knew little in what mould
Each other's mind was fashioned ; and at length,
When once again we met in Grasmere Vale,
Between us there was little other bond
Than common feelings of fraternal love.   75
But thou, a Schoolboy, to the sea hadst carried
Undying recollections ! Nature there
Was with thee; she, who loved us both, she still
Was with thee ; and even so didst thou become
A *silent* Poet ; from the solitude   80
Of the vast sea didst bring a watchful heart
Still couchant, an inevitable ear,
And an eye practised like a blind man's touch.
— Back to the joyless Ocean thou art gone ;
Nor from this vestige of thy musing hours   85
Could I withhold thy honoured name, — and now
I love the fir-grove with a perfect love.
Thither do I withdraw when cloudless suns
Shine hot, or wind blows troublesome and strong ;
And there I sit at evening, when the steep   90
Of Silver-how, and Grasmere's peaceful lake,
And one green island, gleam between the stems
Of the dark firs, a visionary scene !
And, while I gaze upon the spectacle
Of clouded splendour, on this dream-like sight   95
Of solemn loveliness, I think on thee,
My Brother, and on all which thou hast lost.
Nor seldom, if I rightly guess, while Thou,

Muttering the verses which I muttered first
Among the mountains, through the midnight watch 100
Art pacing thoughtfully the vessel's deck
In some far region, here, while o'er my head,
At every impulse of the moving breeze,
The fir-grove murmurs with a sea-like sound,
Alone I tread this path ; — for aught I know, 105
Timing my steps to thine ; and, with a store
Of undistinguishable sympathies,
Mingling most earnest wishes for the day
When we, and others whom we love, shall meet
A second time, in Grasmere's happy Vale. 110

1800–1802.

NOTE. — This wish was not granted; the lamented Person not
long after perished by shipwreck, in discharge of his duty as Commander of the Honourable East India Company's Vessel, the Earl
of Abergavenny.

THE GREEN LINNET.

BENEATH these fruit-tree boughs that shed
Their snow-white blossoms on my head,
With brightest sunshine round me spread
　　Of spring's unclouded weather,
In this sequestered nook how sweet 5
To sit upon my orchard-seat !
And birds and flowers once more to greet,
　　My last year's friends together.

One have I marked, the happiest guest
In all this covert of the blest : 10
Hail to Thee, far above the rest
　　In joy of voice and pinion !

Thou, Linnet! in thy green array,
Presiding Spirit here to-day,
Dost lead the revels of the May;   15
    And this is thy dominion.

While birds, and butterflies, and flowers,
Make all one band of paramours,
Thou, ranging up and down the bowers,
    Art sole in thy employment: 20
A Life, a Presence like the Air,
Scattering thy gladness without care,
Too blest with any one to pair;
    Thyself thy own enjoyment.

Amid yon tuft of hazel trees,   25
That twinkle to the gusty breeze,
Behold him perched in ecstasies,
    Yet seeming still to hover;
There! where the flutter of his wings
Upon his back and body flings   30
Shadows and sunny glimmerings,
    That cover him all over.

My dazzled sight he oft deceives,
A Brother of the dancing leaves;
Then flits, and from the cottage-eaves   35
    Pours forth his song in gushes;
As if by that exulting strain
He mocked and treated with disdain
The voiceless Form he chose to feign,
    While fluttering in the bushes.   40

              1803.

YEW–TREES.

THERE is a Yew-tree, pride of Lorton Vale,
Which to this day stands single, in the midst
Of its own darkness, as it stood of yore ;
Not loth to furnish weapons for the bands
Of Umfraville or Percy ere they marched   5
To Scotland's heaths ; or those that crossed the sea
And drew their sounding bows at Azincour,
Perhaps at earlier Crecy, or Poictiers.
Of vast circumference and gloom profound
This solitary Tree ! a living thing   10
Produced too slowly ever to decay ;
Of form and aspect too magnificent
To be destroyed.   But worthier still of note
Are those fraternal Four of Borrowdale,
Joined in one solemn and capacious grove ;   15
Huge trunks ! and each particular trunk a growth
Of intertwisted fibres serpentine
Up-coiling, and inveterately convolved ;
Nor uninformed with Phantasy, and looks
That threaten the profane ; — a pillared shade,   20
Upon whose grassless floor of red-brown hue,
By sheddings from the pining umbrage tinged
Perennially — beneath whose sable roof
Of boughs, as if for festal purpose decked
With unrejoicing berries — ghostly Shapes   25
May meet at noontide ; Fear and trembling Hope,
Silence and Foresight ; Death the Skeleton
And Time the Shadow ; — there to celebrate,
As in a natural temple scattered o'er
With altars undisturbed of mossy stone,   30
United worship ; or in mute repose

To lie, and listen to the mountain flood
Murmuring from Glaramara's inmost caves.

                                        1803.

AT THE GRAVE OF BURNS. 1803.

SEVEN YEARS AFTER HIS DEATH.

I SHIVER, Spirit fierce and bold,
At thought of what I now behold :
As vapours breathed from dungeons cold
        Strike pleasure dead,
So sadness comes from out the mould   5
        Where Burns is laid.

And have I then thy bones so near,
And thou forbidden to appear ?
As if it were thyself that 's here
        I shrink with pain ;   10
And both my wishes and my fear
        Alike are vain.

Off weight — nor press on weight ! — away
Dark thoughts ! — they came, but not to stay ;
With chastened feelings would I pay   15
        The tribute due
To him, and aught that hides his clay
        From mortal view.

Fresh as the flower, whose modest worth
He sang, his genius " glinted " forth,   20
Rose like a star that touching earth,
        For so it seems,
Doth glorify its humble birth
        With matchless beams.

The piercing eye, the thoughtful brow, 25
The struggling heart, where be they now? —
Full soon the Aspirant of the plough,
    The prompt, the brave,
Slept, with the obscurest, in the low
    And silent grave. 30

I mourned with thousands, but as one
More deeply grieved, for He was gone
Whose light I hailed when first it shone,
    And showed my youth
How Verse may build a princely throne 35
    On humble truth.

Alas! where'er the current tends,
Regret pursues and with it blends, —
Huge Criffel's hoary top ascends
    By Skiddaw seen, — 40
Neighbours we were, and loving friends
    We might have been;

True friends though diversely inclined;
But heart with heart and mind with mind,
Where the main fibres are entwined, 45
    Through Nature's skill,
May even by contraries be joined
    More closely still.

The tear will start, and let it flow;
Thou "poor Inhabitant below," 50
At this dread moment — even so —
    Might we together
Have sate and talked where gowans blow,
    Or on wild heather.

What treasures would have then been placed　　55
Within my reach ; of knowledge graced
By fancy what a rich repast !
　　　　But why go on ? —
Oh ! spare to sweep, thou mournful blast,
　　　　His grave grass-grown.　　　　　　60

There, too, a Son, his joy and pride,
(Not three weeks past the Stripling died,)
Lies gathered to his Father's side,
　　　　Soul-moving sight !
Yet one to which is not denied　　　　65
　　　　Some sad delight :

For *he* is safe, a quiet bed
Hath early found among the dead,
Harboured where none can be misled,
　　　　Wronged, or distrest ;　　　　70
And surely here it may be said
　　　　That such are blest.

And oh for Thee, by pitying grace
Checked oft-times in a devious race,
May He who halloweth the place　　　75
　　　　Where Man is laid
Receive thy Spirit in the embrace
　　　　For which it prayed !

Sighing I turned away ; but ere
Night fell I heard, or seemed to hear,　　80
Music that sorrow comes not near,
　　　　A ritual hymn,
Chaunted in love that casts out fear
　　　　By Seraphim.　　　　1803.

THOUGHTS

<small>SUGGESTED THE DAY FOLLOWING, ON THE BANKS OF NITH,
NEAR THE POET'S RESIDENCE.</small>

Too frail to keep the lofty vow
That must have followed when his brow
Was wreathed — "The Vision" tells us how —
  With holly spray,
He faltered, drifted to and fro,   5
  And passed away.

Well might such thoughts, dear Sister, throng
Our minds when, lingering all too long,
Over the grave of Burns we hung
  In social grief —   10
Indulged as if it were a wrong
  To seek relief.

But, leaving each unquiet theme
Where gentlest judgments may misdeem,
And prompt to welcome every gleam   15
  Of good and fair,
Let us beside this limpid Stream
  Breathe hopeful air.

Enough of sorrow, wreck, and blight;
Think rather of those moments bright   20
When to the consciousness of right
  His course was true,
When Wisdom prospered in his sight
  And virtue grew.

Yes, freely let our hearts expand,   25
Freely as in youth's season bland,
When side by side, his Book in hand,

We wont to stray,
Our pleasure varying at command
    Of each sweet Lay.   30

How oft inspired must he have trod
These pathways, yon far-stretching road !
There lurks his home ; in that Abode,
    With mirth elate,
Or in his nobly-pensive mood,   35
    The Rustic sate.

Proud thoughts that Image overawes,
Before it humbly let us pause,
And ask of Nature, from what cause
    And by what rules   40
She trained her Burns to win applause
    That shames the Schools.

Through busiest street and loneliest glen
Are felt the flashes of his pen ;
He rules 'mid winter snows, and when   45
    Bees fill their hives ;
Deep in the general heart of men
    His power survives.

What need of fields in some far clime
Where Heroes, Sages, Bards sublime,   50
And all that fetched the flowing rhyme
    From genuine springs,
Shall dwell together till old Time
    Folds up his wings ?

Sweet Mercy ! to the gates of Heaven   55
This Minstrel lead, his sins forgiven ;
The rueful conflict, the heart riven

With vain endeavour,
And memory of Earth's bitter leaven,
 Effaced for ever.   60

But why to Him confine the prayer,
When kindred thoughts and yearnings **bear**
On the frail heart the purest share
 With all that live ? —
The best of what we do and **are,**   65
 Just God, forgive !

TO A HIGHLAND GIRL.

AT INVERSNEYDE, UPON LOCH LOMOND.

SWEET Highland Girl, a very shower
Of beauty is thy earthly dower !
Twice seven consenting years have shed
Their utmost bounty on thy head :
And these grey rocks ; that household lawn ;   5
Those trees, a veil just half withdrawn ;
This fall of water that doth make
A murmur near the silent lake ;
This little bay ; a quiet road
That holds in shelter thy Abode —   10
In truth together do ye seem
Like something fashioned in a dream ;
Such Forms as from their covert peep
When earthly cares are laid asleep !
But, O fair Creature ! in the light   15
Of common day, so heavenly bright,
I bless Thee, Vision as thou art,
I bless thee with a human heart ;

God shield thee to thy latest years!
Thee, neither know I, nor thy peers;   20
And yet my eyes are filled with tears.
  With earnest feeling I shall pray
For thee when I am far away:
For never saw I mien, or face,
In which more plainly I could trace   25
Benignity and home-bred sense
Ripening in perfect innocence.
Here scattered, like a random seed,
Remote from men, Thou dost not need
The embarrassed look of shy distress,   30
And maidenly shamefacedness:
Thou wear'st upon thy forehead clear
The freedom of a Mountaineer:
A face with gladness overspread!
Soft smiles, by human kindness bred!   35
And seemliness complete, that sways
Thy courtesies, about thee plays;
With no restraint, but such as springs
From quick and eager visitings
Of thoughts that lie beyond the reach   40
Of thy few words of English speech:
A bondage sweetly brooked, a strife
That gives thy gestures grace and life!
So have I, not unmoved in mind,
Seen birds of tempest-loving kind —   45
Thus beating up against the wind.
  What hand but would a garland cull
For thee who art so beautiful?
O happy pleasure! here to dwell
Beside thee in some heathy dell;   50
Adopt your homely ways, and dress,
A Shepherd, thou a Shepherdess!

But I could frame a wish for thee
More like a grave reality :
Thou art to me but as a wave   55
Of the wild sea ; and I would have
Some claim upon thee, if I could,
Though but of common neighbourhood.
What joy to hear thee, and to see !
Thy elder Brother I would be,   60
Thy Father — anything to thee !
Now thanks to Heaven ! that of its grace
Hath led me to this lonely place.
Joy have I had ; and going hence
I bear away my recompence.   65
In spots like these it is we prize
Our Memory, feel that she hath eyes :
Then, why should I be loth to stir ?
I feel this place was made for her ;
To give new pleasure like the past,   70
Continued long as life shall last.
Nor am I loth, though pleased at heart,
Sweet Highland Girl ! from thee to part :
For I, methinks, till I grow old,
As fair before me shall behold,   75
As I do now, the cabin small,
The lake, the bay, the waterfall ;
And Thee, the Spirit of them all !

1803.

GLEN ALMAIN; OR, THE NARROW GLEN.

IN this still place, remote from men,
Sleeps Ossian, in the NARROW GLEN;
In this still place, where murmurs on
But one meek streamlet, only one :
He sang of battles, and the breath   5
Of stormy war, and violent death ;
And should, methinks, when all was past,
Have rightfully been laid at last
Where rocks were rudely heaped, and rent
As by a spirit turbulent;   10
Where sights were rough, and sounds were wild,
And everything unreconciled;
In some complaining, dim retreat,
For fear and melancholy meet ;
But this is calm; there cannot be   15
A more entire tranquillity.

Does then the Bard sleep here indeed?
Or is it but a groundless creed?
What matters it? — I blame them not
Whose Fancy in this lonely Spot   20
Was moved; and in such way expressed
Their notion of its perfect rest.
A convent, even a hermit's cell,
Would break the silence of this Dell :
It is not quiet, is not ease;   25
But something deeper far than these :
The separation that is here
Is of the grave ; and of austere
Yet happy feelings of the dead ;
And, therefore, was it rightly said   30
That Ossian, last of all his race !
Lies buried in this lonely place.   1803.

STEPPING WESTWARD.

While my Fellow-traveller and I were walking by the side of Loch Ket-
terine, one fine evening after sunset, in our road to a Hut where, in the course
of our Tour, we had been hospitably entertained some weeks before, we met,
in one of the loneliest parts of that solitary region, two well-dressed Women,
one of whom said to us, by way of greeting, "What, you are stepping westward?"

"*What, you are stepping westward?*"—"*Yea.*"
—'T would be a *wildish* destiny,
If we, who thus together roam
In a strange Land, and far from home,
Were in this place the guests of Chance: 5
Yet who would stop, or fear to advance,
Though home or shelter he had none,
With such a sky to lead him on?

The dewy ground was dark and cold;
Behind, all gloomy to behold;   10
And stepping westward seemed to be
A kind of *heavenly* destiny:
I liked the greeting; 't was a sound
Of something without place or bound;
And seemed to give me spiritual right   15
To travel through that region bright.

The voice was soft, and she who spake
Was walking by her native lake:
The salutation had to me
The very sound of courtesy: 20
Its power was felt; and while my eye
Was fixed upon the glowing Sky,
The echo of the voice enwrought
A human sweetness with the thought
Of travelling through the world that lay   25
Before me in my endless way.   1803 (?).

THE SOLITARY REAPER.

BEHOLD her, single in the field,
Yon solitary Highland Lass!
Reaping and singing by herself;
Stop here, or gently pass!
Alone she cuts and binds the grain,   5
And sings a melancholy strain;
O listen! for the Vale profound
Is overflowing with the sound.

No Nightingale did ever chaunt
More welcome notes to weary bands   10
Of travellers in some shady haunt,
Among Arabian sands:
A voice so thrilling ne'er was heard
In spring-time from the Cuckoo-bird,
Breaking the silence of the seas   15
Among the farthest Hebrides.

Will no one tell me what she sings?—
Perhaps the plaintive numbers flow
For old, unhappy, far-off things,
And battles long ago: 20
Or is it some more humble lay,
Familiar matter of to-day?
Some natural sorrow, loss, or pain,
That has been, and may be again?

Whate'er the theme, the Maiden sang   25
As if her song could have no ending;
I saw her singing at her work,
And o'er the sickle bending;—

I listened, motionless and still;
And, as I mounted up the hill   30
The music in my heart I bore,
Long after it was heard no more.

1803 (?).

ADDRESS TO KILCHURN CASTLE, UPON LOCH AWE.

" From the top of the hill a most impressive scene opened upon our view,
— a ruined Castle on an Island (for an Island the flood had made it) at some
distance from the shore, backed by a Cove of the Mountain Cruachan, down
which came a foaming stream. The Castle occupied every foot of the Island
that was visible to us, appearing to rise out of the water, — mists rested upon
the mountain side, with spots of sunshine; there was a mild desolation in the
low grounds, a solemn grandeur in the mountains, and the Castle was wild,
yet stately — not dismantled of turrets — nor the walls broken down, though
obviously a ruin." — *Extract from the Journal of my Companion.*

CHILD of loud-throated War! the mountain Stream
Roars in thy hearing; but thy hour of rest
Is come, and thou art silent in thy age;
Save when the wind sweeps by and sounds are caught
Ambiguous, neither wholly thine nor theirs.   5
Oh! there is life that breathes not; Powers there are
That touch each other to the quick in modes
Which the gross world no sense hath to perceive,
No soul to dream of. What art Thou, from care
Cast off — abandoned by thy rugged Sire,   10
Nor by soft Peace adopted; though, in place
And in dimension, such that thou might'st seem
But a mere footstool to yon sovereign Lord,
Huge Cruachan, (a thing that meaner hills
Might crush, nor know that it had suffered harm;)   15
Yet he, not loth, in favor of thy claims
To reverence, suspends his own; submitting

All that the God of Nature hath conferred,
All that he holds in common with the stars,
To the memorial majesty of Time   20
Impersonated in thy calm decay !
Take then thy seat, Vicegerent unreproved !
Now, while a farewell gleam of evening light
Is fondly lingering on thy shattered front,
Do thou, in turn, be paramount ; and rule   25
Over the pomp and beauty of a scene
Whose mountains, torrents, lake, and woods, unite
To pay thee homage ; and with these are joined,
In willing admiration and respect,
Two Hearts, which in thy presence might be called 30
Youthful as Spring. — Shade of departed Power,
Skeleton of unfleshed humanity,
The chronicle were welcome that should call
Into the compass of distinct regard
The toils and struggles of thy infant years !   35
Yon foaming flood seems motionless as ice ;
Its dizzy turbulence eludes the eye,
Frozen by distance ; so, majestic Pile,
To the perception of this Age, appear
Thy fierce beginnings, softened and subdued   40
And quieted in character — the strife,
The pride, the fury uncontrollable,
Lost on the aërial heights of the Crusades ! [1]

1803 — ?

---

[1] The tradition is, that the Castle was built by a Lady during the absence of her Lord in Palestine.

YARROW UNVISITED.

See the various Poems the scene of which is laid upon the banks of the
Yarrow; in particular, the exquisite Ballad of Hamilton beginning

> " Busk ye, busk ye, my bonny, bonny Bride.
> Busk ye, busk ye, my winsome Marrow ! — "

FROM Stirling castle we had seen
The mazy Forth unravelled ;
Had trod the banks of Clyde, and Tay,
And with the Tweed had travelled ;
And when we came to Clovenford,   5
Then said my " *winsome Marrow,*"
" Whate'er betide, we 'll turn aside,
And see the Braes of Yarrow."

" Let Yarrow folk, *frae* Selkirk town,
Who have been buying, selling,   10
Go back to Yarrow, 't is their own ;
Each maiden to her dwelling !
On Yarrow's banks let herons feed,
Hares couch, and rabbits burrow !
But we will downward with the Tweed,   15
Nor turn aside to Yarrow.

" There 's Galla Water, Leader Haughs,
Both lying right before us ;
And Dryborough, where with chiming Tweed
The lintwhites sing in chorus ;   20
There 's pleasant Tiviot-dale, a land
Made blithe with plough and harrow :
Why throw away a needful day
To go in search of Yarrow ?

"What's Yarrow but a river bare,   25
That glides the dark hills under?
There are a thousand such elsewhere
As worthy of your wonder."
— Strange words they seemed of slight and scorn
My True-love sighed for sorrow;   30
And looked me in the face, to think
I thus could speak of Yarrow!

"Oh! green," said I, "are Yarrow's holms,
And sweet is Yarrow flowing!
Fair hangs the apple frae the rock,   35
But we will leave it growing.
O'er hilly path, and open Strath,
We'll wander Scotland thorough;
But, though so near, we will not turn
Into the dale of Yarrow.   40

"Let beeves and home-bred kine partake
The sweets of Burn-mill meadow;
The swan on still St. Mary's Lake
Float double, swan and shadow!
We will not see them; will not go,   45
To-day, nor yet to-morrow,
Enough if in our hearts we know
There's such a place as Yarrow.

"Be Yarrow stream unseen, unknown!
It must, or we shall rue it: 50
We have a vision of our own;
Ah! why should we undo it?
The treasured dreams of times long past,
We'll keep them, winsome Marrow!
For when we're there, although 'tis fair,
'T will be another Yarrow!   55

"If Care with freezing years should come,
And wandering seem but folly, —
Should we be loth to stir from home,
And yet be melancholy ;
Should life be dull, and spirits low,   60
'T will soothe us in our sorrow,
That earth has something yet to show,
The bonny holms of Yarrow ! "

                1803.

LINES ON THE EXPECTED INVASION, 1803.

COME ye — who, if (which Heaven avert !) the Land
Were with herself at strife, would take your stand,
Like gallant Falkland, by the Monarch's side,
And, like Montrose, make Loyalty your pride —
Come ye — who, not less zealous, might display   5
Banners at enmity with regal sway,
And, like the Pyms and Miltons of that day,
Think that a State would live in sounder health
If Kingship bowed its head to Commonwealth —
Ye too — whom no discreditable fear   10
Would keep, perhaps with many a fruitless tear,
Uncertain what to choose and how to steer —
And ye — who might mistake for sober sense
And wise reserve the plea of indolence —
Come ye — whate'er your creed — O waken all,   15
Whate'er your temper, at your Country's call ;
Resolving (this a free-born Nation can)
To have one soul, and perish to a man,
Or save this honoured Land from every Lord
But British reason and the British sword.   20

"SHE WAS A PHANTOM OF DELIGHT."

She was a Phantom of delight
When first she gleamed upon my sight;
A lovely Apparition, sent
To be a moment's ornament;
Her eyes as stars of Twilight fair;   5
Like Twilight's, too, her dusky hair;
But all things else about her drawn
From May-time and the cheerful Dawn;
A dancing Shape, an Image gay,
To haunt, to startle, and way-lay.   10

I saw her upon nearer view,
A Spirit, yet a Woman too!
Her household motions light and free,
And steps of virgin-liberty;
A countenance in which did meet   15
Sweet records, promises as sweet;
A Creature not too bright or good
For human nature's daily food;
For transient sorrows, simple wiles,
Praise, blame, love, kisses, tears, and smiles.   20

And now I see with eye serene
The very pulse of the machine;
A Being breathing thoughtful breath,
A Traveller between life and death;
The reason firm, the temperate will,   25
Endurance, foresight, strength, and skill;
A perfect Woman, nobly planned,
To warn, to comfort, and command;
And yet a Spirit still, and bright
With something of angelic light.   30

1804.

"I WANDERED LONELY AS A CLOUD."

I WANDERED lonely as a cloud
That floats on high o'er vales and hills,
When all at once I saw a crowd,
A host, of golden daffodils;
Beside the lake, beneath the trees, 5
Fluttering and dancing in the breeze.

Continuous as the stars that shine
And twinkle on the milky way,
They stretched in never-ending line
Along the margin of a bay: 10
Ten thousand saw I at a glance,
Tossing their heads in sprightly dance.

The waves beside them danced; but they
Out-did the sparkling waves in glee:
A poet could not but be gay, 15
In such a jocund company:
I gazed — and gazed — but little thought
What wealth the show to me had brought:

For oft, when on my couch I lie
In vacant or in pensive mood, 20
They flash upon that inward eye
Which is the bliss of solitude;
And then my heart with pleasure fills,
And dances with the daffodils.

     1804.

THE AFFLICTION OF MARGARET ——.

I.

WHERE art thou, my beloved Son,
Where art thou, worse to me than dead?
Oh find me, prosperous or undone!
Or, if the grave be now thy bed,
Why am I ignorant of the same   5
That I may rest; and neither blame
Nor sorrow may attend thy name?

II.

Seven years, alas! to have received
No tidings of an only child;
To have despaired, have hoped, believed,   10
And been for evermore beguiled;
Sometimes with thoughts of very bliss!
I catch at them, and then I miss;
Was ever darkness like to this?

III.

He was among the prime in worth,   15
An object beauteous to behold;
Well born, well bred; I sent him forth
Ingenuous, innocent, and bold:
If things ensued that wanted grace,
As hath been said, they were not base;   20
And never blush was on my face.

IV.

Ah! little doth the young one dream,
When full of play and childish cares,
What power is in his wildest scream,

Heard by his mother unawares !   25
He knows it not, he cannot guess :
Years to a mother bring distress ;
But do not make her love the less.

v.

Neglect me ! no, I suffered long
From that ill thought ; and, being blind   30
Said, " Pride shall help me in my wrong ;
Kind mother have I been, as kind
As ever breathed :" and that is true ;
I 've wet my path with tears like dew,
Weeping for him when no one knew.   35

vi.

My Son, if thou be humbled, poor,
Hopeless of honour and of gain,
Oh ! do not dread thy mother's door ;
Think not of me with grief and pain :
I now can see with better eyes ;   40
And worldly grandeur I despise,
And fortune with her gifts and lies.

vii.

Alas ! the fowls of heaven have wings,
And blasts of heaven will aid their flight ;
They mount — how short a voyage brings   45
The wanderers back to their delight !
Chains tie us down by land and sea ;
And wishes, vain as mine, may be
All that is left to comfort thee.

VIII.

Perhaps some dungeon hears thee groan, 50
Maimed, mangled by inhuman men ;
Or thou upon a desert thrown
Inheritest the lion's den ;
Or hast been summoned to the deep,
Thou, thou and all thy mates, to keep 55
An incommunicable sleep.

IX.

I look for ghosts ; but none will force
Their way to me : 't is falsely said
That there was ever intercourse
Between the living and the dead ; 60
For, surely, then, I should have sight
Of him I wait for day and night,
With love and longings infinite.

X.

My apprehensions come in crowds ;
I dread the rustling of the grass ; 65
The very shadows of the clouds
Have power to shake me as they pass :
I question things and do not find
One that will answer to my mind ;
And all the world appears unkind. 70

XI.

Beyond participation lie
My troubles, and beyond relief :
If any chance to heave a sigh,
They pity me, and not my grief.

Then come to me, my Son, or send   75
Some tidings that my woes may end ;
I havs no other earthly friend !

                                        1804 (?).

────────

ADDRESS TO MY INFANT DAUGHTER, DORA,

ON BEING REMINDED THAT SHE WAS A MONTH OLD THAT DAY,
SEPTEMBER 16.

— HAST thou then survived —
Mild offspring of infirm humanity,
Meek Infant ! among all forlornest things
The most forlorn — one life of that bright star,
The second glory of the Heavens ? — Thou hast,   5
Already hast survived that great decay,
That transformation through the wide earth felt,
And by all nations.   In that Being's sight
From whom the Race of human kind proceed,
A thousand years but are as yesterday;   10
And one day's narrow circuit is to Him
Not less capacious than a thousand years.
But what is time?   What outward glory? neither
A measure is of Thee, whose claims extend
Through "heaven's eternal year." — Yet hail to Thee,   15
Frail, feeble Monthling ! — by that name, methinks,
Thy scanty breathing-time is portioned out
Not idly. — Hadst thou been of Indian birth,
Couched on a casual bed of moss and leaves,
And rudely canopied by leafy boughs,   20
Or to the churlish elements exposed
On the blank plains, — the coldness of the night,
Or the night's darkness, or its cheerful face

Of beauty, by the changing moon adorned,
Would, with imperious admonition, then   25
Have scored thine age, and punctually timed
Thine infant history, on the minds of those
Who might have wandered with thee. — Mother's love,
Nor less than mother's love in other breasts,
Will, among us warm-clad and warmly housed,   30
Do for thee what the finger of the heavens
Doth all too often harshly execute
For thy unblest coevals, amid wilds
Where fancy hath small liberty to grace
The affections, to exalt them or refine ;   35
And the maternal sympathy itself,
Though strong, is, in the main, a joyless tie
Of naked instinct, wound about the heart.
Happier, far happier, is thy lot and ours !
Even now — to solemnise thy helpless state,   40
And to enliven in the mind's regard
Thy passive beauty — parallels have risen,
Resemblances, or contrasts, that connect,
Within the region of a father's thoughts,
Thee and thy mate and sister of the sky.   45
And first ; — thy sinless progress, through a world
By sorrow darkened and by care disturbed,
Apt likeness bears to hers, through gathered clouds,
Moving untouched in silver purity,
And cheering oft-times their reluctant gloom.   50
Fair are ye both, and both are free from stain :
But thou, how leisurely thou fill'st thy horn
With brightness ! leaving her to post along,
And range about, disquieted in change,
And still impatient of the shape she wears.   55
Once up, once down the hill, one journey, Babe,
That will suffice thee ; and it seems that now

Thou hast fore-knowledge that such task is thine ;
Thou travellest so contentedly, and sleep'st
In such a heedless peace. Alas ! full soon   60
Hath this conception, grateful to behold,
Changed countenance, like an object sullied o'er
By breathing mist ; and thine appears to be
A mournful labour, while to her is given
Hope, and a renovation without end.   65
— That smile forbids the thought; for on thy face
Smiles are beginning, like the beams of dawn,
To shoot and circulate ; smiles have there been seen,
Tranquil assurances that Heaven supports
The feeble motions of thy life, and cheers   70
Thy loneliness: or shall those smiles be called
Feelers of love, put forth as if to explore
This untried world, and to prepare thy way
Through a strait passage intricate and dim?
Such are they ; and the same are tokens, signs,   75
Which, when the appointed season hath arrived,
Joy, as her holiest language, shall adopt ;
And Reason's godlike Power be proud to own.

1804.

THE SMALL CELANDINE.

THERE is a Flower, the lesser Celandine,
That shrinks, like many more, from cold and rain ;
And, the first moment that the sun may shine,
Bright as the sun himself, 't is out again !

When hailstones have been falling, swarm on swarm,   5
Or blasts the green field and the trees distrest,
Oft have I seen it muffled up from harm,
In close self-shelter, like a Thing at rest.

But lately, one rough day, this Flower I passed
And recognised it, though an altered form,   10
Now standing forth an offering to the blast,
And buffeted at will by rain and storm.

I stopped, and said with inly-muttered voice,
" It doth not love the shower, nor seek the cold:
This neither is its courage nor its choice,   15
But its necessity in being old.

"The sunshine may not cheer it, nor the dew ;
It cannot help itself in its decay;
Stiff in its members, withered, changed of hue."
And, in my spleen, I smiled that it was grey.   20

To be a Prodigal's Favourite — then, worse truth,
A Miser's Pensioner — behold our lot !
O Man, that from thy fair and shining youth
Age might but take the things Youth needed not !
                                                    1804.

MORNING AMONG THE MOUNTAINS.

(FROM " THE PRELUDE," BOOK IV.)

                              YES, that heartless chase
Of trivial pleasures was a poor exchange
For books and nature at that early age.
'T is true, some casual knowledge might be gained
Of character or life ; but at that time,   5
Of manners put to school I took small note,
And all my deeper passions lay elsewhere.
Far better had it been to exalt the mind
By solitary study, to uphold

Intense desire through meditative peace ; 10
And yet, for chastisement of these regrets,
The memory of one particular hour
Doth here rise up against me. 'Mid a throng
Of maids and youths, old men, and matrons staid,
A medley of all tempers, I had passed 15
The night in dancing, gaiety, and mirth,
With din of instruments and shuffling feet,
And glancing forms, and tapers glittering,
And unaimed prattle flying up and down ;
Spirits upon the stretch, and here and there 20
Slight shocks of young love-liking interspersed,
Whose transient pleasure mounted to the head,
And tingled through the veins.   Ere we retired,
The cock had crowed, and now the eastern sky
Was kindling, not unseen, from humble copse 25
And open field, through which the pathway wound,
And homeward led my steps.   Magnificent
The morning rose, in memorable pomp,
Glorious as e'er I had beheld — in front,
The sea lay laughing at a distance ; near, 30
The solid mountains shone, bright as the clouds,
Grain-tinctured, drenched in empyrean light ;
And in the meadows and the lower grounds
Was all the sweetness of a common dawn —
Dews, vapours, and the melody of birds, 35
And labourers going forth to till the fields.
Ah ! need I say, dear Friend ! that to the brim
My heart was full ; I made no vows, but vows
Were then made for me ; bond unknown to me
Was given that I should be, else sinning greatly, 40
A dedicated Spirit.   On I walked
In thankful blessedness, which yet survives.

1804.

THE ASCENT OF SNOWDON.

(FROM "THE PRELUDE," BOOK XIV.)

IN one of those excursions (may they ne'er
Fade from remembrance !) through the Northern tracts
Of Cambria ranging with a youthful friend,
I left Bethgelert's huts at couching-time,
And westward took my way, to see the sun   5
Rise, from the top of Snowdon.   To the door
Of a rude cottage at the mountain's base
We came, and roused the shepherd who attends
The adventurous stranger's steps, a trusty guide;
Then, cheered by short refreshment, sallied forth.   10

It was a close, warm, breezeless summer night,
Wan, dull, and glaring, with a dripping fog
Low-hung and thick that covered all the sky ;
But, undiscouraged, we began to climb
The mountain-side.   The mist soon girt us round,   15
And, after ordinary travellers' talk
With our conductor, pensively we sank
Each into commerce with his private thoughts :
Thus did we breast the ascent, and by myself
Was nothing either seen or heard that checked   20
Those musings or diverted, save that once
The shepherd's lurcher, who, among the crags,
Had to his joy unearthed a hedgehog, teased
His coiled-up prey with barkings turbulent.
This small adventure, for even such it seemed   25
In that wild place and at the dead of night,
Being over and forgotten, on we wound
In silence as before.   With forehead bent
Earthward, as if in opposition set

Against an enemy, I panted up   30
With eager pace, and no less eager thoughts.
Thus might we wear a midnight hour away,
Ascending at loose distance each from each,
And I, as chanced, the foremost of the band ;
When at my feet the ground appeared to brighten,   35
And with a step or two seemed brighter still ;
Nor was time given to ask or learn the cause,
For instantly a light upon the turf
Fell like a flash, and lo ! as I looked up,
The Moon hung naked in a firmament   40
Of azure without cloud, and at my feet
Rested a silent sea of hoary mist.
A hundred hills their dusky backs upheaved
All over this still ocean ; and beyond,
Far, far beyond, the solid vapours stretched,   45
In headlands, tongues, and promontory shapes,
Into the main Atlantic, that appeared
To dwindle, and give up his majesty,
Usurped upon far as the sight could reach.
Not so the ethereal vault ; encroachment none   50
Was there, nor loss ; only the inferior stars
Had disappeared, or shed a fainter light
In the clear presence of the full-orbed Moon,
Who, from her sovereign elevation, gazed
Upon the billowy ocean, as it lay   55
All meek and silent, save that through a rift —
Not distant from the shore whereon we stood,
A fixed, abysmal, gloomy, breathing-place —
Mounted the roar of waters, torrents, streams
Innumerable, roaring with one voice !   60
Heard over earth and sea, and, in that hour,
For so it seemed, felt by the starry heavens.

When into air had partially dissolved
That vision, given to spirits of the night
And three chance human wanderers, in calm thought   65
Reflected, it appeared to me the type
Of a majestic intellect, its acts
And its possessions, what it has and craves,
What in itself it is, and would become.
There I beheld the emblem of a mind   70
That feeds upon infinity, that broods
Over the dark abyss, intent to hear
Its voices issuing forth to silent light
In one continuous stream ; a mind sustained
By recognitions of transcendent power,   75
In sense conducting to ideal form,
In soul of more than mortal privilege.
One function, above all, of such a mind
Had Nature shadowed there, by putting forth,
'Mid circumstances awful and sublime,   80
That mutual domination which she loves
To exert upon the face of outward things,
So moulded, joined, abstracted, so endowed
With interchangeable supremacy,
That men, least sensitive, see, hear, perceive,   85
And cannot choose but feel.   The power, which all
Acknowledge when thus moved, which Nature thus
To bodily sense exhibits, is the express
Resemblance of that glorious faculty
That higher minds bear with them as their own.   90
This is the very spirit in which they deal
With the whole compass of the universe :
They from their native selves can send abroad
Kindred mutations ; for themselves create
A like existence ; and, whene'er it dawns   95
Created for them, catch it, or are caught

By its inevitable mastery,
Like angels stopped upon the wing by sound
Of harmony from Heaven's remotest spheres.
Them the enduring and the transient both   100
Serve to exhalt; they build up greatest things
From least suggestions ; ever on the watch,
Willing to work and to be wrought upon,
They need not extraordinary calls
To rouse them ; in a world of life they live,   105
By sensible impressions not enthralled,
But by their quickening impulse made more prompt
To hold fit converse with the spiritual world,
And with the generations of mankind
Spread over time, past, present, and to come,   110
Age after age, till Time shall be no more.
Such minds are truly from the Deity,
For they are Powers; and hence the highest bliss
That flesh can know is theirs — the consciousness
Of Whom they are, habitually infused   115
Through every image and through every thought,
And all affections by communion raised
From earth to heaven, from human to divine;
Hence endless occupation for the Soul,
Whether discursive or intuitive ;   120
Hence cheerfulness for acts of daily life,
Emotions which best foresight need not fear,
Most worthy then of trust when most intense.
Hence, amid ills that vex and wrongs that crush
Our hearts — if here the words of Holy Writ   125
May with fit reverence be applied — that peace
Which passeth understanding, that repose
In moral judgments which from this pure source
Must come, or will by man be sought in vain.

THE SIMPLON PASS.

—— Brook and road
Were fellow-travellers in this gloomy Pass,
And with them did we journey several hours
At a slow step.   The immeasurable height
Of woods decaying, never to be decayed,   5
The stationary blasts of waterfalls,
And in the narrow rent, at every turn,
Winds thwarting winds bewildered and forlorn,
The torrents shooting from the clear blue sky,
The rocks that muttered close upon our ears,   10
Black, drizzling crags that spake by the wayside
As if a voice were in them, the sick sight
And giddy prospect of the raving stream,
The unfettered clouds and region of the heavens,
Tumult and peace, the darkness and the light ——   15
Were all like workings of one mind, the features
Of the same face, blossoms upon one tree,
Characters of the great Apocalypse,
The types and symbols of Eternity,
Of first, and last, and midst, and without end.   20

1804.

MIST OPENING IN THE HILLS.

(FROM "THE EXCURSION," BOOK II.)

So was he lifted gently from the ground,
And with their freight homeward the shepherds moved
Through the dull mist, I following —— when a step,
A single step, that freed me from the skirts
Of the blind vapour, opened to my view   5

Glory beyond all glory ever seen
By waking sense or by the dreaming soul !
The appearance, instantaneously disclosed,
Was of a mighty city — boldly say
A wilderness of building, sinking far 10
And self-withdrawn into a boundless depth,
Far sinking into splendour — without end !
Fabric it seemed of diamond and of gold,
With alabaster domes, and silver spires,
And blazing terrace upon terrace, high 15
Uplifted ; here, serene pavilions bright,
In avenues disposed ; there, towers begirt
With battlements that on their restless fronts
Bore stars — illumination of all gems !
By earthly nature had the effect been wrought 20
Upon the dark materials of the storm
Now pacified ; on them, and on the coves
And mountain-steeps and summits, whereunto
The vapours had receded, taking there
Their station under a cerulean sky. 25
Oh, 't was an unimaginable sight !
Clouds, mists, streams, watery rocks and emerald turf,
Clouds of all tincture, rocks and sapphire sky,
Confused, commingled, mutually inflamed,
Molten together, and composing thus, 30
Each lost in each, that marvellous array
Of temple, palace, citadel, and huge
Fantastic pomp of structure without name,
In fleecy folds, voluminous, enwrapped.
Right in the midst, where interspace appeared 35
Of open court, an object like a throne
Under a shining canopy of state
Stood fixed ; and fixed resemblances were seen
To implements of ordinary use,

But vast in size, in substance glorified; 40
Such as by Hebrew Prophets were beheld
In vision — forms uncouth of mightiest power
For admiration and mysterious awe.
This little Vale, a dwelling-place of Man,
Lay low beneath my feet; 't was visible — 45
I saw not, but I felt that it was there.
That which I *saw* was the revealed abode
Of Spirits in beatitude : my heart
Swelled in my breast — " I have been dead," I cried,
" And now I live!   Oh ! wherefore *do* I live ? " 50
And with that pang I prayed to be no more ! —
— But I forget our Charge, as utterly
I then forgot him : — there I stood and gazed :
The apparition faded not away,
And I descended. 55

FRENCH REVOLUTION,

AS IT APPEARED TO ENTHUSIASTS AT ITS COMMENCEMENT.
(REPRINTED FROM "THE FRIEND.")

Oh ! pleasant exercise of hope and joy !
For mighty were the auxiliars which then stood
Upon our side, we who were strong in love !
Bliss was it in that dawn to be alive,
But to be young was very heaven ! — Oh ! times, 5
In which the meagre, stale, forbidding ways
Of custom, law, and statute, took at once
The attraction of a country in romance !
When Reason seemed the most to assert her rights,
When most intent on making of herself 10

A prime Enchantress — to assist the work,
Which then was going forward in her name!
Not favoured spots alone, but the whole earth,
The beauty wore of promise, that which sets
(As at some moment might not be unfelt   15
Among the bowers of paradise itself)
The budding rose above the rose full blown.
What temper at the prospect did not wake
To happiness unthought of?   The inert
Were roused, and lively natures rapt away!   20
They who had fed their childhood upon dreams,
The playfellows of fancy, who had made
All powers of swiftness, subtilty, and strength
Their ministers, — who in lordly wise had stirred
Among the grandest objects of the sense,   25
And dealt with whatsoever they found there
As if they had within some lurking right
To wield it ; — they, too, who, of gentle mood,
Had watched all gentle motions, and to these
Had fitted their own thoughts, schemers more mild,   30
And in the region of their peaceful selves ; —
Now was it that both found, the meek and lofty
Did both find, helpers to their heart's desire,
And stuff at hand, plastic as they could wish ;
Were called upon to exercise their skill,   35
Not in Utopia, subterranean fields,
Or some secreted island, Heaven knows where!
But in the very world, which is the world
Of all of us, — the place where in the end
We find our happiness, or not at all!   40

1804.

ODE TO DUTY.

" Jam non consilio bonus, sed more eò perductus, ut non tantum rectè
facere possim, sed nisi rectè facere non possim."

STERN Daughter of the Voice of God!
O Duty! if that name thou love
Who art a light to guide, a rod
To check the erring, and reprove;
Thou, who art victory and law   5
When empty terrors overawe;
From vain temptations dost set free;
And calm'st the weary strife of frail humanity!

There are who ask not if thine eye
Be on them; who, in love and truth,   10
Where no misgiving is, rely
Upon the genial sense of youth:
Glad Hearts! without reproach or blot
Who do thy work, and know it not:
Oh! if through confidence misplaced   15
They fail, thy saving arms, dread Power! around
    them cast.

Serene will be our days and bright,
And happy will our nature be,
When love is an unerring light,
And joy its own security.   20
And they a blissful course may hold
Even now, who, not unwisely bold,
Live in the spirit of this creed;
Yet seek thy firm support, according to their need.

I, loving freedom, and untried;   25
No sport of every random gust,

Yet being to myself a guide,
Too blindly have reposed my trust :
And oft, when in my heart was heard
Thy timely mandate, I deferred   30
The task, in smoother walks to stray ;
But thee I now would serve more strictly, if I may.

Through no disturbance of my soul,
Or strong compunction in me wrought,
I supplicate for thy control ;   35
But in the quietness of thought :
Me this unchartered freedom tires ;
I feel the weight of chance-desires :
My hopes no more must change their name,
I long for a repose that ever is the same.   40

Stern Lawgiver ! yet thou dost wear
The Godhead's most benignant grace ;
Nor know we anything so fair
As is the smile upon thy face :
Flowers laugh before thee on their beds   45
And fragrance in thy footing treads ;
Thou dost preserve the stars from wrong ;
And the most ancient heavens, through Thee, are
          fresh and strong.

To humbler functions, awful Power !
I call thee : I myself commend   50
Unto thy guidance from this hour ;
Oh, let my weakness have an end !
Give unto me, made lowly wise,
The spirit of self-sacrifice ;
The confidence of reason give ;   55
And in the light of truth thy Bondman let me live !

1805.

TO A SKY-LARK.

Up with me! up with me into the clouds!
    For thy song, Lark, is strong;
Up with me, up with me into the clouds!
      Singing, singing,
With clouds and sky about thee ringing,   5
    Lift me, guide me till I find
That spot which seems so to thy mind!

I have walked through wildernesses dreary,
And to-day my heart is weary;
Had I now the wings of a Faery,   10
Up to thee would I fly.
There is madness about thee, and joy divine
In that song of thine;
Lift me, guide me, high and high,
To thy banqueting-place in the sky.   15

      Joyous as morning,
Thou art laughing and scorning;
Thou hast a nest for thy love and thy rest,
And, though little troubled with sloth,
Drunken Lark! thou would'st be loth   20
To be such a traveller as I.
Happy, happy Liver,
With a soul as strong as a mountain river
Pouring out praise to the Almighty Giver,
    Joy and jollity be with us both!   25

Alas! my journey, rugged and uneven,
Through prickly moors or dusty ways must wind;
But hearing thee, or others of thy kind,
As full of gladness and as free of heaven,

I, with my fate contented, will plod on,   30
And hope for higher raptures, when life's day is
    done.

                      1805.

FIDELITY.

A BARKING sound the Shepherd hears,
A cry as of a dog or fox ;
He halts — and searches with his eyes
Among the scattered rocks :
And now at distance can discern   5
A stirring in a brake of fern ;
And instantly a dog is seen,
Glancing through that covert green.

The Dog is not of mountain breed ;
Its motions, too, are wild and shy ;   10
With something, as the Shepherd thinks,
Unusual in its cry :
Nor is there any one in sight
All round, in hollow or on height ;
Nor shout, nor whistle strikes his ear ;   15
What is the creature doing here ?

It was a cove, a huge recess,
That keeps, till June, December's snow ;
A lofty precipice in front,
A silent tarn [1] below !   20
Far in the bosom of Helvellyn,
Remote from public road or dwelling,
Pathway, or cultivated land ;
From trace of human foot or hand.

[1] Tarn is a *small* Mere, or Lake, mostly high up in the mountains.

There sometimes doth a leaping fish　　　　25
Send through the tarn a lonely cheer ;
The crags repeat the raven's croak,
In symphony austere ;
Thither the rainbow comes — the cloud —
And mists that spread the flying shroud ;　　30
And sunbeams ; and the sounding blast,
That, if it could, would hurry past ;
But that enormous barrier holds it fast.

Not free from boding thoughts, a while
The Shepherd stood ; then makes his way　　35
O'er rocks and stones, following the Dog
As quickly as he may ;
Nor far had gone before he found
A human skeleton on the ground ;
The appalled Discoverer with a sigh　　　40
Looks round, to learn the history.

From those abrupt and perilous rocks
The Man had fallen, that place of fear !
At length upon the Shepherd's mind
It breaks, and all is clear :　　　　　　45
He instantly recalled the name,
And who he was, and whence he came ;
Remembered, too, the very day
On which the Traveller passed this way.

But hear a wonder, for whose sake　　　50
This lamentable tale I tell !
A lasting monument of words
This wonder merits well,
The Dog, which still was hovering nigh,
Repeating the same timid cry,　　　　55
This Dog, had been through three months' space
A dweller in that savage place.

Yes, proof was plain that, since the day
When this ill-fated Traveller died,
The Dog had watched about the spot,   60
Or by his master's side :
How nourished here through such long time
He knows, who gave that love sublime ;
And gave that strength of feeling, great
Above all human estimate !   65

                                    1805.

ELEGIAC STANZAS.

SUGGESTED BY A PICTURE OF PEELE CASTLE, IN A STORM,
PAINTED BY SIR GEORGE BEAUMONT.

I WAS thy neighbour once, thou rugged Pile !
Four summer weeks I dwelt in sight of thee :
I saw thee every day ; and all the while
Thy Form was sleeping on a glassy sea.

So pure the sky, so quiet was the air !   5
So like, so very like, was day to day !
Whene'er I looked, thy Image still was there ;
It trembled, but it never passed away.

How perfect was the calm ! it seemed no sleep ;
No mood, which season takes away, or brings :   10
I could have fancied that the mighty Deep
Was even the gentlest of all gentle Things.

Ah ! THEN, if mine had been the Painter's hand,
To express what then I saw ; and add the gleam,
The light that never was, on sea or land,   15
The consecration, and the Poet's dream ;

I would have planted thee, thou hoary Pile
Amid a world how different from this !
Beside a sea that could not cease to smile ;
On tranquil land, beneath a sky of bliss.   20

Thou shouldst have seemed a treasure-house divine
Of peaceful years ; a chronicle of heaven ; —
Of all the sunbeams that did ever shine
The very sweetest had to thee been given.

A Picture had it been of lasting ease,   25
Elysian quiet, without toil or strife ;
No motion but the moving tide, a breeze,
Or merely silent Nature's breathing life.

Such, in the fond illusion of my heart,
Such Picture would I at that time have made :   30
And seen the soul of truth in every part,
A steadfast peace that might not be betrayed.

So once it would have been, — 't is so no more ;
I have submitted to a new control :
A power is gone, which nothing can restore ;   35
A deep distress hath humanised my Soul.

Not for a moment could I now behold
A smiling sea, and be what I have been :
The feeling of my loss will ne'er be old ;
This, which I know, I speak with mind serene.   40

Then, Beaumont, Friend ! who would have been the
          Friend,
If he had lived, of Him whom I deplore,
This work of thine I blame not, but commend ;
This sea in anger, and that dismal shore.

O 't is a passionate work !— yet wise and well,   45
Well chosen is the spirit that is here ;
That Hulk which labours in the deadly swell,
This rueful sky, this pageantry of fear !

And this huge Castle, standing here sublime,
I love to see the look with which it braves,   50
Cased in the unfeeling armour of old time,
The lightning, the fierce wind, and trampling waves.

Farewell, farewell the heart that lives alone,
Housed in a dream, at distance from the Kind !
Such happiness, wherever it be known,   55
Is to be pitied ; for 't is surely blind.

But welcome fortitude, and patient cheer,
And frequent sights of what is to be borne !
Such sights, or worse, as are before me here, —
Not without hope we suffer and we mourn.   60

1805.

CHARACTER OF THE HAPPY WARRIOR.

WHO is the happy Warrior ?   Who is he
That every man in arms should wish to be ?
— It is the generous Spirit, who, when brought
Among the tasks of real life, hath wrought
Upon the plan that pleased his boyish thought :   5
Whose high endeavours are an inward light
That makes the path before him always bright :
Who, with a natural instinct to discern
What knowledge can perform, is diligent to learn ;
Abides by this resolve, and stops not there,   10
But makes his moral being his prime care ;

Who, doomed to go in company with Pain,
And Fear, and Bloodshed, miserable train!
Turns his necessity to glorious gain ;
In face of these doth exercise a power   15
Which is our human nature's highest dower ;
Controls them and subdues, transmutes, bereaves
Of their bad influence, and their good receives :
By objects, which might force the soul to abate
Her feeling, rendered more compassionate ;   20
Is placable — because occasions rise
So often that demand such sacrifice ;
More skilful in self-knowledge, even more pure,
As tempted more ; more able to endure,
As more exposed to suffering and distress ;   25
Thence, also, more alive to tenderness.
— 'T is he whose law is reason ; who depends
Upon that law as on the best of friends ;
Whence, in a state where men are tempted still
To evil for a guard against worse ill,   30
And what in quality or act is best
Doth seldom on a right foundation rest,
He labours good on good to fix, and owes
To virtue every triumph that he knows :
— Who, if he rise to station of command,   35
Rises by open means ; and there will stand
On honourable terms, or else retire,
And in himself possess his own desire :
Who comprehends his trust, and to the same
Keeps faithful with a singleness of aim ;   40
And therefore does not stoop, nor lie in wait
For wealth, or honours, or for worldly state ;
Whom they must follow ; on whose head must fall,
Like showers of manna, if they come at all :
Whose powers shed round him in the common strife, 45

Or mild concerns of ordinary life,
A constant influence, a peculiar grace;
But who, if he be called upon to face
Some awful moment to which Heaven has joined
Great issues, good or bad for human kind, 50
Is happy as a Lover; and attired
With sudden brightness, like a Man inspired;
And, through the heat of conflict, keeps the law
In calmness made, and sees what he foresaw;
Or if an unexpected call succeed, 55
Come when it will, is equal to the need:
— He who, though thus endued as with a sense
And faculty for storm and turbulence,
Is yet a Soul whose master-bias leans
To homefelt pleasures and to gentle scenes; 60
Sweet images! which, wheresoe'er he be,
Are at his heart; and such fidelity
It is his darling passion to approve;
More brave for this, that he hath much to love:—
'T is, finally, the Man, who, lifted high, 65
Conspicuous object in a Nation's eye,
Or left unthought-of in obscurity, —
Who, with a toward or untoward lot,
Prosperous or adverse, to his wish or not —
Plays, in the many games of life, that one 70
Where what he most doth value must be won:
Whom neither shape of danger can dismay,
Nor thought of tender happiness betray;
Who, not content that former worth stand fast,
Looks forward, persevering to the last, 75
From well to better, daily self-surpast:
Who, whether praise of him must walk the earth
For ever, and to noble deeds give birth,
Or he must fall, to sleep without his fame,

And leave a dead unprofitable name — 80
Finds comfort in himself and in his cause;
And, while the mortal mist is gathering, draws
His breath in confidence of Heaven's applause:
This is the happy Warrior; this is He
That every Man in arms should wish to be. 85

1806.

A COMPLAINT.

THERE is a change — and I am poor;
Your love hath been, not long ago,
A fountain at my fond heart's door,
Whose only business was to flow;
And flow it did: not taking heed 5
Of its own bounty, or my need.

What happy moments did I count!
Blest was I then all bliss above!
Now, for that consecrated fount
Of murmuring, sparkling, living love, 10
What have I? shall I dare to tell?
A comfortless and hidden well.

A well of love — it may be deep —
I trust it is, — and never dry:
What matter? if the waters sleep 15
In silence and obscurity.
— Such change, and at the very door
Of my fond heart, hath made me poor.

1806.

STRAY PLEASURES.

"——Pleasure is spread through the earth
In stray gifts to be claimed by whoever shall find."

By their floating mill,
That lies dead and still,
Behold yon Prisoners three,
The Miller with two Dames, on the breast of the
Thames !
The platform is small, but gives room for them all ;   5
And they're dancing merrily.

From the shore come the notes
To their mill where it floats,
To their house and their mill tethered fast :
To the small wooden isle where, their work to beguile,   10
They from morning to even take whatever is given ;—
And many a blithe day they have past.

In sight of the spires,
All alive with the fires
Of the sun going down to his rest,   15
In the broad open eye of the solitary sky,
They dance, — there are three, as jocund as free,
While they dance on the calm river's breast.

Man and Maidens wheel,
They themselves make the reel,   20
And their music's a prey which they seize ;
It plays not for them, — what matter ? 't is theirs ;
And if they had care, it has scattered their cares,
While they dance, crying, "Long as ye please !"

　　　They dance not for me,　　　　　　　　25
　　　Yet mine is their glee!
Thus pleasure is spread through the earth
In stray gifts to be claimed by whoever shall find;
Thus a rich loving-kindness, redundantly kind,
Moves all nature to gladness and mirth.　　　　30

　　　The showers of the spring
　　　Rouse the birds, and they sing;
If the wind do but stir for his proper delight,
Each leaf, that and this, his neighbour will kiss;
Each wave, one and t' other, speeds after his brother:　　35
They are happy, for that is their right!

　　　　　　　　　　　1806.

POWER OF MUSIC.

An Orpheus! an Orpheus! yes, Faith may grow bold,
And take to herself all the wonders of old;—
Near the stately Pantheon you 'll meet with the same
In the street that from Oxford hath borrowed its name.

His station is there; and he works on the crowd,　　　5
He sways them with harmony merry and loud;
He fills with his power all their hearts to the brim—
Was aught ever heard like his fiddle and him?

What an eager assembly! what an empire is this!
The weary have life, and the hungry have bliss;　　　10
The mourner is cheered, and the anxious have rest;
And the guilt-burthened soul is no longer opprest.

As the Moon brightens round her the clouds of the night,
So He, where he stands, is a centre of light ;
It gleams on the face, there, of dusky-browed Jack,   15
And the pale-visaged Baker's, with basket on back.

That errand-bound 'Prentice was passing in haste —
What matter ! he 's caught — and his time runs to waste ;
The Newsman is stopped, though he stops on the fret ;
And the half-breathless Lamplighter — he 's in the net !   20

The Porter sits down on the weight which he bore ;
The Lass with her barrow wheels hither her store ; —
If a thief could be here he might pilfer at ease ;
She sees the Musician, 't is all that she sees !

He stands, backed by the wall ; — he abates not his din   25
His hat gives him vigour, with boons dropping in,
From the old and the young, from the poorest ; and there !
The one-pennied Boy has his penny to spare.

O blest are the hearers, and proud be the hand
Of the pleasure it spreads through so thankful a band ;   30
I am glad for him, blind as he is ! — all the while
If they speak 't is to praise, and they praise with a smile.

That tall Man, a giant in bulk and in height,
Not an inch of his body is free from delight ;
Can he keep himself still, if he would ? oh, not he !   35
The music stirs in him like wind through a tree.

Mark that Cripple who leans on his crutch ; like a tower
That long has leaned forward, leans hour after hour ! —
That Mother, whose spirit in fetters is bound,
While she dandles the Babe in her arms to the sound.   40

Now, coaches and chariots ! roar on like a stream ;
Here are twenty souls happy as souls in a dream :
They are deaf to your murmurs — they care not for you,
Nor what ye are flying, nor what ye pursue !

                                        1806.

STAR-GAZERS.

WHAT crowd is this ? what have we here ! we must not
        pass it by ;
A Telescope upon its frame, and pointed to the sky :
Long is it as a barber's pole, or mast of little boat,
Some little pleasure-skiff, that doth on Thames's waters
        float.

The Showman chooses well his place, 't is Leicester's busy
        square ;   5
And is as happy in his night, for the heavens are blue and
        fair ;
Calm, though impatient, is the crowd ; each stands ready
        with the fee,
And envies him that's looking ; — what an insight must
        it be !

Yet, Showman, where can lie the cause ?   Shall thy Imple-
        ment have blame,
A boaster, that when he is tried, fails, and is put to
        shame ?   10
Or is it good as others are, and be their eyes in fault ?
Their eyes, or minds ? or, finally, is yon resplendent vault ?

Is nothing of that radiant pomp so good as we have here ?
Or gives a thing but small delight that never can be dear ?

The silver moon with all her vales, and hills of mightiest
    fame,   15
Doth she betray us when they 're seen? or are they but a
    name?

Or is it rather that Conceit rapacious is and strong,
And bounty never yields so much but it seems to do her
    wrong?
Or is it, that when human Souls a journey long have had
And are returned into themselves, they cannot but be
    sad?   20

Or must we be constrained to think that these Spectators
    rude,
Poor in estate, of manners base, men of the multitude,
Have souls which never yet have risen, and therefore
    prostrate lie?
No, no, this cannot be;— men thirst for power and
    majesty!

Does, then, a deep and earnest thought the blissful mind
    employ   25
Of him who gazes, or has gazed? a grave and steady joy,
That doth reject all show of pride, admits no outward
    sign,
Because not of this noisy world, but silent and divine!

Whatever be the cause, 't is sure that they who pry and
    pore
Seem to meet with little gain, seem less happy than
    before: 30
One after One they take their turn, nor have I one espied
That doth not slackly go away, as if dissatisfied.

                1806.

"YES, IT WAS THE MOUNTAIN ECHO."

Yes, it was the mountain Echo,
Solitary, clear, profound,
Answering to the shouting Cuckoo,
Giving to her sound for sound!

Unsolicited reply   5
To a babbling wanderer sent;
Like her ordinary cry,
Like — but oh, how different!

Hears not also mortal Life?
Hear not we, unthinking Creatures!   10
Slaves of folly, love, or strife —
Voices of two different natures?

Have not *we* too? — yes, we have
Answers, and we know not whence;
Echoes from beyond the grave,   15
Recognised intelligence!

Such rebounds our inward ear
Catches sometimes from afar —
Listen, ponder, hold them dear;
For of God, — of God they are.   20

1806.

PERSONAL TALK.

I.

I am not One who much or oft delight
To season my fireside with personal talk, —
Of friends, who live within an easy walk,
Or neighbours, daily, weekly, in my sight:

And, for my chance-acquaintance, ladies bright,   5
Sons, mothers, maidens withering on the stalk,
These all wear out of me, like Forms, with chalk
Painted on rich men's floors, for one feast-night.
Better than such discourse doth silence long,
Long, barren silence, square with my desire ;   10
To sit without emotion, hope, or aim,
In the loved presence of my cottage fire,
And listen to the flapping of the flame,
Or kettle whispering its faint undersong.

II.

" Yet life," you say, " is life ; we have seen and see,   15
And with a living pleasure we describe ;
And fits of sprightly malice do but bribe
The languid mind into activity.
Sound sense, and love itself, and mirth and glee
Are fostered by the comment and the gibe."   20
Even be it so ; yet still among your tribe,
Our daily world's true Worldlings, rank not me !
Children are blest, and powerful ; their world lies
More justly balanced ; partly at their feet,
And part far from them : sweetest melodies   25
Are those that are by distance made more sweet ;
Whose mind is but the mind of his own eyes,
He is a Slave ; the meanest we can meet !

III.

Wings have we, — and as far as we can go,
We may find pleasure : wilderness and wood,   30
Blank ocean and mere sky, support that mood
Which with the lofty sanctifies the low.
Dreams, books, are each a world ; and books, we know,
Are a substantial world, both pure and good :

Round these, with tendrils strong as flesh and blood,　35
Our pastime and our happiness will grow.
There find I personal themes, a plenteous store,
Matter wherein right voluble I am,
To which I listen with a ready ear;
Two shall be named, pre-eminently dear, —　　　40
The gentle Lady married to the Moor;
And heavenly Una with her milk-white Lamb.

IV.

Nor can I not believe but that hereby
Great gains are mine; for thus I live remote
From evil-speaking; rancour, never sought,　　　45
Comes to me not; malignant truth, or lie.
Hence have I genial seasons, hence have I
Smooth passions, smooth discourse, and joyous thought:
And thus from day to day my little boat
Rocks in its harbour, lodging peaceably.　　　50
Blessings be with them — and eternal praise,
Who gave us nobler loves, and nobler cares —
The Poets, who on earth have made us heirs
Of truth and pure delight by heavenly lays!
Oh! might my name be numbered among theirs,　55
Then gladly would I end my mortal days.

1806 (?).

LINES

Composed at Grasmere, during a walk one Evening, after a stormy day, the Author having just read in a Newspaper that the dissolution of Mr. Fox was hourly expected.

LOUD is the Vale! the Voice is up
With which she speaks when storms are gone,
A mighty unison of streams!
Of all her Voices, One!

Loud is the Vale; — this inland Depth   5
In peace is roaring like the Sea;
Yon star upon the mountain-top
Is listening quietly.

Sad was I, even to pain deprest,
Importunate and heavy load![1]   10
The Comforter hath found me here,
Upon this lonely road;

And many thousands now are sad —
Wait the fulfilment of their fear;
For he must die who is their stay,   15
Their glory disappear.

A Power is passing from the earth
To breathless Nature's dark abyss;
But when the great and good depart
What is it more than this —   20

That Man, who is from God sent forth,
Doth yet again to God return? —
Such ebb and flow must ever be,
Then wherefore should we mourn?
                              1806.

[1] Importuna e grave salma. — MICHAEL ANGELO.

ODE.

INTIMATIONS OF IMMORTALITY FROM RECOLLECTIONS OF EARLY CHILDHOOD.

> " The Child is Father of the Man ;
> And I could wish my days to be
> Bound each to each by natural piety."

I.

THERE was a time when meadow, grove, and stream,
The earth, and every common sight,
　　　　To me did seem
　　　Apparelled in celestial light,
The glory and the freshness of a dream.　　　　　　　5
It is not now as it hath been of yore ; —
　　　　Turn wheresoe'er I may,
　　　　　By night or day,
The things which I have seen I now can see no more.

II.

　　The Rainbow comes and goes,　　　　　　10
　　And lovely is the Rose,
　　The Moon doth with delight
Look round her when the heavens are bare,
　　Waters on a starry night
　　Are beautiful and fair ;　　　　　　　　15
　The sunshine is a glorious birth ;
　But yet I know, where'er I go,
That there hath past away a glory from the earth.

III.

Now, while the birds thus sing a joyous song,
　　And while the young lambs bound　　　20
　　　As to the tabor's sound,

To me alone there came a thought of grief;
A timely utterance gave that thought relief,
  And I again am strong:
The cataracts blow their trumpets from the steep;   25
No more shall grief of mine the season wrong;
I hear the Echoes through the mountains throng,
The Winds come to me from the fields of sleep,
  And all the earth is gay;
   Land and sea   30
 Give themselves up to jollity,
  And with the heart of May
Doth every Beast keep holiday; —
  Thou Child of Joy,
Shout round me, let me hear thy shouts, thou
  happy Shepherd-boy!   35

IV.

Ye blessèd Creatures, I have heard the call
 Ye to each other make; I see
The heavens laugh with you in your jubilee:
 My heart is at your festival,   40
 My head hath its coronal,
The fulness of your bliss, I feel — I feel it all.
 Oh evil day! if I were sullen
 While Earth herself is adorning,
  This sweet May-morning,   45
 And the Children are culling
  On every side,
In a thousand valleys far and wide,
Fresh flowers; while the sun shines warm,
And the Babe leaps up on his Mother's arm: —   50
 I hear, I hear, with joy I hear!
 — But there's a Tree, of many, one,
A single Field which I have looked upon,

Both of them speak of something that is gone :
　　The Pansy at my feet　　　　　　　　　　55
　　Doth the same tale repeat :
Whither is fled the visionary gleam ?
Where is it now, the glory and the dream ?

v.

Our birth is but a sleep and a forgetting :
The Soul that rises with us, our life's Star,　　60
　　Hath had elsewhere its setting,
　　　　And cometh from afar :
　　Not in entire forgetfulness,
　　And not in utter nakedness,
But trailing clouds of glory do we come　　65
　　From God, who is our home :
Heaven lies about us in our infancy !
Shades of the prison-house begin to close
　　Upon the growing Boy,
But He beholds the light, and whence it flows,　　70
　　He sees it in his joy ;
The Youth, who daily farther from the east
　　Must travel, still is Nature's Priest,
　　And by the vision splendid
　　Is on his way attended ;　　75
At length the Man perceives it die away,
And fade into the light of common day.

vi.

Earth fills her lap with pleasures of her own ;
Yearnings she hath in her own natural kind,
And, even with something of a Mother's mind,　　80
　　And no unworthy aim,
　　The homely Nurse doth all she can
To make her Foster-child, her Inmate Man,

Forget the glories he hath known,
And that imperial palace whence he came. 85

VII.

Behold the Child among his new-born blisses,
A six years' Darling of a pigmy size !
See, where 'mid work of his own hand he lies,
Fretted by sallies of his mother's kisses,
With light upon him from his father's eyes ! 90
See, at his feet, some little plan or chart,
Some fragment from his dream of human life,
Shaped by himself with newly-learned art ;
    A wedding or a festival,
    A mourning or a funeral ; 95
      And this hath now his heart,
    And unto this he frames his song :
      Then will he fit his tongue
To dialogues of business, love, or strife ;
    But it will not be long 100
    Ere this be thrown aside,
    And with new joy and pride
The little Actor cons another part ;
Filling from time to time his " humorous stage "
With all the Persons, down to palsied Age, 105
That Life brings with her in her equipage ;
    As if his whole vocation
    Were endless imitation.

VIII.

Thou, whose exterior semblance doth belie
    Thy Soul's immensity ; 110
Thou best Philosopher, who yet dost keep
Thy heritage, thou Eye among the blind,
That, deaf and silent, read'st the eternal deep,

Haunted for ever by the eternal **mind**, —
    Mighty Prophet ! Seer blest !   115
    On whom those truths do rest,
Which we are toiling all our lives to find,
In darkness lost, the darkness of the grave ;
Thou, over whom thy Immortality
Broods like the Day, a Master o'er a Slave,   120
A Presence which is not to be put by ;
Thou little Child, yet glorious in the might
Of heaven-born freedom on thy being's height,
Why with such earnest pains dost thou provoke
The years to bring the inevitable yoke,   125
Thus blindly with thy blessedness at strife ?
Full soon thy Soul shall have her earthly freight,
And custom lie upon thee with a weight,
Heavy as frost, and deep almost as life !

IX.

    O joy ! that in our embers   130
    Is something that doth live,
    That nature yet remembers
    What was so fugitive !
The thought of our past years in me doth breed
Perpetual benediction : not indeed   135
For that which is most worthy to be blessed —
Delight and liberty, the simple creed
Of Childhood, whether busy or at rest,
With new-fledged hope still fluttering in his breast : —
    Not for these I raise   140
    The song of thanks and praise ;
  But for those obstinate questionings
  Of sense and outward things,
  Fallings from us, vanishings ;
  Blank misgivings of a Creature   145

Moving about in worlds not realised,
High instincts before which our mortal Nature
Did tremble like a guilty Thing surprised :
    But for those first affections,
    Those shadowy recollections, 150
  Which, be they what they may,
Are yet the fountain light of all our day,
Are yet a master light of all our seeing ;
  Uphold us, cherish, and have power to make
Our noisy years seem moments in the being 155
Of the eternal Silence : truths that wake,
    To perish never ;
Which neither listlessness, nor mad endeavour,
    Nor Man nor Boy,
Nor all that is at enmity with joy, 160
Can utterly abolish or destroy !
    Hence in a season of calm weather
    Though inland far we be,
Our Souls have sight of that immortal sea
    Which brought us hither, 165
    Can in a moment travel thither,
And see the Children sport upon the shore,
And hear the mighty waters rolling evermore.

x.

Then sing, ye Birds, sing, sing a joyous song !
    And let the young Lambs bound 170
    As to the tabor's sound !
We in thought will join your throng,
    Ye that pipe and ye that play,
    Ye that through your hearts to-day
    Feel the gladness of the May ! 175
What though the radiance which was once so bright
Be now for ever taken from my sight,

Though nothing can bring back the hour
Of splendour in the grass, of glory in the flower;
  We will grieve not, rather find   180
  Strength in what remains behind;
  In the primal sympathy
  Which having been must ever be;
  In the soothing thoughts that spring
  Out of human suffering;   185
  In the faith that looks through death,
In years that bring the philosophic mind.

XI.

And O, ye Fountains, Meadows, Hills, and Groves,
Forebode not any severing of our loves!
Yet in my heart of hearts I feel your might; 190
I only have relinquished one delight
To live beneath your more habitual sway.
I love the Brooks which down their channels fret,
Even more than when I tripped lightly as they;
The innocent brightness of a new-born Day 195
   Is lovely yet;
The Clouds that gather round the setting sun
Do take a sober colouring from an eye
That hath kept watch o'er man's mortality;
Another race hath been, and other palms are won. 200
Thanks to the human heart by which we live,
Thanks to its tenderness, its joys, and fears,
To me the meanest flower that blows can give
Thoughts that do often lie too deep for tears.
      1803–6.

"O NIGHTINGALE! THOU SURELY ART."

O NIGHTINGALE! thou surely art
A creature of a "fiery heart" : —
These notes of thine — they pierce and pierce;
Tumultuous harmony and fierce!
Thou sing'st as if the God of wine   5
Had helped thee to a Valentine;
A song in mockery and despite
Of shades, and dews, and silent night;
And steady bliss, and all the loves
Now sleeping in these peaceful groves.   10

I heard a Stock-dove sing or say
His homely tale, this very day;
His voice was buried among trees,
Yet to be come at by the breeze :
He did not cease ; but cooed — and cooed;   15
And somewhat pensively he wooed :
He sang of love, with quiet blending,
Slow to begin, and never ending ;
Of serious faith, and inward glee ;
That was the song — the song for me!   20

1806.

SONG AT THE FEAST OF BROUGHAM CASTLE,

UPON THE RESTORATION OF LORD CLIFFORD, THE SHEPHERD,
TO THE ESTATES AND HONOURS OF HIS ANCESTORS.

HIGH in the breathless Hall the Minstrel sate,
And Emont's murmur mingled with the Song. —
The words of ancient time I thus translate,
A festal strain that hath been silent long : —

" From town to town, from tower to tower,   5
The red rose is a gladsome flower.
Her thirty years of winter past,
The red rose is revived at last ;
She lifts her head for endless spring,
For everlasting blossoming :   10
Both roses flourish, red and white :
In love and sisterly delight
The two that were at strife are blended,
And all old troubles now are ended. —
Joy ! joy to both! but most to her   15
Who is the flower of Lancaster !
Behold her how She smiles to-day
On this great throng, this bright array !
Fair greeting doth she send to all
From every corner of the hall ;   20
But chiefly from above the board
Where sits in state our rightful Lord,
A Clifford to his own restored !
　　They came with banner, spear, and shield,
And it was proved in Bosworth-field.   25
Not long the Avenger was withstood —
Earth helped him with the cry of blood :
St. George was for us, and the might
Of blessed Angels crowned the right.
Loud voice the Land has uttered forth,   30
We loudest in the faithful north :
Our fields rejoice, our mountains ring,
Our streams proclaim a welcoming ;
Our strong-abodes and castles see
The glory of their loyalty.   35
　　How glad is Skipton at this hour —
Though lonely, a deserted Tower ;

Knight, squire, and yeoman, page and groom ·
We have them at the feast of Brough 'm.
How glad Pendragon—though the sleep 40
Of years be on her !—She shall reap
A taste of this great pleasure, viewing
As in a dream her own renewing.
Rejoiced is Brough, right glad I deem
Beside her little humble stream ; 45
And she that keepeth watch and ward
Her statelier Eden's course to guard ;
They both are happy at this hour,
Though each is but a lonely Tower :—
But here is perfect joy and pride 50
For one fair House by Emont's side,
This day, distinguished without peer,
To see her Master and to cheer—
Him, and his Lady-mother dear !

Oh ! it was a time forlorn 55
When the fatherless was born—
Give her wings that she may fly,
Or she sees her infant die !
Swords that are with slaughter wild
Hunt the Mother and the Child. 60
Who will take them from the light ?
— Yonder is a man in sight—
Yonder is a house—but where ?
No, they must not enter there.
To the caves, and to the brooks, 65
To the clouds of heaven she looks ;
She is speechless, but her eyes
Pray in ghostly agonies.
Blissful Mary, Mother mild,
Maid and Mother undefiled, 70
Save a Mother and her Child !

Now Who is he that bounds with joy
On Carrock's side, a Shepherd-boy?
No thoughts hath he but thoughts that pass
Light as the wind along the grass. 75
Can this be He who hither came
In secret, like a smothered flame?
O'er whom such thankful tears were shed
For shelter, and a poor man's bread!
God loves the Child; and God hath willed 80
That those dear words should be fulfilled,
The Lady's words, when forced away,
The last she to her Babe did say:
' My own, my own, thy Fellow-guest
I may not be; but rest thee, rest, 85
For lowly shepherd's life is best!'
    Alas! when evil men are strong
No life is good, no pleasure long.
The Boy must part from Mosedale's groves,
And leave Blencathara's rugged coves, 90
And quit the flowers that summer brings
To Glenderamakin's lofty springs;
Must vanish and his careless cheer
Be turned to heaviness and fear.
— Give Sir Lancelot Threlkeld praise! 95
Hear it, good man, old in days!
Thou tree of covert and of rest
For this young Bird that is distrest;
Among thy branches safe he lay,
And he was free to sport and play, 100
When falcons were abroad for prey.
    A recreant harp, that sings of fear
And heaviness in Clifford's ear!
I said, when evil men are strong,
No life is good, no pleasure long, 105

A weak and cowardly untruth !
Our Clifford was a happy Youth,
And thankful through a weary time,
That brought him up to manhood's prime.
— Again he wanders forth at will,   110
And tends a flock from hill to hill :
His garb is humble ; ne'er was seen
Such garb with such a noble mien ;
Among the shepherd grooms no mate
Hath he, a child of strength and state !   115
Yet lacks not friends for simple glee,
Nor yet for higher sympathy.
To his side the fallow-deer
Came and rested without fear ;
The eagle, lord of land and sea,   120
Stooped down to pay him fealty ;
And both the undying fish that swim
Through Bowscale-tarn did wait on him ;
The pair were servants of his eye
In their immortality ;   125
And glancing, gleaming, dark or bright,
Moved to and fro, for his delight.
He knew the rocks which Angels haunt
Upon the mountains visitant ;
He hath kenned them taking wing :   130
And into caves where Faeries sing
He hath entered ; and been told
By Voices how men lived of old.
Among the heavens his eye can see
The face of thing that is to be ;   135
And, if that men report him right,
His tongue could whisper words of might.
— Now another day is come,
Fitter hope, and nobler doom ;

He hath thrown aside his crook, 140
And hath buried deep his book ;
Armour rusting in his halls
On the blood of Clifford calls ; —
'Quell the Scot,' exclaims the Lance —
Bear me to the heart of France, 145
Is the longing of the Shield—
Tell thy name, thou trembling Field ;
Field of death, where'er thou be,
Groan thou with our victory !
Happy day, and mighty hour, 150
When our Shepherd, in his power,
Mailed and horsed, with lance and sword,
To his ancestors restored
Like a re-appearing Star,
Like a glory from afar, 155
First shall head the flock of war ! "

Alas ! the impassioned minstrel did not know
How, by Heaven's grace, this Clifford's heart was
    framed,
How he, long forced in humble walks to go,
Was softened into feeling, soothed, and tamed. 160

Love had he found in huts where poor men lie ;
His daily teachers had been woods and rills,
The silence that is in the starry sky,
The sleep that is among the lonely hills.

In him the savage virtue of the Race, 165
Revenge, and all ferocious thoughts were dead :
Nor did he change ; but kept in lofty place
The wisdom which adversity had bred.

Glad were the vales, and every cottage hearth ;
The Shepherd-lord was honoured more and more ;   170
And, ages after he was laid in earth,
"The good Lord Clifford" was the name he bore.

1807.

THE FORCE OF PRAYER; OR THE FOUNDING OF BOLTON PRIORY.

A TRADITION.

" *What is good for a bootless bene ?* "
With these dark words begins my Tale ;
And their meaning is, whence can comfort spring
When prayer is of no avail ?

" *What is good for a bootless bene ?* "   5
The Falconer to the Lady said ;
And she made answer " ENDLESS SORROW ! "
For she knew that her Son was dead.

She knew it by the Falconer's words,
And from the look of the Falconer's eye ;   10
And from the love which was in her soul
For her youthful Romilly.

— Young Romilly through Barden woods
Is ranging high and low ;
And holds a greyhound in a leash,   15
To let slip upon buck or doe.

The pair have reached that fearful chasm,
How tempting to bestride !
For lordly Wharf is there pent in
With rocks on either side.   20

The striding-place is called THE STRID,
A name which it took of yore :
A thousand years hath it borne that name,
And shall a thousand more.

And hither is young Romilly come,   25
And what may now forbid
That he, perhaps for the hundredth time,
Shall bound across THE STRID?

He sprang in glee,—for what cared he
That the river was strong, and the rocks were steep?—30
But the greyhound in the leash hung back,
And checked him in his leap.

The Boy is in the arms of Wharf,
And strangled by a merciless force ;
For never more was young Romilly seen   35
Till he rose a lifeless corse.

Now there is stillness in the vale,
And long, unspeaking sorrow :
Wharf shall be to pitying hearts
A name more sad than Yarrow.   40

If for a lover the Lady wept,
A solace she might borrow
From death, and from the passion of death ;—
Old Wharf might heal her sorrow.

She weeps not for the wedding-day   45
Which was to be to-morrow :
Her hope was a further-looking hope,
And hers is a mother's sorrow.

He was a tree that stood alone,
And proudly did its branches wave; 50
And the root of this delightful tree
Was in her husband's grave !

Long, long in darkness did she sit,
And her first words were, " Let there be
In Bolton, on the field of Wharf, 55
A stately Priory ! "

The stately Priory was reared ;
And Wharf, as he moved along,
To matins joined a mournful voice,
Nor failed at evensong. 60

And the Lady prayed in heaviness
That looked not for relief !
But slowly did her succour come,
And a patience to her grief.

Oh ! there is never sorrow of heart 65
That shall lack a timely end,
If but to God we turn, and ask
Of Him to be our friend !

1807.

CHARACTERISTICS OF A CHILD THREE YEARS OLD.

LOVING she is, and tractable, though wild;
And Innocence hath privilege in her
To dignify arch looks and laughing eyes ;
And feats of cunning ; and the pretty round
Of trespasses, affected to provoke 5
Mock-chastisement and partnership in play.

And, as a faggot sparkles on the hearth,
Not less if unattended and alone
Than when both young and old sit gathered round
And take delight in its activity;   10
Even so this happy Creature of herself
Is all-sufficient; solitude to her
Is blithe society, who fills the air
With gladness and involuntary songs.
Light are her sallies as the tripping fawn's   15
Forth-startled from the fern where she lay couched;
Unthought-of, unexpected, as the stir
Of the soft breeze ruffling the meadow-flowers,
Or from before it chasing wantonly
The many-coloured images imprest   20
Upon the bosom of a placid lake.

                                            1811.

SOURCES OF SPIRITUAL STRENGTH.

(FROM "THE EXCURSION," BOOK IV.)

'T IS, by comparison, an easy task
Earth to despise; but to converse with heaven—
This is not easy:— to relinquish all
We have, or hope, of happiness and joy,
And stand in freedom loosened from this world,   5
I deem not arduous : but must needs confess
That 't is a thing impossible to frame
Conceptions equal to the soul's desires;
And the most difficult of tasks to *keep*
Heights which the soul is competent to gain.   10
— Man is of dust : ethereal hopes are his,
Which, when they should sustain themselves aloft,

Want due consistence ; like a pillar of smoke,
That with majestic energy from earth
Rises ; but having reached the thinner air, 15
Melts, and dissolves, and is no longer seen.
From this infirmity of mortal kind
Sorrow proceeds, which else were not ; at least,
If grief be something hallowed and ordained,
If, in proportion, it be just and meet, 20
Yet, through this weakness of the general heart,
Is it enabled to maintain its hold
In that excess which conscience disapproves.
For who could sink and settle to that point
Of selfishness ; so senseless who could be 25
As long and perseveringly to mourn
For any object of his love, removed
From this unstable world, if he could fix
A satisfying view upon that state
Of pure, imperishable blessedness, 30
Which reason promises, and holy writ
Ensures to all believers ? — Yet mistrust
Is of such incapacity, methinks,
No natural branch ; despondency far less;
And least of all, is absolute despair. 35
— And, if there be whose tender frames have drooped
Even to the dust ; apparently, through weight
Of anguish unrelieved, and lack of power
An agonizing sorrow to transmute ;
Deem not that proof is here of hope withheld 40
When wanted most ; a confidence impaired
So pitiably, that, having ceased to see
With bodily eyes, they are borne down by love
Of what is lost, and perish through regret.
Oh ! no, the innocent Sufferer often sees 45
Too clearly ; feels too vividly ; and longs

To realize the vision, with intense
And over-constant yearning ; — there — there lies
The excess, by which the balance is destroyed.
Too, too contracted are these walls of flesh,   50
This vital warmth too cold, these visual orbs,
Though inconceivably endowed, too dim
For any passion of the soul that leads
To ecstasy ; and, all the crooked paths
Of time and change disdaining, takes its course   55
Along the line of limitless desires.
I, speaking now from such disorder free,
Nor rapt, nor craving, but in settled peace,
I cannot doubt that they whom you deplore
Are glorified ; or, if they sleep, shall wake   60
From sleep, and dwell with God in endless love.
Hope, below this, consists not with belief
In mercy, carried infinite degrees
Beyond the tenderness of human hearts :
Hope, below this, consists not with belief   65
In perfect wisdom, guiding mightiest power,
That finds no limits but her own pure will.

Here then we rest ; not fearing for our creed
The worst that human reasoning can achieve,
To unsettle or perplex it : yet with pain   70
Acknowledging, and grievous self-reproach,
That, though immovably convinced, we want
Zeal, and the virtue to exist by faith
As soldiers live by courage ; as, by strength
Of heart, the sailor fights with roaring seas.   75
Alas ! the endowment of immortal power
Is matched unequally with custom, time,
And domineering faculties of sense
In *all ;* in most, with superadded foes,

Idle temptations ; open vanities,   80
Ephemeral offspring of the unblushing world;
And, in the private regions of the mind,
Ill-governed passions, ranklings of despite,
Immoderate wishes, pining discontent,
Distress and care.   What then remains? — To seek   85
Those helps for his occasions ever near
Who lacks not will to use them ; vows, renewed
On the first motion of a holy thought;
Vigils of contemplation ; praise ; and prayer—
A stream, which, from the fountain of the heart   90
Issuing, however feebly, nowhere flows
Without access of unexpected strength.
But, above all, the victory is most sure
For him, who, seeking faith by virtue, strives
To yield entire submission to the law   95
Of conscience — conscience reverenced and obeyed,
As God's most intimate presence in the soul,
And his most perfect image in the world.
— Endeavour thus to live; these rules regard ;
These helps solicit ; and a stedfast seat   100
Shall then be yours among the happy few
Who dwell on earth, yet breathe empyreal air
Sons of the morning.   For your nobler part,
Ere disencumbered of her mortal chains,
Doubt shall be quelled and trouble chased away ;   105
With only such degree of sadness left
As may support longings of pure desire ;
And strengthen love, rejoicing secretly
In the sublime attractions of the grave.

                              1808–1811 (?).

GREEK DIVINITIES.

(FROM "THE EXCURSION," BOOK IV.)

ONCE more to distant ages of the world
Let us revert, and place before our thoughts
The face which rural solitude might wear
To the unenlightened swains of pagan Greece.
— In that fair clime, the lonely herdsman, stretched   5
On the soft grass through half a summer's day,
With music lulled his indolent repose :
And, in some fit of weariness, if he,
When his own breath was silent, chanced to hear
A distant strain, far sweeter than the sounds   10
Which his poor skill could make, his fancy fetched,
Even from the blazing chariot of the sun,
A beardless Youth, who touched a golden lute,
And filled the illumined groves with ravishment.
The nightly hunter, lifting a bright eye   15
Up towards the crescent moon, with grateful heart
Called on the lovely wanderer who bestowed
That timely light, to share his joyous sport :
And hence, a beaming Goddess with her Nymphs,
Across the lawn and through the darksome grove,   20
Not unaccompanied with tuneful notes
By echo multiplied from rock or cave,
Swept in the storm of chase ; as moon and stars
Glance rapidly along the clouded heaven,
When winds are blowing strong.   The traveller slaked   25
His thirst from rill or gushing fount, and thanked
The Naiad.   Sunbeams, upon distant hills
Gliding apace, with shadows in their train,
Might, with small help from fancy, be transformed
Into fleet Oreads sporting visibly.   30
The Zephyrs fanning, as they passed, their wings,

Lacked not, for love, fair objects whom they wooed
With gentle whisper.   Withered boughs grotesque,
Stripped of their leaves and twigs by hoary age,
From depth of shaggy covert peeping forth   35
In the low vale, or on steep mountain side ;
And, sometimes, intermixed with stirring horns
Of the live deer, or goat's depending beard,—
These were the lurking Satyrs, a wild brood
Of gamesome Deities ; or Pan himself,   40
The simple shepherd's awe-inspiring God !

                              1808–1811 (?).

THE SEA-SHELL.

(FROM "THE EXCURSION," BOOK IV.)

                              I HAVE seen
A curious child, who dwelt upon a tract
Of inland ground, applying to his ear
The convolutions of a smooth-lipped shell ;
To which, in silence hushed, his very soul   5
Listened intensely ; and his countenance soon
Brightened with joy ; for from within were heard
Murmurings, whereby the monitor expressed
Mysterious union with its native sea.
Even such a shell the universe itself   10
Is to the ear of Faith ; and there are times,
I doubt not, when to you it doth impart
Authentic tidings of invisible things ;
Of ebb and flow, and ever-during power ;
And central peace, subsisting at the heart   15
Of endless agitation.   Here you stand,
Adore, and worship, when you know it not ;
Pious beyond the intention of your thought ;
Devout above the meaning of your will.

— Yes, you have felt, and may not cease to feel.   2c
The estate of man would be indeed forlorn
If false conclusions of the reasoning power
Made the eye blind, and closed the passages
Through which the ear converses with the heart.
Has not the soul, the being of your life,   25
Received a shock of awful consciousness,
In some calm season, when these lofty rocks
At night's approach bring down the unclouded sky,
To rest upon their circumambient walls ;
A temple framing of dimensions vast,   30
And yet not too enormous for the sound
Of human anthems, — choral song, or burst
Sublime of instrumental harmony,
To glorify the Eternal !   What if these
Did never break the stillness that prevails   35
Here, — if the solemn nightingale be mute,
And the soft woodlark here did never chant
Her vespers, — Nature fails not to provide
Impulse and utterance.   The whispering air
Sends inspiration from the shadowy heights,   40
And blind recesses of the caverned rocks ;
The little rills, and waters numberless,
Inaudible by daylight, blend their notes
With the loud streams : and often, at the hour
When issue forth the first pale stars, is heard,   45
Within the circuit of this fabric huge,
One voice — the solitary raven, flying
Athwart the concave of the dark blue dome,
Unseen, perchance above all power of sight —
An iron knell ! with echoes from afar   50
Faint — and still fainter — as the cry, with which
The wanderer accompanies her flight
Through the calm region, fades upon the ear,

Diminishing by distance till it seemed
To expire; yet from the abyss is caught again,   55
And yet again recovered !

1808–1811 (?).

LAODAMIA.

" WITH sacrifice before the rising morn
Vows have I made by fruitless hope inspired ;
And from the infernal Gods, 'mid shades forlorn
Of night, my slaughtered Lord have I required :
Celestial pity I again implore; —   5
Restore him to my sight — great Jove, restore ! "

So speaking, and by fervent love endowed
With faith, the Suppliant heavenward lifts her hands ;
While, like the sun emerging from a cloud,
Her countenance brightens — and her eye expands ;   10
Her bosom heaves and spreads, her stature grows ;
And she expects the issue in repose.

O terror ! what hath she perceived ? — O joy !
What doth she look on ? — whom doth she behold ?
Her Hero slain upon the beach of Troy ?   15
His vital presence ? his corporeal mould ?
It is — if sense deceive her not — 't is He !
And a God leads him, wingèd Mercury !

Mild Hermes spake — and touched her with his wand
That calms all fear ; " Such grace hath crowned thy   20
        prayer,
Laodamía ! that at Jove's command
Thy Husband walks the paths of upper air :
He comes to tarry with thee three hours' space ;
Accept the gift, behold him face to face ! "

Forth sprang the impassioned Queen her Lord to clasp; 25
Again that consummation she essayed;
But unsubstantial Form eludes her grasp
As often as that eager grasp was made.
The Phantom parts — but parts to re-unite,
And re-assume his place before her sight.   30

"Protesiláus, lo! thy guide is gone!
Confirm, I pray, the vision with thy voice:
This is our palace, — yonder is thy throne;
Speak, and the floor thou tread'st on will rejoice.
Not to appal me have the gods bestowed   35
This precious boon; and blest a sad abode."

"Great Jove, Laodamía! doth not leave
His gifts imperfect :— Spectre though I be,
I am not sent to scare thee or deceive;
But in reward of thy fidelity.   40
And something also did my worth obtain;
For fearless virtue bringeth boundless gain.

"Thou knowest, the Delphic oracle foretold
That the first Greek who touched the Trojan strand
Should die; but me the threat could not withhold: 45
A generous cause a victim did demand;
And forth I leapt upon the sandy plain;
A self-devoted chief — by Hector slain."

"Supreme of Heroes — bravest, noblest, best!
Thy matchless courage I bewail no more,   50
Which then, when tens of thousands were deprest
By doubt, propelled thee to the fatal shore;
Thou found'st — and I forgive thee — here thou art —
A nobler counsellor than my poor heart.

"But thou, though capable of sternest deed,   55
Wert kind as resolute, and good as brave ;
And he, whose power restores thee, hath decreed
Thou should'st elude the malice of the grave :
Redundant are thy locks, thy lips as fair
As when their breath enriched Thessalian air.   60

"No Spectre greets me, — no vain Shadow this ;
Come, blooming Hero, place thee by my side !
Give, on this well-known couch, one nuptial kiss
To me, this day, a second time thy bride ! "
Jove frowned in heaven : the conscious Parcæ threw   65
Upon those roseate lips a Stygian hue.

"This visage tells thee that my doom is past :
Nor should the change be mourned, even if the joys
Of sense were able to return as fast
And surely as they vanish.   Earth destroys   70
Those raptures duly— Erebus disdains :
Calm pleasures there abide — majestic pains.

"Be taught, O faithful Consort, to control
Rebellious passion : for the Gods approve
The depth, and not the tumult, of the soul ;   75
A fervent, not ungovernable, love.
Thy transports moderate ; and meekly mourn
When I depart, for brief is my sojourn — "

"Ah, wherefore ? — Did not Hercules by force
Wrest from the guardian Monster of the tomb   80
Alcestis, a reanimated corse,
Given back to dwell on earth in vernal bloom ?
Medea's spells dispersed the weight of years,
And Æson stood a youth 'mid youthful peers.

" The Gods to us are merciful — and they   85
Yet further may relent : for mightier far
Than strength of nerve and sinew, or the sway
Of magic potent over sun and star,
Is love, though oft to agony distrest,
And though his favourite seat be feeble woman's breast. 90

" But if thou goest, I follow — " " Peace ! " he said,—
She looked upon him and was calmed and cheered ;
The ghastly colour from his lips had fled ;
In his deportment, shape, and mien, appeared
Elysian beauty, melancholy grace,   95
Brought from a pensive though a happy place.

He spake of love, such love as Spirits feel
In worlds whose course is equable and pure ;
No fears to beat away — no strife to heal —
The past unsighed for, and the future sure ;   100
Spake of heroic arts in graver mood
Revived, with finer harmony pursued ;

Of all that is most beauteous — imaged there
In happier beauty ; more pellucid streams,
An ampler ether, a diviner air,   105
And fields invested with purpureal gleams ;
Climes which the sun, who sheds the brightest day
Earth knows, is all unworthy to survey.

Yet there the Soul shall enter which hath earned
That privilege by virtue. — " Ill," said he,   110
" The end of man's existence I discerned,
Who from ignoble games and revelry
Could draw, when we had parted, vain delight,
While tears were thy best pastime, day and night ;

" And while my youthful peers before my eyes   115
(Each hero following his peculiar bent)
Prepared themselves for glorious enterprise
By martial sports, — or, seated in the tent,
Chieftains and kings in council were detained ;
What time the fleet at Aulis lay enchained.   120

" The wished-for wind was given : — I then revolved
The oracle, upon the silent sea ;
And, if no worthier led the way, resolved
That, of a thousand vessels, mine should be
The foremost prow in pressing to the strand, —   125
Mine the first blood that tinged the Trojan sand.

" Yet bitter, oft-times bitter, was the pang
When of thy loss I thought, belovèd Wife !
On thee too fondly did my memory hang,
And on the joys we shared in mortal life, —   130
The paths which we had trod — these fountains, flowers,
My new-planned cities, and unfinished towers.

" But should suspense permit the Foe to cry,
' Behold they tremble ! — haughty their array,
Yet of their number no one dares to die ' ?   135
In soul I swept the indignity away :
Old frailties then recurred : — but lofty thought,
In act embodied, my deliverance wrought.

" And Thou, though strong in love, art all too weak
In reason, in self-government too slow ;   140
I counsel thee by fortitude to seek
Our blest re-union in the shades below.
The invisible world with thee hath sympathised ;
Be thy affections raised and solemnised.

"Learn, by a mortal yearning, to ascend — 145
Seeking a higher object. Love was given,
Encouraged, sanctioned, chiefly for that end ;
For this the passion to excess was driven —
That self might be annulled : her bondage prove
The fetters of a dream, opposed to love." —— 150

Aloud she shrieked ! for Hermes reappears !
Round the dear Shade she would have clung — 'tis
    vain :
The hours are past — too brief had they been years ;
And him no mortal effort can detain :
Swift, toward the realms that know not earthly day, 155
He through the portal takes his silent way,
And on the palace-floor a lifeless corse She lay.

Thus all in vain exhorted and reproved,
She perished ; and, as for a wilful crime,
By the just Gods whom no weak pity moved, 160
Was doomed to wear out her appointed time,
Apart from happy Ghosts, that gather flowers
Of blissful quiet 'mid unfading bowers.

— Yet tears to human suffering are due ;
And mortal hopes defeated and o'erthrown 165
Are mourned by man, and not by man alone,
As fondly he believes. — Upon the side
Of Hellespont (such faith was entertained)
A knot of spiry trees for ages grew
From out the tomb of him for whom she died ; 170
And ever, when such stature they had gained
That Ilium's walls were subject to their view,

The trees' tall summits withered at the sight ;
A constant interchange of growth and blight ! [1]

1814.

YARROW VISITED.

SEPTEMBER, 1814.

(See page 181.)

AND is this — Yarrow ? — *This* the Stream
Of which my fancy cherished,
So faithfully, a waking dream ?
An image that hath perished !
O that some Minstrel's harp were **near,**   5
To utter notes of gladness,
And chase this silence from the **air,**
That fills my heart with sadness !

Yet why ? — a silvery current flows
With uncontrolled meanderings ;   10
Nor have these eyes by greener hills
Been soothed, in all my wanderings.
And, through her depths, Saint Mary's Lake
Is visibly delighted ;
For not a feature of those hills   15
Is in the mirror slighted.

[1] For the account of these long-lived trees, see Pliny's *Natural History*, lib. xvi. cap. 44 ; and for the features in the character of Protesilaus, see the *Iphigenia in Aulis* of Euripides.   Virgil places the Shade of Laodamia in a mournful region, among unhappy Lovers,

"—— His Laodamia,
It comes. —— "

A blue sky bends o'er Yarrow vale,
Save where that pearly whiteness
Is round the rising sun diffused,
A tender hazy brightness ;   20
Mild dawn of promise ! that excludes
All profitless dejection ;
Though not unwilling here to admit
A pensive recollection.

Where was it that the famous Flower   25
Of Yarrow Vale lay bleeding ?
His bed perchance was yon smooth mound
On which the herd is feeding :
And haply from this crystal pool,
Now peaceful as the morning,   30
The Water-wraith ascended thrice —
And gave his doleful warning.

Delicious is the Lay that sings
The haunts of happy Lovers,
The path that leads them to the grove,   35
The leafy grove that covers :
And Pity sanctifies the Verse
That paints, by strength of sorrow,
The unconquerable strength of love ;
Bear witness, rueful Yarrow !   40

But thou, that didst appear so fair
To fond imagination,
Dost rival in the light of day
Her delicate creation :
Meek loveliness is round thee spread,   45
A softness still and holy ;
The grace of forest charms decayed,
And pastoral melancholy.

That region left, the vale unfolds
Rich groves of lofty stature,   50
With Yarrow winding through the pomp
Of cultivated nature ;
And, rising from those lofty groves,
Behold a Ruin hoary !
The shattered front of Newark's Towers,   55
Renowned in Border story.

Fair scenes for childhood's opening bloom,
For sportive youth to stray in ;
For manhood to enjoy his strength ;
And age to wear away in !   60
Yon cottage seems a bower of bliss,
A covert for protection
Of tender thoughts, that nestle there —
The brood of chaste affection.

How sweet, on this autumnal day,   65
The wild-wood fruits to gather,
And on my True-love's forehead plant
A crest of blooming heather !
And what if I enwreathed my own !
'T were no offence to reason ;   70
The sober Hills thus deck their brows
To meet the wintry season.

I see — but not by sight alone,
Loved Yarrow, have I won thee ;
A ray of fancy still survives —   75
Her sunshine plays upon thee !
Thy ever-youthful waters keep
A course of lively pleasure ;
And gladsome notes my lips can breathe,
Accordant to the measure.   80

The vapours linger round the Heights,
They melt, and soon must vanish;
One hour is theirs, nor more is mine —
Sad thought, which I would banish,
But that I know, where'er I go,   85
Thy genuine image, Yarrow!
Will dwell with me — to heighten joy,
And cheer my mind in sorrow.

                                        1814.

DION.

I.

SERENE, and fitted to embrace,
Where'er he turned, a swan-like grace
Of haughtiness without pretence,
And to unfold a still magnificence,
Was princely Dion, in the power   5
And beauty of his happier hour.
And what pure homage *then* did wait
On Dion's virtues, while the lunar beam
Of Plato's genius, from its lofty sphere,
Fell round him in the grove of Academe,   10
Softening their inbred dignity austere —
    That he, not too elate
    With self-sufficing solitude,
But with majestic lowliness endued,
    Might in the universal bosom reign,   15
And from affectionate observance gain
Help, under every change of adverse fate.

II.

Five thousand warriors — O the rapturous day !
Each crowned with flowers, and armed with spear and
    shield,
Or ruder weapon which their course might yield,   20
To Syracuse advance in bright array.
Who leads them on ? — The anxious people see
Long-exiled Dion, marching at their head,
He also crowned with flowers of Sicily,
And in a white, far-beaming corselet clad !   25
Pure transport undisturbed by doubt or fear
The gazers feel; and, rushing to the plain,
Salute those strangers as a holy train
Or blest procession (to the Immortals dear)
That brought their precious liberty again.   30
Lo ! when the gates are entered, on each hand,
Down the long street, rich goblets filled with wine
      In seemly order stand,
On tables set, as if for rights divine ; —
And, as the great Deliverer marches by,   35
   He looks on festal ground with fruits bestrown ;
And flowers are on his person thrown
    In boundless prodigality ;
Nor doth the general voice abstain from prayer,
Invoking Dion's tutelary care,   40
As if a very Deity he were !

III.

Mourn, hills and groves of Attica ! and mourn
Ilissus, bending o'er thy classic urn !
Mourn, and lament for him whose spirit dreads
Your once sweet memory, studious walks and shades ! 45
For him who to divinity aspired,

Not on the breath of popular applause,
But through dependence on the sacred laws
Framed in the schools where Wisdom dwelt retired,
Intent to trace the ideal path of right   50
(More fair than heaven's broad causeway paved with
    stars)
Which Dion learned to measure with sublime delight ; —
But He hath overleaped the eternal bars ;
And, following guides whose craft holds no consent
With aught that breathes the ethereal element,   55
Hath stained the robes of civil power with blood,
Unjustly shed, though for the public good.
Whence doubts that came too late, and wishes vain,
Hollow excuses, and triumphant pain ;
And oft his cogitations sink as low   60
As, through the abysses of a joyless heart,
The heaviest plummet of despair can go —
But whence that sudden check ? that fearful start !
    He hears an uncouth sound —
    Anon his lifted eyes   65
Saw, at a long-drawn gallery's dusky bound,
A Shape of more than mortal size
And hideous aspect, stalking round and round !
    A woman's garb the Phantom wore,
    And fiercely swept the marble floor, —   70
    Like Auster whirling to and fro,
    His force on Caspian foam to try ;
Or Boreas when he scours the snow
That skins the plains of Thessaly,
Or when aloft on Mænalus he stops   75
His flight, 'mid eddying pine-tree tops !

IV.

So, but from toil less sign of profit reaping,
The sullen Spectre to her purpose bowed,
        Sweeping — vehemently sweeping —
No pause admitted, no design avowed !   80
" Avaunt, inexplicable Guest ! — avaunt,"
Exclaimed the Chieftain —" let me rather see
The coronal that coiling vipers make ;
The torch that flames with many a lurid flake,
And the long train of doleful pageantry   85
Which they behold, whom vengeful Furies haunt ;
Who, while they struggle from the scourge to flee,
Move where the blasted soil is not unworn,
And, in their anguish, bear what other minds have
        borne ! "

V.

But Shapes that come not at an earthly call,   90
Will not depart when mortal voices bid ;
Lords of the visionary eye whose lid,
Once raised, remains aghast, and will not fall !
Ye Gods, thought He, that servile Implement
Obeys a mystical intent !   95
Your Minister would brush away
The spots that to my soul adhere ;
But should she labour night and day,
They will not, cannot disappear ;
Whence angry pertubations, — and that look   100
Which no Philosophy can brook !

VI.

Ill-fated Chief ! there are whose hopes are built
Upon the ruins of thy glorious name ;
Who, through the portal of one moment's guilt,

Pursue thee with their deadly aim !
O matchless perfidy ! portentous lust
Of monstrous crime ! — that horror-striking blade,
Drawn in defiance of the Gods, hath laid
The noble Syracusan low in dust !
Shuddered the walls — the marble city wept —   110
And sylvan places heaved a pensive sigh ;
But in calm peace the appointed Victim slept,
As he had fallen in magnanimity ;
Of spirit too capacious to require
That Destiny her course should change ; too just   115
To his own native greatness to desire
That wretched boon, days lengthened by mistrust.
So were the hopeless troubles, that involved
The soul of Dion, instantly dissolved.
Released from life and cares of princely state,   120
He left this moral grafted on his Fate ;
" Him only pleasure leads, and peace attends,
Him, only him, the shield of Jove defends,
Whose means are fair and spotless as his ends."
                                        1816.

THE SWAN ON LOCARNO.

(ORIGINALLY THE OPENING STANZA OF DION.)

FAIR is the Swan, whose majesty, prevailing
O'er breezeless water, on Locarno's lake,
Bears him on while proudly sailing
He leaves behind a moon-illumined wake :
Behold ! the mantling spirit of reserve   5
Fashions his neck into a goodly curve ;
An arch thrown back between luxuriant wings

Of whitest garniture, like fir-tree boughs
To which, on some unruffled morning, clings
A flaky weight of winter's purest snows !   10
— Behold ! — as with a gushing impulse heaves
That downy prow, and softly cleaves
The mirror of the crystal flood,
Vanish inverted hill, and shadowy wood,
And pendent rocks, where'er, in gliding state,   15
Winds the mute Creature without visible Mate
Or Rival, save the Queen of night
Showering down a silver light,
From heaven, upon her chosen Favourite !

                                                                    1816.

ODE TO LYCORIS. MAY, 1817.

I.

An age hath been when Earth was proud
Of lustre too intense
To be sustained ; and Mortals bowed
The front in self-defence.
Who *then*, if Dian's crescent gleamed,   5
Or Cupid's sparkling arrow streamed
While on the wing the Urchin played,
Could fearlessly approach the shade ?
— Enough for one soft vernal day,
If I, a bard of ebbing time,   10
And nurtured in a fickle clime,
May haunt this hornèd bay ;
Whose amorous water multiplies
The flitting halcyon's vivid dyes ;
And smooths her liquid breast — to show   15
These swan-like specks of mountain snow,

White as the pair that slid along the plains
Of heaven, when Venus held the reins!

II.

In youth we love the darksome lawn
Brushed by the owlet's wing;　　　　　　　　20
Then, Twilight is preferred to Dawn,
And Autumn to the Spring.
Sad fancies do we then affect,
In luxury of disrespect
To our own prodigal excess　　　　　　　　25
Of too familiar happiness.
Lycoris (if such name befit
Thee, thee my life's celestial sign!)
When Nature marks the year's decline,
Be ours to welcome it;　　　　　　　　　30
Pleased with the harvest hope that runs
Before the path of milder suns;
Pleased while the sylvan world displays
Its ripeness to the feeding gaze;
Pleased when the sullen winds resound the knell　35
Of the resplendent miracle.

III.

But something whispers to my heart
That, as we downward tend,
Lycoris! life requires an *art*
To which our souls must bend;　　　　　　40
A skill — to balance and supply;
And, ere the flowing fount be dry,
As soon it must, a sense to sip,
Or drink, with no fastidious lip.
Then welcome, above all, the Guest　　　　45
Whose smiles, diffused o'er land and sea,

Seem to recall the Deity
Of youth into the breast:
May pensive Autumn ne'er present
A claim to her disparagement! 50
While blossoms and the budding spray
Inspire us in our own decay;
Still, as we nearer draw to life's dark goal,
Be hopeful Spring the favourite of the Soul!

    1817.

THE LONGEST DAY.

ADDRESSED TO MY DAUGHTER.

LET us quit the leafy arbour,
And the torrent murmuring by;
For the sun is in his harbour,
Weary of the open sky.

Evening now unbinds the fetters 5
Fashioned by the glowing light;
All that breathe are thankful debtors
To the harbinger of night.

Yet by some grave thoughts attended
Eve renews her calm career: 10
For the day that now is ended,
Is the longest of the year.

Dora! sport, as now thou sportest,
On this platform, light and free;
Take thy bliss, while longest, shortest, 15
Are indifferent to thee!

Who would check the happy feeling
That inspires the linnet's song?
Who would stop the swallow, wheeling
On her pinions swift and strong?   20

Yet at this impressive season,
Words which tenderness can speak
From the truths of homely reason,
Might exalt the loveliest cheek;

And, while shades to shades succeeding   25
Steal the landscape from the sight,
I would urge this moral pleading,
Last forerunner of "Good night!"

SUMMER ebbs;—each day that follows
Is a reflux from on high,   30
Tending to the darksome hollows
Where the frosts of winter lie.

He who governs the creation,
In his providence, assigned
Such a gradual declination   35
To the life of human kind.

Yet we mark it not;—fruits redden,
Fresh flowers blow as flowers have blown,
And the heart is loth to deaden
Hopes that she so long hath known.   40

Be thou wiser, youthful Maiden!
And when thy decline shall come,
Let not flowers, or boughs fruit-laden,
Hide the knowledge of thy doom.

Now, even now, ere wrapped in slumber, 45
Fix thine eyes upon the sea
That absorbs time, space, and number;
Look thou to Eternity !

Follow thou the flowing river
On whose breast are thither borne 50
All deceived, and each deceiver,
Through the gates of night and morn;

Through the year's successive portals ;
Through the bounds which many a star
Marks, not mindless of frail mortals 55
When his light returns from far.

Thus when thou with Time hast travelled
Toward the mighty gulf of things,
And the mazy stream unravelled
With thy best imaginings ; 60

Think, if thou on beauty leanest,
Think how pitiful that stay,
Did not virtue give the meanest
Charms superior to decay.

Duty, like a strict preceptor, 65
Sometimes frowns, or seems to frown ;
Choose her thistle for thy sceptre,
While youth's roses are thy crown.

Grasp it, — if thou shrink and tremble,
Fairest damsel of the green, 70
Thou wilt lack the only symbol
That proclaims a genuine queen ;

And ensures those palms of honour
Which selected spirits wear,
Bending low before the Donor,   75
Lord of heaven's unchanging year!

1817.

COMPOSED UPON AN EVENING OF EXTRAORDINARY SPLENDOUR AND BEAUTY.

I.

HAD this effulgence disappeared
With flying haste, I might have sent,
Among the speechless clouds, a look
Of blank astonishment;
But 'tis endued with power to stay,   5
And sanctify one closing day,
That frail Mortality may see —
What is? — ah no, but what *can* be!
Time was when field and watery cove
With modulated echoes rang,   10
While choirs of fervent Angels sang
Their vespers in the grove;
Or, crowning, star-like, each some sovereign height,
Warbled, for heaven above and earth below,
Strains suitable to both. — Such holy rite,   15
Methinks, if audibly repeated now
From hill or valley, could not move
Sublimer transport, purer love,
Than doth this silent spectacle — the gleam —
The shadow — and the peace supreme!   20

II.

No sound is uttered, — but a deep
And solemn harmony pervades
The hollow vale from steep to steep,
And penetrates the glades.
Far-distant images draw nigh,   25
Called forth by wondrous potency
Of beamy radiance, that imbues
Whate'er it strikes, with gem-like hues!
In vision exquisitely clear,
Herds range along the mountain side ;   30
And glistening antlers are descried ;
And gilded flocks appear.
Thine is the tranquil hour, purpureal Eve !
But long as god-like wish, or hope divine,
Informs my spirit, ne'er can I believe   35
That this magnificence is wholly thine !
— From worlds not quickened by the sun
A portion of the gift is won ;
An intermingling of Heaven's pomp is spread
On ground which British shepherds tread !   40

III.

And, if there be whom broken ties
Afflict, or injuries assail,
Yon hazy ridges to their eyes
Present a glorious scale,
Climbing suffused with sunny air,   45
To stop — no record hath told where !
And tempting Fancy to ascend,
And with immortal Spirits blend ![1]
— Wings at my shoulders seem to play ;

[1] See Note.

But, rooted here, I stand and gaze 50
On those bright steps that heavenward raise
Their practicable way.
Come forth, ye drooping old men, look abroad,
And see to what fair countries ye are bound !
And if some traveller, weary of his road, 55
Hath slept since noon-tide on the grassy ground,
Ye Genii ! to his covert speed ;
And wake him with such gentle heed
As may attune his soul to meet the dower
Bestowed on this transcendent hour ! 60

IV.

Such hues from their celestial Urn
Were wont to stream before mine eye,
Where'er it wandered in the morn
Of blissful infancy.
This glimpse of glory, why renewed ? 65
Nay, rather speak with gratitude ;
For, if a vestige of those gleams
Survived, 't was only in my dreams.
Dread Power ! whom peace and calmness serve
No less than Nature's threatening voice, 70
If aught unworthy be my choice,
From THEE if I would swerve ;
Oh, let thy grace remind me of the light
Full early lost, and fruitlessly deplored ;
Which, at this moment, on my waking sight 75
Appears to shine, by miracle restored ;
My soul, though yet confined to earth,
Rejoices in a second birth !
— 'T is past, the visionary splendour fades ;
And night approaches with her shades. 80

1818.

NOTE.— The multiplication of mountain-ridges, described at the commencement of the third Stanza of this Ode, as a kind of Jacob's Ladder, leading to Heaven, is produced either by watery vapours, or sunny haze ; — in the present instance by the latter cause. Allusions to the Ode, entitled "Intimations of Immortality," pervade the last stanza of the foregoing Poem.

SEPTEMBER, 1819.

THE sylvan slopes with corn-clad fields
Are hung, as if with golden shields,
Bright trophies of the sun !
Like a fair sister of the sky,
Unruffled doth the blue lake lie,   5
The mountains looking on.

And, sooth to say, yon vocal grove,
Albeit uninspired by love,
By love untaught to ring,
May well afford to mortal ear   10
An impulse more profoundly dear
Than music of the Spring.

For *that* from turbulence and heat
Proceeds, from some uneasy seat
In nature's struggling frame,   15
Some region of impatient life :
And jealousy, and quivering strife,
Therein a portion claim.

This, this is holy ; — while I hear
These vespers of another year,   20
This hymn of thanks and praise,

My spirit seems to mount above
The anxieties of human love,
And earth's precarious days.

But list ! — though winter storms be nigh, 25
Unchecked is that soft harmony :
There lives Who can provide
For all his creatures ; and in Him,
Even like the radiant Seraphim,
These choristers confide. 30

———

UPON THE SAME OCCASION.

DEPARTING summer hath assumed
An aspect tenderly illumed,
The gentlest look of spring ;
That calls from yonder leafy shade
Unfaded, yet prepared to fade, 5
A timely carolling.

No faint and hesitating trill,
Such tribute as to winter chill
The lonely redbreast pays !
Clear, loud, and lively is the din, 10
From social warblers gathering in
Their harvest of sweet lays.

Nor doth the example fail to cheer
Me, conscious that my leaf is sere,
And yellow on the bough : — 15
Fall, rosy garlands, from my head !
Ye myrtle wreaths, your fragrance shed
Around a younger brow !

Yet will I temperately rejoice ;
Wide is the range, and free the choice   20
Of undiscordant themes ;
Which, haply, kindred souls may prize
Not less than vernal ecstasies,
And passion's feverish dreams.

For deathless powers to verse belong,   25
And they like Demi-gods are strong
On whom the Muses smile ;
But some their function have disclaimed,
Best pleased with what is aptliest framed
To enervate and defile.   30

Not such the initiatory strains
Committed to the silent plains
In Britain's earliest dawn :
Trembled the groves, the stars grew pale,
While all-too-daringly the veil   35
Of nature was withdrawn !

Nor such the spirit-stirring note
When the live chords Alcæus smote,
Inflamed by sense of wrong ;
Woe ! woe to Tyrants ! from the lyre   40
Broke threateningly, in sparkles dire
Of fierce vindictive song.

And not unhallowed was the page
By wingèd Love inscribed, to assuage
The pangs of vain pursuit ;
Love listening while the Lesbian Maid   45
With finest touch of passion swayed
Her own Æolian lute.

O ye, who patiently explore
The wreck of Herculanean lore,   50
What rapture ! could ye seize
Some Theban fragment, or unroll
One precious, tender-hearted scroll,
Of pure Simonides.

That were, indeed a genuine birth   55
Of poesy ; a bursting forth
Of genius from the dust:
What Horace gloried to behold,
What Maro loved, shall we enfold?
Can haughty Time be just !   60

                                        1819.

TO THE REV. DR. WORDSWORTH.

(WITH THE SONNETS TO THE RIVER DUDDON, AND OTHER POEMS
IN THIS COLLECTION, 1820.)

THE Minstrels played their Christmas tune
To-night beneath my cottage-eaves ;
While, smitten by a lofty moon,
The encircling laurels, thick with leaves,
Gave back a rich and dazzling sheen,   5
That overpowered their natural green.

Through hill and valley every breeze
Had sunk to rest with folded wings :
Keen was the air, but could not freeze,
Nor check, the music of the strings ;   10
So stout and hardy were the band
That scraped the chords with strenuous hand ;

And who but listened?—till was paid
Respect to every Inmate's claim :
The greeting given, the music played,   15
In honour of each household name,
Duly pronounced with lusty call,
And "merry Christmas" wished to all!

O Brother! I revere the choice
That took thee from thy native hills ;   20
And it is given thee to rejoice :
Though public care full often tills
(Heaven only witness of the toil)
A barren and ungrateful soil.

Yet, would that Thou, with me and mine,   25
Hadst heard this never-failing rite ;
And seen on other faces shine
A true revival of the light
Which Nature and these rustic Powers,
In simple childhood, spread through ours.   30

For pleasure hath not ceased to wait
On these expected annual rounds ;
Whether the rich man's sumptuous gate
Call forth the unelaborate sounds,
Or they are offered at the door   35
That guards the lowliest of the poor.

How touching, when at midnight, sweep
Snow-muffled winds, and all is dark,
To hear—and sink again to sleep !
Or, at an earlier call, to mark,   40
By blazing fire, the still suspense
Of self-complacent innocence ;

The mutual nod, — the grave disguise
Of hearts with gladness brimming o'er ;
And some unbidden tears that rise   45
For names once heard, and heard no more ;
Tears brightened by the serenade
For infant in the cradle laid.

Ah ! not for emerald fields alone,
With ambient streams more pure and bright   50
Than fabled Cytherea's zone
Glittering before the Thunderer's sight,
Is to my heart of hearts endeared
The ground where we were born and reared !

Hail, ancient Manners ! sure defence,   55
Where they survive, of wholesome laws ;
Remnants of love whose modest sense
Thus into narrow room withdraws ;
Hail, Usages of pristine mould,
And ye that guard them, Mountains old !   60

Bear with me, Brother ! quench the thought
That slights this passion, or condemns ;
If thee fond Fancy ever brought
From the proud margin of the Thames,
And Lambeth's venerable towers,   65
To humbler streams, and greener bowers.

Yes, they can make, who fail to find,
Short leisure even in busiest days ;
Moments, to cast a look behind,
And profit by those kindly rays   70
That through the clouds do sometimes steal,
And all the far-off past reveal.

Hence, while the imperial City's din
Beats frequent on thy satiate ear,
A pleased attention I may win   75
To agitations less severe,
That neither overwhelm nor cloy,
But fill the hollow vale with joy !

TO THE LADY FLEMING.

ON SEEING THE FOUNDATION PREPARING FOR THE ERECTION OF
RYDAL CHAPEL, WESTMORELAND.

I.

BLEST is this Isle — our native Land ;
Where battlement and moated gate
Are objects only for the hand
Of hoary Time to decorate ;
Where shady hamlet, town that breathes   5
Its busy smoke in social wreaths,
No rampart's stern defence require,
Nought but the heaven-directed spire,
And steeple tower (with pealing bells
Far-heard) — our only citadels.   10

II.

O Lady ! from a noble line
Of chieftains sprung, who stoutly bore
The spear, yet gave to works divine
A bounteous help in days of yore,
(As records mouldering in the Dell   15
Of Nightshade[1] haply yet may tell)

[1] Bekangs Ghyll — or the Dell of Nightshade — in which stands
St. Mary's Abbey in Low Furness.

Thee kindred aspirations moved
To build, within a vale beloved,
For Him upon whose high behests
All peace depends, all safety rests.   20

III.

How fondly will the woods embrace
This daughter of thy pious care,
Lifting her front with modest grace
To make a fair recess more fair ;
And to exalt the passing hour ;   25
Or soothe it with a healing power
Drawn from the Sacrifice fulfilled,
Before this rugged soil was tilled,
Or human habitation rose
To interrupt the deep repose !   30

IV.

Well may the villagers rejoice !
Nor heat, nor cold, nor weary ways,
Will be a hindrance to the voice
That would unite in prayer and praise ;
More duly shall wild wandering Youth   35
Receive the curb of sacred truth,
Shall tottering Age, bent earthward, hear
The Promise, with uplifted ear ;
And all shall welcome the new ray
Imparted to their sabbath-day.   40

V.

Nor deem the Poet's hope misplaced,
His fancy cheated — that can see
A shade upon the future cast,
Of time's pathetic sanctity ;

Can hear the monitory clock 45
Sound o'er the lake with gentle shock
At evening, when the ground beneath
Is ruffled o'er with cells of death ;
Where happy generations lie,
Here tutored for eternity. 50

VI.

Lives there a man whose sole delights
Are trivial pomp and city noise,
Hardening a heart that loathes or slights
What every natural heart enjoys?
Who never caught a noon-tide dream 55
From murmur of a running stream ;
Could strip, for aught the prospect yields
To him, their verdure from the fields ;
And take the radiance from the clouds
In which the sun his setting shrouds. 60

VII.

A soul so pitiably forlorn,
If such do on this earth abide,
May season apathy with scorn,
May turn indifference to pride;
And still be not unblest— compared 65
With him who grovels, self-debarred
From all that lies within the scope
Of holy faith and christian hope ;
Or, shipwrecked, kindles on the coast
False fires, that others may be lost. 70

VIII.

Alas ! that such perverted zeal
Should spread on Britain's favoured ground !

That public order, private weal,
Should e'er have felt or feared a wound
From champions of the desperate law　　　75
Which from their own blind hearts they draw;
Who tempt their reason to deny
God, whom their passions dare defy,
And boast that they alone are free
Who reach this dire extremity!　　　80

IX.

But turn we from these " bold bad " men ;
The way, mild Lady ! that hath led
Down to their " dark opprobrious den,"
Is all too rough for Thee to tread.
Softly as morning vapours glide　　　85
Down Rydal-cove from Fairfield's side,
Should move the tenor of *his* song
Who means to charity no wrong ;
Whose offering gladly would accord
With this day's work, in thought and word.　　　90

X.

Heaven prosper it ! may peace, and love,
And hope, and consolation, fall,
Through its meek influence, from above,
And penetrate the hearts of all ;
All who, around the hollowed Fane,　　　95
Shall sojourn in this fair domain ;
Grateful to Thee, while service pure,
And ancient ordinance, shall endure,
For opportunity bestowed
To kneel together, and adore their God !　　　100

1823.

TO ———.

O DEARER far than light and life are dear,
Full oft our human foresight I deplore ;
Trembling, through my unworthiness, with fear
That friends, by death disjoined, may meet no more !

Misgivings, hard to vanquish or control,   5
Mix with the day, and cross the hour of rest ;
While all the future, for thy purer soul,
With "sober certainties" of love is blest.

That sigh of thine, not meant for human ear,
Tells that these words thy humbleness offend;   10
Yet bear me up — else faltering in the rear
Of a steep march : support me to the end.

Peace settles where the intellect is meek,
And Love is dutiful in thought and deed ;
Through Thee communion with that Love I seek :   15
The faith Heaven strengthens where *he* moulds the
    Creed.   1824.

WRITTEN IN A BLANK LEAF OF MACPHERSON'S OSSIAN.

OFT have I caught, upon a fitful breeze,
Fragments of far-off melodies,
With ear not coveting the whole,
A part so charmed the pensive soul.
While a dark storm before my sight   5
Was yielding, on a mountain height
Loose vapours have I watched, that won
Prismatic colours from the sun ;

Nor felt a wish that heaven would show
The image of its perfect bow.   10
What need, then, of these finished Strains?
Away with counterfeit Remains!
An abbey in its lone recess,
A temple of the wilderness,
Wrecks though they be, announce with feeling   15
The majesty of honest dealing.
Spirit of Ossian! if imbound
In language thou may'st yet be found,
If aught (intrusted to the pen
Or floating on the tongues of men,   20
Albeit shattered and impaired)
Subsist thy dignity to guard,
In concert with memorial claim
Of old grey stone, and high-born name
That cleaves to rock or pillared cave   25
Where moans the blast, or beats the wave,
Let Truth, stern arbitress of all,
Interpret that Original,
And for presumptuous wrongs atone; —
Authentic words be given, or none!   30
    Time is not blind; — yet He, who spares
Pyramid pointing to the stars,
Hath preyed with ruthless appetite
On all that marked the primal flight
Of the poetic ecstasy   35
Into the land of mystery.
No tongue is able to rehearse
One measure, Orpheus! of thy verse;
Musæus, stationed with his lyre
Supreme among the Elysian quire,   40
Is, for the dwellers upon earth,
Mute as a lark e'er morning's birth.

Why grieve for these, though past away
The music, and extinct the lay?
When thousands, by severer doom,　　　　　　45
Full early to the silent tomb
Have sunk, at Nature's call; or strayed
From hope and promise, self-betrayed;
The garland withering on their brows;
Stung with remorse for broken vows;　　　50
Frantic — else how might they rejoice?
And friendless, by their own sad choice!

　　Hail, Bards of mightier grasp! on you
I chiefly call, the chosen Few,
Who cast not off the acknowledged guide,　　55
Who faltered not, nor turned aside;
Whose lofty genius could survive
Privation, under sorrow thrive;
In whom the fiery Muse revered
The symbol of a snow-white beard,　　　　60
Bedewed with meditative tears
Dropped from the lenient cloud of years.

　　Brothers in soul! though distant times
Produced you nursed in various climes,
Ye, when the orb of life had waned,　　　　65
A plenitude of love retained:
Hence, while in you each sad regret
By corresponding hope was met,
Ye lingered among human kind,
Sweet voices for the passing wind,　　　　70
Departing sunbeams, loth to stop,
Though smiling on the last hill top!
Such to the tender-hearted maid
Even ere her joys begin to fade;
Such, haply, to the rugged chief　　　　　75
By fortune crushed, or tamed by grief;

Appears, on Morven's lonely shore,
Dim-gleaming through imperfect lore,
The Son of Fingal ; such was blind
Mæonides of ampler mind ;   80
Such Milton, to the fountain head
Of glory by Urania led !
                                                   1824.

TO A SKY-LARK.

ETHEREAL minstrel ! pilgrim of the sky !
Dost thou despise the earth where cares abound ?
Or, while the wings aspire, are heart and eye
Both with thy nest upon the dewy ground ?
Thy nest which thou canst drop into at will,   5
Those quivering wings composed, that music still !

Leave to the nightingale her shady wood ;
A privacy of glorious light is thine ;
Whence thou dost pour upon the world a flood
Of harmony, with instinct more divine ;   10
Type of the wise who soar, but never roam ;
True to the kindred points of Heaven and Home !
                                                   1825.

"THE DAISY SLEEPS." [1]

(A FRAGMENT.)

THE daisy sleeps upon the dewy lawn,
Not lifting yet the head that evening bowed ;
But *He* is risen, a later star of dawn,
Glittering and twinkling near yon rosy cloud ;

[1] See Note, p. 476.

Bright gem instinct with music, vocal spark;   5
The happiest bird that sprang out of the Ark!

Hail, blest above all kinds! — Supremely skilled
Restless with fixed to balance, high with low,
Thou leav'st the halcyon free her hopes to build
On such forbearance as the deep may show;   10
Perpetual flight, unchecked by earthly ties,
Leav'st to the wandering bird of paradise.

Faithful, though swift as lightning, the meek dove;
Yet more hath Nature reconciled in thee;
So constant with thy downward eye of love,   15
Yet, in aërial singleness, so free;
So humble, yet so ready to rejoice
In power of wing and never-wearied voice.

To the last point of vision, and beyond,
Mount, daring warbler! — that love-prompted strain,   20
('Twixt thee and thine a never-failing bond)
Thrills not the less the bosom of the plain:
Yet might'st thou seem, proud privilege! to sing
All independent of the leafy spring.

How would it please old Ocean to partake,   25
With sailors longing for a breeze in vain,
The harmony thy notes most gladly make
Where earth resembles most his own domain!
Urania's self might welcome with pleased ear
These matins mounting towards her native sphere.   30

Chanter by heaven attracted, whom no bars
To day-light known deter from that pursuit,
'Tis well that some sage instinct, when the stars

Come forth at evening, keeps Thee still and mute ;
For not an eyelid could to sleep incline   35
Wert thou among them, singing as they shine !

                                        1828.

TO MAY.

Though many suns have risen and set
    Since thou, blithe May, wert born,
And Bards, who hailed thee, may forget
    Thy gifts, thy beauty scorn ;
There are who to a birthday strain   5
    Confine not harp and voice,
But evermore throughout thy reign
    Are grateful and rejoice !

Delicious odours ! music sweet,
    Too sweet to pass away !   10
Oh for a deathless song to meet
    The soul's desire — a lay
That, when a thousand years are told,
    Should praise thee, genial Power !
Through summer heat, autumnal cold,   15
    And winter's dreariest hour.

Earth, sea, thy presence feel, — nor less,
    If yon ethereal blue
With its soft smile the truth express,
    The heavens have felt it too.   20
The inmost heart of man if glad
    Partakes a livelier cheer ;
And eyes that cannot but be sad
    Let fall a brightened tear.

Since thy return, through days and weeks 25
  Of hope that grew by stealth,
How many wan and faded cheeks
  Have kindled into health !
The Old by thee revived, have said,
  " Another year is ours " ; 30
And wayworn Wanderers, poorly fed
  Have smiled upon thy flowers.

Who tripping lisps a merry song
  Amid his playful peers?
The tender Infant who was long 35
  A prisoner of fond fears ;
But now, when every sharp-edged blast
  Is quiet in its sheath,
His Mother leaves him free to taste
  Earth's sweetness in thy breath. 40

Thy help is with the weed that creeps
  Along the humblest ground ;
No cliff so bare but on its steeps
  Thy favours may be found ;
But most on some peculiar nook 45
  That our own hands have drest,
Thou and thy train are proud to look,
  And seem to love it best.

And yet how pleased we wander forth
  When May is whispering, " Come ! 50
" Choose from the bowers of virgin earth
  " The happiest for your home ;
" Heaven's bounteous love through me is spread
  " From sunshine, clouds, winds, waves,
" Drops on the mouldering turret's head, 55
  " And on your turf-clad graves ! "

Such greeting heard, away with sighs
　　For lilies that must fade,
Or " the rathe primrose as it dies
　　Forsaken " in the shade !　　　　　　　　60
Vernal fruitions and desires
　　Are linked in endless chase ;
While, as one kindly growth retires,
　　Another takes its place.

And what if thou, sweet May, hast known,　　65
　　Mishap by worm and blight ;
If expectations newly blown
　　Have perished in thy sight ;
If loves and joys, while up they sprung,
　　Were caught as in a snare ;　　　　　　　70
Such is the lot of all the young,
　　However bright and fair.

Lo ! Streams that April could not check
　　Are patient of thy rule ;
Gurgling in foamy water-break,　　　　　　75
　　Loitering in glassy pool ;
By thee, thee only, could be sent
　　Such gentle mists as glide,
Curling with unconfirmed intent,
　　On that green mountain's side.　　　　　80

How delicate the leafy veil
　　Through which yon house of God
Gleams, mid the peace of this deep dale
　　By few but shepherds trod !
And lowly huts, near beaten ways,　　　　　85
　　No sooner stand attired
In thy fresh wreaths, than they for praise
　　Peep forth, and are admired.

Season of fancy and of hope,
   Permit not for one hour,   90
A blossom from thy crown to drop,
   Nor add to it a flower !
Keep, lovely May, as if by touch
   Of self-restraining art,
This modest charm of not too much,   95
   Part seen, imagined part !

1826-1834.

THE WISHING-GATE.

In the vale of Grasmere, by the side of the old high-way leading to Amble-side, is a gate, which, time out of mind, has been called the Wishing-gate, from a belief that wishes formed or indulged there have a favourable issue.

HOPE rules a land forever green :
All powers that serve the bright-eyed Queen
   Are confident and gay ;
Clouds at her bidding disappear ;
Points she to aught ? — the bliss draws near,   5
   And Fancy smooths the way.

Not such the land of Wishes — there
Dwell fruitless day-dreams, lawless prayer,
   And thoughts with things at strife ;
Yet how forlorn, should *ye* depart   10
Ye superstitions of the *heart*,
   How poor, were human life !

When magic lore abjured its might,
Ye did not forfeit one dear right,
   One tender claim abate ;   15

Witness this symbol of your sway,
Surviving near the public way
　　The rustic Wishing-gate !

Inquire not if the faery race
Shed kindly influence on the place,　　　　　20
　　Ere northward they retired ;
If here a warrior left a spell,
Panting for glory as he fell ;
　　Or here a saint expired.

Enough that all around is fair,　　　　　25
Composed with Nature's finest care,
　　And in her fondest love —
Peace to embosom and content —
To overawe the turbulent,
　　The selfish to reprove.　　　　　30

Yea ! even the Stranger from afar,
Reclining on this moss-grown bar,
　　Unknowing, and unknown,
The infection of the ground partakes,
Longing for his Beloved — who makes　　　　　35
　　All happiness her own.

Then why should conscious Spirits fear
The mystic stirrings that are here,
　　The ancient faith disclaim ?
The local Genius ne'er befriends　　　　　40
Desires whose course in folly ends,
　　Whose just reward is shame.

Smile if thou wilt, but not in scorn,
If some, by ceaseless pains outworn,
　　Here crave an easier lot ;　　　　　45

If some have thirsted to renew
A broken vow, or bind a true,
   With firmer, holier knot.

And not in vain, when thoughts are cast
Upon the irrevocable past,   50
   Some Penitent sincere
May for a worthier future sigh,
While trickles from his downcast eye
   No unavailing tear.

The Worldling, pining to be freed   55
From turmoil, who would turn or speed
   The current of his fate,
Might stop before this favoured scene,
At Nature's call, nor blush to lean
   Upon the Wishing-gate.   60

The Sage, who feels how blind, how weak
Is man, though loth such help to *seek*,
   Yet, passing, here might pause,
And thirst for insight to allay
Misgiving, while the crimson day   65
   In quietness withdraws ;

Or when the church-clock's knell profound
To Time's first step across the bound
   Of midnight makes reply ;
Time pressing on with starry crest,   70
To filial sleep upon the breast
   Of dread eternity.

                1828.

"IN THESE FAIR VALES HATH MANY A TREE."

In these fair vales hath many a Tree
   At Wordsworth's suit been spared;
And from the builder's hand this Stone,
For some rude beauty of its own,
   Was rescued by the Bard: 5
So let it rest; and time will come
   When here the tender-hearted
May heave a gentle sigh for him,
   As one of the departed.

                 1830.

THE PRIMROSE OF THE ROCK.

A Rock there is whose homely front
   The passing traveller slights;
Yet there the glow-worms hang their lamps,
   Like stars, at various heights;
And one coy Primrose to that Rock   5
   The vernal breeze invites.

What hideous warfare hath been waged,
   What kingdoms overthrown,
Since first I spied that Primrose-tuft
   And marked it for my own;   10
A lasting link in Nature's chain
   From highest heaven let down!

The flowers, still faithful to the stems,
   Their fellowship renew;
The stems are faithful to the root,   15
   That worketh out of view;

And to the rock the root adheres
  In every fibre true.

Close clings to earth the living rock,
  Though threatening still to fall;   20
The earth is constant to her sphere ;
  And God upholds them all :
So blooms this lonely Plant, nor dreads
  Her annual funeral.

     .   .   .   .

Here closed the meditative strain ;   25
  But air breathed soft that day,
The hoary mountain-heights were cheered,
  The sunny vale looked gay;
And to the Primrose of the Rock
  I gave this after-lay.   30

I sang — Let myriads of bright flowers,
  Like Thee, in field and grove
Revive unenvied ; — mightier far,
  Than tremblings that reprove
Our vernal tendencies to hope,   35
  Is God's redeeming love ;

That love which changed — for wan disease,
  For sorrow that had bent
O'er hopeless dust, for withered age—
  Their moral element,   40
And turned the thistles of a curse
  To types beneficent.

Sin-blighted though we are, we too,
  The reasoning Sons of Men,
From one oblivious winter called   45
  Shall rise, and breathe again ;

And in eternal summer lose
    Our threescore years and ten.

To humbleness of heart descends
    This prescience from on high,   50
The faith that elevates the just,
    Before and when they die ;
And makes each soul a separate heaven,
    A court for Deity.

                    1831.

YARROW REVISITED.

The following Stanzas are a memorial of a day passed with Sir Walter Scott and other Friends visiting the Banks of the Yarrow under his guidance, immediately before his departure from Abbotsford, for Naples.

    The title *Yarrow Revisited* will stand in no need of explanation for Readers acquainted with the Author's previous poems suggested by that celebrated Stream.

THE gallant Youth, who may have gained,
    Or seeks, a "winsome Marrow,"
Was but an Infant in the lap
    When first I looked on Yarrow ;
Once more, by Newark's Castle-gate   5
    Long left without a warder,
I stood, looked, listened, and with Thee,
    Great Minstrel of the Border !

Grave thoughts ruled wide on that sweet day,
    Their dignity installing   10
In gentle bosoms, while sere leaves
    Were on the bough, or falling ;
But breezes played, and sunshine gleamed —
    The forest to embolden ;
Reddened the fiery hues, and shot   15
    Transparence through the golden.

For busy thoughts the Stream flowed on
   In foamy agitation ;
And slept in many a crystal pool
   For quiet contemplation :   20
No public and no private care
   The freeborn mind enthralling,
We made a day of happy hours,
   Our happy days recalling.

Brisk Youth appeared, the Morn of youth,   25
   With freaks of graceful folly, —
Life's temperate Noon, her sober Eve,
   Her Night not melancholy ;
Past, present, future, all appeared
   In harmony united,   30
Like guests that meet, and some from far,
   By cordial love invited.

And if, as Yarrow, through the woods
   And down the meadow ranging,
Did meet us with unaltered face,   35
   Though we were changed and changing ;
If, *then*, some natural shadows spread
   Our inward prospect over,
The soul's deep valley was not slow
   Its brightness to recover.   40

Eternal blessings on the Muse,
   And her divine employment!
The blameless Muse, who trains her Sons
   For hope and calm enjoyment ;
Albeit sickness, lingering yet,   45
   Has o'er their pillow brooded ;
And Care waylays their steps — a Sprite
   Not easily eluded.

For thee, O SCOTT! compelled to change
   Green Eildon-hill and Cheviot   50
For warm Vesuvio's vine-clad slopes;
   And leave thy Tweed and Tiviot
For mild Sorento's breezy waves ;
   May classic Fancy, linking
With native Fancy her fresh aid,   55
   Preserve thy heart from sinking !

Oh ! while they minister to thee,
   Each vying with the other,
May Health return to mellow Age
   With Strength, her venturous brother;   60
And Tiber, and each brook and rill
   Renowned in song and story,
With unimagined beauty shine,
   Nor lose one ray of glory!

For Thou, upon a hundred streams,   65
   By tales of love and sorrow,
Of faithful love, undaunted truth,
   Hast shed the power of Yarrow;
And streams unknown, hills yet unseen,
   Wherever they invite Thee,   70
At parent Nature's grateful call,
   With gladness must requite Thee.

A gracious welcome shall be thine,
   Such looks of love and honour
As thy own Yarrow gave to me   75
   When first I gazed upon her ;
Beheld what I had feared to see,
   Unwilling to surrender
Dreams treasured up from early days,
   The holy and the tender.   80

And what, for this frail world, were all
   That mortals do or suffer,
Did no responsive harp, no pen,
   Memorial tribute offer?
Yea, what were mighty Nature's self?   85
   Her features, could they win us,
Unhelped by the poetic voice
   That hourly speaks within us?

Nor deem that localised Romance
   Plays false with our affections;   90
Unsanctifies our tears — made sport
   For fanciful dejections:
Ah, no! the visions of the past
   Sustain the heart in feeling
Life as she is — our changeful Life,   95
   With friends and kindred dealing.

Bear witness, Ye, whose thoughts that day
   In Yarrow's groves were centred;
Who through the silent portal arch
   Of mouldering Newark entered;   100
And clomb the winding stair that once
   Too timidly was mounted
By the " last Minstrel," (not the last!)
   Ere he his Tale recounted.

Flow on for ever, Yarrow Stream!   105
   Fulfil thy pensive duty,
Well pleased that future Bards should chant
   For simple hearts thy beauty;
To dream-light dear while yet unseen,
   Dear to the common sunshine,   110
And dearer still, as now I feel,
   To memory's shadowy moonshine!

DEVOTIONAL INCITEMENTS.

" Not to the earth confined,
Ascend to heaven."

WHERE will they stop, those breathing Powers,
The Spirits of the new-born flowers?
They wander with the breeze, they wind
Where'er the streams a passage find;
Up from their native ground they rise   5
In mute aërial harmonies;
From humble violet — modest thyme —
Exhaled, the essential odours climb,
As if no space below the sky
Their subtle flight could satisfy: 10
Heaven will not tax our thoughts with pride
If like ambition be *their* guide.

    Roused by this kindliest of May-showers,
The spirit-quickener of the flowers,
That with moist virtue softly cleaves   15
The buds, and freshens the young leaves,
The birds pour forth their souls in notes
Of rapture from a thousand throats—
Here checked by too impetuous haste,
While there the music runs to waste,   20
With bounty more and more enlarged,
Till the whole air is overcharged;
Give ear, O Man! to their appeal
And thirst for no inferior zeal,
Thou, who canst *think* as well as feel.   25

    Mount from the earth; aspire! aspire!
So pleads the town's cathedral quire,
In strains that from their solemn height
Sink, to attain a loftier flight;
While incense from the altar breathes   30

Rich fragrance in embodied wreaths ;
Or, flung from swinging censer, shrouds
The taper-lights, and curls in clouds
Around angelic Forms, the still
Creation of the painter's skill,   35
That on the service wait concealed
One moment, and the next revealed
— Cast off your bonds, awake, arise,
And for no transient ecstasies !
What else can mean this visual plea   40
Of still or moving imagery —
The iterated summons loud,
Not wasted on the attendant crowd,
Nor wholly lost upon the throng
Hurrying the busy streets along?   45
  Alas ! the sanctities combined
By art to unsensualise the mind,
Decay and languish ; or, as creeds
And humours change, are spurned like weeds :
The priests are from their altars thrust ;   50
Temples are levelled with the dust;
And solemn rites and awful forms
Founder amid fanatic storms.
Yet evermore, through years renewed
In undisturbed vicissitude   55
Of seasons balancing their flight
On the swift wings of day and night,
Kind Nature keeps a heavenly door
Wide open for the scattered Poor.
Where flower-breathed incense to the skies   60
Is wafted in mute harmonies ;
And ground fresh-cloven by the plough
Is fragrant with a humbler vow ;
Where birds and brooks from leafy dells

Chime forth unwearied canticles,　　　　65
And vapours magnify and spread
The glory of the sun's bright head —
Still constant in her worship, still
Conforming to the eternal Will,
Whether men sow or reap the fields,　　　70
Divine monition Nature yields,
That not by bread alone we live,
Or what a hand of flesh can give;
That every day should leave some part
Free for a sabbath of the heart:　　　75
So shall the seventh be truly blest,
From morn to eve, with hallowed rest.

1832.

"CALM IS THE FRAGRANT AIR."

(An Evening Voluntary.)

CALM is the fragrant air, and loth to lose
Day's grateful warmth, tho' moist with falling dews.
Look for the stars, you'll say that there are none;
Look up a second time, and, one by one,
You mark them twinkling out with silvery light,　　　5
And wonder how they could elude the sight!
The birds, of late so noisy in their bowers,
Warbled a while with faint and fainter powers,
But now are silent as the dim-seen flowers:
Nor does the village Church-clock's iron tone　　　10
The time's and season's influence disown;
Nine beats distinctly to each other bound
In drowsy sequence — how unlike the sound
That, in rough winter, oft inflicts a fear
On fireside listeners, doubting what they hear!　　　15

The shepherd, bent on rising with the sun,
Had closed his door before the day was done,
And now with thankful heart to bed doth creep,
And joins his little children in their sleep.
The bat, lured forth where trees the lane o'ershade,   20
Flits and reflits along the close arcade ;
The busy dor-hawk chases the white moth
With burring note, which Industry and Sloth
Might both be pleased with, for it suits them both.
A stream is heard — I see it not, but know   25
By its soft music whence the waters flow :
Wheels and the tread of hoofs are heard no more;
One boat there was, but it will touch the shore
With the next dipping of its slackened oar ;
Faint sound, that, for the gayest of the gay,   30
Might give to serious thought a moment's sway,
As a last token of man's toilsome day !

1832.

"IF THIS GREAT WORLD OF JOY AND PAIN."

IF this great world of joy and pain
    Revolve in one sure track ;
If freedom, set, will rise again,
    And virtue, flown, come back ;
Woe to the purblind crew who fill   5
    The heart with each day's care ;
Nor gain, from past or future, skill
    To bear, and to forbear !

1833.

ON A HIGH PART OF THE COAST OF CUMBERLAND,

EASTER SUNDAY, APRIL 7, THE AUTHOR'S SIXTY-THIRD BIRTHDAY.

(An Evening Voluntary.)

THE Sun, that seemed so mildly to retire,
Flung back from distant climes a streaming fire,
Whose blaze is now subdued to tender gleams,
Prelude of night's approach with soothing dreams.
Look round; — of all the clouds not one is moving;   5
'T is the still hour of thinking, feeling, loving.
Silent, and stedfast as the vaulted sky,
The boundless plain of waters seems to lie: —
Comes that low sound from breezes rustling o'er
The grass-crowned headland that conceals the shore?   10
No ; 't is the earth-voice of the mighty sea,
Whispering how meek and gentle he *can* be !

    Thou Power supreme ! who, arming to rebuke
Offenders, dost put off the gracious look,
And clothe thyself with terrors like the flood   15
Of ocean roused into its fiercest mood,
Whatever discipline thy Will ordain
For the brief course that must for me remain;
Teach me with quick-eared spirit to rejoice
In admonitions of thy softest voice !   20
Whate'er the path these mortal feet may trace,
Breathe through my soul the blessing of thy grace,
Glad, through a perfect love, a faith sincere
Drawn from the wisdom that begins with fear,
Glad to expand ; and, for a season, free   25
From finite cares, to rest absorbed in Thee !

                              1833.

"NOT IN THE LUCID INTERVALS OF LIFE."

(An Evening Voluntary.)

Not in the lucid intervals of life
That come but as a curse to party-strife;
Not in some hour when Pleasure with a sigh
Of languor puts his rosy garland by;
Not in the breathing-times of that poor slave   5
Who daily piles up wealth in Mammon's cave —
Is Nature felt, or can be; nor do words,
Which practised talent readily affords,
Prove that her hand has touched responsive chords;
Nor has her gentle beauty power to move   10
With genuine rapture and with fervent love
The soul of Genius, if he dare to take
Life's rule from passion craved for passion's sake;
Untaught that meekness is the cherished bent
Of all the truly great and all the innocent.   15

But who is innocent? By grace divine,
Not otherwise, O Nature! we are thine,
Through good and evil thine, in just degree
Of rational and manly sympathy.
To all that Earth from pensive hearts is stealing,   20
And Heaven is now to gladdened eyes revealing,
Add every charm the Universe can show
Through every change its aspects undergo —
Care may be respited, but not repealed;
No perfect cure grows on that bounded field.   25
Vain is the pleasure, a false calm the peace,
If He, through whom alone our conflicts cease,
Our virtuous hopes without relapse advance,
Come not to speed the Soul's deliverance;
To the distempered Intellect refuse   30
His gracious help, or give what we abuse.

1834.

TO A CHILD.

WRITTEN IN HER ALBUM.

SMALL service is true service while it lasts :
Of humblest Friends, bright Creature! scorn not one :
The Daisy, by the shadow that it casts,
Protects the lingering dew-drop from the Sun.

1834.

WRITTEN AFTER THE DEATH OF CHARLES LAMB.

To a good Man of most dear memory
This Stone is sacred.   Here he lies apart
From the great city where he first drew breath,
Was reared and taught ; and humbly earned his bread,
To the strict labours of the merchant's desk   5
By duty chained.   Not seldom did those tasks
Tease, and the thought of time so spent depress
His spirit, but the recompence was high ;
Firm Independence, Bounty's rightful sire ;
Affections, warm as sunshine, free as air ;   10
And when the precious hours of leisure came,
Knowledge and wisdom, gained from converse sweet
With books, or while he ranged the crowded streets
With a keen eye, and overflowing heart :
So genius triumphed over seeming wrong,   15
And poured out truth in works by thoughtful love
Inspired — works potent over smiles and tears.
And as round mountain-tops the lightning plays,
Thus innocently sported, breaking forth
As from a cloud of some grave sympathy,   20
Humour and wild instinctive wit, and all

The vivid flashes of his spoken words.
From the most gentle creature nursed in fields
Had been derived the name he bore — a name,
Wherever Christian altars have been raised,   25
Hallowed to meekness and to innocence ;
And if in him meekness at times gave way,
Provoked out of herself by troubles strange,
Many and strange, that hung about his life ;
Still, at the centre of his being, lodged   30
A soul by resignation sanctified :
And if too often, self-reproached, he felt
That innocence belongs not to our kind,
A power that never ceased to abide in him,
Charity, 'mid the multitude of sins   35
That she can cover, left not his exposed
To an unforgiving judgment from just Heaven.
Oh, he was good, if e'er a good Man lived !

.   .   .   .

From a reflecting mind and sorrowing heart
Those simple lines flowed with an earnest wish,   40
Though but a doubting hope, that they might serve
Fitly to guard the precious dust of him
Whose virtues called them forth.   That aim is missed ;
For much that truth most urgently required
Had from a faltering pen been asked in vain :   45
Yet, haply, on the printed page received,
The imperfect record, there, may stand unblamed
As long as verse of mine shall breathe the air
Of memory, or see the light of love.
     Thou wert a scorner of the fields, my Friend,   50
But more in show than truth ; and from the fields,
And from the mountains, to thy rural grave
Transported, my soothed spirit hovers o'er

Its green untrodden turf, and blowing flowers;
And taking up a voice shall speak (tho' still   55
Awed by the theme's peculiar sanctity
Which words less free presumed not even to touch)
Of that fraternal love, whose heaven-lit lamp
From infancy, through manhood, to the last
Of threescore years, and to thy latest hour,   60
Burnt on with ever-strengthening light, enshrined
Within thy bosom.
                    "Wonderful" hath been
The love established between man and man,
"Passing the love of women"; and between
Man and his help-mate in fast wedlock joined   65
Through God, is raised a spirit and soul of love
Without whose blissful influence Paradise
Had been no Paradise; and earth were now
A waste where creatures bearing human form,
Direst of savage beasts, would roam in fear,   70
Joyless and comfortless.   Our days glide on;
And let him grieve who cannot choose but grieve
That he hath been an Elm without his Vine,
And her bright dower of clustering charities,
That, round his trunk and branches, might have clung 75
Enriching and adorning.   Unto thee,
Not so enriched, not so adorned, to thee
Was given (say rather, thou of later birth
Wert given to her) a Sister — 'tis a word
Timidly uttered, for she *lives*, the meek,   80
The self-restraining, and the ever-kind;
In whom thy reason and intelligent heart
Found — for all interests, hopes, and tender cares,
All softening, humanising, hallowing powers,
Whether withheld, or for her sake unsought —   85
More than sufficient recompence!

Her love
(What weakness prompts the voice to tell it here?)
Was as the love of mothers; and when years,
Lifting the boy to man's estate, had called
The long-protected to assume the part 90
Of a protector, the first filial tie
Was undissolved; and, in or out of sight,
Remained imperishably interwoven
With life itself. Thus, 'mid a shifting world,
Did they together testify of time 95
And season's difference— a double tree
With two collateral stems sprung from one root;
Such were they— such thro' life they *might* have been
In union, in partition only such;
Otherwise wrought the will of the Most High; 100
Yet, thro' all visitations and all trials,
Still they were faithful; like two vessels launched
From the same beach one ocean to explore
With mutual help, and sailing— to their league
True, as inexorable winds, or bars 105
Floating or fixed of polar ice, allow.

But turn we rather, let my spirit turn
With thine, O silent and invisible Friend!
To those dear intervals, nor rare nor brief,
When reunited, and by choice withdrawn 110
From miscellaneous converse, ye were taught
That the remembrance of foregone distress,
And the worse fear of future ill (which oft
Doth hang around it, as a sickly child
Upon its mother) may be both alike 115
Disarmed of power to unsettle present good
So prized, and things inward and outward held
In such an even balance, that the heart
Acknowledges God's grace, his mercy feels,

And in its depth of gratitude is still.   120
  O gift divine of quiet sequestration !
The hermit, exercised in prayer and praise,
And feeding daily on the hope of heaven,
Is happy in his vow, and fondly cleaves
To life-long singleness ; but happier far   125
Was to your souls, and, to the thoughts of others,
A thousand times more beautiful appeared,
Your *dual* loneliness.   The sacred tie
Is broken; yet why grieve ? for Time but holds
His moiety in trust, till Joy shall lead   130
To the blest world where parting is unknown.

                                        1835.

EXTEMPORE EFFUSION UPON THE DEATH OF
JAMES HOGG.

WHEN first, descending from the moorlands,
I saw the Stream of Yarrow glide
Along a bare and open valley,
The Ettrick Shepherd was my guide.

When last along its banks I wandered,   5
Through groves that had begun to shed
Their golden leaves upon the pathways,
My steps the Border-minstrel led.

The mighty Minstrel breathes no longer,
'Mid mouldering ruins low he lies ;   10
And death upon the braes of Yarrow,
Has closed the Shepherd-poet's eyes :

Nor has the rolling year twice measured,
From sign to sign, its stedfast course,

Since every mortal power of Coleridge   15
Was frozen at its marvellous source;

The rapt One, of the godlike forehead,
The heaven-eyed creature sleeps in earth :
And Lamb, the frolic and the gentle,
Has vanished from his lonely hearth.   20

Like clouds that rake the mountain-summits,
Or waves that own no curbing hand,
How fast has brother followed brother
From sunshine to the sunless land !

Yet I, whose lids from infant slumber   25
Were earlier raised, remain to hear
A timid voice, that asks in whispers,
" Who next will drop and disappear ? "

Our haughty life is crowned with darkness,
Like London with its own black wreath,   30
On which with thee, O Crabbe ! forthlooking,
I gazed from Hampstead's breezy heath.

As if but yesterday departed,
Thou too art gone before ; but why,
O'er ripe fruit, seasonably gathered,   35
Should frail survivors heave a sigh ?

Mourn rather for that holy Spirit,
Sweet as the spring, as ocean deep;
For Her who, ere her summer faded,
Has sunk into a breathless sleep.   40

No more of old romantic sorrows,
For slaughtered Youth or love-lorn Maid !
With sharper grief is Yarrow smitten,
And Ettrick mourns with her their Poet dead.

Nov., 1835.

SONNETS.

POLITICAL SONNETS.

COMPOSED BY THE SEASIDE, NEAR CALAIS,
AUGUST, 1802.

FAIR Star of evening, Splendour of the west,
Star of my Country ! — on the horizon's brink
Thou hangest, stooping, as might seem, to sink
On England's bosom ; yet well pleased to rest,
Meanwhile, and be to her a glorious crest   5
Conspicuous to the Nations.   Thou, I think,
Should'st be my Country's emblem ; and should'st wink,
Bright Star ! with laughter on her banners, drest
In thy fresh beauty.   There ! that dusky spot
Beneath thee, that is England ; there she lies.   10
Blessings be on you both ! one hope, one lot,
One life, one glory ! — I, with many a fear
For my dear Country, many heartfelt sighs,
Among men who do not love her, linger here.

CALAIS, AUGUST, 1802.

Is it a reed that 's shaken by the wind,
Or what is it that ye go forth to see ?
Lords, lawyers, statesmen, squires of low degree,

Men known, and men unknown, sick, lame, and blind,
Post forward all, like creatures of one kind,   5
With first-fruit offerings crowd to bend the knee
In France, before the new-born Majesty.
'Tis ever thus.   Ye men of prostrate mind,
A seemly reverence may be paid to power;
But that's a loyal virtue, never sown   10
In haste, nor springing with a transient shower:
When truth, when sense, when liberty were flown,
What hardship had it been to wait an hour?
Shame on you, feeble Heads, to slavery prone!

1801.

I GRIEVED for Buonaparté, with a vain
And an unthinking grief! The tenderest mood
Of that Man's mind—what can it be? what food
Fed his first hopes? what knowledge could *he* gain?
'Tis not in battles that from youth we train   5
The Governor who must be wise and good,
And temper with the sternness of the brain
Thoughts motherly, and meek as womanhood.
Wisdom doth live with children round her knees:
Books, leisure, perfect freedom, and the talk   10
Man holds with week-day man in the hourly walk
Of the mind's business; these are the degrees
By which true Sway doth mount; this is the stalk
True Power doth grow on; and her rights are these.

                                        1802.

ON THE EXTINCTION OF THE VENETIAN REPUBLIC.

ONCE did She hold the gorgeous east in fee ;
And was the safeguard of the west : the worth
Of Venice did not fall below her birth,
Venice, the eldest Child of Liberty.
She was a maiden City, bright and free ;   5
No guile seduced, no force could violate ;
And, when she took unto herself a Mate,
She must espouse the everlasting Sea.
And what if she had seen those glories fade,
Those titles vanish, and that strength decay ;   10
Yet shall some tribute of regret be paid
When her long life hath reached its final day :
Men are we, and must grieve when even the Shade
Of that which once was great is passed away.

1802.

TO TOUSSAINT L'OUVERTURE.

TOUSSAINT, the most unhappy man of men !
Whether the whistling Rustic tend his plough
Within thy hearing, or thy head be now
Pillowed in some deep dungeon's earless den ; —
O miserable Chieftain ! where and when   5
Wilt thou find patience ? Yet die not ; do thou
Wear rather in thy bonds a cheerful brow :
Though fallen thyself, never to rise again,
Live, and take comfort. Thou hast left behind
Powers that will work for thee ; air, earth, and skies ;   10
There 's not a breathing of the common wind
That will forget thee ; thou hast great allies ;

Thy friends are exultations, agonies,
And love, and man's unconquerable mind.

1802.

SEPTEMBER, 1802, NEAR DOVER.

INLAND, within a hollow vale, I stood ;
And saw, while sea was calm and air was clear,
The coast of France — the coast of France how near !
Drawn almost into frightful neighbourhood.
I shrunk ; for verily the barrier flood   5
Was like a lake, or river bright and fair,
A span of waters ; yet what power is there !
What mightiness for evil and for good !
Even so doth God protect us if we be
Virtuous and wise.   Winds blow, and waters roll,   10
Strength to the brave, and Power, and Deity ;
Yet in themselves are nothing !   One decree
Spake laws to *them*, and said that by the soul
Only, the Nations shall be great and free.

THOUGHT OF A BRITON ON THE SUBJUGATION OF SWITZERLAND.

Two Voices are there ; one is of the sea,
One of the mountains ; each a mighty Voice :
In both from age to age thou didst rejoice,
They were thy chosen music, Liberty !
There came a Tyrant, and with holy glee   5
Thou fought'st against him ; but hast vainly striven :
Thou from thy Alpine holds at length art driven,

Where not a torrent murmurs heard by thee.
Of one deep bliss thine ear hath been bereft:
Then cleave, O cleave to that which still is left;　　10
For, high-souled Maid, what sorrow would it be
That Mountain floods should thunder as before,
And Ocean bellow from his rocky shore,
And neither awful Voice be heard by thee.

　　　　　　　　　　　　　1806.

WRITTEN IN LONDON, September, 1802.

O Friend! I know not which way I must look
For comfort, being, as I am, opprest,
To think that now our life is only drest
For show ; mean handy-work of craftsman, cook,
Or groom !—We must run glittering like a brook　　5
In the open sunshine, or we are unblest:
The wealthiest man among us is the best :
No grandeur now in nature or in book
Delights us.　Rapine, avarice, expense,
This is idolatry ; and these we adore :　　10
Plain living and high thinking are no more :
The homely beauty of the good old cause
Is gone ; our peace, our fearful innocence,
And pure religion breathing household laws.

LONDON, 1802.

Milton ! thou should'st be living at this hour :
England hath need of thee : she is a fen
Of stagnant waters : altar, sword, and pen,
Fireside, the heroic wealth of hall and bower,

Have forfeited their ancient English dower   5
Of inward happiness.   We are selfish men ;
Oh ! raise us up, return to us again ;
And give us manners, virtue, freedom, power.
Thy soul was like a Star, and dwelt apart :
Thou hadst a voice whose sound was like the sea :   10
Pure as the naked heavens, majestic, free,
So didst thou travel on life's common way,
In cheerful godliness ; and yet thy heart
The lowliest duties on herself did lay.

It is not to be thought of that the Flood
Of British freedom, which, to the open sea
Of the world's praise, from dark antiquity
Hath flowed, "with pomp of waters, unwithstood,"
Roused though it be full often to a mood   5
Which spurns the check of salutary bands,
That this most famous Stream in bogs and sands
Should perish ; and to evil and to good
Be lost forever.   In our halls is hung
Armoury of the invincible Knights of old :   10
We must be free or die, who speak the tongue
That Shakspeare spake ; the faith and morals hold
Which Milton held. — In every thing we are sprung
Of Earth's first blood, have titles manifold.

1802.

When I have borne in memory what has tamed
Great Nations, how ennobling thoughts depart
When men change swords for ledgers, and desert

The student's bower for gold, some fears unnamed
I had, my Country ! — am I to be blamed? 5
Now, when I think of thee, and what thou art,
Verily, in the bottom of my heart,
Of those unfilial fears I am ashamed.
For dearly must we prize thee ; we who find
In thee a bulwark for the cause of men ; 10
And I by my affection was beguiled:
What wonder if a Poet now and then,
Among the many movements of his mind,
Felt for thee as a lover or a child !

1802.

OCTOBER, 1803.

THESE times strike monied worldlings with dismay :
Even rich men, brave by nature, taint the air
With words of apprehension and despair :
While tens of thousands, thinking on the affray,
Men unto whom sufficient for the day 5
And minds not stinted or untilled are given,
Sound, healthy, children of the God of heaven,
Are cheerful as the rising sun in May.
What do we gather hence but firmer faith
That every gift of noble origin 10
Is breathed upon by Hope's perpetual breath ;
That virtue and the faculties within
Are vital, — and that riches are akin
To fear, to change, to cowardice, and death ?

IN THE PASS OF KILLICRANKY,

AN INVASION BEING EXPECTED, OCTOBER, 1803.

Six thousand veterans practised in war's game,
Tried men, at Killicranky were arrayed
Against an equal host that wore the plaid,
Shepherds and herdsmen. — Like a whirlwind came
The Highlanders, the slaughter spread like flame ;   5
And Garry, thundering down his mountain-road,
Was stopped, and could not breathe beneath the load
Of the dead bodies. — 'Twas a day of shame
For them whom precept and the pedantry
Of cold mechanic battle do enslave.   10
O for a single hour of that Dundee
Who on that day the word of onset gave !
Like conquest would the Men of England see
And her Foes find a like inglorious grave.

TO THE MEN OF KENT, OCTOBER, 1803.

Vanguard of Liberty, ye men of Kent,
Ye children of a Soil that doth advance
Her haughty brow against the coast of France,
Now is the time to prove your hardiment !
To France be words of invitation sent !   5
They from their fields can see the countenance
Of your fierce war, may ken the glittering lance,
And hear you shouting forth your brave intent.
Left single, in bold parley, ye, of yore,
Did from the Norman win a gallant wreath ;   10
Confirmed the charters that were yours before ; —
No parleying now !   In Britain is one breath ;

We all are with you now from shore to shore : —
Ye men of Kent, 't is victory or death !

NOVEMBER, 1806.

ANOTHER year ! — another deadly blow !
Another mighty Empire overthrown !
And We are left, or shall be left, alone ;
The last that dare to struggle with the Foe.
'T is well ! from this day forward we shall know   5
That in ourselves our safety must be sought ;
That by our own right hands it must be wrought ;
That we must stand unpropped, or be laid low.
O dastard whom such foretaste doth not cheer !
We shall exult, if they who rule the land   10
Be men who hold its many blessings dear,
Wise, upright, valiant ; not a servile band,
Who are to judge of danger which they fear
And honour which they do not understand.

TO THOMAS CLARKSON,

ON THE FINAL PASSING OF THE BILL FOR THE ABOLITION OF
THE SLAVE TRADE.

MARCH, 1807.

CLARKSON ! it was an obstinate hill to climb :
How toilsome — nay, how dire — it was, by thee
Is known ; by none, perhaps, so feelingly :
But thou, who, starting in thy fervent prime,
Didst first lead forth that enterprise sublime,   5

Hast heard the constant Voice its charge repeat,
Which, out of thy young heart's oracular seat,
First roused thee. — O true yolk-fellow of Time,
Duty's intrepid liegeman, see, the palm
Is won, and by all Nations shall be worn !   10
The blood-stained Writing is for ever torn ;
And thou henceforth wilt have a good man's calm,
A great man's happiness ; thy zeal shall find
Repose at length, firm friend of human kind !

COMPOSED BY THE SIDE OF GRASMERE LAKE.

1807.

CLOUDS, lingering yet, extend in solid bars
Through the grey west ; and lo ! these waters, steeled
By breezeless air to smoothest polish, yield
A vivid repetition of the stars ;
Jove, Venus, and the ruddy crest of Mars   5
Amid his fellows beauteously revealed
At happy distance from earth's groaning field,
Where ruthless mortals wage incessant wars.
Is it a mirror ? — or the nether Sphere
Opening to view the abyss in which she feeds   10
Her own calm fires ? — But list ! a voice is near ;
Great Pan himself low-whispering through the reeds,
" Be thankful, thou ; for, if unholy deeds
Ravage the world, tranquillity is here ! "

COMPOSED WHILE THE AUTHOR WAS ENGAGED IN WRITING A TRACT, OCCASIONED BY THE CONVENTION OF CINTRA.

1808.

NOT 'mid the World's vain objects that enslave
The free-born Soul — that World whose vaunted skill
In selfish interest perverts the will,
Whose factions lead astray the wise and brave —
Not there ; but in dark wood and rocky cave,   5
And hollow vale which foaming torrents fill
With omnipresent murmur as they rave
Down their steep beds, that never shall be still ;
Here, mighty Nature ; in this school sublime
I weigh the hopes and fears of suffering Spain :   10
For her consult the auguries of time,
And through the human heart explore my way ;
And look and listen — gathering, whence I may,
Triumph, and thoughts no bondage can restrain.

ALAS ! what boots the long laborious quest
Of moral prudence, sought through good and ill ;
Or pains abstruse — to elevate the will,
And lead us on to that transcendent rest
Where every passion shall the sway attest   5
Of Reason, seated on her sovereign hill ;
What is it but a vain and curious skill,
If sapient Germany must lie deprest,
Beneath the brutal sword ? — Her haughty Schools
Shall blush ; and may not we with sorrow say,   10
A few strong instincts and a few plain rules,
Among the herdsmen of the Alps, have wrought
More for mankind at this unhappy day
Than all the pride of intellect and thought ?   1809.

1811.

THE power of Armies is a visible thing,
Formal, and circumscribed in time and space ;
But who the limits of that power shall trace
Which a brave People into light can bring
Or hide, at will, — for freedom combating   5
By just revenge inflamed ?   No foot may chase,
No eye can follow, to a fatal place
That power, that spirit, whether on the wing
Like the strong wind, or sleeping like the wind
Within its awful caves. — From year to year   10
Springs this indigenous produce far and near ;
No craft this subtle element can bind,
Rising like water from the soil, to find
In every nook a lip that it may cheer.

1811.

HERE pause : the poet claims at least this praise,
That virtuous Liberty hath been the scope
Of his pure song, which did not shrink from hope
In the worst moment of these evil days ;
From hope, the paramount *duty* that Heaven lays,   5
For its own honour, on man's suffering heart.
Never may from our souls one truth depart —
That an accursed thing it is to gaze
On prosperous tyrants with a dazzled eye ;
Nor — touched with due abhorrence of *their* guilt   10
For whose dire ends tears flow, and blood is spilt,
And justice labours in extremity —
Forget thy weakness, upon which is built,
O wretched man, the throne of tyranny !

MISCELLANEOUS SONNETS.

COMPOSED UPON WESTMINSTER BRIDGE,
SEPT. 3, 1802.

EARTH has not anything to show more fair :
Dull would he be of soul who could pass by
A sight so touching in its majesty :
This City now doth, like a garment, wear
The beauty of the morning ; silent, bare,   5
Ships, towers, domes, theatres, and temples lie
Open unto the fields, and to the sky ;
All bright and glittering in the smokeless air.
Never did sun more beautifully steep
In his first splendour, valley, rock, or hill ;   10
Ne'er saw I, never felt, a calm so deep !
The river glideth at his own sweet will :
Dear God ! the very houses seem asleep ;
And all that mighty heart is lying still !

IT is a beauteous evening, calm and free,
The holy time is quiet as a Nun
Breathless with adoration ; the broad sun
Is sinking down in its tranquillity ;
The gentleness of heaven broods o'er the Sea :   5
Listen ! the mighty Being is awake,
And doth with his eternal motion make

A sound like thunder—everlastingly.
Dear Child! dear Girl! that walkest with me here,
If thou appear untouched by solemn thought,   10
Thy nature is not therefore less divine:
Thou liest in Abraham's bosom all the year;
And worship'st at the Temple's inner shrine,
God being with thee when we know it not.

1802.

COMPOSED AFTER A JOURNEY ACROSS THE HAM-BLETON HILLS, YORKSHIRE.

DARK and more dark the shades of evening fell;
The wished-for point was reached—but at an hour
When little could be gained from that rich dower
Of prospect, whereof many thousands tell.
Yet did the glowing west with marvellous power   5
Salute us; there stood Indian citadel,
Temple of Greece, and minster with its tower
Substantially expressed—a place for bell
Or clock to toll from!   Many a tempting isle,
With groves that never were imagined, lay   10
'Mid seas how steadfast! objects all for the eye
Of silent rapture; but we felt the while
We should forget them; they are of the sky,
And from our earthly memory fade away.

1802.

—— "they are of the sky,
And from our earthly memory fade away."

THOSE words were uttered as in pensive mood
We turned, departing from that solemn sight:
A contrast and reproach to gross delight,

And life's unspiritual pleasures daily wooed !
But now upon this thought I cannot brood ;   5
It is unstable as a dream of night ;
Nor will I praise a cloud, however bright,
Disparaging Man's gifts, and proper food.
Grove, isle, with every shape of sky-built dome,
Though clad in colours beautiful and pure,   10
Find in the heart of man no natural home :
The immortal Mind craves objects that endure :
These cleave to it ; from these it cannot roam,
Nor they from it : their fellowship is secure.

Before 1807.

COMPOSED AT [NEIDPATH] CASTLE.

DEGENERATE Douglas ! oh, the unworthy Lord !
Whom mere despite of heart could so far please,
And love of havoc, (for with such disease
Fame taxes him,) that he could send forth word
To level with the dust a noble horde,   5
A brotherhood of venerable Trees,
Leaving an ancient dome, and towers like these,
Beggared and outraged ! — Many hearts deplored
The fate of those old Trees ; and oft with pain
The traveller, at this day, will stop and gaze   10
On wrongs, which Nature scarcely seems to heed :
For sheltered places, bosoms, nooks, and bays,
And the pure mountains, and the gentle Tweed,
And the green silent pastures, yet remain.

1803.

Nuns fret not at their convent's narrow room ;
And hermits are contented with their cells ;
And students with their pensive citadels ;
Maids at the wheel, the weaver at his loom,
Sit blithe and happy ; bees that soar for bloom,   5
High as the highest Peak of Furness-fells,
Will murmur by the hour in foxglove bells :
In truth the prison, unto which we doom
Ourselves, no prison is : and hence for me,
In sundry moods, 't was pastime to be bound   10
Within the Sonnet's scanty plot of ground ;
Pleased if some Souls (for such there needs must be)
Who have felt the weight of too much liberty,
Should find brief solace there, as I have found.

Before 1807.

ADMONITION.

Intended more particularly for the perusal of those who may have happened
to be enamoured of some beautiful Place of Retreat, in the Country of the
Lakes.

Well may'st thou halt — and gaze with brightening eye !
The lovely Cottage in the guardian nook
Hath stirred thee deeply ; with its own dear brook,
Its own small pasture, almost its own sky !
But covet not the Abode : — forbear to sigh,   5
As many do, repining while they look ;
Intruders — who would tear from Nature's book
This precious leaf, with harsh impiety.
Think what the Home must be if it were thine,
Even thine, though few thy wants ! — Roof, window, door,   10
The very flowers are sacred to the Poor,
The roses to the porch which they entwine :

Yea, all, that now enchants thee, from the day
On which it should be touched, would melt away.

Before 1807.

THE world is too much with us: late and soon.
Getting and spending, we lay waste our powers:
Little we see in Nature that is ours ;
We have given our hearts away, a sordid boon !
This Sea that bares her bosom to the moon ;   5
The winds that will be howling at all hours,
And are up-gathered now like sleeping flowers ;
For this, for every thing, we are out of tune ;
It moves us not. — Great God ! I 'd rather be
A Pagan suckled in a creed outworn ;   10
So might I, standing on this pleasant lea,
Have glimpses that would make me less forlorn ;
Have sight of Proteus rising from the sea ;
Or hear old Triton blow his wreathèd horn.

Before 1807.

TO SLEEP.

A FLOCK of sheep that leisurely pass by,
One after one ; the sound of rain, and bees
Murmuring ; the fall of rivers, winds and seas,
Smooth fields, white sheets of water, and pure sky ;
I have thought of all by turns, and yet do lie   5
Sleepless ! and soon the small birds' melodies
Must hear, first uttered from my orchard trees ;
And the first cuckoo's melancholy cry.
Even thus last night, and two nights more, I lay,

And could not win thee, Sleep! by any stealth :   10
So do not let me wear to-night away :
Without Thee what is all the morning's wealth?
Come, blessed barrier between day and day,
Dear mother of fresh thoughts and joyous health !

Before 1807.

WHERE lies the Land to which yon Ship must go?
Fresh as a lark mounting at break of day,
Festively she puts forth in trim array ;
Is she for tropic suns, or polar snow?
What boots the inquiry? — Neither friend nor foe   5
She cares for ; let her travel where she may,
She finds familiar names, a beaten way
Ever before her, and a wind to blow.
Yet still I ask, what haven is her mark?
And, almost as it was when ships were rare,   10
(From time to time, like Pilgrims, here and there
Crossing the waters) doubt, and something dark,
Of the old Sea some reverential fear,
Is with me at thy farewell, joyous Bark !

Before 1807.

TO THE MEMORY OF RAISLEY CALVERT.

CALVERT! it must not be unheard by them
Who may respect my name, that I to thee
Owed many years of early liberty.
This care was thine when sickness did condemn
Thy youth to hopeless wasting, root and stem —   5

That I, if frugal and severe, might stray
Where'er I liked ; and finally array
My temples with the Muse's diadem.
Hence, if in freedom I have loved the truth ;
If there be aught of pure, or good, or great,   10
In my past verse ; or shall be, in the lays
Of higher mood which now I meditate :—
It gladdens me, O worthy, short-lived, Youth !
To think how much of this will be thy praise.

Before 1807.

METHOUGHT I saw the footsteps of a throne
Which mists and vapours from mine eyes did shroud —
Nor view of who might sit thereon allowed;
But all the steps and ground about were strown
With sights the ruefullest, that flesh and bone   5
Ever put on ; a miserable crowd,
Sick, hale, old, young, who cried before that cloud,
"Thou art our king, O Death ! to thee we groan."
Those steps I clomb ; the mists before me gave
Smooth way: and I beheld the face of one   10
Sleeping alone within a mossy cave,
With her face up to heaven ; that seemed to have
Pleasing remembrance of a thought foregone ;
A lovely Beauty in a summer grave !

Before 1807.

BROOK ! whose society the Poet seeks,
Intent his wasted spirits to renew ;
And whom the curious Painter doth pursue
Through rocky passes, among flowery creeks,
And tracks thee dancing down thy waterbreaks ;   5

If wish were mine some type of thee to view,
Thee, and not thee thyself, I would not do
Like Grecian Artists, give thee human cheeks,
Channels for tears; no Naiad should'st thou be, —
Have neither limbs, feet, feathers, joints nor hairs: 10
It seems the Eternal Soul is clothed in thee
With purer robes than those of flesh and blood,
And hath bestowed on thee a safer good;
Unwearied joy, and life without its cares.

1806.

TO LADY BEAUMONT.

LADY! the songs of Spring were in the grove
While I was shaping beds for winter flowers;
While I was planting green unfading bowers,
And shrubs — to hang upon the warm alcove,
And sheltering wall; and still, as Fancy wove   5
The dream, to time and nature's blended powers
I gave this paradise for winter hours,
A labyrinth, Lady! which your feet shall rove.
Yes! when the sun of life more feebly shines,
Becoming thoughts, I trust, of solemn gloom   10
Or of high gladness you shall hither bring;
And these perennial bowers and murmuring pines
Be gracious as the music and the bloom
And all the mighty ravishment of spring.

1807.

UPON THE SIGHT OF A BEAUTIFUL PICTURE.

PAINTED BY SIR G. H. BEAUMONT, BART.

PRAISED be the Art whose subtle power could stay
Yon cloud, and fix it in that glorious shape ;
Nor would permit the thin smoke to escape,
Nor those bright sunbeams to forsake the day ;
Which stopped that band of travellers on their way,   5
Ere they were lost within the shady wood ;
And showed the Bark upon the glassy flood
For ever anchored in her sheltering bay.
Soul-soothing Art ! whom Morning, Noontide, Even,
Do serve with all their changeful pageantry ;   10
Thou, with ambition modest yet sublime,
Here, for the sight of mortal man, hast given
To one brief moment caught from fleeting time
The appropriate calm of blest eternity.

1811.

SURPRISED by joy—impatient as the Wind
I turned to share the transport—Oh ! with whom
But Thee, deep buried in the silent tomb,
That spot which no vicissitude can find ?
Love, faithful love, recalled thee to my mind—   5
But how could I forget thee ! Through what power,
Even for the least division of an hour,
Have I been so beguiled as to be blind
To my most grievous loss ?—That thought's return
Was the worst pang that sorrow ever bore,   10
Save one, one only, when I stood forlorn,
Knowing my heart's best treasure was no more ;

That neither present time, nor years unborn
Could to my sight that heavenly face restore.

After June, 1812; before 1815.

HAIL, Twilight, sovereign of one peaceful hour!
Not dull art Thou as undiscerning Night;
But studious only to remove from sight
Day's mutable distinctions. — Ancient Power!
Thus did the waters gleam, the mountains lower,   5
To the rude Briton, when, in wolf-skin vest
Here roving wild, he laid him down to rest
On the bare rock, or through a leafy bower
Looked ere his eyes were closed.   By him was seen
The self-same Vision which we now behold,   10
At thy meek bidding, shadowy Power! brought forth;
These mighty barriers, and the gulf between;
The flood, the stars, — a spectacle as old
As the beginning of the heavens and earth!

Before 1815.

I WATCH, and long have watched, with calm regret
Yon slowly-sinking star — immortal Sire
(So might he seem) of all the glittering quire!
Blue ether still surrounds him — yet — and yet;
But now the horizon's rocky parapet   5
Is reached, where, forfeiting his bright attire,
He burns — transmuted to a dusky fire —
Then pays submissively the appointed debt
To the flying moments, and is seen no more.
Angels and gods!   We struggle with our fate,   10
While health, power, glory, from their height decline,
Depressed; and then extinguished; and our state,

In this, how different, lost Star, from thine,
That no to-morrow shall our beams restore!

Between 1815 and 1819.

TO B. R. HAYDON.

HIGH is our calling, Friend! — Creative Art
(Whether the instrument of words she use,
Or pencil pregnant with ethereal hues,)
Demands the service of a mind and heart,
Though sensitive, yet, in their weakest part,   5
Heroically fashioned — to infuse
Faith in the whispers of the lonely Muse,
While the whole world seems adverse to desert.
And, oh! when Nature sinks, as oft she may,
Through long-lived pressure of obscure distress,   10
Still to be strenuous for the bright reward,
And in the soul admit of no decay,
Brook no continuance of weak-mindedness —
Great is the glory, for the strife is hard!

1815.

NOVEMBER 1.

How clear, how keen, how marvellously bright
The effluence from yon distant mountain's head,
Which, strewn with snow smooth as the sky can shed,
Shines like another sun — on mortal sight
Uprisen, as if to check approaching Night,   5
And all her twinkling stars. Who now would tread,
If so he might, yon mountain's glittering head —
Terrestrial, but a surface, by the flight

Of sad mortality's earth-sullying wing,
Unswept, unstained?   Nor shall the aërial Powers   10
Dissolve that beauty, destined to endure,
White, radiant, spotless, exquisitely pure,
Through all vicissitudes, till genial Spring
Has filled the laughing vales with welcome flowers.

1815.

THE RIVER DUDDON.

I.

SOLE listener, Duddon ! to the breeze that played
With thy clear voice, I caught the fitful sound
Wafted o'er sullen moss and craggy mound —
Unfruitful solitudes, that seemed to upbraid
The sun in heaven !— but now, to form a shade   5
For Thee, green alders have together wound
Their foliage ; ashes flung their arms around ;
And birch-trees risen in silver colonnade.
And thou hast also tempted here to rise,
'Mid sheltering pines, this Cottage rude and grey ;   10
Whose ruddy children, by the mother's eyes
Carelessly watched, sport through the summer day,
Thy pleased associates : — light as endless May
On infant bosoms lonely Nature lies.

II.

THE PLAIN OF DONNERDALE.

THE old inventive Poets, had they seen,
Or rather felt, the entrancement that detains
Thy waters, Duddon ! 'mid these flowery plains —

The still repose, the liquid lapse serene,
Transferred to bowers imperishably green,   5
Had beautified Elysium !   But these chains
Will soon be broken ; — a rough course remains,
Rough as the past ; where Thou, of placid mien,
Innocuous as a firstling of the flock,
And countenanced like a soft cerulean sky,   10
Shalt change thy temper ; and with many a shock
Given and received in mutual jeopardy,
Dance, like a Bacchanal, from rock to rock,
Tossing her frantic thyrsus wide and high !

III.

RETURN, Content ! for fondly I pursued,
Even when a child, the Streams — unheard, unseen ;
Through tangled woods, impending rocks between ;
Or, free as air, with flying inquest viewed
The sullen reservoirs whence their bold brood —   5
Pure as the morning, fretful, boisterous, keen,
Green as the salt-sea billows, white and green —
Poured down the hills, a choral multitude !
Nor have I tracked their course for scanty gains ;
They taught me random cares and truant joys,   10
That shield from mischief and preserve from stains
Vague minds, while men are growing out of boys ;
Maturer Fancy owes to their rough noise
Impetuous thoughts that brook not servile reins.

IV.

AFTER–THOUGHT.

I THOUGHT of Thee, my partner and my guide,
As being past away. — Vain sympathies !
For, backward, Duddon ! as I cast my eyes,
I see what was, and is, and will abide ;
Still glides the Stream, and shall for ever glide ;   5
The Form remains, the Function never dies ;
While we, the brave, the mighty, and the wise,
We Men, who in our morn of youth defied
The elements, must vanish ; — be it so !
Enough, if something from our hands have power   10
To live, and act, and serve the future hour ;
And if, as toward the silent tomb we go,
Through love, through hope, and faith's transcendent
          dower,
We feel that we are greater than we know.

Between 1806 and 1820.

BETWEEN NAMUR AND LIEGE.

WHAT lovelier home could gentle Fancy choose ?
Is this the stream, whose cities, heights, and plains,
War's favourite playground, are with crimson stains
Familiar, as the Morn with pearly dews ?
The Morn, that now, along the silver MEUSE,   5
Spreading her peaceful ensigns, calls the swains
To tend their silent boats and ringing wains,
Or strip the bough whose mellow fruit bestrews
The ripening corn beneath it.   As mine eyes
Turn from the fortified and threatening hill,   10
How sweet the prospect of yon watery glade,
With its grey rocks clustering in pensive shade —

That, shaped like old monastic turrets, rise
From the smooth meadow-ground, serene and still !

1821.

THE MONUMENT COMMONLY CALLED LONG MEG AND HER DAUGHTERS, NEAR THE RIVER EDEN.

A WEIGHT of awe, not easy to be borne,
Fell suddenly upon my Spirit — cast
From the dread bosom of the unknown past,
When first I saw that family forlorn.
Speak Thou, whose massy strength and stature scorn   5
The power of years — pre-eminent, and placed
Apart, to overlook the circle vast —
Speak, Giant-mother ! tell it to the Morn
While she dispels the cumbrous shades of Night;
Let the Moon hear, emerging from a cloud;   10
At whose behest uprose on British ground
That Sisterhood, in hieroglyphic round
Forth-shadowing, some have deemed, the infinite
The inviolable God, that tames the proud !

1821.

SECLUSION.

LANCE, shield, and sword relinquished, at his side
A bead-roll, in his hand a claspèd book,
Or staff more harmless than a shepherd's crook,
The war-worn Chieftain quits the world — to hide
His thin autumnal locks where Monks abide   5
In cloistered privacy.   But not to dwell

In soft repose he comes : within his cell,
Round the decaying trunk of human pride,
At morn, and eve, and midnight's silent hour,
Do penitential cogitations cling ;　　　　　　　　10
Like ivy, round some ancient elm, they twine
In grisly folds and strictures serpentine ;
Yet, while they strangle, a fair growth they bring,
For recompence — their own perennial bower.

CONTINUED.

METHINKS that to some vacant hermitage
My feet would rather turn — to some dry nook
Scooped out of living rock, and near a brook
Hurled down a mountain-cove from stage to stage,
Yet tempering, for my sight, its bustling rage　　　5
In the soft heaven of a translucent pool ;
Thence creeping under sylvan arches cool,
Fit haunt of shapes whose glorious equipage
Would elevate my dreams.　A beechen bowl,
A maple dish, my furniture should be ;　　　　　10
Crisp, yellow leaves my bed ; the hooting owl
My night-watch : nor should e'er the crested fowl
From thorp or vill his matins sound for me,
Tired of the world and all its industry.
　　　　　　　　　　　　　　　　1821.

RURAL CEREMONY.

Content with calmer scenes around us spread
And humbler objects, give we to a day
Of annual joy one tributary lay;
This day, when, forth by rustic music led,
The village Children, while the sky is red   5
With evening lights, advance in long array
Through the still churchyard, each with garland gay,
That, carried sceptre-like, o'ertops the head
Of the proud Bearer.   To the wide church-door,
Charged with these offerings which their fathers bore   10
For decoration in the Papal time,
The innocent procession softly moves : —
The spirit of Laud is pleased in heaven's pure clime,
And Hooker's voice the spectacle approves !

1821.

MUTABILITY.

From low to high doth dissolution climb,
And sink from high to low, along a scale
Of awful notes, whose concord shall not fail;
A musical but melancholy chime,
Which they can hear who meddle not with crime,   5
Nor avarice, nor over-anxious care.
Truth fails not; but her outward forms that bear
The longest date do melt like frosty rime,
That in the morning whitened hill and plain
And is no more ; drop like the tower sublime   10
Of yesterday, which royally did wear
His crown of weeds, but could not even sustain
Some casual shout that broke the silent air,
Or the unimaginable touch of Time.

INSIDE OF KING'S COLLEGE CHAPEL, CAMBRIDGE.

TAX not the royal Saint with vain expense,
With ill-matched aims the Architect who planned —
Albeit labouring for a scanty band
Of white-robed Scholars only — this immense
And glorious Work of fine intelligence !   5
Give all thou canst ; high Heaven rejects the lore
Of nicely-calculated less or more ;
So deemed the man who fashioned for the sense
These lofty pillars, spread that branching roof
Self-poised, and scooped into ten thousand cells,   10
Where light and shade repose, where music dwells
Lingering — and wandering on as loth to die ;
Like thoughts whose very sweetness yieldeth proof
That they were born for immortality.

THE SAME.

WHAT awful pérspective ! while from our sight
With gradual stealth the lateral windows hide
Their Portraitures, their stone-work glimmers, dyed
In the soft chequerings of a sleepy light.
Martyr, or King, or sainted Eremite,   5
Whoe'er ye be, that thus, yourselves unseen,
Imbue your prison-bars with solemn sheen,
Shine on, until ye fade with coming Night ! —
But, from the arms of silence — list ! O list !
The music bursteth into second life ;   10
The notes luxuriate, every stone is kissed
By sound, or ghost of sound, in mazy strife ;
Heart-thrilling strains, that cast, before the eye
Of the devout, a veil of ecstasy !

CONTINUED.

THEY dreamt not of a perishable home
Who thus could build.   Be mine, in hours of fear
Or grovelling thought, to seek a refuge here ;
Or through the aisles of Westminster to roam :
Where bubbles burst, and folly's dancing foam   5
Melts, if it cross the threshold ; where the wreath
Of awe-struck wisdom droops : or let my path
Lead to that younger Pile, whose sky-like dome
Hath typified by reach of daring art
Infinity's embrace ; whose guardian crest,   10
The silent Cross, among the stars shall spread
As now, when She hath also seen her breast
Filled with mementos, satiate with its part
Of grateful England's overflowing Dead.

                                        1820–21.

A PARSONAGE IN OXFORDSHIRE.

WHERE holy ground begins, unhallowed ends,
Is marked by no distinguishable line ;
The turf unites, the pathways intertwine ;
And, wheresoe'er the stealing footstep tends,
Garden, and that domain where kindred, friends,   5
And neighbours rest together, here confound
Their several features, mingled like the sound
Of many waters, or as evening blends
With shady night.   Soft airs from shrub and flower,
Waft fragrant greetings to each silent grave ;   10
And while those lofty poplars gently wave
Their tops, between them comes and goes a sky
Bright as the glimpses of eternity,
To saints accorded in their mortal hour.

                                        1820.

A VOLANT Tribe of Bards on earth are found,
Who, while the flattering Zephyrs round them play,
On " coignes of vantage " hang their nests of clay ;
How quickly from that aëry hold unbound,
Dust for oblivion !   To the solid ground   5
Of nature trusts the Mind that builds for aye ;
Convinced that there, there only, she can lay
Secure foundations.   As the year runs round,
Apart she toils within the chosen ring ;
While the stars shine, or while day's purple eye   10
Is gently closing with the flowers of spring ;
Where even the motion of an Angel's wing
Would interrupt the intense tranquillity
Of silent hills, and more than silent sky.

1823, or earlier.

NOT Love, not War, nor the tumultuous swell,
Of civil conflict, nor the wrecks of change,
Nor Duty struggling with afflictions strange —
Not these *alone* inspire the tuneful shell ;
But where untroubled peace and concord dwell,   5
There also is the Muse not loth to range,
Watching the twilight smoke of cot or grange,
Skyward ascending from a woody dell.
Meek aspirations please her, lone endeavour,
And sage content, and placid melancholy ;   10
She loves to gaze upon a crystal river —
Diaphanous because it travels slowly ;
Soft is the music that would charm for ever ;
The flower of sweetest smell is shy and lowly.

1823, or earlier.

TO [LADY FITZGERALD], IN HER SEVENTIETH YEAR.

SUCH age how beautiful ! O Lady bright,
Whose mortal lineaments seem all refined
By favouring Nature and a saintly Mind
To something purer and more exquisite
Than flesh and blood ; whene'er thou meet'st my sight,   5
When I behold thy blanched unwithered cheek,
Thy temples fringed with locks of gleaming white,
And head that droops because the soul is meek,
Thee with the welcome Snowdrop I compare ;
That child of winter, prompting thoughts that climb   10
From desolation toward the genial prime ;
Or with the Moon conquering earth's misty air,
And filling more and more with crystal light
As pensive Evening deepens into night.

1824.

SCORN not the Sonnet ; Critic, you have frowned,
Mindless of its just honours ; with this key
Shakspeare unlocked his heart : the melody
Of this small lute gave ease to Petrarch's wound ;
A thousand times this pipe did Tasso sound ;   5
With it Camoëns soothed an exile's grief ;
The Sonnet glittered a gay myrtle leaf
Amid the cypress with which Dante crowned
His visionary brow : a glow-worm lamp,
It cheered mild Spenser, called from Faeryland   10
To struggle through dark ways ; and, when a damp
Fell round the path of Milton, in his hand
The Thing became a trumpet ; whence he blew
Soul-animating strains — alas, too few !

Before 1827.

TO ROTHA QUILLINAN.

ROTHA, my Spiritual Child! this head was grey
When at the sacred font for thee I stood;
Pledged till thou reach the verge of womanhood,
And shalt become thy own sufficient stay:
Too late, I feel, sweet Orphan! was the day 5
For stedfast hope the contract to fulfil;
Yet shall my blessing hover o'er thee still,
Embodied in the music of this Lay,
Breathed forth beside the peaceful mountain Stream
Whose murmur soothed thy languid Mother's ear 10
After her throes, this Stream of name more dear
Since thou dost bear it, — a memorial theme
For others; for thy future self, a spell
To summon fancies out of Time's dark cell.

Before 1827.

IN my mind's eye a Temple, like a cloud
Slowly surmounting some invidious hill,
Rose out of darkness: the bright Work stood still:
And might of its own beauty have been proud,
But it was fashioned and to God was vowed 5
By Virtues that diffused, in every part,
Spirit divine through forms of human art:
Faith had her arch — her arch, when winds blow loud,
Into the consciousness of safety thrilled;
And Love her towers of dread foundation laid 10
Under the grave of things; Hope had her spire
Star-high, and pointing still to something higher;
Trembling I gazed, but heard a voice — it said,
" Hell-gates are powerless Phantoms when *we* build."

Before 1827.

ON THE DEPARTURE OF SIR WALTER SCOTT FROM ABBOTSFORD, FOR NAPLES.

A TROUBLE, not of clouds, or weeping rain,
Nor of the setting sun's pathetic light
Engendered, hangs o'er Eildon's triple height :
Spirits of Power, assembled there, complain
For kindred Power departing from their sight ;   5
While Tweed, best pleased in chanting a blithe strain,
Saddens his voice again, and yet again.
Lift up your hearts, ye Mourners ! for the might
Of the whole world's good wishes with him goes ;
Blessings and prayers, in nobler retinue   10
Than sceptred king or laurelled conqueror knows
Follow this wondrous Potentate.   Be true,
Ye winds of ocean, and the midland sea,
Wafting your Charge to soft Parthenope !

1831.

THE TROSSACHS.

THERE'S not a nook within this solemn Pass
But were an apt confessional for One
Taught by his summer spent, his autumn gone,
That Life is but a tale of morning grass
Withered at eve.   From scenes of art which chase   5
That thought away, turn, and with watchful eyes
Feed it 'mid Nature's old felicities,
Rocks, rivers, and smooth lakes more clear than glass
Untouched, unbreathed upon.   Thrice happy quest,
If from a golden perch of aspen spray   10
(October's workmanship to rival May)
The pensive warbler of the ruddy breast

That moral sweeten by a heaven-taught lay,
Lulling the year, with all its cares, to rest!

1831.

THE pibroch's note, discountenanced or mute;
The Roman kilt, degraded to a toy
Of quaint apparel for a half-spoilt boy;
The target mouldering like ungathered fruit;
The smoking steam-boat eager in pursuit,   5
As eagerly pursued; the umbrella spread
To weather-fend the Celtic herdsman's head —
All speak of manners withering to the root,
And of old honours, too, and passions high:
Then may we ask, though pleased that thought should
          range   10
Among the conquests of civility,
Survives imagination — to the change
Superior?   Help to virtue does she give?
If not, O Mortals, better cease to live!

1831.

EAGLES.

COMPOSED AT DUNOLLIE CASTLE IN THE BAY OF OBAN.

DISHONOURED Rock and Ruin! that, by law
Tyrannic, keep the Bird of Jove embarred
Like a lone criminal whose life is spared.
Vexed is he, and screams loud.   The last I saw
Was on the wing; stooping, he struck with awe   5
Man, bird, and beast; then, with a consort paired,
From a bold headland, their loved aery's guard,
Flew high above Atlantic waves, to draw

Light from the fountain of the setting sun.
Such was this Prisoner once ; and, when his plumes   10
The sea-blast ruffles as the storm comes on,
Then, for a moment, he, in spirit, resumes
His rank 'mong freeborn creatures that live free,
His power, his beauty, and his majesty.

1831.

HIGHLAND HUT.

SEE what gay wild flowers deck this earth-built Cot,
Whose smoke, forth-issuing whence and how it may,
Shines in the greeting of the sun's first ray
Like wreaths of vapour without stain or blot.
The limpid mountain-rill avoids it not ;   5
And why shouldst thou ? — If rightly trained and bred,
Humanity is humble, finds no spot
Which her Heaven-guided feet refuse to tread.
The walls are cracked, sunk is the flowery roof,
Undressed the pathway leading to the door ;   10
But love, as Nature loves, the lonely Poor ;
Search, for their worth, some gentle heart wrong-proof,
Meek, patient, kind, and, were its trials fewer,
Belike less happy. — Stand no more aloof !

1831.

TO THE PLANET VENUS, AN EVENING STAR.

COMPOSED AT LOCH LOMOND.

THOUGH joy attend Thee orient at the birth
Of dawn, it cheers the lofty spirit most
To watch thy course when Day-light, fled from earth,

In the grey sky hath left his lingering Ghost,
Perplexed as if between a splendour lost   5
And splendour slowly mustering.   Since the Sun,
The absolute, the world-absorbing One,
Relinquished half his empire to the host
Emboldened by thy guidance, holy Star,
Holy as princely — who that looks on thee,   10
Touching, as now, in thy humility
The mountain borders of this seat of care,
Can question that thy countenance is bright,
Celestial Power, as much with love as light?

                                             1831.

ROMAN ANTIQUITIES.

FROM THE ROMAN STATION AT OLD PENRITH.

How profitless the relics that we cull,
Troubling the last holds of ambitious Rome,
Unless they chasten fancies that presume
Too high, or idle agitations lull !
Of the world's flatteries if the brain be full,   5
To have no seat for thought were better doom,
Like this old helmet, or the eyeless skull
Of him who gloried in its nodding plume.
Heaven out of view, our wishes what are they?
Our fond regrets, tenacious in their grasp?   10
The Sage's theory? the Poet's lay?
Mere Fibulæ without a robe to clasp;
Obsolete lamps, whose light no time recalls;
Urns without ashes, tearless lacrymals !

                                             1831.

TO THE AUTHOR'S PORTRAIT.

Painted at Rydal Mount, by W. Pickersgill, Esq., for St. John's College, Cambridge.

Go, faithful Portrait ! and where long hath knelt
Margaret, the Saintly Foundress, take thy place;
And, if Time spare the colours for the grace
Which to the work surpassing skill hath dealt,
Thou, on thy rock reclined, though kingdoms melt   5
And states be torn up by the roots, wilt seem
To breathe in rural peace, to hear the stream,
And think and feel as once the Poet felt.
Whate'er thy fate, those features have not grown
Unrecognized through many a household tear   10
More prompt, more glad, to fall than drops of dew
By morning shed around a flower half-blown ;
Tears of delight, that testified how true
To life thou art, and, in thy truth how dear !

1832.

IN SIGHT OF THE TOWN OF COCKERMOUTH.

A POINT of life between my Parent's dust,
And yours, my buried Little-ones ! am I ;
And to those graves looking habitually
In kindred quiet I repose my trust.
Death to the innocent is more than just,   5
And, to the sinner, mercifully bent ;
So may I hope, if truly I repent
And meekly bear the ills which bear I must :
And You, my Offspring ! that do still remain,
Yet may outstrip me in the appointed race,   10
If e'er, through fault of mine, in mutual pain

We breathed together for a moment's space,
The wrong, by love provoked, let love arraign,
And only love keep in your hearts a place.

1833.

MARY QUEEN OF SCOTS.

LANDING AT THE MOUTH OF THE DERWENT, WORKINGTON.

DEAR to the Loves, and to the Graces vowed,
The Queen drew back the wimple that she wore;
And to the throng, that on the Cumbrian shore
Her landing hailed, how touchingly she bowed!
And like a Star (that, from a heavy cloud   5
Of pine-tree foliage poised in air, forth darts,
When a soft summer gale at evening parts
The gloom that did its loveliness enshroud)
She smiled; but Time, the old Saturnian seer,
Sighed on the wing as her foot pressed the strand,   10
With step prelusive to a long array
Of woes and degradations hand in hand —
Weeping captivity, and shuddering fear
Stilled by the ensanguined block of Fotheringay!

1833.

DESIRE we past illusions to recall?
To reinstate wild Fancy, would we hide
Truths whose thick veil Science has drawn aside?
No, — let this Age, high as she may, instal
In her esteem the thirst that wrought man's fall,   5
The universe is infinitely wide;
And conquering Reason, if self-glorified,

Can nowhere move uncrossed by some new wall
Or gulf of mystery, which thou alone,
Imaginative Faith ! canst overleap,.   10
In progress toward the fount of Love, — the throne
Of Power whose ministers the records keep
Of periods fixed, and laws established, less
Flesh to exalt than prove its nothingness.

1833.

BY THE SEASHORE, ISLE OF MAN.

WHY stand we gazing on the sparkling Brine,
With wonder smit by its transparency,
And all-enraptured with its purity ? —
Because the unstained, the clear, the crystalline,
Have ever in them something of benign ;   5
Whether in gem, in water, or in sky,
A sleeping infant's brow, or wakeful eye
Of a young maiden, only not divine.
Scarcely the hand forbears to dip its palm
For beverage drawn as from a mountain-well ;   10
Temptation centres in the liquid Calm ;
Our daily raiment seems no obstacle
To instantaneous plunging in, deep Sea !
And revelling in long embrace with thee.[1]

1833.

"THERE !" said a Stripling, pointing with meet pride
Towards a low roof with green trees half concealed,
"Is Mosgiel Farm ; and that's the very field

[1] The sea-water on the coast of the Isle of Man is singularly pure and beautiful.

Where Burns ploughed up the Daisy." Far and wide
A plain below stretched seaward, while, descried   5
Above sea-clouds, the Peaks of Arran rose ;
And, by that simple notice, the repose
Of earth, sky, sea, and air, was vivified.
Beneath " the random *bield* of clod or stone "
Myriads of daisies have shone forth in flower   10
Near the lark's nest, and in their natural hour
Have passed away ; less happy than the One
That, by the unwilling ploughshare, died to prove
The tender charm of poetry and love.

1833.

TRANQUILLITY ! the sovereign aim wert thou
In heathen schools of philosophic lore ;
Heart-stricken by stern destiny of yore
The Tragic Muse thee served with thoughtful vow ;
And what of hope Elysium could allow   5
Was fondly seized by Sculpture, to restore
Peace to the Mourner. But when He who wore
The crown of thorns around his bleeding brow
Warmed our sad being with celestial light,
Then Arts which still had drawn a softening grace   10
From shadowy fountains of the Infinite,
Communed with that Idea face to face :
And move around it now as planets run,
Each in its orbit round the central Sun.

1833.

MOST sweet it is with unuplifted eyes
To pace the ground, if path be there or none,
While a fair region round the traveller lies

Which he forbears again to look upon ;
Pleased rather with some soft ideal scene, 5
The work of Fancy, or some happy tone
Of meditation, slipping in between
The beauty coming and the beauty gone.
If Thought and Love desert us, from that day
Let us break off all commerce with the Muse : 10
With Thought and Love companions of our way,
Whate'er the senses take or may refuse,
The Mind's internal heaven shall shed her dews
Of inspiration on the humblest lay.

1833.

COMPOSED ON A MAY MORNING,
1838.

LIFE with yon Lambs, like day, is just begun,
Yet Nature seems to them a heavenly guide.
Does joy approach ? they meet the coming tide ;
And sullenness avoid, as now they shun
Pale twilight's lingering glooms, — and in the sun 5
Couch near their dams, with quiet satisfied ;
Or gambol — each with his shadow at his side,
Varying its shape wherever he may run.
As they from turf yet hoar with sleepy dew
All turn, and court the shining and the green, 10
Where herbs look up, and opening flowers are seen ;
Why to God's goodness cannot We be true,
And so, His gifts and promises between,
Feed to the last on pleasures ever new ?

A Poet! — He hath put his heart to school,
Nor dares to move unpropped upon the staff
Which Art hath lodged within his hand — must laugh
By precept only, and shed tears by rule.
Thy Art be Nature ; the live current quaff,   5
And let the groveller sip his stagnant pool,
In fear that else, when Critics grave and cool
Have killed him, Scorn should write his epitaph.
How does the Meadow-flower its bloom unfold ?
Because the lovely little flower is free   10
Down to its root, and, in that freedom, bold ;
And so the grandeur of the Forest-tree
Comes not by casting in a formal mould,
But from its *own* divine vitality.

> Before 1842.

THE PINE OF MONTE MARIO AT ROME.

I saw far off the dark top of a Pine
Look like a cloud — a slender stem the tie
That bound it to its native earth — poised high
'Mid evening hues, along the horizon line,
Striving in peace each other to outshine.   5
But when I learned the Tree was living there,
Saved from the sordid axe by Beaumont's care,
Oh, what a gush of tenderness was mine !
The rescued Pine-Tree, with its sky so bright
And cloud-like beauty, rich in thoughts of home,   10
Death-parted friends, and days too swift in flight,
Supplanted the whole majesty of Rome
(Then first apparent from the Pincian Height)
Crowned with St. Peter's everlasting Dome.

> 1840 (?).

TO A PAINTER.

ALL praise the Likeness by thy skill portrayed;
But 'tis a fruitless task to paint for me,
Who, yielding not to changes Time has made,
By the habitual light of memory see
Eyes unbedimmed, see bloom that cannot fade,   5
And smiles that from their birth-place ne'er shall flee
Into the land where ghosts and phantoms be :
And, seeing this, own nothing in its stead.
Couldst thou go back into far-distant years,
Or share with me, fond thought ! that inward eye,   10
Then, and then only, Painter ! could thy Art
The visual powers of Nature satisfy,
Which hold, whate'er to common sight appears,
Their sovereign empire in a faithful heart.

1840.

ON THE SAME SUBJECT.

THOUGH I beheld at first with blank surprise
This Work, I now have gazed on it so long
I see its truth with unreluctant eyes ;
O, my Belovèd !   I have done thee wrong,
Conscious of blessedness, but, whence it sprung,   5
Ever too heedless, as I now perceive :
Morn into noon did pass, noon into eve,
And the old day was welcome as the young,
As welcome, and as beautiful — in sooth
More beautiful, as being a thing more holy :   10
Thanks to thy virtues, to the eternal youth
Of all thy goodness, never melancholy ;
To thy large heart and humble mind, that cast
Into one vision, future, present, past.

1840.

WANSFELL![1] this Household has a favoured lot,
Living with liberty on thee to gaze,
To watch while Morn first crowns thee with her rays,
Or when along thy breast serenely float
Evening's angelic clouds.   Yet ne'er a note   5
Hath sounded (shame upon the Bard!) thy praise
For all that thou, as if from heaven, hast brought
Of glory lavished on our quiet days.
Bountiful Son of Earth! when we are gone
From every object dear to mortal sight,   10
As soon we shall be, may these words attest
How oft, to elevate our spirits, shone
Thy visionary majesties of light,
How in thy pensive glooms our hearts found rest.

DEC. 24, 1842.

[1] The hill that rises to the south-east, above Ambleside.

NOTES.

NOTES.

Figures Referring to Lines.

"IF THOU INDEED."

ALL we know as to the date of these lines is that Wordsworth said "they were written some time after we had become residents at Rydal Mount," 1813, and that they were printed in 1827. First placed among the "Poems of Sentiment and Reflection," this poem in 1837 was prefixed to that group, and in 1845 Wordsworth decided to give it a more important place, as an inscription prefixed to his entire poetical works. "I mean it," he wrote, "to serve as a sort of Preface." In the earliest form it consists of eleven lines ; l. 2, l. 4, and the last three lines were added in 1837, when also some slight changes of text were made in the earlier lines. The poem may well be compared with that beginning "It is no Spirit who from heaven hath flown," in which Hesperus, the "ambitious Star," prompts the thought that the Poet may one day ascend to the heights and shine there unreproved. The added lines in the present poem are an exhortation of the Poet to himself to occupy no more and no less than his allotted place :

> to the measure of that heaven-born light,
> Shine, Poet!

Lines **3, 4,** page **2.** Compare in the "Fragment from *The Recluse*," ll. 87–90 :

> upon me bestow
> A gift of genuine insight ; that my Song
> With star-like virtue in its place may shine,
> Shedding benignant influence.

10. An untended watch-fire. In the sonnet beginning "I watched, and long have watched," a star reaching the rocky parapet is described as "transmuted to a dusky fire."

LINES

Left upon a Seat in a Yew-tree.

Dated by Wordsworth, 1795, but written in part when he was at school at Hawkshead before October, 1787; published in 1798. The Yew-tree has disappeared; " it stood on the eastern shore of Esthwaite-water, about three-quarters of a mile from Hawkshead " (Knight). " This spot," said Wordsworth, " was my favourite walk in the evenings during the latter part of my school-time." The person whose character is here given was " a gentleman of the neighbourhood, a man of talent and learning, who had been educated at one of the Universities, and returned to pass his time in seclusion on his own estate."

4. Before 1832, with a less simple collocation of words: " What if these barren boughs the bee not loves? "

11. This line in 1800 replaced the 1798 reading: " Now wild, to bend its arms in circling shade," thus leaving the Yew-tree bower still intact.

13-24. In 1798 these lines stood thus:

> In youth, by genius nurs'd,
> And big with lofty views, he to the world
> Went forth, pure in his heart, against the taint
> Of dissolute tongues, 'gainst jealousy, and hate,
> And scorn, against all enemies prepared,
> All but neglect: and so, his spirit damped
> At once, with rash disdain he turned away,
> And with the food of pride sustained his soul
> In solitude.

In 1800 the lines were almost as now, except that between " neglect " and " with indignation," the following (altered in 1802) was introduced:

> The world, for so it thought,
> Owed him no service: he was like a plant
> Fair to the sun, the darling of the winds,
> But hung with fruit which no one that passed by
> Regarded, and, his spirit damped at once,

The image of the " plant," following the description of the Yew-tree, was somewhat confusing or distracting to the imagination.

27. This line returns (1820) to the first text; in 1815:

> The stone-chat, or the sand-lark, restless Bird,
> Piping along the margin of the lake;

Lamb in 1815 complained of the loss of the 1798 line, — " a line quite alive."

30.   Downcast in 1800 replaced the less correct " downward " of 1798.

38.   This line was added in 1800; " added by Coleridge " (Knight).

43.   Before 1836: " With mournful joy, to think that others felt." Wordsworth doubtless conceived that " mournful joy " disturbed the feeling of the lines with a paradox.

The poem, when considered in connection with its early date, is remarkable as embodying much that is characteristic of the writer in its moral wisdom.   Something, though with many differences, of the character of the Solitary in " The Excursion " is anticipated in these lines. For an interesting criticism of the poem, see Sir Henry Taylor's article on " Wordsworth's Poetical Works." (Taylor's Works, vol. V, pp. 18–23, ed. 1878.)

MARGARET; OR THE RUINED COTTAGE.

This is a portion of " The Excursion," Bk. i.   After line 37 follow 400 lines — here omitted — which give an account of the Old Man's boyhood, education, and manner of life.   He is a pedlar, born in Scotland, well educated, and of lofty character, devout temper, and philosophic intellect.

This portion of " The Excursion " was begun in 1795, and was substantially complete in 1798, though we find that Wordsworth was again engaged upon it in 1801.   " The Excursion " was published in 1814. There is a certain sanction for presenting this fragment by itself, for originally Wordsworth seems to have designed " The Ruined Cottage " (such being his intended title) for a separate poem.

The text of " The Excursion " was revised for the edition of 1827, was retouched in 1832, again revised in 1837, and again in 1845.   In 1827 Wordsworth, upon the whole, pruned and condensed ; in 1845 he made a few interesting additions, some of these expressing more clearly his Christian faith.

There is little or nothing in this poem that calls for explanation or comment, but a few of the many changes of text may be noted.

16, 17.   Before 1827 the reading was :

> By that impending covert made more soft,
> More low and distant !

94–98. These lines are the result of several revisions. In 1814 and 1820 we have a text far inferior in beauty :

> Green with the moss of years ; a pensive sight
> That moved my heart !— recalling former days
> When I could never pass that road but She
> Who lived within these walls, at my approach,

165. **Her dwelling** in 1827 replaced " his dwelling." Several like changes in the sex of birds may be noticed in Wordsworth's revision of his poems.

175. **Amusing** means distracting — diverting him from melancholy.

176. **Mingled** in 1837 replaced the less correct " blended " of earlier texts.

197. **Tuneful hum** is a late correction, 1845 ; in earlier texts, " Is filling all the air with melody." Wordsworth perceived that " melody" is not a happy word to describe the murmur of flies. At the same time, in the next line, " cheek " replaced " eye."

247. In edd. 1814 and 1820 the Old Man does not lift the latch, but, on reaching the door, knocks. His confidence in the later reading enhances the surprise of sorrow.

303. **" Trotting brooks,"** from Burns's " To William Simpson," " Adoun some trottin' burn's meander."

307. In edd. 1814 and 1820, " Towards the wane of Summer ; when the wheat "

344. **Dull red stains** caused by the " reddle," with which the several owners of sheep on the common had marked their animals.

374. **God** in 1832 replaced " heaven."

415. **When** : a late alteration, 1845 ; previously " Ere," making the wanderer's visit earlier in the year ; compare note on l. 307, where a change of the opposite kind was made. In each instance the season is made more joyous than as at first conceived.

534–540, and also **552–555,** changes were made, late in Wordsworth's life, in 1845, to give clearer expression to his Christian faith. Before that date two lines stood in the place of 534–540 :

> Be wise and chearful ; and no longer read
> The forms of things with an unworthy eye.

And for 552–555 stood :

> Appeared an idle dream, that could not live
> Where meditation was.   I turned away

THE REVERIE OF POOR SUSAN.

Dated by Wordsworth, 1797, and published in 1800. "This arose," said Wordsworth, "out of my observations of the affecting music of these birds hanging in this way in the London streets during the freshness and stillness of the Spring morning." Until 1815 the name was "Poor Susan." In a note in that edition (vol. I, p. 329) Wordsworth describes it as "strictly a Reverie," and says that it would not have been placed among "Poems of the Imagination" except to avoid a needless multiplication of classes among his poems. The noteworthy changes of text are two : in l. 2, "Hangs" was substituted in 1820 for "There's"; and in 1802 a stanza, which closed the poem in 1800, was judiciously omitted.

> Poor Outcast ! return — to receive thee once more
> The house of thy Father will open its door,
> And thou once again, in thy plain russet gown,
> May'st hear the thrush sing from a tree of its own.

Myers speaks of Wordsworth as "the poet not of London considered as London, but of London considered as a part of the country." In a letter of 1815, from Lamb to Wordsworth (Lamb's Letters, ed. Ainger, I, 286), he speaks of "The Farmer of Tilsbury Vale" as a charming counterpart to "Poor Susan"; "*Susan* stood for the representative of poor *Rus in urbe*. . . . The last verse of Susan was to be got rid of, at all events. It threw a kind of dubiety upon Susan's moral conduct. Susan is a servant maid. I see her trundling her mop, and contemplating the whirling phenomenon through blurred optics; but to term her 'a poor outcast' seems as much as to say that poor Susan was no better than she should be, which I trust was not what you meant to express. Robin Goodfellow supports himself without that *stick* of a moral which you have thrown away."

1. **Wood Street,** off Cheapside, London.
7. **Lothbury,** a street behind the Bank of England.

A NIGHT PIECE.

The date is Jan. 25, 1798, when Dorothy Wordsworth writes in her Journal, "Went to Poole's after tea. The sky spread over with one continuous cloud, whitened by the light of the moon, which, though her dim shape was seen, did not throw forth so strong a light as to chequer the earth with shadows. At once the clouds seemed to cleave asunder, and left her in the centre of a black-blue vault. She sailed along, followed by multitudes of stars, small, and bright, and sharp ; their brightness seemed concentrated." Perhaps Dorothy's words did not suggest, but were derived from the poem, for Wordsworth, in 1843, said that it was composed extempore on the road, — " I distinctly recollect the very moment when I was struck, as described." Lines in Coleridge's " Christabel " may have been suggested on the same occasion (or possibly on Jan. 31 ; see Dorothy's Journal) :

> The thin gray cloud is spread on high,
> It covers but not hides the sky.
> The moon is behind, and at the full ;
> And yet she looks both small and dull.

Compare the sonnet beginning " The shepherd looking eastward," and that beginning " With how sad steps, O Moon," as other " Night Pieces " of Wordsworth in which the play of clouds around the moon, its sudden brightness, and the hurrying and sparkling stars are described.

13. Note the happy fall of the accent on " clear " and " glory."

WE ARE SEVEN.

This poem was composed in 1798, while Wordsworth was walking in the grove at Alfoxden, and was published in the same year in " Lyrical Ballads." " I composed," said Wordsworth, " the last stanza first, having begun with the last line." When it was all but finished, he recited the poem to his sister Dorothy and Coleridge, and expressed his desire to add a prefatory stanza. Coleridge immediately threw off the first stanza, beginning with the line, " A little child, dear brother Jem." Wordsworth objected to " Jem," but they all enjoyed " hitching in " the name of a friend who was familiarly called Jem, and until 1815 the first line remained " A simple child, dear brother Jim." The little girl who is the heroine had been met by Wordsworth within the area of Goodrich Castle, upon his visit to the river Wye, in 1793.

The text was little altered. In l. 49 " little Jane " stood in place of " sister Jane " until 1836 ; the word " little " had occurred in l. 47, and perhaps Wordsworth thought that one small child would hardly speak of another as " little." L. 54 until 1827 was " And all the summer dry." L. 63, " Quick was the little maid's reply " (1836), gains on the earlier " The little Maiden did reply " in vigour of meaning and of expression.

The idea of the poem — the incapacity of a child to conceive of death — has much in common with the "Ode: Intimations of Immortality in Early Childhood." The opening stanza attributes this incapacity to the child's vivid sense of physical life. The "Ode" discovers other and deeper causes; and perhaps the best comment on this poem may be found in Wordsworth's "Essay on Epitaphs," in which he maintains that the inability of children to realise the thought of death proceeds from a higher source than mere ignorance or animal vivacity: "Forlorn, and cut off from communication with the best part of his nature must that man be, who should derive the sense of immortality, as it exists in the mind of a child, from the same unthinking gaiety or liveliness of animal spirits with which the lamb in the meadow, or any other irrational creature is endowed." (The passage is too long to quote in full.)

SIMON LEE.

Written in 1798, and published in the same year. "This Old Man," says Wordsworth, "had been huntsman to the squires of Alfoxden, which, at the time we occupied it, belonged to a minor. The Old Man's cottage stood upon the common, a little way from the entrance to Alfoxden Park. . . . The expression when the hounds were out, 'I dearly love their voice,' was word for word from his own lips."

No poem of Wordsworth's underwent so many and perplexing changes as "Simon Lee." The last five stanzas, indeed, were little altered; but the first seven, which nearly reached their final form in 1832, are found in different texts and different sequence in 1798, 1802, 1820, 1827, 1832. Condensation was effected, words and lines were altered, stanzas were shifted in position, and new stanzas were constructed by connecting the halves of certain stanzas with the halves of others. It would hardly be profitable to trace here all these curious changes; they will be found recorded in my edition of Wordsworth in the Aldine Poets. I shall here do no more than give the earliest form of those stanzas which were most considerably rehandled:

> In the sweet shire of Cardigan,
> Not far from pleasant Ivor-hall,
> An old man dwells, a little man,
> I've heard he once was tall.
> Of years he has upon his back,
> No doubt a burthen weighty;
> He says he is three score and ten,
> But others say he's eighty.

A long blue livery-coat has he,
That 's fair behind, and fair before;
Yet, meet him where you will, you see
At once that he is poor.
Full five and twenty years he lived
A running huntsman merry;
And, though he has but one eye left,
His cheek is like a cherry.

No man like him the horn could sound,
And no man was so full of glee;
To say the least, four counties round
Had heard of Simon Lee;
His master's dead, and no one now
Dwells in the hall of Ivor;
Men, dogs, and horses, all are dead;
He is the sole survivor.

His hunting feats have him bereft
Of his right eye, as you may see:
And then what limbs those feats have left
To poor old Simon Lee!
He has no son, he has no child;
His wife, an aged woman,
Lives with him, near the waterfall,
Upon the village common.

And he is lean and he is sick,
His little body 's half awry,
His ancles they are swoln and thick;
His legs are thin and dry.
When he was young he little knew
Of husbandry, or tillage;
And now he 's forced to work, though weak,
— The weakest in the village.

He all the country could outrun,
Could leave both man and horse behind;
And often, ere the race was done,
He reeled and was stone-blind.
And still there 's something in the world
At which his heart rejoices;
For when the chiming hounds are out,
He dearly loves their voices!

Old Ruth works out of doors with him,
And does what Simon cannot do;
For she, not over stout of limb,
Is stouter of the two.
And though you with your utmost skill
From labour could not wean them,
Alas! 't is very little, all
Which they can do between them.

Beside their moss-grown hut of clay,
Not twenty paces from the door,
A scrap of land they have, but they
Are poorest of the poor.
This scrap of land he from the heath
Enclosed when he was stronger;
But what avails the land to them,
Which they can till no longer?

Evidently, Wordsworth felt that for the pathos of the poem it was not necessary to make Simon so grotesque a figure as he had been at first, and felt also that he had insisted too much upon certain trivial details. Simon is no longer deprived of an eye; his long blue livery coat is left to the imagination. Enough details of the old man's weakness and poverty remain, of his joyous youth and infirm age; and every detail tends to the central point, the pathetic significance of the incident which closes the poem.

LINES WRITTEN IN EARLY SPRING ("I heard," etc.).

Written and published in 1798. "Actually composed," said Wordsworth, "while I was sitting by the side of the brook that runs down from the Comb, in which stands the village of Alford [*i.e.*, Holford, in Somerset], through the grounds of Alfoxden. It was a chosen resort of mine. The brook ran down a sloping rock so as to make a waterfall considerable for that country, and across the pool below had fallen a tree, an ash, if I rightly remember, from which rose perpendicularly boughs in search of the light intercepted by the deep shade above. The boughs bore leaves of green that, for want of sunshine, had faded into almost lily-white, and from the under side of this natural sylvan bridge depended long and beautiful tresses of ivy, which waved gently in the breeze that might, poetically speaking, be called the breath of the waterfall."

In revising his poems, Wordsworth, in many instances, replaced the word "sweet" by some other adjective ; so, in l. 9, "green bower" in 1837 replaced the earlier "sweet bower."

Lines 21, 22 were originally — with a meaning too subjective, and hence altered —

> If I these thoughts may not prevent,
> If such be of my creed the plan,

In 1820 the present text (except that "is" stood for "be") was introduced. In 1827 the order of words was "From Heaven if this belief be sent." Probably Wordsworth wished to separate "*be*lief" from "*be* sent."

Anyone who glances at a chronological table of the poems of 1798 will see how they fall into two chief groups, — those radiant with joy, which tell of what this poem calls "Nature's holy plan," and those which interpret the sufferings of humanity, telling "what man has made of man."

TO MY SISTER ("It is the first").

This poem was composed in front of Alfoxden House, near Nether Stowey, in the year of publication, 1798. "My little boy-messenger on this occasion ['Edward' of l. 13, who, in the earlier titles, is said to have taken the poem to the writer's sister] was the son of Basil Montagu. The larch mentioned in the first stanza was standing when I revisited the place in May, 1841, more than forty years after."

The only change of text deserving of notice is in l. 26, which, until 1837, was "Than fifty years of reason," — the definite extravagance of which challenged opposition.

EXPOSTULATION AND REPLY.

Composed in front of Alfoxden House in the spring of 1798, the year of publication. The text remained unaltered.

The scene is placed "by Esthwaite Lake" (west of Windermere), because the schoolmaster, William Taylor, from whom some features of "Matthew" are derived, taught at the neighbouring village of Hawkshead, where Wordsworth had been his pupil. The plea for the study of books is put appropriately into the schoolmaster's mouth.

THE TABLES TURNED.

Composed and published in 1798. The only variation of text requiring notice is in the first stanza, where previous to 1820 the third and fourth lines came first and second.

The stanza beginning "One impulse from a vernal wood" has been censured for exaggeration, but Wordsworth means that in communion with external nature a moment may come which will evoke from the heart more moral energy that can be taught by books. The contrast is not merely between books and nature, but also between the genial temper of mind induced by external nature, when rightly observed and felt, and the temper of the mere analytic intellect. Compare ll. 21–32 of "To my Sister."

THE COMPLAINT OF A FORSAKEN INDIAN WOMAN.

Written for "Lyrical Ballads," at Alfoxden, in 1798, and published in the same year. The substance of what Hearne writes is conveyed by Wordsworth into his note prefixed to the poem, but he does not mention that Hearne tells of a woman left behind by his Indian companions, who three times succeeded in coming up with them. "At length, poor creature! she dropt behind, and no one attempted to go back in search of her." Chap. vii.

4. This is the earliest text, restored in 1836. From 1815 to 1832 the reading was of less imaginative power, — "The stars were mingled with my dreams."

5, 6. From 1798 to 1815:

> In sleep did I behold the skies,
> I saw the crackling flashes drive;

Wordsworth noticed that "crackling" needed the verb to hear, and substituted the present text in 1820, with only the difference "I heard, and saw" (altered in 1827).

23, 24. Before 1815:

> Too soon despair o'er me prevailed;
> Too soon my heartless spirit failed;

The reproach of l. 24 adds an idea; the original l. 24 only repeated the idea of l. 23.

30. **Dear friends :** before 1845, " My friends."

36. Before 1815 : " A most strange something did I see ; "

40. Before 1815 : "like a little child." The change brings out the child's inability to accomplish what seemed its desire.

61-70. This stanza was omitted, to the loss of the poem, from ed. 1815 to ed. 1832 ; restored in 1836. Line 61, from 1798 to 1805, was " My journey will be shortly run " (altered in 1836). In l. 68 " thought," before 1836 was " thoughts," and the closing lines were :

> I feel my body die away,
> I shall not see another day.

THE OLD CUMBERLAND BEGGAR.

Wordsworth dates this poem 1798 ; published in 1800. It was written, he says, at Racedown and Alfoxden, *i.e.*, between 1796 and 1798. Of the subject he says, " observed, and with great benefit to my own heart when I was a child. The political economists were about that time beginning their war upon mendicity in all its forms, and by implication, if not directly, on almsgiving also." For Wordsworth's views as to the treatment of pauperism, see among his " Prefaces," etc., the " Postscript 1835 " (Aldine edition, vol. V, p. 299).

15. **Ate,** a correction of 1805 ; previously " eat."

26, 27. Altered in 1837, perhaps to avoid the awkward compound " horseman-traveller " (which, however, is retained in " Ruth "), or perhaps to get rid of " does throw " ; previously :

> The sauntering horseman-traveller does not throw
> With careless hand

31. Before 1827 : " Towards this aged Beggar turns a look." The more dwelling sense of " watches " is a gain.

39. **Thus warned** in 1827 replaced " perchance."

54. **Seldom** in 1827 replaced " never." The power of this poem lies in its absolute truthfulness and freedom from exaggeration. See the change in ll. 186–189.

62. **Has :** before 1837, " have."

72. **Or :** before 1837, " and." The proud, of whom Wordsworth speaks, may found their pride on either talents, or power, or wisdom.

79-88. The most important alteration in the poem. Before 1837 only two lines :

> Inseparably linked. While thus he creeps
> From door to door the villagers in him

104. In 1832 the soul was made feminine ; previously "itself," not "herself." Compare the sonnet "Milton, thou shouldst be living," where a like change was made in 1820. "No writer," says Coventry Patmore ("The Rod, the Root, and the Flower," p. 8), "sacred or profane, ever uses the word 'he' or 'him' of the soul. It is always 'she' or 'her,' so universal is the intuitive knowledge that the soul, with regard to God who is her life, is feminine."

109. Even such minds in 1827 replaced "minds like these," to avoid a repeated "like" in 109 and 111, at the same time l. 111 being substituted for the earlier "This helpless Wanderer, have perchance received."

138, 139. A line was omitted in 1827 ; previously:

> . . . negligent,
> Meanwhile, in any tenderness of heart
> Or act of love

Perhaps Wordsworth thought that neglect properly applies to "acts," but not to a state of heart.

157. Store: before 1827, "chest."

164. Borne: a needed correction of 1827 ; previously "led," an inappropriate word to connect with "tide."

175. The chartered wind, privileged wind, — probably a reminiscence from Shakespeare's "King Henry V," i. 1. 48, "the air, a chartered libertine."

184, 185. Lamb in a letter to Wordsworth of January, 1801, notes "the delicate and curious feeling in the wish for the Cumberland Beggar that he may have about him the melody of birds, although he hear them not."

186-189. Before 1815 :

> if his eyes, which now
> Have been so long familiar with the earth,
> No more behold the horizontal sun

The exaggeration is corrected. See note on l. 54.

193. On a in 1837 replaced "by the," to avoid the "th" sound occurring thrice in the line.

In this poem Wordsworth takes a human being who seems to have reached the lowest point of utility, in the vulgar meaning of that word, and shows how he confers real service on his fellows in receiving service, and has a just claim on the charities of man as well as the unfailing charities of nature.

ANIMAL TRANQUILLITY AND DECAY.

Written and published in 1798. The original title was "Old Man Travelling; Animal Tranquillity and Decay, A Sketch." The only change in the present lines was, l. 10, "hath such" in 1805 replacing "has such," to avoid the clash of sibilants. But at first these lines were succeeded by the following:

> I asked him whither he was bound, and what
> The object of his journey; he replied
> "Sir! I am going many miles to take
> A last leave of my son, a mariner
> Who from a sea-fight has been brought to Falmouth,
> And there is dying in an hospital."

These lines were slightly altered in 1800, and were omitted in 1815. Poems on the sorrows of the poor caused by war are numerous in Southey and other writers between 1790 and 1800. Here the virtue of the poem lies in its mere presentation of an old man, his tranquillity and decay, and the added piece of narrative rather lessened its imaginative effect.

LINES COMPOSED A FEW MILES ABOVE TINTERN ABBEY, etc.

This poem was written in 1798 and published in the same year, being the last poem of "Lyrical Ballads," a volume which opens with Coleridge's "Ancient Mariner." "No poem of mine," said Wordsworth (*Fenwick note*), "was composed under circumstances more pleasant for me to remember than this. I began it upon leaving Tintern, after crossing the Wye, and concluded it just as I was entering Bristol in the evening, after a ramble of four or five days with my sister. Not a line of it was altered, and not any part of it written down till I reached Bristol."

Wordsworth had visited the Wye in the summer of 1793, to which fact he refers in the opening lines.

4. **Soft inland murmur:** before 1845, "sweet inland murmur." Wordsworth in his earlier poems had used the word "sweet" too frequently and indiscriminately, and at a later time he grew perhaps overfastidious as to the word, which disappeared from a large number of passages.

13, 14. The text is of 1845. In 1798–1800 :

> Among the woods and copses lose themselves,
> Nor, with their green and simple hue, disturb
> The wild green landscape.

In 1802–43 :

> Are clad in one green hue, and lose themselves
> Among the woods and copses, nor disturb
> The wild green landscape.

Perhaps Wordsworth thought the earlier reading too analytic in its characterizing of landscape for the mood of mind expressing itself in these lines.

The reader of " Lyrical Ballads," 1798, should notice that a line coming between l. 18 and l. 19 in that edition, " And the low copses — coming from the trees," is cancelled in the " errata."

22, 23. Before 1827 :

> Though absent long,
> These forms of beauty.

The absence was that of Wordsworth ; in the earlier text the word " absent " might be supposed to belong to " forms of beauty."

32. Before 1820, " As may have had no trivial influence." Wordsworth generalizes the reflection, and does not wish to identify his own life with " the good man's life " of l. 33.

84. Aching joys. In a suppressed stanza of " Ruth " occur the words

> with delight
> The heart of Ruth would ache.

106. The words of Young referred to in Wordsworth's footnote occur in " The Complaint," " Night Thoughts," VI, 423–5 :

> At a small inlet, which a grain might close,
> And half create the wondrous world they see.
> Our *senses*, as our *reason*, are divine.

With respect to the changes which Wordsworth's feeling for nature underwent, this poem may be read in connection with the " Ode : Intimations of Immortality," etc. Here he describes the mere animal enjoyment of nature in boyhood ; the later period, when beauty and sublimity, reaching him through the eye and ear, became a passion ; later still, the tranquillising, and also the elevating and spiritual influences of nature ; and now, a feeling for nature, touched and chastened by humanity, and, at the same time, a deeper communion with the spiritual Presence at work both through nature and in man. We might name these periods that of the blood, that of the senses, that of the imagination, and that of the soul. In the development of feeling something was lost, but more was gained. "Wordsworth," writes Myers, "has shown by the subtle intensity of his own emotion how the contemplation of Nature can be made a revealing agency, like Love or Prayer, — an opening, if indeed there be any opening, into the transcendent world." In a note, ed. 1800, Wordworth writes : "I have not ventured to call this Poem an Ode; but it was written with a hope that in the transitions, and the impassioned music of the versification, would be found the principal requisites of that species of composition."

THERE WAS A BOY.

Written in Germany late in 1798; the receipt of a MS. copy is acknowledged from Ratzeburg, on December 10, by Coleridge, who writes "That

> 'uncertain heaven received
> Into the bosom of the steady lake'

I should have recognized anywhere; and had I met these lines running wild in the deserts of Arabia, I should have instantly screamed out, 'Wordsworth!'" The poem was first published in 1800. When in 1804 Wordsworth was at work on "The Prelude," he made this poem a part of Bk. v (ll. 364–397). The Boy's name is unknown. He has erroneously been identified with Wordsworth's school-fellow, William Raincock of Rayrigg.

2. Winander, Windermere or Winandermere in Westmoreland.

3. Before 1815 : "At evening, when the stars had just begun "

15. Concourse wild, a correction of 1805 ; previously " a wild scene " ; but while " visible scene " of l. 21 is correct, a " scene of din " misapplies the word.

16, 17. Before 1836:

> Of mirth and jocund din ! And, when it chanced
> That pauses of deep silence mocked his skill,

In " The Prelude ":

> and, when a lengthened pause
> Of silence came, and baffled his best skill,

The idea of mockery disturbs the feeling of the lines which follow.

26-34. In 1800 and 1802 the lines corresponding to these were the following :

> Fair are the woods, and beauteous is the spot,
> The vale where he was born ; the Church-yard **hangs**
> Upon a slope above the village school,
> And there along that bank when I have pass'd
> At evening, I believe, that near his grave
> A full half-hour together I have stood,
> Mute — for he died when he was ten years old.

In 1805 Wordsworth felt that the last words were a bald addition, informing the reader of the Boy's age and nothing more. He therefore announced the Boy's death as in the present ll. 26, 27, except that he remained of the age of " ten " (where now "full twelve " — 1815 — stands). The passage continued " Fair are," etc., as in 1800, until we reach l. 32 :

> At evening, I believe, that oftentimes
> A full half-hour together I have stood
> Mute — looking at the grave in which he lies. (1805.)

Lines 28, 29 are of 1845. In 1827 (and in " The Prelude ") Words-worth substituted for the reading of 1800 :

> Fair is the spot, most beautiful the vale
> Where he was born ; the grassy church-yard hangs

In 1840 the original text was restored; but still dissatisfied, Wordsworth in 1845 wrote ll. 28, 29 as we now have them. Lines 31-33 received their final form in 1836. " A long half-hour " was substituted in 1815 for " A full half-hour." Compare " To a Butterfly," l. 1, where " a short half-hour " was changed to " a full half-hour."

In " The Waggoner " Wordsworth speaks of the Windermere owls :

> The jolly bird hath learned his cheer
> On the banks of Windermere ;
> Where a tribe of them make merry,
> Mocking the man that keeps the ferry.

The poem might have closed without a sense of incompleteness at the line " Into the bosom of the steady lake," but the contrast between the " concourse wild of jocund din " and the silence of the grave heightens and deepens the impression which it makes.

"STRANGE FITS OF PASSION HAVE I KNOWN."

This poem was written in Germany early in 1799, and was published in 1800.   The following variations of text may be noted:
Lines 5, 6 replaced in 1836 the earlier

> When she I loved was strong and gay
> And like a rose in June,

Line 8, "an evening moon" in 1836 replaced "the evening moon"; "the," following "beneath," produced a disagreeable juxtaposition of the "th" sound.

Line 11 in 1836 replaced "My horse trudg'd on, and we drew nigh." The quickening pace corresponds better with a lover's feeling.

Lines 15, 16 previous to 1836 were

> Towards the roof of Lucy's cot
> The moon descended still.

The use of "towards" as a dissyllable was at this time condemned by Wordsworth.

Line 24.   In this line the word "planet," applied to the moon, was altered in 1815 to "bright moon."

The Lucy of other poems of this date dies (see "She dwelt among the untrodden ways"), and so the lover's omen was confirmed.   Aubrey de Vere questioned Wordsworth as to why he had not written more love-poems.   "Had I been a writer of love-poetry," Wordsworth replied, "it would have been natural to me to write it with a degree of warmth which could hardly have been approved by my principles."

"SHE DWELT AMONG THE UNTRODDEN WAYS."

Written in Germany in 1799 and published in 1800.   The text is as it has stood in all editions except 1802, when l. 4 was "A very few to love."

The river Dove rises on the borders of Derby and Stafford, near Buxton and Axedge Hill.   It is not known whether any original of Lucy existed, or whether the poems connected with her are wholly of the imagination.

"I TRAVELLED AMONG UNKNOWN MEN."

Written in 1799, probably on returning from Germany, but not published until 1807. Other poems connected with Lucy appeared in 1800.

Sara Coleridge writes of the last stanza as one " in which the poet, as it were, *spreads day and night* over the object of his affections, and seems, under the influence of his passionate feeling, to think of England, whether in light or darkness, only as Lucy's play-place and verdant home."

In 1807 Wordsworth directed his printer to insert the poem after " A Slumber did my Spirit Seal."

"THREE YEARS SHE GREW."

Composed in the Hartz Forest in 1799 and published in 1800 ; printed also in *The Morning Post*, Mar. 2, 1801.

With the exception of one line, the 23d, the poem is now as originally published. Line 23 in 1800 was " A beauty that shall mould her form"; *grace* of motion is correct, and the repetition of *beauty* in two successive stanzas is avoided. The change was made in 1802. At the same time Wordsworth altered ll. 7, 8, reading :

> Her Teacher I myself will be,
> She is my darling ;— and with me

Happily he reverted in 1805 to the earlier texts ; the conception of Nature as pedagogue is far less suitable and less significant than that of Nature as " law and impulse." In the account of Ruth's lover (p. 64) we read of Nature as an impulse, but without the restraining law. The third stanza expounds the meaning of " law and impulse " ; the fourth tells of education through visible beauty ; the fifth of impulses from sound; the sixth of the vital joy communicated by the life of Nature. Prof. Knight says that l. 23 of ed. 1800 is replaced in the errata by the present reading. It is not so in the errata of my copy of that edition.

"A SLUMBER DID MY SPIRIT SEAL."

Written in Germany in 1799; published in 1800. The text was never altered. One of the " Lucy " group of poems. Mr. Aubrey de Vere calls this poem " a dirge, which those who confound the passionate with the exclamatory will do well to pass by, but which to others will represent, in its stern brevity, the tragic rising to the terrible."

A POET'S EPITAPH.

Composed in the winter of 1798–99, in Germany, during Wordsworth's walks on the ramparts of Goslar; published in 1800.

1. **Statist**: substituted in 1837 for the earlier "Statesman," doubtless to avoid the jingle of "man" and "van."

6–8. Before 1820 :

> Go, carry to some other place
> The hardness of thy coward eye,
> The falsehood of thy sallow face.

See Lamb's comment below.

9–12. The "Doctor" of this stanza is not a physician, but a divine, accustomed to kneel at prayers on a luxurious "cushion."

13. Before 1820 : "Art thou a man of gallant pride "; altered to vary from the opening words of the preceding stanza.

14. The soldier is represented as less alien to the poet than the other typical personages.

18. Is the "Philosopher" the same person as the "Physician"? Observe the note of exclamation, not of interrogation, after "Philosopher !" But the query is not repeated in l. 25.

24. In 1837 this replaced the reading of 1815–32 : "That abject thing, thy soul, away," which itself replaced the reading of 1800–5, "Thy pin-point of a soul away." See Lamb's comment below.

30. **Great or small**, a correction of 1837; previously "nor."

31. **Self-sufficing**. So in 1800, but in 1802 and 1805 "self-sufficient"; "self-sufficing" restored in 1815.

38. The "russet brown" is probably a reminiscence from Thomson's "Castle of Indolence," where the bard is "in russet brown bedight."

Lamb, in a letter of 1801, wrote: "The 'Poet's Epitaph' is disfigured, to my taste, by the common satire upon parsons and lawyers in the beginning, and the coarse epithet of 'pin-point' in the sixth stanza. All the rest is eminently good, and your own."

LUCY GRAY.

Written in 1799 at Goslar in Germany ; published in the second volume of "Lyrical Ballads," 1800. "It was founded," says Wordsworth, "on a circumstance told me by my Sister, of a little girl, who, not far from Halifax in Yorkshire, was bewildered in a snowstorm. Her footsteps were traced by her parents to the middle of the lock of a canal, and no other vestige of her, backward or forward, could be traced. The body, however, was found in the canal." In Crabb Robinson's Diary, Sept. 11, 1816, the writer, recording a conversation with Wordsworth, notes that the poet's object was "to exhibit poetically entire *solitude*, and he represents the child as observing the day-moon, which no town or village girl would ever notice." Wordsworth remarks that the way in which the incident was treated and "the spiritualizing of the character" might furnish hints for contrasting the imaginative influences which he endeavoured to throw over common life with Crabbe's matter-of-fact style of treating subjects of the same kind. In 1827 Wordsworth altered, in l. 45, the words "Then downward" to "Half breathless," but restored "Then downwards" at a later date.

The chief departure from the real incident is that Lucy Gray's body is not found; this gives opportunity for the rumours that she is still alive, and the supposed confirmation of these rumours by her apparition on the wild. For Wordsworth's treatment of the supernatural, compare his poem "The Danish Boy," where the spirit walks or sits at noonday in a moorland dell, warbling songs of war that seem songs of love :

> For calm and gentle is his mien;
> Like a dead Boy he is serene.

"The Danish Boy," like "Lucy Gray," was written in Germany in 1799. If in either poem there be terror, the terror is almost lost in beauty.

RUTH.

Written in Germany in 1799; published in 1800. "Suggested," says Wordsworth, "by an account I had of a wanderer in Somersetshire."

The changes of text are many and perplexing. In 1802 Wordsworth rehandled the poem. Stanza 3 (ll. 13–18) was then added, with the reading in ll. 17, 18 (altered in 1827) :

> She passed her time; and in this way
> Grew up to woman's height.

Stanza 39 (ll. 229–234) was also then added, with the reading in ll. 229, 230 (altered in 1805):

> The neighbours grieve for her, and say
> That she will, long before her day,

But the chief change in 1802 was an insertion between stanza 10 and stanza 11 (*i.e.*, between l. 60 and l. 61). Three stanzas (now ll. 127–144) were altered from third to first person, and were removed from their place in 1800, — a place which they resumed in 1805, — and these three stanzas were preceded by two new stanzas, and followed by two also new. Of these four new stanzas two have been retained and two were omitted from all the editions after 1805. The retained stanzas are now the 28th (ll. 163–168) and the 30th (ll. 175–180); they came as second and sixth of the insertion of 1802, and the two stanzas not now retained, which stood first and last in the inserted passage, were as follows:

> Of march and ambush, siege and fight,
> Then did he tell; and with delight
> The heart of Ruth would ache;
> Wild histories they were, and dear:
> But 't was a thing of heaven to hear
> When of himself he spake. (Stanza 11 of 1802.)

> " It is a purer, better mind :
> O Maiden innocent and kind
> What sights I might have seen !
> Even now upon my eyes they break !"
> — And he again began to speak
> Of Lands where he had been. (Stanza 17 of 1802.)

In 1805 the three transposed stanzas (ll. 127–144) were put back in their former place; a new stanza, now the 29th (ll. 169–174), was written for the inserted passage between l. 60 and l. 61, and it was placed as the third stanza of the insertion, the order being (1) " Of march and ambush," (2) " Sometimes most earnestly," (3) " Before me shone," (4) " No more of this," (5) " It is a purer." In 1815 these five stanzas were omitted. In 1820 those numbered 2, 3, 4, were restored and placed as now, while 1 and 5 were never restored.

3, 4. In 1800 (only) :

> And so, not seven years old,
> The slighted Child.

8, 9. Before 1836 :

> And from that oaten pipe could draw
> All sounds

An exaggeration corrected.

26. Before 1836 : " Ah, no !" — the pathetic " Ah " being inappropriate here. In l. 27, " bore " before 1805 was " bare."

55–57. Before 1836 :

> He spake of plants divine and strange
> That every hour [1802 ; " day " 1800] their blossoms change,
> Ten thousand lovely hues !

73. Before 1836: " And then he said, ' How sweet it were.' " " Sweet " had been over-used by Wordsworth in early editions, and was banished from many passages. See l. 79 and l. 98.

75–77. Before 1836 :

> "A gardener in the shade,
> Still wandering with an easy mind,
> To build "

The ideas of " a gardener " and of " wandering " did not harmonize ; edition 1836 read " In sunshine or through shade " (altered as now, 1845).

79. Before 1836: " sweet years." See notes on l. 73 and l. 98.

86. Before 1832 : " Dear thoughts " ; altered because " dearer " occurs in l. 90.

98. Before 1820: " Sweet Ruth alone " ; altered to avoid repetition of l. 91.

133. In 1802 (only): " unhallow'd " replaced " voluptuous."

135. Before 1845 : " lovely flowers." And at the same time, 1845, in l. 138, " gorgeous bowers " (1815–43) — itself a substitute for the earlier " magic bowers " — became " favoured bowers," thus allowing the change to be made in l. 135.

140. " Sometimes " in 1805 replacing " often," 1802, returned to the reading of 1800. So also in l. 142, " linked to " replaced " amid," and in l. 143 " needs must have " replaced " wanted not," returning to the original text.

145. In 1802 (only): " Ill did he live."

167, 168. In 1802 (only): " thoughtlessness " in place of " confidence." From 1820 to 1836 :

> " When first, in confidence and pride,
> I crossed "

169–171. Before 1840 :

> " It was a fresh and glorious world —
> A banner bright that was [' shone,' 1836] unfurled
> Before me suddenly : "

175–180. This stanza, written in 1802 for the insertion between l. 60 and l. 61, was originally :

> " So it was then, and so is now :
> For Ruth ! with thee I know not how,
> I feel my spirit burn
> Even as the east when day comes forth ;
> And to the west, and south, and north,
> The morning doth return."

From 1805 to 1843, the first two lines :

> " But wherefore speak of this ? For now
> Sweet [' Dear,' 1836–43] Ruth ! "

The last three lines remained as in 1802 until 1836, when the present text appeared. The alterations bring the lines into closer sequence with the preceding stanza.

181. Before 1820 : " But now the pleasant dream was gone." From 1820 to 1843 : " Full soon that purer mind was gone " (altered, 1845).

196–198. Before 1820 :

> And there, exulting in her wrongs,
> Among the music of her songs
> She fearfully carous'd.

Lamb objected that this use of " carouse " was not English. In 1820–32 :

> And there she sang tumultuous songs,
> By recollection of her wrongs
> To fearful passion roused.

The present text is of 1836. " Certainly ' to carouse cups,' that is, to empty them, " wrote Wordsworth, " is the genuine English." So in " Othello," II, 3, 55 : " Roderigo . . . caroused potations."

203. Clear brook in 1836 replaced " wild brook." " Wild " occurs in the same line of the preceding stanza.

214, 215. In 1800 (only) :

> And to the pleasant banks of Tone
> She took her way, to dwell alone

This expressed too much deliberation for a wild creature of chance. Tone is a river in county Somerset, which joins the Parret at Borough Bridge.

217. In 1800 (only) : " engines of her grief."

226. In 1800 and 1802 : " (And in this tale we all agree)," — altered to prevent the intrusion of a personal element.

Both Coleridge and Wordsworth, in the Nether Stowey and Alfoxden days, were readers of William Bartram's " Travels through North and South Carolina," etc., — a delightful book. The "feathers" bought by Ruth's lover from the Cherokees, l. 21, appear in Bartram's frontispiece,— a portrait of " Mico-Chlucco, the Long Warrior," and the Cherokee head-dress is described, p. 499. The Indian girls gathering strawberries and singing (ll. 49–54) are from Bartram, p. 355, and the plants of ll. 55–60 are derived from Bartram's description (pp. 159, 160) of the *Gordonia lasianthus*, which " may be said to change and renew its garments every morning throughout the year, and every day appears with unfading lustre."

Wordsworth has written many poems in which the influence of nature as "law and impulse" is shown in its beneficent working. Here the dangers to the heart and life arising from nature as impulse, apart from its restraining power, are exhibited. The Georgian youth sinks into moral degradation ; Ruth, whom he has wronged, is incapable of moral fortitude, yet she finds, in her distraction, some healing influences from the woods and streams to which, in girlhood, she had abandoned herself in "thoughtless freedom."

De Quincey ("Autobiographic Sketches," vol. II, p. 305, ed. 1854) says that the story of Ruth is founded on fact: "Wordsworth himself told me, in general terms, that the case which suggested the poem was that of an American lady, whose husband forsook her at the very place of embarkation from England, under circumstances and under expectations, upon her part, very much the same as those of Ruth."

INFLUENCES OF BEAUTY AND FEAR IN BOYHOOD.

[From " The Prelude," Bk. i, ll. 301–400.]

This passage from the first book of " The Prelude " immediately precedes that given separately by Wordsworth, with the title " Influence of Natural Objects," etc., which in the present selection follows next. The same title would indeed be appropriate, but in order to distinguish the extract I have named it " Influences of Beauty and Fear in Boyhood."

With the description of the moving mountains, as seen from the boat, compare Browning's lines in " The Englishman in Italy ":

> Oh, those mountains, their infinite movement,
>   Still moving with you ;
> For ever some new head or breast of them
>   Thrusts into view
> To observe the intruder.

INFLUENCE OF NATURAL OBJECTS.

Written in 1799, being an extract from "The Prelude," Bk. i. The extract was first printed in Coleridge's periodical *The Friend*, Dec. 28, 1809, where it follows Coleridge's prose description of skating on the lake of Ratzeburg. The frozen lake of the poem is Esthwaite; the village, Hawkshead, where Wordsworth was a schoolboy.

17. **Valleys**: in "The Prelude," "valley."

27. In "The Prelude," "The cottage windows blazed through twilight gloom."

37. **The pack loud-chiming**: until 1840, "The pack loud bellowing." Compare Kingsley, of hounds, "Chime, ye dappled darlings!"

40. **Smitten** in 1836 replaced "Meanwhile," — a gain in vividness.

50–52. The text dates from 1827. Before 1820:

> To cut across the image of a Star
> That gleam'd upon the ice; and oftentimes

In 1820:

> To cross the bright reflection of a Star,
> Image, that, flying still before me — gleamed
> Upon the glassy plain: and oftentimes

In "The Prelude":

> To cut across the reflex of a star,
> That fled, and flying still, etc.

By reverting to "cut across," Wordsworth retained the vivid description of motion on skates; "reflex" made the sense clear, and the pursuit of the flying image was an added observation of 1820.

63. In "The Prelude," "Till all was tranquil as a dreamless sleep." Perhaps Wordsworth thought — surely erroneously — that "summer sea" was inappropriate as the close of a description of the midwinter frozen lake.

NUTTING.

Written in Germany in 1799; published in 1800. It was intended at first for part of "The Prelude," but was struck out "as not being wanted there." "Like most of my school-fellows," said Wordsworth, "I was an impassioned nutter. For this pleasure the vale of Esthwaite, abounding in coppice wood, furnished a very wide range. These verses arose out of the remembrance of feelings I had often had when a boy, and particularly in the extensive woods that still [1843] stretch from the side of Esthwaite Lake towards Graythwaite, the seat of the ancient family of Sandys."

2. This line was added in 1802.

4. This line was added in 1827, before which date l. 5 was "when forth I sallied from our cottage door." The cottage was Anne Tyson's, where Wordsworth boarded in his school days.

6. Before 1815: "And with a wallet." The "and" was superfluous; the "huge" adds picturesqueness.

8. Tow'rd some far-distant wood: before 1836, "Towards the distant woods"; altered because Wordsworth had come to view "toward" as a monosyllable.

9-12. Before 1815:

> of Beggar's weeds
> Put on for the occasion, by advice
> And exhortation of my frugal Dame.
> Motley accoutrements! ["accoutrement," 1802-5.]

The "beggar's weeds" were felt by Wordsworth to be too suggestive of a feeling of disgust.

14-16. Before 1836 less vividly descriptive :

> Among the woods
> And o'er the pathless rocks, I forc'd my way
> Until, at length, I came

20. Tempting clusters: before 1845, "milk-white clusters."

36. Notice the choice of the word "fleeced" to harmonize with the image of a flock of sheep. In this line "under" replaced "beneath" in 1845, perhaps to vary from "beneath" in l. 25 and l. 30, and also to avoid the repeated sound of "th."

50. Before 1836: "Even then, when from the bower"; altered probably to avoid the thrice-repeated "en" sound in the opening words.

53. In 1836 "saw" was inserted, probably to remove the stress on "the" in "the intruding sky."

The poem — a fragment of autobiography — illustrates the processes and incidents by which Wordsworth's animal joy in nature in boyhood was gradually purified and spiritualised.

MATTHEW.

Written in 1799 and published in 1800. The text is unchanged, except that in l. 24 "dew" in 1815 replaced "oil." The Rev. William Taylor, schoolmaster at Hawkshead, close to Esthwaite Lake, taught Wordsworth from 1782 to 1786. In the ' Address to the Scholars of the Village School of ——," Wordsworth speaks of Taylor as "our common Friend and Father." And in "The Prelude," Bk. x, ll. 532–544, he tells how he turned aside to seek Taylor's grave. Some features of the character of Matthew are derived from Taylor, but it is an ideal construction, not a portrait. "This and other poems connected with Matthew," said Wordsworth (*Fenwick note*), "would not gain by a literal detail of facts. Like the Wanderer in "The Excursion," this Schoolmaster was made up of several, both of his class and men of other occupations. I do not ask pardon for what there is of untruth in such verses, considered strictly as matters of fact. It is enough if, being true and consistent in spirit, they move and teach in a manner not unworthy of a Poet's calling." Wordsworth dealt with landscape in the same ideal way, bringing together features from several places and harmonising them into unity. With the opening stanza compare the second and third stanzas of the "Ode to Duty." De Quincey writes ("On Wordsworth's Poetry"): "Whosoever looks searchingly into the characteristic genius of Wordsworth, will see that he does not willingly deal with a passion in its direct aspect, or presenting an unmodified contour, but in forms more complex and oblique, and when passing under the shadow of some secondary passion. Joy, for instance, that wells up from constitutional sources, joy that is ebullient from youth to age, and cannot cease to sparkle, he yet exhibits in the person of Matthew, the village schoolmaster, as touched and overgloomed by memories of sorrow." Taylor died in 1786, aged 32.

32. Of thee returns (1815) to original text from 1805 "to thee."

THE TWO APRIL MORNINGS.

Written in 1799 and published in 1800. See note on last poem.
25–28. In 1802 this stanza replaced the following of 1800 :

> " And on that slope of springing corn
> The self-same crimson hue
> Fell from the sky that April morn,
> The same which now I view !"

Did Wordsworth believe that he had misstated the fact of nature when he described a crimson hue falling from the sky upon a slope of corn?

29, 30. Before 1815 :

> " With rod and line my silent sport
> I plied by Derwent's wave,"

31. In 1837 Wordsworth substituted this line for the earlier " And, coming to the church, stopped short "; altered lest for a moment the grave should be supposed to be within the church.

58. A bough: before 1827, " his bough."

" Some of Wordsworth's pieces," writes Pater (" Appreciations," p. 57), " pieces prompted by a sort of half-playful mysticism, like the *Daffodils* and *The Two April Mornings*, are distinguished by a certain quaint gaiety of metre, and rival by their perfect execution, in this respect, similar pieces among our own Elizabethan or contemporary French poetry."

THE FOUNTAIN.

Written in 1799 and published in 1800. See note on " Matthew."

9. Before 1820: " Now, Matthew, let us try to match." The " said I " of the present text is a convenient explanation.

21. Before 1837: " Down to the vale this water steers." Probably Wordsworth doubted the propriety of the word " steers," or thought that by being somewhat unusual in this application it diverted feeling from the spirit of the passage. The stanza was often rehandled in MS. by Wordsworth, several of which experiments are printed in Knight's " Wordsworth," vol. II, p. 77.

37, 38. Before 1837 :

> " The blackbird in the summer trees,
> The lark upon the hill,"

The alteration got **rid** of one of four " th " sounds in the two short lines, and rightly described the lark as " above," not " upon," the hill.

58–60. The identity of rhyme — " plains," " plains " — possibly escaped Wordsworth's observation.

63. He grasped my hand replaced in 1815 the earlier " he grasped his hands," which some readers may prefer as a more instinctive expression of grief.

HART–LEAP WELL.

Written early in 1800 at Town-end, Grasmere, and published in the same year. "The first eight stanzas," says Wordsworth, "were composed extempore one winter evening in the cottage; when, after having tired myself with laboring at an awkward passage in 'The Brothers,' I started with a sudden impulse to this to get rid of the other, and finished it in a day or two. My sister and I had passed the place a few weeks before in our wild winter journey from Sockburn on the banks of the Tees to Grasmere. A peasant whom we met near the spot told us the story so far as concerned the name of the Well and the Hart, and pointed out the Stones. Both the Stones and the Well are objects that may easily be missed; the tradition by this time [1843] may be extinct in the neighborhood; the man who related it to us was very old." The well is three and a half miles from Richmond in Yorkshire. The aspens and the pillars have disappeared. For miles around there is a barren moor. The water still falls into the "cup of stone."

This poem of animal anguish has something in its motive in common with Coleridge's " The Ancient Mariner." The newly awakened sensibility and humanity of the 18th century overflowed on the lower animals. Passages in Sterne, in Cowper, and in Burns give an earlier expression to this feeling. With Wordsworth the hart is viewed, not merely as an independent, individual creature, but as a member of the great fraternity of nature, and sympathised with in its sufferings by

> The Being that is in the clouds and air,
> That is in the green leaves among the groves.

1. **Wensley Moor,** in the North Riding of Yorkshire.

3, 4. Before 1836 :

> He turned aside towards a Vassal's door,
> And " Bring another," etc.

Altered to avoid the dissyllabic " towards."

19. **Blanch** in 1827 replaced " Brach," a general name for a kind of hunting-dog (commonly used of a female). " Music " was the name of the Hutchinsons' dog, celebrated in verse by Wordsworth. " Brach " occurs in " King Lear," and one of Lear's dogs was " Blanch," whence, perhaps, the name.

20. In 1800 (only) : " weary up the mountain."

21. Before 1827 : " chid and cheer'd," — but he would first " cheer," and, that failing, would " chide."

25–27. In 1800 (only): " chase " was the word in l. 25 and " race " (twice) in l. 27.

35. Cracked : before 1820, " smack'd."

38–40. Before 1820 l. 40 was " And foaming like a mountain cataract," rhyming with " glorious act " in l. 38. Perhaps Wordsworth thought l. 40 an exaggeration ; no doubt he was glad to avoid " act " so soon after " cracked."

42. Before 1820 : " His nose half-touch'd." " Nostril " is more correct in speaking of a hart.

46. Before 1820: " Was never man in such a joyful case "; with which " place " rhymed in l. 48. Probably altered to avoid the repeated sound of " gazed," " gazed," and " place."

49. In 1800 (only) : " And turning."

50. An extravagance of all earlier editions, " nine roods " was removed in 1845.

51. In 1800 (only): " Three several marks which with his hoofs the Beast "; altered, probably, because the statement " with his hoofs " was awkward.

52. Before 1820 : " verdant ground."

54. Before 1836 : " living eyes "; by the alteration past generations are more obviously included.

65. Before 1827: " gallant brute !"

70. Paramour, lady-love ; not used in an evil sense.

75, 76. Swale, a tributary of the river Ure ; by their junction they form the Yorkshire Ouse.

79, 80. Before 1815 :

> And soon the Knight perform'd what he had said,
> The fame whereof through many a land did ring.

The exaggeration of " many a land " is removed.

90. Before 1820: " journey'd with his Paramour." The alteration adds an idea in " wondering."

98. In 1800 (only) : " To curl the blood "; altered because " curdle " is the correct form, and yet did not metrically suit the line.

100. Before 1815 : " to thanking hearts "; a song may be *for* the heart, but it must be *to* the ear.

101. Hawes . . . Richmond, towns in Yorkshire.

113. Before 1815 : " hills "; but for the imagination there was only the one hill.

142. The text in 1815 replaced clumsy lines of earlier date ; in 1800, " To this place from the stone upon the steep "; in 1802, " From the stone upon the summit of the steep."

150. Before 1832 : " this fountain."

153. Before 1836: " scented thorn."

157. Before 1827 : " But now here 's neither grass." In general, in later editions, Wordsworth avoids such contractions as " here 's."

168. Before 1815: " For them the quiet creatures."

The changes, it will be seen, were nearly all in details of workmanship.

THE BROTHERS.

Written in 1800 and published in the same year. On August 1, Dorothy Wordsworth " copied ' The Brothers.' " It is therefore a little earlier in chronological order than " Michael." In earlier editions the following note — omitted in 1832 — appeared : " This Poem was intended to be the concluding poem of a series of pastorals, the scene of which was laid among the mountains of Cumberland and Westmoreland. I mention this to apologise for the abruptness with which the poem begins." In the *Fenwick note* Wordsworth tells us that the poem was composed in a grove at the northeastern end of Grasmere Lake, since in great part destroyed by making the road. " The poem arose out of the fact mentioned to me at Ennerdale that a shepherd had fallen asleep upon the top of the rock called The Pillar, and perished as here described, his staff being left midway on the rock." This, says Knight, is the only poem of Wordsworth's referring to Ennerdale ; but the places are treated ideally. Wordsworth's " Pillar " cannot be the Pillar Rock, a crag difficult of ascent, nor does it quite agree with the Pillar Mountain.

The retouches are numerous, and some of them are interesting:

6-8. Before 1827 :

> " Upon the forehead of a jutting crag
> Sit perched with book and pencil on their knee
> And look "

Altered to describe the sketcher's attitude more correctly, — " pencil in hand," not " on the knee."

24-26. Less vividly before 1836:

> Who turn'd her large round wheel in the open air
> With back and forward steps.

Probably the change was suggested by the desire to treat " Towards " in l. 26 as a monosyllable as in l. 80, which before 1836 was " Towards the church-yard he had turn'd aside."

31. Snow-white in 1802 replaced "snowy"; altered to confine the resemblance to colour.

39–44. Leonard's age was changed in 1815, partly to allow time for the growth of such deep affection between the brothers. See note on l. 297. Before 1815 as follows:

> . . . who ere his thirteenth year
> Had changed his calling, with the mariners
> A fellow-mariner, and so had fared
> Through twenty seasons.

56. The broad blue wave: before 1840, "the broad green wave," — a descriptive error. Some of the features of Leonard's character, and especially his feeling when at sea for rural pleasures, are taken from Wordsworth's brother John. See the poem, "When to the attractions of the busy world."

88. Even to hope: until 1832, "he had hopes," which went badly in immediate connection with the "he had seen" of l. 89. Altered in 1832 to "hope was his"; present reading, 1836.

96. Imagined that he saw: before 1815, "he thought that he perceiv'd."

99. Everlasting hills: less correctly before 1820, "the eternal hills"; in 1820 "everlasting" replaced "eternal," and in 1827 "the" was omitted.

103. Perused him: before 1815, "He scanned him," where the "he" and "him," referring to different persons, were defective in clearness.

139. Pike, a peak, hill, summit.

143, 144. More like an omen in editions before 1827:

> Companions for each other: ten years back,
> Close to those brother fountains, the huge crag
> Was rent with lightning — one is dead and gone,

"Dead and gone" are words hardly appropriate to a spring of water. A note was added from 1800 to 1805: "The impressive circumstance here described actually took place some years ago in this country, upon an eminence called Kidstow Pike, one of the highest of the mountains that surround Hawes-water. The summit of the Pike was stricken by lightning; and every trace of one of the fountains disappeared, while the other continued to flow as before."

169. This fine line was added in 1802. Leonard dare not say " a brother could not find his brother's grave."

182, 183. In edd. 1800 to 1805 a note was given: "There is not anything more worthy of remark in the manners of the inhabitants of these mountains than the tranquillity, I might say indifference, with which they think and talk upon the subject of death. Some of the country church-yards, as here described, do not contain a single tomb-stone, and most of them have a very small number."

187. For eight-score winters past, added in 1802. Perhaps inadvertently omitted in 1800.

213. Kept up: in 1800, "preserv'd"; altered in 1802, perhaps to bring out the idea of resistance to difficulty.

244–247. Before 1815 two lines:

> The only kinsman near them in the house,
> Yet he being old, they had much love to spare,

Perhaps Wordsworth thought there was a want of tenderness in attributing to Walter Ewbank's old age the fact that the boys had love to spare.

269. Before 1836: "The finest Sunday that the Autumn saw"; altered, probably, to avoid the crowding of the "th" sounds.

275. Before 1836: "Where foot could come, to one or both of them." Perhaps Wordsworth considered this and the next line too heavy with monosyllables.

283. House and field: before 1827, "twenty pounds." The change makes the Priest's wager more remote from actual betting.

297. Before 1815: "And, though a very stripling, twelve years old." See note on ll. 39–44.

312. Joyous festival: before 1836, "very festival."

320. Youth. Here, in l. 381 and l. 386, "youth" was substituted in 1815 for "lad." So in "Michael," l. 299.

323–325. Before 1836 less closely connected with the churchyard:

> If ever the day came when he was rich,
> He would return, and on his Father's land
> He would grow old among us.

327. Happy: in 1800, "as happy"; altered for sake of the metre in 1802.

349. Dwelt: before 1827, "liv'd"; altered, perhaps, because "lived" had been used in l. 343.

359–365. The prosaic text of earlier editions was elevated to poetry in 1820; previously:

> With two or three companions, whom it chanc'd
> Some further business summon'd to a house
> Which stands at the Dale-head.   James, tir'd perhaps,
> Or from some other cause remain'd behind.
> You see yon Precipice — it almost looks
> Like some vast building

369–375.   This passage was straggling and prosaic in 1800; it was slightly touched in 1802 and 1815.   Coleridge in "Biographia Literaria" (1817) spoke of it as a string of prosaisms in metre.   It was recast in 1820, further improved in 1827, but not set finally right until 1836.   The earliest form, 1800, may here suffice:

> James, pointing to its summit, over which
> They all had purpos'd to return together,
> Inform'd them that he there would wait for them :
> They parted, and his comrades pass'd that way
> Some two hours after, but they did not find him
> At the appointed place, a circumstance
> Of which they took no heed : but one of them
> Going by chance, at night, into the house
> Which at this time was James's home, there learn'd

379.   In 1800 : "Some went, and some towards the lake : ere noon"; in 1820 : "Some hastened, some towards the lake : ere noon"; altered to the present text in 1836, when Wordsworth treated "towards" as a monosyllable.

397.   On the soft heath : before 1836, "Upon the grass."   The "aery summit crowned with heath," l. 369, was introduced in 1820.   Wordsworth now makes this passage agree with the description in l. 369.   On the Pillar Mountain heath may be found, but not on the Pillar Rock.

401–405.   Before 1836 as follows:

> And so no doubt he perish'd : at the time,
> We guess, that in his hands he must have had ["held," 1827–32]
> His Shepherd's staff; for midway in the cliff
> It had been caught; and there for many years
> It hung — and mouldered there.

406–408.   Before 1815 as follows:

> but he felt
> Tears rushing in; both left the spot in silence.

413.   Altered in 1836 to avoid "towards" as a dissyllable; previously : "Pointing towards the Cottage, he entreated."

415.   Earnest voice : before 1836, "fervent voice"; altered, perhaps, to avoid the idea of heat.

422. Before 1836: " Were with him in his heart; his cherish'd hopes " ; the alteration adds meaning.

428. Before 1836: " He travelled on to Egremont." Egremont, a market town of County Cumberland, five miles southeast of Whitehaven.

429. In 1800 : " That night, address'd a letter to the Priest "; altered in 1802, perhaps because " address'd a letter " is a somewhat prosaic expression.

" The mountains," writes Mr. Leslie Stephen, " are not with Wordsworth a symbol of anti-social feeling. On the contrary, they are in their proper place as the background of the simple domestic affections. He loves his native hills, not in the Byronic fashion, as a savage wilderness, but as the appropriate framework in which a healthy social order can permanently maintain itself. That, for example, is, as he tells us, the thought which inspired *The Brothers*, a poem which excells all modern idylls in weight of meaning and depth of feeling, by virtue of the idea thus embodied," — and see what follows, " Hours in a Library," XIII (*Cornhill Magazine*), " Wordsworth's Ethics."

THE PET-LAMB.

Written at Town-end, Grasmere, in 1800, and published the same year. Barbara Lewthwaite was " one of two most lovely sisters "; but she was not, in fact, the child whom Wordsworth had seen and overheard as described in the poem. The name was chosen because Barbara was so beautiful: " Were those two Angels that I have just seen ? " asked Wordsworth's brother John, when he visited his brother at Grasmere for the first time. Barbara, who was vain of the distinction conferred on her by the poem, was living at Ambleside in 1843.

The text was hardly altered. Line 5, before 1836, opened thus: " No other sheep were near."

17. **Right towards** replaced in 1836 " Towards," to bring it to a monosyllabic pronunciation. The other retouches are too slight to deserve record, with the exception of ll. 57–60 which in 1802 replaced the 1800 reading:

> " Here thou need'st not dread the raven in the sky,
> He will not come to thee, our Cottage is hard by,
> Night and day thou art safe as living thing can be,
> Be happy then and rest, what is 't that aileth thee ? "

The gain in diversifying the rhyme sounds may have been one motive for the change.

"IT WAS AN APRIL MORNING: FRESH AND CLEAR."

Written at Grasmere in 1800 and published in the same year. "The poem," says Wordsworth, "was suggested on the banks of the brook that runs through Easedale, which is, in some parts of its course, as wild and beautiful as brook can be. I have composed thousands of verses by the side of it."

9–13. Before 1845:

> The budding groves appear'd as if in haste
> To spur the steps of June ; as if their shades
> Of *various* green were hindrances that stood
> Between them and their object : yet, meanwhile
> There was such deep contentment in the air

It may be doubted that this alteration of Wordsworth's old age effected any real gain.

15. Before 1845 : " Yet leafless, seemed as though the countenance." "Seemed" being introduced in l. 9, now disappeared from l. 15.

"Emma" is Dorothy Wordsworth. Compare the "Emmeline" of "To a Butterfly" and "The Sparrow's Nest." The walk into Easedale was found by Wordsworth and his sister three days after they entered their Grasmere cottage. "This long remained," says Wordsworth, "our favourite haunt." Compare ll. 40, 41. In several of the "Poems on the Naming of Places" there is some appropriateness to the person after whom the place was named. Lines in the poem "Composed a few miles above Tintern Abbey," addressed to his sister, perhaps suggest what was the appropriateness here:

> When thy mind
> Shall be a mansion for all lovely forms,
> Thy memory be as a dwelling-place
> For all sweet sounds and harmonies.

TO JOANNA.

Written at Grasmere in 1800 and published in the same year. Dorothy Wordsworth writes in her Journal, Aug. 23, 1800: "W. read ' Peter Bell ' and the poem of 'Joanna' beside the Rothay by the road-side." Joanna was Joanna Hutchinson, the sister of Wordsworth's wife; she was not, in fact, city-bred, nor could she have been absent from Grasmere for two years (l. 13), for Wordsworth had only settled in Grasmere in December, 1799. The "steeple-tower" (l. 20) is that of Grasmere; the firs (l. 19) — now gone — were by the roadside near the church; the "lofty barrier" (l. 44) is part of Helm-crag. It is not known whether Wordsworth actually carved Joanna's name, or did not. The echoing of Joanna's laugh, he admits, "is an extravagance, though the effect of the reverberation of voices in some parts of the mountains is very striking"; and he refers to the description of the echo of a lamb's bleat in "The Excursion," Bk. iv, ll. 402–412, as un-exaggerated.

6. Altered in 1836 to avoid a dissyllabic "towards"; previously: "Is slow towards [toward, 1827] the sympathies of them."

15. Be : before 1836, "are"; altered to subjunctive mood after "if."

28. Runic. Runes were phonetic signs of our Teutonic ancestors; the alphabet is called, from its first six letters, "futhork."

32–34. These lines mean that although the speaker had true love for Joanna, he had also a little malicious pleasure in telling of the re-venge of the echoes for her laughter at his look of ravishment (ll. 52, 53). In l. 33 "between" in 1836 replaced "betwixt," a change made in several other passages.

43, 44. Another change made to avoid a dissyllabic "towards"; before 1836:

> Which looks towards [toward, 1827] the East, I there stopp'd short
> And trac'd

57. Hammar-scar, a name now disused, applied to some rocks on the flank of Silver-how, to the wood around them, and also to the gorge between Silver-how and Loughrigg. From old Norse *hamar*, a steep broken rock (Knight).

72. Before 1827 : "Is not for me to tell; but sure I am." Possibly Wordsworth thought this line too heavily monosyllabic.

83. Before 1845: "Joanna's name upon the living stone." The chiselling was "into" not "upon" the stone."

We know that Wordsworth was acquainted with Drayton's "Polyol-bion" (see notes on "At the Grave of Burns"); and in the Thirtieth Song, which, as treating of Westmoreland and Cumberland, Words-worth would have known especially well, occur lines which probably suggested the extravagance of the echoed laugh :

> Which Copland scarce had spoke, but quickly every hill,
> Upon her verge that stands, the neighboring vallies fill;
> Helvillon from his height, it through the mountains threw,
> From whom as soon again, the sound Dunbalrase drew,
> From whose stone-trophied head, it on to Wendross went,
> Which tow'rds the sea again, resounded it to Dent,

That Brodwater therewith within her banks astound,
In sailing to the sea, told it to Egremound,
Whose buildings, walks, and streets, with echoes loud and long,
Did mightily commend old Copland for her song.

"THERE IS AN EMINENCE — OF THESE OUR HILLS."

Written in 1800 and published in that year. Wordsworth confesses that the " Eminence " could not, in fact, be seen from the orchard-seat. " It rises above the road by the side of Grasmere Lake, towards Keswick, and its name is Stone-Arthur."

5. **Peak:** before 1845, " cliff."

17. Before 1815 : " Hath said, this lonesome Peak shall bear my Name." Wordsworth's contemplative passion for solitude and also his life of the affections are expressed or signified in this poem.

THE CHILDLESS FATHER.

Written at Town-end, Grasmere ; dated by Wordsworth 1800, and published on January 30 of that year in *The Morning Post ;* again, in " Lyrical Ballads," 1800. Wordsworth (*Fenwick note*) says that the funeral basin was in use at Cockermouth when he was a child ; it was placed upon a table covered with white cloth in front of the house. " The huntings on foot," he adds, " in which the old man is supposed to join as here described, were of common, almost habitual, occurrence in our vales when I was a boy."

9, 10. These lines are of 1827. In the earliest version, 1800, the table appears :

> The bason of boxwood, just six months before,
> Had stood on the table at Timothy's door ;

In 1820 Wordsworth thought that " bason of boxwood " might be supposed to be a basin made of boxwood, and he explains the custom in the text as well as the note :

> The bason had offered, just six months before,
> Fresh sprigs of green boxwood at Timothy's door.

The reserve of passion in this poem heightens the pathos ; the old joy of the chase still lives in Timothy's heart ; the new sorrow is signified only by a tear and the necessary act of making fast the cottage door.

MICHAEL.

This poem was written at Town-end, Grasmere, between October and December, 1800, and was published in the second volume of " Lyrical Ballads," which is dated 1800.   In Dorothy Wordsworth's Journal for the 11th Oct., 1800, we read: " After dinner we walked up Greenhead Gill in search of a sheepfold. . . .   The sheepfold is falling away.   It is built nearly in the form of a heart unequally divided."   Other entries tell us of Wordsworth's working at " the sheepfold poem " until November 12, and when she writes on December 9, " W. finished his poem to-day," the reference is probably to " Michael."   Greenhead Ghyll is not far from Dove Cottage, Grasmere; when Wordsworth in 1843 dictated the *Fenwick notes*, the ruins of the sheepfold remained.   The precise spot cannot now be identified.   " Michael's cottage stood," says Professor Knight, " where the coach-house and stables of ' the Hollins ' now stand."   The name of the Evening Star was not in fact given to this house, but to another on the same side of the valley, more to the north.   " The character and circumstances of Luke," said Wordsworth (*Fenwick note*), " were taken from a family to whom had belonged, many years before, the house we lived in at Town-end, along with some fields and woodlands on the eastern shore of Grasmere."   Wordsworth told Thomas Poole of Nether Stowey that in writing the poem he had Poole's character, as suggesting features for that of Michael, often before his eyes, and sometimes thought he was delineating such a man as Poole would have been under the same circumstances (Mrs. Sandford's " Thomas Poole and his Friends," vol. II, p. 55).   " I have attempted," he writes to Poole, " to give a picture of a man of strong mind and lively sensibility, agitated by two of the most powerful affections of the human heart, — the parental affection and the love of property, *landed* property, including the feelings of inheritance, home and personal and family independence."   And to Charles James Fox he wrote, Jan. 14, 1801 : " In the two poems, ' The Brothers ' and ' Michael,' I have attempted to draw a picture of the domestic affections, as I know they exist among a class of men who are now almost confined to the north of England.   They are small independent *proprietors* of land, here called statesmen [*i.e.*, estates-men], men of respectable education, who daily labour on their little properties. . . .   Their little tract of land serves as a kind of rallying-point for their domestic feelings, as a tablet upon which they are written, which makes them objects of memory in a thousand instances, when they would otherwise be forgotten."

When the volume containing " Michael " was published, in the early days of January, 1801, Wordsworth was troubled to find that the printer had omitted fifteen lines following l. 191. He tells Poole in April that half a sheet had been reprinted to amend the error; a copy which gives the lines is in the possession of the Rev. T. Hutchinson.

In Professor Knight's ," Life of Wordsworth," vol. I, pp. 382–388, and also in my edition of his poetical works (Aldine Series, vol. V, pp. 182–187), will be found fragments intended for " Michael," recovered from a MS. book of Dorothy Wordsworth's. The greater portion of these fragments are occupied with an episode, judiciously omitted, which tells of the search made in late autumn by Michael and his son for a stray sheep. The boy discovers it on an island of the brook to which he leaps, but the sheep springs into the stream. Luke is found by Michael on the island, and with the aid of his father's staff Luke regains the bank.

One passage of these fragments is of peculiar interest, as giving Wordsworth's answer to the question, " What feeling for external nature has such a man as Michael ? " It corresponds to the passage of the poem, ll. 62–77 :

> No doubt if you in terms direct had asked
> Whether he loved the mountains, true it is
> That with blunt repetition of your words
> He might have stared at you, and said that they
> Were frightful to behold, but had you then
> Discoursed with him . . . . .
> Of his own business, and the goings on
> Of earth and sky, then truly had you seen
> That in his thoughts there were obscurities,
> Wonder, and admiration, things that wrought
> Not less than a religion of his heart.

And the passage proceeds for fifteen lines more in the same spirit. In ed. 1805 Wordsworth omitted the following lines, which in edd. 1800 and 1802 followed l. 128 :

> Not with a waste of words, but for the sake
> Of pleasure, which I know that I shall give
> To many living now, I of this Lamp
> Speak thus minutely : for there are no few
> Whose memories will bear witness to my tale.
> The Light was famous, etc.

A recast of these lines was sent to Poole in April, 1801, and it was then intended that they should immediately succeed the following passage, in which, it will be observed, some words appear identical with those which have just been given from Dorothy Wordsworth's MS. book ; this passage, slightly varied, also appears in the MS. book with the added lines which I place in brackets :

> Though in these occupations they would pass
> Whole hours with but small interchange of speech,
> Yet were there times in which they did not want
> Discourse both wise and prudent, shrewd remarks
> Of daily providence, clothed in images
> Lively and beautiful, in rural forms
> That made their conversation fresh and fair
> As is a landscape : — And the shepherd oft
> Would draw out of his heart, the obscurities
> And admirations that were there, of God
> And of his works, or, yielding to the bent
> Of his peculiar humour, would let loose
> The tongue and give it the wind's freedom, — then
> Discoursing on remote imaginations, strong
> Conceits, devices, day-dreams, thoughts and schemes,
> [Of alterations human hands might make
> Among the mountains, fens which might be drained,
> Mines opened, forests planted, and rocks split,]
> The fancies of a solitary man.

The version of these lines sent to Poole is later than that in the MS. book, where in place of the word " obscurities," transferred to Poole's version from another experimental passage quoted above, the word " mysteries " is found. These lines sent to Poole were to follow l. 128 of the poem (" Murmur as with the sound of summer flies ").

A bold passage of the poem as originally printed, 1800, was altered in 1802. Lines 405–410 stood thus :

> When thou art gone away, should evil men
> Be thy companions, let this Sheep-fold be
> Thy anchor and thy shield ; amid all fear
> And all temptation, let it be to thee
> An emblem of the life thy Fathers liv'd.

Probably Wordsworth thought that to name the sheepfold an anchor and a shield was overbold, or was inappropriate in a shepherd's life.

2. **Ghyll.** Wordsworth explains the word — of Scandinavian origin — in a note of 1800 on " The Idle Shepherd Boys " as " in the dialect of Cumberland and Westmoreland, a short and, for the most part, a steep narrow valley with a stream running through it."

6. **Around** in 1827 replaced the earlier " beside."

51. **Subterraneous music.** I am not sure that I understand this aright. Does it mean the sound of the wind under overhanging cliffs and in hollows of the hills ?

73, 74. Before 1832 as follows :

> So grateful in themselves, the certainty
> Of honourable gain [" gains," 1800–2] ; these fields, these hills,
> Which were his living Being, even more
> Than his own blood — what could they less ? — had laid

The narration which follows shows that the fields and hills were not more a part of Michael's being than was his son.

78, 79. Before 1815 as follows :

> He had not passed his days in singleness.
> He had a Wife, a comely Matron, old —

Altered, probably, to avoid the recurring " he had " in two different uses, at the beginning of two successive lines.

112. Before 1836 : " Did with a huge projection overbrow "; altered to avoid the enfeebling expletive " did."

125. **Far** in 1836 replaced " late," going better with the preposition " into."

134. **Easedale,** near Grasmere. **Dunmail-Raise,** the pass on the way from Grasmere to Keswick.

147. This line was added in 1836.

150. After this line the following lines were omitted in 1827 :

> From such, and other causes, to the thoughts
> Of the old Man, his only Son was now
> The dearest object that he knew on earth.

155. **Pastime** in 1827 replaced the less masculine " dalliance."

158. A possible objection was anticipated by the insertion in 1836 of " as."

163–166 replaced in 1836 the following :

> Had work by his own door, or when he sate
> With sheep before him on his Shepherd's stool
> Beneath that large old Oak, which near their door
> Stood, and from its enormous breadth of shade,

207. In 1800 : " While this good household thus were living on." In 1802 and 1805 :

> While in the fashion which I have described
> This simple Household thus were living on.

221–223. Before 1836:

> As soon as he had gathered so much strength,
> That he could look his trouble in the face,
> It seemed that his sole refuge was to sell

Altered, perhaps, to vary the position of the pauses.

233. The sun himself in 1827 replaced "the Sun itself." A like change was often made as Wordsworth came to perceive the uses of poetic personification.

258. Richard Bateman. In edd. 1802–5 Wordsworth gives a note : "The story alluded to is well known in the country. The chapel is called Ings Chapel; and it is on the right-hand side of the road leading from Kendal to Ambleside." The date when Bateman rebuilt the chapel was 1743.

290. Last two nights : corrected in 1836 ; previously, "two last."

299. Youth in 1815 replaced "lad." See note on "The Brothers," l. 320

304. With daylight in 1820 replaced the less expressive "Next morning" of earlier texts.

324. Sheepfold. In edd. 1800–5 Wordsworth gives a note: "It may be proper to inform some readers that a sheepfold in these mountains is an unroofed building of stone walls, with different divisions. It is generally placed by a brook, for the convenience of washing the sheep; but it is also useful as a shelter for them, and as a place to drive them into, to enable the shepherds conveniently to single out one or more for any particular purpose."

338, 339. Touch on replaced in 1836 "speak of."

340. As oft befalls replaced in 1827 "as it befalls," which was hardly true to fact.

373. Threescore replaced in 1827 "sixty."

390. Hale replaced in 1827 "stout," the meaning of which was ambiguous.

424, 425. An improvement of 1815; previously, one line : "Next morning, as had been resolv'd, the Boy."

450. Before 1820 this line was "Would break the heart :— Old Michael found it so."

456. From 1800 to 1827 the line closed with "up upon the sun"; in 1832 the fault was emended by the reading "up towards the sun." But when making the revision for 1836, Wordsworth decided uniformly to treat "towards" as a monosyllable, and accordingly he substituted the present reading.

Several changes of text of a less interesting kind are here unrecorded. Of this poem Sir Henry Taylor says : "The poet writes in his confidence to impart interest to the realities of life, deriving both the confidence and the power from the deep interest which he feels in them. It is an attribute of unusual susceptibility of imagination to need no extraordinary provocatives; and when this is combined with intensity of observation and peculiarity of language, it is the high privilege of the poet so endowed to rest upon the common realities of life and to dispense with its anomalies."

FRAGMENT FROM THE RECLUSE.

BOOK I.

" The Recluse " was the general title given to a great philosophical poem designed by Wordsworth, which was never completed. Its principal subject was to be the sensations and opinions of a Poet living in retirement, and it was to express his views of Man, Nature, and Society. The autobiographical poem, " The Prelude," published after Wordsworth's death, was intended to be preparatory to the whole ; " The Excursion " formed its second part. The third part, to consist, like the first, chiefly of meditations in the Author's own person, was never written. The date at which the first book of " The Recluse " was written is uncertain ; perhaps it was written as early as 1800. Professor Knight dates it 1805, which may be right. An extract or an addition was published by Wordsworth with the title " Water-Fowl," and is dated by him 1812.

The extract here given forms the conclusion of Book I. It was printed in 1814, in the Preface to " The Excursion," and Wordsworth says " it may be acceptable as a kind of Prospectus of the design and scope of the whole Poem." In fact it may be called a prospectus of all his work as a poet. The first book of " The Recluse " was published in 1888. The text of the extract is identical in the volume of 1888 with that printed in 1814.

13. **Numerous verse,** verse consisting of poetical numbers ; the expression occurs in " Paradise Lost," V, 150, and in P. Fletcher's " Piscatory Eclogues," 1633.

23. **Fit audience,** etc. : from " Paradise Lost," VII, 31, where Milton invokes the muse Urania; see l. 25.

48. Plato's Atlantis was an imaginary island in the Atlantic Ocean. Homer made the Atlanticas two, — the Hesperides and the Elysian Fields.

86. Metropolitan, of the mother city. The word has special ecclesiastical associations, Metropolitan (*noun*) meaning bishop of a mother church.

THE SPARROW'S NEST.

Written in the orchard, Town-end, Grasmere, and dated by Wordsworth 1801; first published in 1807. "At the end of the garden," says Wordsworth (*Fenwick note* on this poem), "of my father's house at Cockermouth was a high terrace that commanded a fine view of the river Derwent and Cockermouth Castle. This was our favourite playground. The terrace-wall, a low one, was covered with closely clipt privet and roses, which gave an almost impervious shelter to birds that built their nests there."

In 1807 (only) the following lines opened the poem :

> Look, five blue eggs are gleaming there !
> Few visions have I seen more fair,
> Nor many prospects of delight
> More pleasing than that simple sight !

which had an unpleasant air of self-consciousness, and were happily omitted.

Until 1845 ll. 11, 12 stood thus :

> She look'd at it as if she fear'd it ;
> Still wishing, dreading to be near it,

with a faulty rhyme.

In "The Prelude," XI, 335–370, Wordsworth tells how at a later time his sister led him back, after the downfall of his hopes for France, to "sweet counsels between head and heart," and preserved him still a Poet. On the name "Emmeline," see note on "To a Butterfly." In the original manuscript "Dorothy" is written.

TO A YOUNG LADY ("Dear Child," etc.).

This poem — which may have been written in 1801 — originally appeared in *The Morning Post* for Feb. 11, 1802, with the title "To a beautiful Young Lady who had been harshly spoken of on account of her fondness for taking long walks in the country." It was included among the "Poems," 1807. Wordsworth afterwards dated it 1803, and said in the *Fenwick note* that it was "composed at the same time and on the same view as 'I met Louisa in the shade'; indeed they were designed to make one piece." "Louisa" he dated 1805. Evidently his memory deceived him. There is a MS. copy written out for the "Lyrical Ballads" of 1802. Professor Knight and I supposed that the young lady was idealised from Wordsworth's sister Dorothy. Mr. T. Hutchinson conjectures that Joanna, Wordsworth's sister-in-law, was meant. Mr. Ernest H. Coleridge (*The Athenæum*, Sept. 16, 1893) argues that Mary Hutchinson, whom Wordsworth married on Oct. 4, 1802, was meant. She was at Dove Cottage, Grasmere (Wordsworth's home), in the late autumn of 1801, and on December 28 she accompanied the Wordsworths on foot to Keswick. A second visit to Grasmere was paid in January, 1802. "The poem ' Louisa,'" says Mr. Coleridge, "is evidently addressed by a lover to his betrothed," and here the young lady is promised heart-stirring days as a wife (to Wordsworth) and friend (to Dorothy). The reproaches, Mr. Coleridge supposes, may have come from Mrs. Coleridge, then at Greta Hall, to which Mary Hutchinson walked from Grasmere; Mrs. Coleridge "did not appreciate long walks." Dorothy Wordsworth was, however, a noted pedestrian, and was reproached for her long walks. "The Glowworm" of Wordsworth, in which Lucy is spoken of as "my Love," was suggested, in fact, by an incident in which his sister was Lucy's original. In "Yarrow Unvisited" Wordsworth's sister is, for poetical purposes, transformed to his "true love" and "winsome Marrow." Miss Quillinan stated that the lines were addressed to Dorothy, and I still believe this to be the truth. The poem should be read with "Louisa."

In l. 5 "heart-stirring" replaced in 1837 the earlier "delightful"; altered, probably, to avoid the clash of "delightful" with "light" in the next line.

Lines 8, 9 previous to 1827 were :

> As if thy heritage were joy,
> And pleasure were thy trade.

In l. 16 "serene" in 1815 replaced the earlier "alive."

ALICE FELL.

Written Mar. 12 and 13, 1802; published 1807. The incident happened to Mr. Graham of Glasgow (brother of the author of "The Sabbath") who urged Wordsworth, for humanity's sake, to put it into verse. In Dorothy Wordsworth's Journal of Feb. 16, 1802, she records the incident as told on that day by Graham; the poem closely agrees with the entry in the Journal. On its appearance the critics ridiculed the poem, and out of policy Wordsworth for a time excluded it from his "Poetical Works"; it was restored at the request of friends, in particular of Edward Quillinan, the poet's son-in-law.

The text was retouched in many lines in 1836, and assumed its final form in 1845.

3, 4. Before 1845 thus:

> When suddenly I seem'd to hear
> A moan, a lamentable sound.

Altered to render the sound, as first heard, more vague, and to avoid the repeated "seemed" in l. 3 and l. 7.

21. In 1807: "'My cloak!' the word was last and first," rhyming with l. 23, "As if her very heart would burst" ("burst" being also the word used in Dorothy's Journal). When in 1836 l. 21 became "'My cloak!' no other word she spoke," l. 23 did not rhyme, "As if her innocent heart would burst." There was an objection to rhyming with "spoke," the word "spoke" in another sense rhyming in the next stanza but one. The present text is of 1840.

29–31. In 1807:

> 'T was twisted between nave and spoke;
> Her help she lent, and with good heed
> Together we released the Cloak;
> A wretched, wretched rag indeed!

Other variations of text, less important, remain unnoticed. The poem may be contrasted with "Lucy Gray," the one being literal and realistic, while "Lucy Gray" is an ideal treatment of the actual incident.

BEGGARS.

Written at Town-end, Grasmere, on Mar. 13 and 14, 1802; published in 1807. Dorothy Wordsworth writes in her Journal of March 13: "William finished 'Alice Fell' [like this, a poem of poverty] and then wrote the poem of 'The Beggar Woman,' taken from a woman whom I had seen in May (now nearly two years ago), when John and he were at Gallow Hill [with the Hutchinson's]. . . . After tea I read to William [from the Journal] that account of the little boy belonging to the tall woman, and an unlucky thing it was, for he could not escape from those very words, and so he could not write the poem. He left it unfinished, and went tired to bed. In our walk from Rydal he had got warmed with the subject, and had half cast the poem. *Sunday Morning*. William . . . got up at nine o'clock, but before he rose he had finished 'The Beggar Boy.'"

In this poem we have an excellent opportunity of studying both Wordsworth's dealing with his material and the manner in which he criticised and rehandled his own work. He had not himself seen the beggars; the following is his sister's account of the incident: "*May 27* [1800]. A very tall woman, tall much beyond the measure of tall women, called at the door. She had on a very long brown cloak, and a very white cap without bonnet. Her face was excessively brown, but it had plainly once been fair. She led a little barefooted child, about two years old, by the hand, and said her husband, who was a tinker, was gone before with the other children. I gave her a piece of bread. Afterwards, on my way to Ambleside, beside the bridge at Rydal, I saw her husband sitting at the roadside, his two asses standing beside him, and the two young children at play upon the grass. The man did not beg. I passed on, and about a quarter of a mile farther, I saw two boys, one about ten, the other about eight years old, at play chasing a butterfly. They were wild figures, not very ragged, but without shoes or stockings. The hat of the elder was wreathed round with yellow flowers; the younger, whose hat was only a rimless crown, had stuck it round with laurel leaves. They continued at play till I drew very near, and then they addressed me with the begging cant and the whining voice of sorrow. I said, 'I served your mother this morning' (the boys were so like the woman who had called at our door that I could not be mistaken). 'O!' says the elder, 'you could not serve my mother, for she's dead, and my father's on at the next town — he's a potter.' I persisted in my assertion, and that I would give them nothing. Says the elder, 'Come, let's away,' and away they flew like lightning."

Wordsworth omits the husband, the asses, the child of two, and concentrates attention on the woman and the boys.

The poem was little touched (but see note on ll. 29, 30) until 1827. In a letter to Barron Field the motive of rehandling is stated by Wordsworth: "I have aimed at giving more eloquence and dignity to this poem, partly on its own account, and partly that it might harmonise better with the one appended to it."

The present text of stanza 1 is of 1845. In 1807:

> She had a tall Man's height, or more;
> No bonnet screen'd her from the heat;
> A long drab-colour'd Cloak she wore,
> A Mantle reaching to her feet;

> What other dress she had I could not know;
> Only she wore a Cap that was as white as snow.

The fifth of these lines is called by Wordsworth, in his letter to Barron Field, "a villainous line, one of the very worst in my whole writings." In 1827 the stanza stood thus :

> Before me as the Wanderer stood,
> No bonnet screened her from the heat;
> Nor claimed she service from the hood
> Of a blue mantle, to her feet
> Depending with a graceful flow;
> Only she wore a cap pure as unsullied snow.

" Nor claimed she service," etc., Wordsworth thought "too pompous for the occasion." In 1832 :

> Before my eyes a Wanderer stood ;
> Her face from summer's noon-day heat
> Nor [" No," 1836–43] bonnet shaded, nor the hood
> Of that [" the," 1836–43] blue cloak which to her feet
> Depended with a graceful flow ;
> Only she wore a cap as white as new-fallen snow.

Happily, Wordsworth reverted to the first line as originally written.

7–12. This stanza was reached in 1827 (except l. 11, where " head " instead of " lead " stood until 1836 ; excluding " head " from l. 11 made possible the insertion in 1845 of " head " in l. 6). Lines 7–10 before 1827 were :

> In all my walks through field or town,
> Such Figure had I never seen :
> Her face was of Egyptian brown :
> Fit person was she for a Queen.

" In all my walks " Wordsworth thought "obtrusively personal."
The third stanza is of 1845. In 1807 :

> Before me begging did she stand,
> Pouring out sorrows like a sea;
> Grief after grief :— on English land
> Such woes I knew could never be;

" Sea," Wordsworth says, " clashes with ' was beautiful to see ' "in l. 18. In 1827 the lines became :

> Her suit no faltering scruples checked;
> Forth did she pour, in current free,
> Tales that could challenge no respect
> But from a blind credulity;

In 1832-43 :

> She begged an alms; no scruple checked
> The current of her ready plea,
> Words that could challenge, etc.

18. **A weed of glorious feature** is from Spenser's " Muiopotmos, or the Fate of the Butterfly," l. 213, and was in quotation marks before 1827.

29-30. A change of 1820 ; previously :

> Two Brothers seem'd they, eight and ten years old;
> And like that Woman's face as gold is like to gold.

31-36. This stanza was added in 1827 with " Precursors of ['to,' 1836] " in its fourth line.

37. Before 1827 : " They bolted on me thus, and lo ! "

42. Before 1827 : "'Nay but I gave her pence, and she will buy you bread.'"

44. The text is of 1845. In 1807-20, and again 1836-43 : "'Sweet Boys, you're telling me a lie'"; in 1827-32: "'Sweet Boys! Heaven hears that rash reply,'" which Wordsworth thought "somewhat too refined."

48. Before 1827 : " Off to some other play they both together flew."

Various experiments at improvement of the poem are given from MS. by Professor Knight.

Part of the virtue of this poem resides in a series of beautiful surprises. The title " Beggars " hardly prepares us for the dignity of an Amazonian queen and the joy and beauty of the " precursors of Aurora's car " ; their trade of misery is only a profitable assumption masking a life of gladness and freedom, and the lie of the conscienceless creatures is so superficial — not one of those lies which Bacon describes as " sinking and settling in the mind "— that we are almost relieved, and glad to be relieved, from the duty of moral condemnation. It seems only a gaiety and piece of their " ready wit." The interpretation of the whole is given in the " Sequel " which follows.

SEQUEL TO THE FOREGOING (*i.e.*, Beggars).

Written in 1817 ; published in 1827.

2. **Dædal,** curiously adorned.

13, 14. Between these two lines occurred the following before 1836 ; in that year four of the lines were transferred to a later part of the poem (ll. 32-35), in an invocation of Spirits :

> Spirits of beauty and of grace:
> Associates in that eager chase;
> Ye, by a course to nature true,
> The sterner judgment can subdue;
> And waken a relenting smile
> When she encounters fraud or guile;
> And sometimes ye can charm away
> The inward mischief, or allay,
> Ye, who within the blameless mind,
> Your favourite seat of empire find!

27, 28.   Before 1836:

> . . . . is still endeared
> The faith

and at the same time l. 31 replaced " Or, if such thoughts," etc.

TO A BUTTERFLY (" Stay near me ").

Written in the orchard, Town-end, Grasmere, on Mar. 14, 1802; first published in 1807. Dorothy Wordsworth writes in her Journal : " While we were at breakfast . . . he wrote the poem 'To a Butterfly.' . . . The thought first came upon him as we were talking about the pleasure we both always felt at the sight of a butterfly. I told him that I used to chase them a little, but that I was afraid of brushing the dust off their wings, and did not catch them. He told me how he used to kill all the white ones when he went to school, because they were Frenchmen." The text is unaltered. In "The Sparrow's Nest" Wordsworth again names his sister "Emmeline," and in the sonnet " There is a little unpretending rill " and the first poem " On the Naming of Places " (" It was an April morning "), " Emma."

TO THE CUCKOO (" O blithe New-comer ! ").

This poem, written on Mar. 23–26, 1802, in the orchard, Town-end, Grasmere, was first published in 1807. In Dorothy Wordsworth's Journal for 1802, which gives us the date of the poem, occur several references to the cuckoo. On May 1 : " William tired himself with seeking an epithet for the cuckoo "; on June 3 : " The cuckoo sang in Easedale; after dinner we read the life and some of the writings of poor Logan." The well-known poem, " To the Cuckoo," containing the stanza

> Sweet bird! thy bower is ever green,
> Thy sky is ever clear;
> Thou hast no sorrow in thy song,
> No winter in thy year,

is claimed for Michael Bruce as well as for John Logan.

Wordsworth, in several poems, has written of the cuckoo. A sonnet, " To the Cuckoo," tells of the joy on hearing this first spring summons, the " erratic voice," and "twin notes inseparably paired." In " The Excursion," Bk. vii, l. 408, one of the chief losses sustained by the dalesman born deaf is that "not for his delight The vernal cuckoo shouted." Again in " The Excursion," Bk. ii, ll. 346–348, we find :

> . . . only from the neighbouring vales
> The cuckoo, straggling up to the hill-tops
> Shouteth faint tidings of some gladder place.

The same word " shout " occurs in " Yes, it was the mountain Echo," the echo "answering to the *shouting* cuckoo." In one of the sonnets to Sleep, the early morning cry of the bird, heard after a sleepless night, is " the first cuckoo's melancholy cry." A poem on " The Cuckoo-clock " tells of the joyous associations connected with the bird's voice (the cuckoo-clock at Rydal Mount was shouting twelve, at noon, on Apr. 23, 1850, when Wordsworth died). In "Memorials of a Tour in Italy, 1837," is a blank-verse poem, " The Cuckoo at Laverna," in which Wordsworth imagines the Franciscan monks reminded by the bird's voice of " the Voice of One crying amid the wilderness," with a prophecy of a spiritual springtime. He modernised the poem, inaccurately ascribed to Chaucer, " The Cuckoo and the Nightingale."

In his " Guide to the Lakes " he writes, much in the spirit of the present poem : " There is also an imaginative influence in the voice of the cuckoo, when that voice has taken possession of a deep mountain valley."

The second stanza, which appears as simple as a drop of dew, was the result of many revisions, and was reached after more than forty years from the original date of composition. In 1802 it was as follows :

> While I am lying on the grass,
> I hear thy restless shout:
> From hill to hill it seems to pass,
> About, and all about.

The last line was greatly improved in 1815 by the change to " At once far off and near," and the rhyming word " shout " in l. 2 was sacrificed,

that line becoming " Thy loud note smites my ear ! "   In 1820 Wordsworth attacked the third line, which became " It seems to fill the whole
air's space."   One day he noticed that the voice of a cuckoo, heard
from a tree at a great distance, did not seem any louder when he
approached the tree, and he resolved to record this fact.   He also desired to recover the word " shout," and to distinguish it as the cuckoo's
by the epithet " twofold."   Accordingly, in 1827, the stanza became :

> While I am lying on the grass,
> Thy twofold shout I hear,
> That seems to fill the whole air's space,
> As loud far off as near.

Finally in 1845 he reverted to the original third line of 1807, " From
hill to hill it seems to pass," and to the 1815 form of l. 4, " At once far
off and near."

The third stanza, which in its present form dates from 1827, was in
1807 :

> To me no Babbler with a tale
> Of sunshine and of flowers,
> Thou tellest, Cuckoo ! in the Vale
> Of visionary hours.

The rhyming words of the first and third lines were transposed in 1815,
and the idea brought out more clearly :

> I hear thee babbling to the Vale
> Of sunshine and of flowers ;
> And [" But," 1820] unto me thou bring'st a tale
> Of visionary hours.

The present text makes the contrast still more clear.

15.   " No bird, but an invisible thing."   So in " The Cuckoo at
Laverna," " Although invisible as Echo's self."

31, 32 :

> An unsubstantial fairy place ;
> That is fit home for Thee !

So in " The Cuckoo at Laverna ":

> Voice of the Desert, fare-thee-well ; sweet Bird !
> If that substantial title please thee more.

In the Preface to the ed. of 1815 Wordsworth comments on
ll. 3, 4 of this poem : " This concise interrogation characterises
the seeming ubiquity of the cuckoo, and dispossesses the creature

almost of corporeal existence ; the Imagination being tempted to this exertion of her power by a consciousness in the memory that the cuckoo is almost perpetually heard throughout the season of spring, but seldom becomes an object of sight."

"MY HEART LEAPS UP."

Written on Mar. 26, 1802, at Town-end, Grasmere; first published in 1807. Dorothy Wordsworth writes in her Journal : "While I was getting into bed he wrote 'The Rainbow'"; and again on May 14, 1802 : "William very nervous. After he was in bed, haunted with altering 'The Rainbow.'" The printed text was never altered. In the "Ode: Intimations of Immortality from Recollections of Early Childhood," Wordsworth tells of "the glory and the freshness of a dream" which arrayed the aspects of nature for him in childhood, and which faded in maturer years (the rainbow is especially mentioned) ; and he goes on to show how his early feeling for nature is not lost, but is deepened by human experiences, including the sorrow of mature years. In his own arrangement of his Poems "My heart leaps up" is placed first (if we omit the "Poems written in Youth"), and the "Ode" — having for its motto the last three lines of this poem — is placed last, kindred thoughts and feelings thus rounding his entire work. "The Cuckoo" was written on the same day as "My heart leaps up," and expresses the same thought as to the "natural piety" of carrying on the feelings of childhood into later life. There is a special propriety in the word "piety," in the Latin sense of filial reverence, the child here being the father of the man, and the man feeling such reverence for his parent.

WRITTEN IN MARCH, etc.

This poem — a favourite with Joanna Baillie — was composed with speed ("extempore," says Wordsworth) near Brothers' Water, on Apr. 16, 1802. The text was never altered. Dorothy Wordsworth writes in her Journal : "When we came to the foot of Brothers' Water I left William sitting on the bridge. . . . When I returned I found William writing a poem descriptive of the sights and sounds we saw and heard. There was the gentle flowing of the stream, the glittering, lively lake, green fields, without a single creature to be seen on them ; behind us a flat pasture with forty-two cattle feeding. . . . The people were at work ploughing, harrowing, and sowing ; lasses working, a dog barking now and then ; cocks crowing, birds twittering ; the snow in patches at the top of the highest hill. . . . William finished his poem before we got to the foot of Kirkstone."

THE REDBREAST CHASING THE BUTTERFLY.

This poem was written in the orchard, Town-end, Grasmere. The date is given in Dorothy Wordsworth's Journal, Apr. 18, 1802 : " A mild grey morning with rising vapours. We sate in the orchard. William wrote the poem on "The Robin and the Butterfly." . . . William met me at Rydal with the conclusion of the poem to the Robin. I read it to him in bed. We left out some lines." The poem was published in 1807.

The reader should compare the poem of 1834, "The Redbreast (suggested in a Westmoreland Cottage)."

2. The pious bird. The pious deed, by which the bird dyed its breast in taking a thorn from the crucified Saviour's crown, is referred to in the poem of 1834.

9. The bird that : one of Wordsworth's latest corrections, in the ed. of 1849 ; "the bird whom," 1807–20 ; "the bird who," 1827–45.

20. This line remained in 1815 when one preceding and one following it were omitted :

> His little heart is throbbing :
> Can this be the Bird, to man so good,
> Our consecrated Robin ?

35, 36. Date from 1815. In 1807, three lines :

> Like the hues of thy breast
> His beautiful wings in crimson are drest,
> A brother he seems of thine own :

In 1832 the reading in the text, but cancelled in errata, is :

> His beautiful bosom is drest,
> In crimson as bright as thine own.

Wordsworth's desire was to make the butterfly resemble the redbreast as closely as possible, but on consideration he thought it absurd to speak of a butterfly's bosom, and so he retained the reading of 1815. Matthew Arnold, probably by an oversight, prints the cancelled text of 1832.

TO A BUTTERFLY ("I 've watched you").

Written in the orchard, Town-end, Grasmere, on Apr. 20, 1802; first published in 1807. Dorothy Wordsworth's Journal gives us the date of the poem, which she calls "a conclusion to the poem of the 'Butter-fly,'" that is, to the poem beginning "Stay near me" (p. 135). The stanza of both poems is identical in form. When printed the poems appeared separately. Perhaps "The Redbreast chasing the Butterfly" (Apr. 18, 1802) recalled the butterfly poem written on March 14. The first line is now as it originally stood, but in 1836 Wordsworth substituted "a short half-hour," — "short" carries the reader away from the butterfly to Wordsworth's mood of mind, and he happily reverted to the earlier text. It also suggested a point which Wordsworth did not intend, — a contrast between the "short" passage of time now and the "long" days of childhood (ll. 18, 19).

12, 13. In ed. 1807 (only) were:

> Stop here whenever you are weary,
> And rest as in a sanctuary!

To connect the butterfly at rest in the sun with "frozen seas" (l. 5) is an example of the "abstracting power" of the imagination, of which Wordsworth speaks in his Preface to the ed. of 1815; the one common characteristic on which the imagination concentrates itself is the motionlessness of both butterfly and ocean.

TO THE SMALL CELANDINE.

Written Apr. 30, 1802, at Town-end, Grasmere, and published in 1807. Dorothy Wordsworth writes in her Journal: "We came into the orchard directly after breakfast and sat there. The lake was calm, the sky cloudy. William began to write the poem of The Celandine. . . . I walked backwards and forwards with William. He repeated his poem to me. Then he got to work again and would not give over." Wordsworth notes as remarkable that "this flower, coming out so early in the spring as it does, and so bright and beautiful and in such profusion, should not have been noticed earlier in English verse. What adds much to the interest that attends it is its habit of shutting itself up and opening out according to the degree of light and temperature of the air." Southey, however, in a sonnet ("Thou lingerest, Spring!") written in 1799, had written:

> Scarce doth the glossy celandine appear
> Starring the sunny bank.

The most interesting fact about the text is that in the ed. of 1836 and until that of 1843 a stanza appeared between the present fifth and sixth stanzas, which in 1845 Wordsworth transferred with an altered text to the next following poem, "To the Same Flower," where it appears as the last stanza but one ("Drawn by what peculiar spell").

16. **Sage astronomer** in 1836 replaced "great astronomer."

27. **Her nest**: before 1832, "its nest."

58. Too strongly put before 1836: "Scorn'd and slighted upon earth."

61, 62. Before 1836:

> Singing at my heart's command,
> In the lanes my thoughts pursuing,

Altered, probably, because the "singing" anticipates "I will sing" in l. 63, and to avoid the identity of rhyme in "ensuing," "pursuing."

TO THE SAME FLOWER ("Pleasures newly found").

Dorothy Wordsworth's Journal gives the date of composition, May 1, 1802: "William wrote The Celandine, second part." Published in 1807.

There are interesting variations of text in ll. 51–53; in 1807:

> Let, as old Magellen ["Magellan," 1815] did,
> Others roam about the sea;
> Build who will a pyramid.

In 1820:

> Let, with bold advent'rous skill,
> Others thrid the polar sea;
> Rear a pyramid who will.

In 1827 as now, except with "Adventurer" for "Discoverer" (1845). Wordsworth at one time intended to restore "old Magellan."

For the transference of the sixth stanza, see notes on the last poem. As found 1836–43 in the preceding poem, it stood thus:

> Drawn by what peculiar spell,
> By what charm for sight or smell,
> Do those wingèd dim-eyed creatures,
> Labourers sent from waxen cells,
> Settle on thy brilliant features,
> In neglect of buds and bells
> Opening daily at thy side,
> By the season multiplied?

It was well to erase the unhappy " Settle on thy brilliant features."

14. Rising sun: 1807–32, " risen sun."

20. 'Kerchief-plots, plots no larger than a handkerchief.

38. Sheltering hold: 1807–27, " shelter'd hold."

39. Previous to 1845 this line was " Bright as any of the train."

50. Beneath our shoon. Rolfe compares, *Comus* 634, the herb " hæmony " with its " bright golden flower," on which the " dull swain " treads daily " with his clouted shoon."

Wordsworth in 1804 wrote a third poem on " The Small Celandine," in a sadder strain. See p. 191.

RESOLUTION AND INDEPENDENCE.

Written at Town-end, Grasmere, between May 3 and July 4, 1802; published in 1807. Dorothy Wordsworth's Journal gives the dates, and tells how Wordsworth, on certain days, worked almost incessantly at " The Leech-Gatherer," and " tired himself to death." The incident on which the poem was founded was recorded by Dorothy on Oct. 3, 1800. The encounter with the Leech-Gatherer was probably on September 26. Not far from Dove Cottage the brother and sister met " an old man almost double," carrying a bundle ; he wore an apron and night-cap ; " his face was interesting ; he had dark eyes and a long nose." The man was of Scotch parents, and he had been in the army ; his wife and nine out of ten children were dead. " His trade was to gather leeches, but now leeches were scarce, and he had not strength for it. He lived by begging, and was making his way to Carlisle where he should buy a few godly books to sell." " I was in the state of feeling described in the beginning of the poem," says Wordsworth (*Fenwick note*), " while crossing over Barton Fell from Mr. Clarkson's at the foot of Ullswater, towards Askham. The image of the hare I then observed on the ridge of the Fell." In a letter to friends [probably to Mary and Sara Hutchinson, June 14, 1802] Wordsworth writes : " I will explain to you in prose my feelings in writing *that* poem. . . . I describe myself as having been exalted to the highest pitch of delight by the joyousness and beauty of nature ; and then as depressed, even in the midst of those beautiful objects, to the lowest dejection and despair. A young poet in the midst of the happiness of nature is described as overwhelmed by the thoughts of the miserable reverses which have befallen the happiest of all men, *viz.*, poets. I think of this till I am so deeply impressed with it, that I consider the manner in which I was rescued from my dejection and despair almost as an interposition of Providence. A person reading the poem with feelings like mine will have been awed and controlled, expecting something spiritual or supernatural. What is brought forward ? A lonely place, 'a pond by which an old man *was*, far from all house or home' [the text was subsequently altered]; not *stood*, nor *sat*, but *was* — the figure presented in the most naked simplicity possible. The feeling of spirituality or supernaturalness is again referred to as being strong in my mind in this passage. How came he here? thought I, or what can he be doing? I then described him, whether ill or well is not for me to judge with perfect confidence ; but this I *can* confidently affirm, that though I believe God has given me a strong imagination, I cannot conceive a figure more impressive than that of an old man like this, the survivor of a wife and ten children, travelling alone among the mountains and all lonely places, carrying with him his own fortitude and the necessities which an unjust state of society has laid upon him."

1. In Dorothy Wordsworth's Journal, Feb. 1, 1798, we find " The trees almost *roared*."

5. Stock-dove. Wordsworth confuses the stock-dove and the wood-pigeon. See note on " The Nightingale."

6. The jay imitates the notes of other birds.

29. Warbling in 1820 replaced " singing."

44. His pride in 1815 replaced "its pride." In the sonnet on Milton the change was from "itself" to "herself" (of the soul). Chatterton and Burns, when Wordsworth wrote, afforded very recent examples of the misery of poets.

46. Following his plough : before 1820, " Behind his plough."

53, 54. The reading before 1820 is much less impressive :

> When up and down my fancy thus was driven,
> And I with these untoward thoughts had striven,

56. After stanza 8 in early editions appeared a stanza censured by Coleridge in " Biographia Literaria " in 1817, and omitted in 1820:

> **My** course I stopped as soon as I espied
> The Old Man in this naked wilderness:
> Close by a Pond, upon the further side,
> He stood alone: a minute's space I guess
> I watch'd him, he continuing motionless:
> To the Pool's further margin then I drew;
> He being all the while before me full in **view.**

57–63. Of this and the next stanza Wordsworth wrote in the Preface to ed. 1815: "In these images, the conferring, the abstracting, and the modifying powers of the Imagination immediately and mediately acting, are all brought into conjunction. The Stone is endowed with something of the power of life to approximate it to the Sea-beast; and the Sea-beast stripped of some of its vital qualities to assimilate it to the Stone; which intermediate image is thus treated for the purpose of bringing the original image, that of the Stone, to a nearer resemblance to the figure and condition of the aged Man; who is divested of so much of the indications of life and motion as to bring him to the point where the two objects unite and coalesce in just comparison. After what has been said, the image of the Cloud need not be commented upon."

67. In life's pilgrimage: an improvement of 1820 on the earlier 'in their pilgrimage."

71. Made more vivid in 1836; previously, "Himself he propped, his body, limbs, and face."

74. Before 1820: "Beside the little pond or moorish flood."

77, 78. Between stanzas 11 and 12 a stanza is found in manuscript describing the man as pale of face, wearing a cloak, and carrying a pack. See Knight's "Wordsworth," vol. II, p. 318 (ed. 1896).

82. Before 1820: "And now such freedom as I could I took"; altered because to accost the old man was rather a courtesy than a liberty.

88. Before 1820: "What kind of work is that which you pursue?"

90, 91. In 1807 and 1815:

> He answered me with pleasure and surprize,
> And there was, while he spake, a fire about his **eyes.**

In 1820 the idea of pleasure was excluded, and the lines stood as now, except the first three words, which were "He answer'd, while." Wordsworth in 1836 makes the eyes flash before the lips speak.

99. In edd. 1807 to 1820 an awkward, monosyllabic line: "He told me that he to this pond had come"; altered in 1827.

112. **By apt admonishment** in 1827 replaced the earlier "and [' by,' 1820] strong admonishment," 1807–15. The timeliness of the admonishment was the source of its strength.

117. In 1807: "And now, not knowing what the Old Man said"; in 1815: "But now, perplex'd by what the Old Man had said." Altered in 1820.

123. **Pools** in 1827 replaced "ponds."

STANZAS WRITTEN IN MY POCKET-COPY OF THOMSON'S CASTLE OF INDOLENCE.

Composed in the orchard, Town-end, Grasmere, May 9–11, 1802; published in 1815. In Dorothy Wordsworth's Journal we find: "May 9th . . . After tea he wrote two stanzas in the manner of Thomson's 'Castle of Indolence,' and was tired out." "May 11th. William finished the stanzas about C. [Coleridge] and himself." Wordsworth states that Coleridge's son, Hartley, said "that his father's character and habits are here preserved in a livelier way than anything that has been written about him." Although, probably in consequence of confusion in De Quincey's recollection of this poem, questions have been raised as to the identity of the persons described, and Matthew Arnold, Mr. Stopford Brooke, and others have erred in the matter, I hold it for certain that in the first four stanzas Wordsworth describes himself and in the last four S. T. Coleridge. The evidence — too long to state here — has been collected by Mr. T. Hutchinson in an admirable article in *The Fortnightly Review*, November, 1894. It may be added that Wordsworth's biographer, the Bishop of Lincoln, Sara Coleridge, and others always understood the poem aright. Mr. E. H. Coleridge (" Letters of Coleridge," vol. I, p. 345, *n.*) maintains that the portraits are composite — that of the earlier stanzas "a blended portrait of Wordsworth and Coleridge," that of the later a blended portrait of Coleridge and William Calvert.

5. This mood of Wordsworth's is presented in "Expostulation" and "The Tables Turned," pp. 32–34.

15. Before 1836: "Oft did." This stanza describes Wordsworth's restless wanderings among the hills, engaged in the exciting toil of composition.

19. Dorothy Wordsworth's Journal again and again refers to the extreme exhaustion suffered by Wordsworth after the excitement of poetical composition.

27. **A naked Indian.** Perhaps Wordsworth had in his mind the orchard bower described in " A Farewell " as an " Indian shed."

37. The description of Coleridge's appearance in this stanza is confirmed in every detail by other observers and by portraits.

55–63. In 1801 Coleridge had been engaged with his friend William Calvert in studies in natural and experimental science.

60. Before 1827: " The beetle with his radiance manifold."

62. Before 1827: "And cups of flowers and herbage green and gold."

66, 67. Before 1836:

> And, sooth, these two did love each other dear,
> As far as love in such a place could be;

It should be noticed that Wordsworth placed these stanzas, not among " Poems of the Imagination," but upon those " Founded on the Affections."

Parallels between Beattie's description of his " Minstrel " and Wordsworth's account of himself in this poem have been noticed.

A FAREWELL.

Written shortly before Wordsworth and his sister left Grasmere in the summer of 1802, in anticipation of Wordsworth's marriage (October 4) to Mary Hutchinson; published in 1815. Dorothy Wordsworth's Journal gives the precise date: " May 29th. . . . William finished his poem on going for Mary "; and "June 13th. William . . . has been altering the poem to Mary this morning." The Journal gives delightful pictures of the " little nook of mountain-ground." " It is," writes Professor Knight, " in very much the same condition as it was in 1802. The ' flowering shrubs ' and the ' rocky well ' still exist, and the ' steep rock's breast ' is ' thronged with primroses ' in spring. . . . The ' Bower ' is gone, and where it used to be a seat is now erected." Since these words were written, Dove Cottage and garden have passed into the guardianship of trustees, who keep it as a national memorial of Wordsworth. It is worth quoting Dorothy's farewell, entered in her Journal (July 8) just before she and her brother left Dove Cottage on this occasion. " O beautiful place! Dear Mary, William. The hour is come . . . I must prepare to go. The swallows I must leave them, the wall, the garden, the roses, all. Dear creatures! they sang last night after I was in bed; seemed to be singing to one another, just before they settled to rest for the night. Well, I must go. Farewell."

10. Before 1836: " And safely she will ride."

11. Before 1836: "The flowering shrubs that decorate our door." The expression was somewhat too stately for a cottage.

18. Two months. In fact the absence was one of three months — July 9 to October 6.

22. Gowan. The colour of the flower — saffron — shows that the common daisy cannot be meant. "Gowan appears in different parts of Scotland to be applied to the various buttercups, the marsh-marigold, the dandelion, the hawkweeds, the corn-marigold, the globe-flower, and indeed to almost any that is yellow." Prior's "Popular Names of British Plants."

43. On thy face. Before 1827: "in thy face."

56. The poem "The Sparrow's Nest." But in fact that poem refers to the garden at Cockermouth, not at Grasmere. "Sang" before 1832 was "sung."

TO H. C.

Dated by Wordsworth 1802; first published in 1807.

The subject of the poem is Hartley Coleridge, who was born Sept. 19, 1796. His brother Derwent thus describes him: "Seated upon Jacky's [Mr. Jackson, Hartley's godfather] knee, or standing by Wilsy's [Mrs. Wilson, the housekeeper at Greta Hall] apron, . . . the chirp of whose knitting-needles formed an accompaniment to the chirrup of his voice, with flashing eyes, which those who have seen will not easily forget, the child Hartley would pour out his strange speculations and weave his wild inventions, believing in his own tale." His father described Hartley as "a strange, strange boy, 'exquisitely wild,' an utter visionary, like the moon among their clouds he moves in a circle of his own making. He alone is a light of his own." Hartley inherited some of his father's infirmity of will, and though always loved and lovable, he did not fulfil the promise of his early years. His best sonnets are admirable, and show the influence of Wordsworth. He died on Jan. 6, 1849.

The text is unaltered except l. 28 (now as in 1827), which at first stood thus: "Not doom'd to jostle with unkindly shocks," and in 1815, "Not framed to undergo unkindly shocks." In the first reading 'jostle" was ungraceful; in the second "undergo" was unhappy, the idea requiring "sustain."

In 1807 Wordsworth acknowledged that he owed something to Jonathan Carver's "Travels." In describing Lake Superior, Carver writes: "The water in general appeared to be on a bed of rocks.

When it was calm, and the sun shone bright, I could sit in my canoe, where the depth was upward of six fathoms, and plainly see huge piles of stone at the bottom, of different shapes, some of which appeared as if they were hewn. The water at this time was pure and transparent as air, and my canoe seemed as if it hung suspended in that element." (Pp. 132, 133, ed. 1781.) Compare ll. 6–8.

In a pathetic sonnet beginning

> How long I sail'd, and never took a thought
> To what port I was bound,

Hartley Coleridge has lines which probably were written with a reminiscence of this poem addressed to him by Wordsworth:

> And watch the sunbeams dallying with the waves;
> Or haply dream what realms beneath may lie
> Where the clear ocean is an emerald sky.

TO THE DAISY ("In youth from rock to rock").

This poem was composed in the orchard, Town-end, Grasmere, in 1802, and was published in 1807. The lines from Wither were prefixed in 1815.

7, 8. In 1840 these lines of 1807 were restored; in 1836:

> And Nature's love of thee partake,
> Her much-loved Daisy!

Altered to avoid the tautology of "love" and "loved"; and here "sweet," frequently cancelled, was happily introduced.

9–12. The present text is of 1836. In 1807:

> When soothed a while by milder airs,
> Thee Winter in the garland wears
> That thinly shades his few gray hairs;
> Spring cannot shun thee;

The idea of Spring shunning the daisy was not happy, and in 1827 the lines became:

> When Winter decks his few gray hairs
> Thee in the scanty wreath he wears;
> Spring parts the clouds with softest airs,
> That she may sun thee;

17. Morrice train. A morris was a rustic dance performed in spring and summer time; said to be derived from the Moors or Moriscoes, with whom it originated; a morris train, a train of morris dancers.

19–21. The text is of 1836. In 1807:

> If welcome [" welcom'd," 1815, 1820] once thou count'st it gain;
>   Thou art not daunted,
> Nor car'st if thou be set at naught;

25. Mews, from French *mue*, moulting; hence a cage; hence an enclosed place, and specially stables; hence a lane or alley in which stables are situated, and so a lane or alley; the idea of a retired place is the dominant one here.

57–64. In 1807 the stanza stood thus:

> When, smitten by the morning ray,
> I see thee rise alert and gay,
> Then, chearful Flower! my spirits play
>   With kindred motion:
> At dusk I 've seldom mark'd thee press
> The ground, as if in thankfulness,
> Without some feeling, more or less,
>   Of true devotion.

The last five of these lines were altered to the present text in 1815; the " more or less " was a superfluity, ridiculed by the *Edinburgh Review*. The first two lines of the stanza were amended in 1836; as they previously stood, " smitten," etc., belonged rather to " I " than to " thee."

73–80. This stanza, as we have it, dates from 1836. In 1807:

> Child of the Year! that round dost run
> Thy course, bold lover of the sun,
> And chearful when the day 's begun
>   As morning Leveret,
> Thou long the Poet's praise shalt gain;
> Thou wilt be more belov'd by men
> In times to come; thou not in vain
>   Art Nature's Favourite.

The idea of regaining lost praise is of 1815:

> Thy long-lost praise thou shalt regain;
> Dear shalt thou be to future men
> As in old time;

There is something to regret in the loss of the fine expression " bold lover of the sun," but probably Wordsworth thought that the idea of running a planetary course round the sun might be suggested, which he did not intend.

Leveret is a young hare.

TO THE SAME FLOWER ("With little here").

The date of composition is 1802 (see note on "To the Daisy," the poem beginning "In youth from rock to rock I went"). Wordsworth's date — 1805 — in edd. 1836-49 is erroneous; first published, 1807.

3. In edd. 1807-32: "Sweet Daisy! oft I talk to thee." Here, and in l. 41 where the first reading was "Sweet Flower!" Wordsworth in 1836 removed the word "Sweet" and read from 1836 until 1845, when the present text was adopted, "Yet once again I talk to thee."

9, 10. The text is of 1820. In 1807-15:

> Oft do I sit by thee at ease
> And weave a web of similies.

The poem is classed by Wordsworth under the head "Poems of the Fancy." In the Preface to ed. 1815 he writes: "The law under which the processes of Fancy are carried on is as capricious as the accidents of things, and the effects are surprising, playful, ludicrous, amusing, tender, or pathetic, as the objects happen to be oppositely produced or fortunately combined. Fancy depends upon the rapidity and profusion with which she scatters her thoughts and images; trusting that their number, and the felicity with which they are linked together, will make amends for the want of individual value; or she prides herself upon the curious subtilty and the successful elaboration with which she can detect their lurking affinities."

Writing of stanzas 3, 5, 6 in "Modern Painters," part III, sect. ii, chap. v, Ruskin writes: "Observe how spiritual, yet how wandering and playful the fancy is in the first two stanzas, and how far she flies from the matter in hand, never stopping to brood on the character of any one of the images she summons, and yet for a moment truly seeing and believing in them all; while in the last stanza the imagination returns with its deep feeling to the heart of the flower, and *cleaves fast* to that."

TO THE DAISY ("Bright Flower!").

This is one of three poems to the Daisy written in 1802 at Town-end, Grasmere; Wordsworth fell at a later time into errors respecting the dates (see Aldine ed. of "Wordsworth," vol. II, p. 263). He described ("Poems," 1807) this poem, and also that beginning "With little here to do and see," as "overflowings of the mind in composing" the poem to the Daisy, beginning "In youth from rock to rock I went." In these stanzas, however, fancy is not, as in the other Daisy poems, the predominant faculty, and they were placed among " Poems of Sentiment and Reflection."

The third stanza was omitted in edd. 1827 and 1832, perhaps because the words "thy function apostolical " had been censured as little less than profane. "The word [apostolical]," said Wordsworth to Miss Fenwick, " is adopted with reference to its derivation, implying something sent out on a mission ; and assuredly this little flower, especially when the subject of verse, may be regarded, in its humble degree, as administering both to moral and spiritual purposes."

2. Until 1840 was perhaps better: " A Pilgrim bold in Nature's care," and in 1827 and 1832 l. 3 was " And oft, the long year through, the heir." In 1837 an unhappy opening (repented of in 1840) appears :

> Confiding Flower, by Nature's care
> Made bold, — who, lodging here or there,
> Art all, etc.

and at the same time l. 6 became " Communion with humanity."

9. Is as it originally stood ; but in edd. 1827 and 1832, " And wherefore? Man is soon deprest." The earlier reading was restored in 1837.

Matthew Arnold prints the 1832 text, from which stanza 3 was omitted.

The three Daisy poems of Wordsworth should be read in connection with one another, and with them James Montgomery's " A Field Flower," which has some thoughts in common with these poems. Montgomery's poem is of 1803, but it was written before the publication of the poems of Wordsworth to the daisy.

WHEN TO THE ATTRACTIONS OF THE BUSY WORLD.

Wordsworth in 1815 and 1820 dated this poem 1802; in 1836 he gave the date 1805, but probably in order to connect the poem with those relating to his brother John's death, which took place at midnight of Feb. 5, 1805. We might without hesitation accept the date 1802, for the poem was certainly written before John Wordsworth's death (see closing lines and Wordsworth's note), were it not for references in Dorothy Wordsworth's Journal of 1800 (when John was staying at Grasmere) to a poem which she calls " The Fir-grove," and

to a poem which she speaks of as an "inscription about the path":
"Sept. 1. W. read 'Joanna' and 'The Fir-grove' to Coleridge," and two
days previously: "I left William to compose an inscription, that about
the path." On the following day (August 30): "William finished his
inscription of the Pathway." It seems highly probable that the poem
was partly written in August, 1800, and was carried farther, and to the
present close, in 1802. Professor Knight conjectures that in 1800 it
closed at l. 66. The poem was published in 1815.

"The Fir-grove," writes Knight, "still exists. It is between Wishing
Gate and White-Moss Common, and almost exactly opposite the
former." Wordsworth pointed out the single beech-tree (l. 18) to Miss
Cookson a few days before Dora Wordsworth's death. "John's grove"
was "a favourite haunt with us all," says Wordsworth, "while we lived
at Town-end."

1–5. The time spoken of is the opening of 1800.

36. **Beneath** in 1836 replaced "between."

39–41. In 1815:

> And, baffled thus, before the Storm relaxed,
> I ceased that ["the" 1827] Shelter to frequent,

Altered in 1836. Wordsworth wished to bring out the fact that there
was a series of storms.

51–61. In 1815:

> Much wondering at my own simplicity
> How I could e'er have made a fruitless search
> For what was now so obvious. At the sight
> Conviction also flashed upon my mind
> That this same path (within the shady grove
> Begun and ended) by my Brother's steps
> Had been impressed. To sojourn a short while
> Beneath my roof He from the barren seas
> Had newly come — a cherished Visitant!
> And much did it delight me to perceive
> That, to this opportune recess allured,
> He had surveyed it with a finer eye,
> A heart more wakeful; that, more loth to part
> From place so lovely, he had worn the track.

The change was made in 1827, leaving only two words to correct — in
l. 54, "Under" in 1845 replacing "Beneath," and in the same line
"gladly" in 1840 replacing "newly." A MS. note of Wordsworth's
shows that "newly" was removed because time was needed to trace a

visible path. The chief object of the change in this passage was to inform the reader of John Wordsworth's presence before telling of the conviction that the path was made by his footsteps.

64–66. Before 1845:

> With which the Sailor measures o'er and o'er
> His short domain upon the vessel's deck,
> While she is travelling through the dreary sea.

Wordsworth did not think "travelling" the best word to apply to a ship.

67. Esthwaite's pleasant shore, where the brothers were at the Hawkshead school.

72. Mind was: a correction of 1836; previously, "minds were."

76, 77. Compare Leonard's feelings at sea in "The Brothers."

80. A silent Poet. Compare the passage in Bk. i of "The Excursion," beginning at l. 77.

82. Inevitable ear, an ear which no sound can elude.

84–87. Before 1827:

> art gone;
> And now I call the path-way by thy name
> And love

91. Peaceful: before 1827, "placid."

101. Thoughtfully: before 1827, "to and fro." John Wordsworth took a deep interest in his brother's poetry. On board ship he was known as "the Philosopher."

THE GREEN LINNET.

Written in 1803; published in 1807. The birds in the orchard at Dove Cottage, Grasmere, suggested the poem.

1–8. In 1807 this stanza was as follows:

> The May is come again:—how sweet
> To sit upon my Orchard-seat!
> And Birds and Flowers once more to greet,
>   My last year's Friends together;
> My thoughts they all by turns employ;
> A whispering Leaf is now my joy,
> And then a Bird will be the toy
>   That doth my fancy tether.

The change was made in 1815 (with "flowers and birds" in l. 7 until 1827). The self-conscious personal element ceased to intrude, and the descriptive power was increased.

25. **Amid** was substituted in 1845 for "Upon."

33–40. This stanza stood thus in 1807:

> While thus before my eyes he gleams,
> A Brother of the Leaves he seems;
> When in a moment forth he teems
>   His little song in gushes:
> As if it pleas'd him to disdain
> And mock the form which he did feign
> While he was dancing with the train
>   Of Leaves among the bushes.

In 1820 the sixth line of this stanza became "The voiceless form he chose to feign." The *Edinburgh Review* objected to the "toy" and "tether" of stanza 1 and the "teems" of this stanza. Wordsworth after a time came round to his critic's view. In 1827 the last stanza was altered to the present text, except its first two lines, which cost Wordsworth many "poetic pains":

> My sight he dazzles, half deceives,
> A bird so like the dancing Leaves; (1827.)

After slight alterations in 1832 and 1840, the present text was reached in 1845.

Mr. Wintringham writes in "The Birds of Wordsworth," p. 123: "Of all English birds, the greenfinch — or the green grosbeak — is best adapted to its position in nature. Its colour makes it almost imperceptible to all who are not adepts in ornithology. The bright gamboge yellow of its primary feathers and the bright golden-green of the least wing-coverts do not foil the hiding powers of its other plumage, but rather complete than destroy the bird's perfect adaptation."

YEW–TREES.

Written at Grasmere in 1803; published in 1815. The text is unchanged. The yew-trees of Borrowdale still exist. A favorite excursion from Keswick is to Buttermere by Borrowdale, returning by the Vale of Lorton. Wordsworth considered this — and justly — one of the most imaginative of his poems; it is cited by Coleridge to prove that Wordsworth possessed "imagination in the highest and strictest sense of the word." Ruskin (" Modern Painters, part III, sect. ii, chap. iv) calls it " the most vigorous and solemn bit of forest landscape ever painted."

5. **Umfraville or Percy.** Percy is remembered in connection with the Ballad of Chevy Chase. A Sir Ingram Umfraville fought with Edward at Bannockburn; a Sir Robert Umfraville, vice-admiral of England, invaded Scotland in 1410.

11. This prophecy of the undecaying life of the tree has not been fulfilled.

15. **Fraternal four.** Compare the sonnet beginning " Degenerate Douglas ! " l. 6, " A brotherhood of venerable trees."

18. **Inveterately,** by virtue of old habit ; Lat., *in* and *veterare*, to grow or become old.

22. **Pining,** decaying. Coleridge, in giving these lines in " Biographia Literaria," printed the word " pinal," meaning perhaps " of pine-trees." See quotation from Ruskin which follows.

23–28. Perhaps the mythology of these lines was suggested by Virgil, Æneid VI, 273–284 ; but it is also evidently influenced by the associations of the yew with church-yards.

33. **Glaramara** is a rugged mountain rising out of the Borrowdale valley. Ruskin (" Modern Painters," part IV, chap. xvii), having described how three or four different persons will variously regard a group of pine-trees, comes to " the man who has most the power of contemplating the thing itself " : " He will not see the colours of the tree so well as the artist, nor its fibres so well as the engineer ; he will not altogether share the emotion of the sentimentalist, nor the trance of the idealist ; but fancy, and feeling, and perception, and imagination will all obscurely meet and balance themselves in him, and he will see the pine-trees somewhat in this manner " (quoting Wordsworth's lines, " Worthier still of note," etc.). Perhaps Ruskin forgot that Wordsworth is describing yews and not pines.

AT THE GRAVE OF BURNS (" I shiver," etc.).

This poem is connected with Wordsworth's tour in Scotland, 1803, and may have been written then or soon after ; but it was not published until 1842. In illustration of the poem, Wordsworth gives in a note a long extract from his sister's Journal. The travellers reached Dumfries late on August 17, and next day visited the grave of Burns. There was no stone to mark the spot ; not long afterwards the body was moved from its first resting-place to the mausoleum. " We looked at the grave with melancholy and painful reflections, repeating to each other his own verses, 'Is there a man whose judgment clear,' etc." They afterwards visited Burns's house; Mrs. Burns was absent, and the servant said she was in great sorrow for the death of her son Wallace. Proceeding to Ellisland, they saw from within half a mile of Burns's dwelling-place the Cumberland mountains. "Drayton has prettily described the connexion which this neighborhood has with ours when he makes Skiddaw say:

> ' Scurfell [Criffel] from the sky,
> That Anadale [Annandale] doth crown, with a most amorous eye,
> Salutes me every day, or at my pride looks grim,
> Oft threatning me with clouds, as I oft threatning him '

These lines recurred to William's memory, and we talked of Burns and of the prospect he must have had, perhaps from his own door, of Skiddaw and his companions, indulging ourselves in the fancy that we *might* have been personally known to each other, and he have looked upon those objects with more pleasure for our sakes." Compare ll. 37–48.

In 1816 Wordsworth printed as a pamphlet his " Letter to a Friend of Robert Burns," in which he criticises Dr. Currie's " Life of Burns," attempts to fix the principles on which information as to the lives of authors should be given or withheld, and writes generously of his brother poet.

In the poems relating to Burns, the favourite stanza of the Scottish poet is adopted. Lines 19, 20 refer to Burns's poem " To a Mountain Daisy," from which " glinted forth " is taken. Lines 31–34 previous to 1845 were:

> Well might I mourn that He was gone
> Whose light I hailed when first it shone,
> When, breaking forth as nature's own
> It showed my youth

Wordsworth's grief was not peculiar to himself, except in its degree.

39. **Criffel** or Crowfell, a mountain in the county of Kirkcudbright, above 1800 feet high.

50. **Poor Inhabitant below,** from Burns's "A Bard's Epitaph," which Wordsworth and his sister had been repeating to each other at the grave.

77, 78. The reference is to Burns's poem " To Ruin," stanza ii (see its last line).

THOUGHTS SUGGESTED THE DAY FOLLOWING.

This poem was not written until many years after 1803; the date is uncertain; it was first published in 1842. Wordsworth tells Prof. Henry Reed in a letter of Dec. 23, 1839, that he had very lately added the last stanza (" But why to Him.") The text was never altered.

3. Burns in his poem " The Vision " imagines the Scottish muse crowning his head with holly.

7-12. See note on last poems.

TO A HIGHLAND GIRL.

Written, as Dorothy Wordsworth states in her Journal, "not long after our return [Sept. 25, 1803] from Scotland"; first published in 1807; placed in edd. 1815 and 1820 among " Poems of the Imagination." On Sunday, Aug. 28, 1803, Wordsworth, with his sister and Coleridge, when descending a hill towards Loch Lomond, overtook two gray-plaided girls, one " exceedingly beautiful." " They answered us," Dorothy writes, "so sweetly that we were quite delighted, at the same time that they stared at us with an innocent look of wonder. I think I never heard the English language sound more sweetly than from the mouth of the elder of these girls, while she stood at the gate answering our inquiries, her face flushed with the rain; her pronunciation was clear and distinct; without difficulty, yet slow, like that of a foreign speech " (see ll. 38–46). They were the sister and sister-in-law of the ferryman. The day was one of drenching rain; at the ferry-house the wanderers dried their clothes and obtained food, while the waterfall hard by " was roaring at the end of the hut," and the waves were dashing against the shore. After some time the ferry-boat, laden with some twenty men and women in bright attire, arrived; " there was a joyous bustle surrounding the boat, which even imparted something of the same character to the waterfall in its tumult, and the restless grey waves; the young men laughed and shouted, the lasses laughed, and the older folks seemed to be in a bustle to be away." Coleridge, in his Journal (see " Letters of Coleridge," I, 432, *n.*), tells also of the " two little lassies " who " did everything with such sweetness, and one, 14, with such native elegance. Oh! she was a divine creature! " She reminded Wordsworth and Dorothy (says Coleridge) of the Highland girl in " Peter Bell."

Wordsworth, in the *Fenwick note*, says : "The sort of prophecy with which the verses conclude has, through God's goodness, been realised, and now, approaching the close of my 73rd year, I have a most vivid remembrance of her and the beautiful objects with which she was surrounded. She is alluded to in the poem of ' The Three Cottage Girls ' in my Continental Memorials." The lines from this poem of 1820 are the following :

> Sweet Highland Girl! a very shower
> Of beauty was thy earthly dower,
> When thou didst flit before mine eyes,
> Gay vision under sullen skies,
> While Hope and Love around thee played,
> Near the rough Falls of Inversneyd!
> Have they, who nursed the blossom, seen
> No breach of promise in the fruit?
> Was joy, in following joy, as keen
> As grief can be in grief's pursuit ?
> When youth had flown did hope still bless
> Thy goings — or the cheerfulness
> Of innocence survive to mitigate distress?

The ideality of the poem "To a Highland Girl" required a transformation of the actual facts ; we hear nothing of the poet's or the girl's companions; nothing of the crowded ferry-boat, the drenching rain, the "tumult and storm," of which Dorothy's Journal tells.

The division of the poem into four sections, each closing with a triplet, imparts to it something of the character of a poem in stanzas; and in the sequence of thought and feeling it bears a resemblance to "She was a Phantom of delight," the germ of which, Wordsworth stated, "was four lines composed as a part of the verses on the Highland Girl." In both poems a "Phantom" or "Vision" (stanza and section 1) is discovered (stanza 2) to be a "Woman," and this again (stanza 3) is heightened and dignified. The "Highland Girl" closes with a characteristically Wordsworthian return upon the poet himself.

5, 6. Wordsworth's care for his text is illustrated by the variations in these lines. "These" and "this," 1807-32, gave place in 1836-43 to "those" and "that"; the present reading was attained in 1845.

11. This, the earliest text, was restored in 1845, after "ye do seem" 1815-32, and the unhappy reading of 1836-43 "In truth, unfolding thus, ye seem."

15-17. For these three lines of 1845-49 stood in earlier edd. only one: "Yet dream and [' or,' 1836-43] Vision as thou art." Wordsworth desired to bring the vision and the reality into closer conjunction before the concluding lines of this section.

20. An improvement of 1845 on the earlier "I neither know Thee, nor thy peers," where the emphasis fell more on "know" than on "Thee."

66–78. With this assertion of the abiding gain for Memory, compare Dorothy Wordsworth's Journal: "I never think of the two girls but the whole image of that romantic spot is before me a living image, as it will be to my dying day."

GLEN ALMAIN.

Written probably in 1803 and published in 1807. On Sept. 9, 1803, Wordsworth, with his sister, walked through Glen Almond — known locally as "the Sma' Glen" — in Perthshire. Knight says he does not know that it was ever called "Glen Almain" till Wordsworth gave it "that remarkably un-Scottish name." The form "Almon" is found, and it is said to be a corrupted spelling of the Gaelic "Avon" = river. Dorothy Wordsworth describes it as "a very sweet scene, a green valley, not very narrow, with a few scattered trees and huts, almost invisible in a misty green of afternoon light"; it became very narrow as they advanced — "everything is simple and undisturbed." She speaks of "its own peculiar character of removedness from the world," and adds: "The poem was written by William on hearing of a tradition relating to it, which we did not know when we were there."

Only two words were changed in the poem: in l. 21 "such" was "this" before 1827 (altered to avoid the recurrence of "this" in ll. 20, 21); and "Yet" in l. 29, where before 1827 stood "And." See on Wordsworth and Ossian the poem "Written on a blank leaf of Macpherson's Ossian," and the notes to that poem. Wordsworth never accepted as genuine remains of antiquity the Ossianic poems given to the world by Macpherson.

STEPPING WESTWARD.

Written at some date between 1803 and April–May, 1805 (when Dorothy Wordsworth copied it for her Journal); first published, 1807. The text is unchanged, except that in l. 19 the copy in the Journal gives "was" in place of "had." The date of the incident is Sunday, Sept. 11, 1803. "We have never had a more delightful walk," Dorothy writes,

" than this evening. Ben Lomond and the three pointed-topped mountains of Loch Lomond, which we had seen from the Garrison, were
very majestic under the clear sky, the lake perfectly calm, the air sweet
and mild. . . . The sun had been set for some time, when, being within
a quarter of a mile of the ferryman's hut, our path having led us close
to the shore of the calm lake, we met two neatly dressed women, without hats, who had probably been taking their Sunday evening's walk.
One of them said to us in a friendly, soft tone of voice, ' What ! you
are stepping westward ? ' I cannot describe how affecting this simple
expression was in that remote place, with the western sky in front, yet
glowing with the departed sun. William wrote the following poem
long after, in remembrance of his feelings and mine." Here, as in " The
Solitary Reaper," the visionary and the human are blended ; the woman's
question is at once an oracular utterance and a courteous salutation.

THE SOLITARY REAPER.

Written at some date between Sept. 13, 1803 and May, 1805 (when
Dorothy Wordsworth copied it for her Journal); first published, 1807.
It is a " Poem of the Imagination," and was placed under that heading
1815–20; but it is rightly included in " Memorials of a Tour in Scotland, 1803," although no such reaper was seen and no such song was
heard by the poet. Dorothy Wordsworth writes in her Journal of the
Tour, under the date September 13 : " As we descended [the pedestrians
were near Loch Voil], the scene became more fertile, our way being
pleasantly varied — through coppices or open fields, and passing farm-
houses, though always with an intermixture of uncultivated ground. It
was harvest-time, and the fields were quietly — might I be allowed to
say pensively ? — enlivened by small companies of reapers. It is not
uncommon in the more lonely parts of the Highlands to see a single
person so employed. The following poem was suggested to William
by a beautiful sentence in Thomas Wilkinson's ' Tour of Scotland.' "
This fact is mentioned by Wordsworth in a note, ed. 1807, where he
adds : " A MS. Tour in Scotland by a Friend, the last line being taken
from it *verbatim*." Wilkinson, whose spade became the subject of a
poem by Wordsworth, was a member of the Society of Friends, proprietor of a small hereditary estate near Yanwath, upon the banks of
the Emont. His " Tours to the British Mountains, with the Descriptive
Poems of Lowther and Emont Vale," was published in 1824. The
sentence (p. 12) which suggested Wordsworth's " Solitary Reaper " is

the following: "Passed a female who was reaping alone; she sung in Erse as she bended over her sickle; the sweetest human voice I ever heard; her strains were tenderly melancholy, and felt delicious, long after they were heard no more."

Wordsworth's ear, though so finely organised for sensibility to the sounds of nature, was not capable of much musical delight. In this poem, as Mr. W. A. Heard has written, the singer's voice "becomes almost a part of nature, working a human sweetness into the landscape. . . . We feel the song to be the very soul of the valley." ("Wordsworthiana," p. 235.)

4. "Her *strains* were tenderly *melancholy*."—Wilkinson.

10. Previous to 1827 was "So sweetly to reposing bands," and l. 13, "No sweeter voice was ever heard." Compare Wilkinson's "The sweetest human voice," etc. Wordsworth believed that he had used the word "sweet" to excess throughout his poems, and in 1827 he removed it from ten passages; in later editions from fifteen additional passages. In 1827 l. 13 became "Such thrilling voice was never heard"; the present reading dates from 1837. In his "Guide to the Lakes," Wordsworth speaks of "an imaginative influence in the voice of the cuckoo, when that voice has taken possession of a deep mountain valley." Here the sense of solitude must be predominant, and it is enhanced by the "silence of the seas" (a phrase almost identical occurs in "The Ancient Mariner") and the silence of the desert.

17. Wordsworth has not imported from his source a mention of the fact that the song was in Erse.

19. **Old, unhappy, far-off things.** In her diary for the day which includes this poem Dorothy Wordsworth notes: "William here conceived the notion of writing an ode upon the affecting subject of those relics of human society found in that grand and solitary region."

25. The alternate rhymes cease in the concluding stanza, and the form of the opening stanza is resumed in this, which closes the poem.

29. In 1807 and 1815 (with the characteristic boldness of Wordsworth's earlier texts): "I listen'd till I had my fill"; in the next line "as" became "when" in 1827 ; "as" was happily restored in 1836.

It may be noted that in his selections from Wordsworth Matthew Arnold manufactures a text from several editions, assuredly not a legitimate process. He retains "So sweetly to reposing bands" from 1807–20; adopts "A voice so thrilling ne'er was heard" from 1836–49; retains "I listen'd till I had my fill" from 1807–15; and gives "when" in l. 30, which is found only in 1827–32.

ADDRESS TO KILCHURN CASTLE.

The first three lines, Wordsworth says, were "thrown off at the moment I first caught sight of the Ruin," *i.e.*, on Aug. 31, 1803; "the rest was added many years after." The poem was first published in 1827. "We were very lucky," writes Dorothy Wordsworth, "in seeing it after a great flood; for its enchanting effect was chiefly owing to its situation in the lake, a decayed palace rising out of the plain of waters!"

10. **Thy rugged Sire,** War (as in l. 1).

19. **Holds:** before 1836, "has."

35. **Infant years** in 1845 replaced "infancy."

The idea of the poem — the majesty of nature yielding to a venerable memorial of humanity — is not of frequent occurrence in the writings of Wordsworth.

YARROW UNVISITED ("From Stirling Castle").

Written in 1803 and published in 1807. The text is unchanged. On September 17 Wordsworth and his sister walked through the Glen of Roslin, past Hawthornden, to Scott's house at Lasswade. Scott promised to meet them two days afterwards at Melrose. Next day they walked from Peebles by the Tweed, and Wordsworth wrote the fine sonnet "Degenerate Douglas!" (p. 317). "We left the Tweed," writes Dorothy, "when we were within about a mile and a half or two miles of Clovenford. . . . At Clovenford, being so near to the Yarrow, we could not but think of the possibility of going thither, but came to the conclusion of reserving the pleasure for some future time, in consequence of which, after our return [*i.e.*, to Grasmere], William wrote the poem."

When Wordsworth refers to the "various poems the scene of which is laid upon the banks of Yarrow," he doubtless had in his mind Logan's pathetic bailad "The Braes of Yarrow" (of which each stanza, as with Wordsworth's poem and others, closes with the word "Yarrow") and probably "Willie's Drowned in Yarrow," "The Douglas Tragedy," "The Lament of the Border Widow," and "The Dowie Dens of Yarrow." See Veitch's "History and Poetry of the Scottish Border."

6. **Winsome Marrow.** "Marrow," a partner; perhaps a corruption of French *mari*.

17. The Gala flows into the Tweed near Abbotsford, below Galashiels. It is celebrated in Scottish ballads. The Leader gives its name

to Lauder-Dale, and joins the Tweed near Melrose. **Haughs** means holms, low-lying lands, which may be occasionally overflowed.

20.   Lintwhites, linnets.

35.   Fair hangs the apple frae the rock, from "The Braes of Yarrow," by Hamilton of Bangour. The "apple" is probably the red berry of the rowan or mountain-ash.

37.   Strath, a valley through which a river runs.

43.   St. Mary's Lake, the reservoir from which the Yarrow takes its rise. In the Introduction to Canto II of "Marmion," Scott describes "lone St. Mary's silent lake." See "The Feeling for Nature in Scottish Poetry" by Professor Veitch, vol. II, p. 196. "In the winter," writes Scott, "it is still frequented by flights of wild swans; hence my friend Mr. Wordsworth's lines :

> The swan on sweet St. Mary's lake
> Floats double, swan and shadow.   (Notes to "Marmion.")

Wordsworth said to Aubrey de Vere : "Scott misquoted in one of his novels my lines on Yarrow. He makes me write —

> The swans on sweet St. Mary's lake
> Float double, swans and shadow.

But I wrote 'The *swan* on *still* St. Mary's lake.' Never could I have written 'swans' in the plural. The scene, when I saw it, with its still and dim lake, under the dusky hills, was one of utter loneliness; there was *one* swan, and one only, stemming the water, and the pathetic loneliness of the region gave importance to the one companion of that swan — its own white image in the water." De Vere's "Essays," vol. II, p. 277.

This poem — a plea for preserving the ideal Yarrow of imagination rather than looking on the real Yarrow — should be read with "Yarrow Visited" and "Yarrow Revisited." When in 1814 Wordsworth saw the romantic stream, the real was, as he says, "won," and yet the ideal was not lost.

LINES ON THE EXPECTED INVASION.

Written in 1803, but not published until 1842. The text is unchanged. Compare the sonnets "To the Men of Kent" and "In the Pass of Killicranky, an Invasion being expected."

3.   Falkland, Lucius Cary, second Viscount Falkland, who died fighting for King Charles I at the battle of Newbury, Sept. 20, 1643.

4. **Montrose,** James Graham, fifth Earl and first Marquis of Montrose, who fought on the Royalist side, and was hanged in the Grassmarket, Edinburgh, May 21, 1650.

7. **Pym,** John Pym, who was conspicuous in the proceedings against Strafford and Laud. He died Dec. 8, 1643.

"SHE WAS A PHANTOM OF DELIGHT."

Written in 1804 at Town-end, Grasmere, and published in 1807. Wordsworth stated that the germ of the poem was four lines composed as a part of the verses on the Highland girl. See as to similarity of plan in both poems the note on " To a Highland Girl," p. 424. " Though beginning in this way," said Wordsworth, " it was written from my heart, as is sufficiently obvious "—meaning that it has reference to his wife. In " The Prelude," Bk. vi, Mary Hutchinson is described in a like way:

> By her exulting outside look of youth
> And placid under-countenance first endeared.

For a closer parallel, see " The Prelude," Bk. xiv, l. 268. In the last line of this poem " angelic light " replaced in 1845 the earlier " an angel light."

8. Became in 1836 " From May-time's brightest, liveliest dawn," but the earlier reading was happily restored.

The idea which appears in the " Ode: Intimations of Immortality " and in the " Elegiac Stanzas suggested by a Picture of Peele Castle " of a visionary glory passing away or being taken up into a graver feeling for life is present here in another connection.

22. " The very pulse of the machine " has been an offence to some lovers of this poem. Does Wordsworth mean by machine merely the body, as Hamlet does in his signature of the letter to Ophelia : " Thine . . . whilst this machine is to him " ? I rather think the whole woman with all her household routine is conceived as the organism of which the thoughtful soul is the animating principle. In Bartram's " Travels," a book which Wordsworth used for his " Ruth," I find the following : " At the return of the morning, by the powerful influence of light, the *pulse* of nature becomes more active, and the universal vibration of life insensibly and irresistibly moves the wondrous *machine*."

Wordsworth told Crabb Robinson that the poems " Our walk was far," etc., " She was a Phantom," and the two sonnets " To a Painter " should be read in succession " as exhibiting the different phases of affection to his wife."

"I WANDERED LONELY," etc.

Written in 1804 at Town-end, Grasmere. First published in 1807. The place of the poem is in Gowbarrow Park, Ullswater, where the daffodils were seen on Apr. 15, 1802. Dorothy Wordsworth writes in her Journal : "I never saw daffodils so beautiful. They grew among the mossy stones, about and above them; some rested their heads upon these stones, as on a pillow for weariness; and the rest tossed and reeled and danced, and seemed as if they verily laughed with the wind that blew directly over the lake to them. They looked so gay, ever glancing, ever changing. . . . There was here and there a little knot, and a few stragglers higher up; but they were so few as not to disturb the simplicity, unity, and life of that one busy highway. We rested again and again. The bays were stormy, and we heard the waves at different distances, and in the middle of the water, like the sea."

The second stanza was an afterthought, added in ed. 1815, after which date the text remained (finally) unaltered.

In 1807, in l. 4, "dancing" stood where we have "golden," and in l. 16, "laughing" (from Dorothy's Journal) where we have "jocund."

Again, in 1807, l. 5, "Along" stood in place of "Beside," and the next line was "Ten thousand dancing," etc.

The two admirable lines 21, 22 were contributed by Mary Wordsworth, the poet's wife. In 1815 Wordsworth described the subject of the stanzas as "rather an elementary feeling and single impression (approaching to the nature of an ocular spectrum) upon the imaginative faculty than an *exertion* of it." The facts are idealized; Wordsworth did not wander "lonely as a cloud"; his sister accompanied him; the host of daffodils were not at first seen. "We saw," says Miss Wordsworth, "a few daffodils close to the water side"; the sense of the "jocund company" is enhanced by the preceding solitude, and the unity of the joyous impression depends partly on the completeness and suddenness of the surprise.

THE AFFLICTION OF MARGARET ——.

Written in 1804 at Town-end, Grasmere; published in 1807, with the title "The Affliction of Margaret —— of —— "; in 1820 "The Affliction of Margaret "; and in 1845 the present title, perhaps to indicate that it was not a poem wholly of imaginative invention. It was "taken," Wordsworth says, "from the case of a poor widow who lived in the town of Penrith. Her sorrow was well known to Mrs. Wordsworth, to my sister, and, I believe, to the whole town. She kept a shop, and when she saw a stranger passing by, she was in the habit of going into the street to enquire of him after her son.

10, 11. Before 1836 :

> To have despair'd, and have believ'd,
> And be for evermore beguil'd ;

24. Before 1827: " What power hath even his wildest scream."

56. Incommunicable sleep. Mr. Myers interprets this (in an unusual sense of " incommunicable ") as a sleep that cannot be communicated with. Perhaps this is right ; but may it not mean a sleep that can make no communication? The reference to " all thy mates " adds to the idea of the solitude and isolation of this sleep of death.

Coleridge in " Biographia Literaria " speaks of this poem as " that most affecting composition, which no mother, and, if I may judge by my own experience, no parent can read without a tear."

60. As in other passages, " Between " was substituted in 1832 for " Betwixt."

ADDRESS TO MY INFANT DAUGHTER DORA.

Written Sept. 16, 1804, and published in 1815. Dora's birthday, August 16, was also that of her mother. The name Dora was added to the title in 1849, after her death. So in " The Kitten and the Falling Leaves," and also in " The Longest Day," in 1849 " Laura " was changed to " Dora." The text was never altered.

4. That bright star, the moon. So Dante, " Paradiso," II, 30 (of the moon) :

> Fix gratefully thy mind
> On God, who unto the first star has brought us

— *la prima stella.* *Cf.* Hamlet, I, i, 118, " the moist star."

15. " Heaven's eternal year," from Dryden's " Ode to the Memory of Mrs. Anne Killigrew."

This poem is placed by Wordsworth among " Poems of the Fancy," not those " Founded on the Affections," probably on the ground of the parallels suggested between the moon's monthly progress and the life of the infant. In the closing lines Wordsworth's favourite thought of the continuity of human life — the gladness and love of infancy passing into the maturer joy and reasonable passion of older years — is touched on.

THE SMALL CELANDINE ("There is a Flower").

Written in 1804; published in 1807. This was subsequently placed by Wordsworth among "Poems referring to the Period of Old Age." The text is unchanged, except that in l. 4 "himself" in 1837 replaced "itself," and in l. 17 "cheer" in 1827 replaced "bless."

MORNING AMONG THE MOUNTAINS.

[From "The Prelude," Bk. iv.]

The fourth book of "The Prelude" was written in 1804. The time to which the incident belongs was a summer vacation from studies at Cambridge. The "dear Friend" of the close of the extract was Coleridge, to whom "The Prelude" was addressed.

ASCENT OF SNOWDON.

[From "The Prelude," Bk. xiv.]

1. Those excursions. The excursion referred to was in the summer and autumn of 1793. Wordsworth had explored North Wales previously in 1791. On both occasions he was accompanied by his friend Robert Jones.

3. Cambria, Latin for Wales.

4. Bethgelert, in the county of Carnarvon, six miles from Snowdon. The name means "the grave of Gelert," where a priory is said to have been founded by Llewellyn, the last king of Wales, in memory of the hound which had saved his child from a wolf, and was rashly killed by the king.

22. Lurcher, a cross between a shepherd's dog and a greyhound.

47. Main Atlantic, the ocean of mist.

51-53. In Pope's translation of the celebrated moonlight scene in the "Iliad," he fails to recognize the dwindling of the lesser stars in the light of the moon. Wordsworth in his prose "Essay, Supplementary to the Preface to 'Lyrical Ballads'" points to this passage as showing to what a low state knowledge of the most obvious phenomena of nature had sunk in early eighteenth-century poetry.

86-111. Compare Wordsworth's analysis of the power of the Imagination in his Preface to the edition of 1815.

120. Discursive or intuitive, that is, having relation to processes of reasoning or to direct intuition.

Stopford Brooke says of this passage : " It is one of the finest speci-
mens of Wordsworth's *grand style.* It is as sustained and stately as
Milton, but differs from Milton's style in the greater simplicity of
diction."

THE SIMPLON PASS.

Probably written in 1804, the date of " The Prelude," Bk. vi, from
which it is an extract, but dated by Wordsworth 1799, as the year in
which " The Prelude " was begun ; first published in 1845. Wordsworth crossed the Alps, with his friend Jones, in the University summer
vacation of 1790.

2. " The Prelude" for " Pass " reads " strait," and in l. 4 reads
" pace " for " step."

18. Characters, etc., the letters of that revelation of the spirit
which works in and through nature.

MIST OPENING IN THE HILLS.

[From " The Excursion," Bk. ii.]

The date at which the second book of " The Excursion " was
written cannot be certainly determined ; but in December, 1804, Wordsworth wrote to Sir George Beaumont of 2000 lines of " The Pedler " as
in existence. These probably formed the first two books of " The Excursion."

The Solitary has related how an old man, lost by night among the
mountains, was found by the peasants amid the ruins of a mountain
chapel. The title for the extract I have accepted from Dean Church
(Ward's " The English Poets," vol. IV, p. 77).

FRENCH REVOLUTION.

This extract from " The Prelude," Bk. xi, was probably written in
December, 1804, or early in 1805; it was given in *The Friend,* Oct.
26, 1809, and was reprinted in Wordsworth's Poems, 1815.

3. We : in " The Prelude " " us."

11. Enchantress : in *The Friend,* 1809, " Enchanter." Lines 9–
11 are very well applicable to Godwin's treatise " Political Justice," in
which all professes to be based on reason, while it puts forth the most
visionary views of future social progress.

13. The French Revolution spoke of the rights, not of any particular country, but of man as man.

15, 16. Before 1832:

> (To take an image which was felt no doubt
> Among the bowers of paradise itself)

It was hardly correct to speak of an "image" as "felt." The reading was found fault with as prosaic and self-conscious in "Guesses at Truth" by the brothers Hare; and Wordsworth, before altering it, had probably heard the criticism. See "Guesses at Truth," second series, p. 108, ed. 1848.

36. Subterranean in 1832 replaced "subterraneous."

37. Some secreted island, such as Plato's Atlantis or Bacon's New Atlantis.

39, 40. The opposition is not between this life and a future life, but between the real world and a world of the imagination.

ODE TO DUTY.

Written in 1805; published in 1807. "The ode," says Wordsworth, "is on the model of Gray's 'Ode to Adversity,' which is copied from Horace's 'Ode to Fortune.'" The stanza is the same as that of Gray; and as Gray does honour to the benign character of Adversity, so Wordsworth shows the "benignant grace" of the "stern Lawgiver," Duty.

The Ode exists in two states, differing considerably from its final form; one of these is the published text of 1807; the other is a version of the Ode printed for the poems of 1807, but cancelled while those volumes were going through the press. It was discovered by Mr. Tutin of Hull. The published text of 1807 gives a stanza — retained in no subsequent edition — which came between the present fifth and sixth stanzas; it dwells on the gain of uniting choice with duty and freedom with law :

> Yet not the less would I throughout
> Still act according to the voice
> Of my own wish; and feel past doubt
> That my submissiveness was choice:
> Not seeking in the school of pride
> For "precepts over dignified,"
> Denial and restraint I prize
> No farther than they breed a second Will more wise.

The cancelled version agrees in its last four stanzas with the published text of 1807.   The first four stanzas are the following:

> There are who tread a blameless way
> In purity, and love, and truth,
> Though resting on no better stay
> Than on the genial sense of youth:
> Glad Hearts! without reproach or blot;
> Who do the right, and know it not;
> May joy be theirs while life shall last
> And may a genial sense remain when youth is past.
>
> Serene would be our days and bright;
> And happy would our nature be;
> If Love were an unerring light;
> And Joy its own security.
> And bless'd are they who in the main
> This creed, even now, do entertain,
> Do in this spirit live; yet know
> That Man hath other hopes; strength which elsewhere must grow.
>
> I, loving freedom, and untried;
> No sport of every random gust,
> Yet being to myself a guide,
> Too blindly have reposed my trust;
> Resolv'd that nothing e'er should press
> Upon my present happiness,
> I shov'd unwelcome tasks away:
> But henceforth I would serve; and strictly if I may.
>
> O Power of DUTY! sent from God
> To enforce on earth his high behest,
> And keep us faithful to the road
> Which Conscience hath pronounc'd the best:
> Thou, who art Victory and Law
> When empty terrors overawe;
> From vain temptations dost set free,
> From Strife, and from Despair, a glorious Ministry!

The last of these stanzas became first, with a greatly ennobled text, in the published version.

8.   In 1807 (only) the last line was retained from stanza 4 of the cancelled version: " From strife and from despair; a glorious ministry."

15, 16.   The final text — 1837 — was preceded by two earlier readings; in 1807–20:

> May joy be theirs while life shall last!
> And Thou, if they should totter, teach them to stand fast!

In 1827–32:

> Long may the kindly impulse last!
> But Thou, etc.

Wordsworth's sense of the dangers attending the impulsive temperament had grown stronger with his maturer experience.

21, 22. Before 1827:

> And bless'd are they who in the main
> This faith, even now, do entertain:

To "entertain" a faith "in the main" was not a happy form of expression.

24. The text is of 1845. In 1807–32: "Yet find that other strength, according to their need." In 1837: "Yet find thy firm support."

29–31. The text is of 1827. In 1807 the three lines of the cancelled version, given above, were retained: "Resolv'd that nothing," etc. In 1815:

> Full oft when in my heart was heard
> Thy timely mandate, I deferred
> The task imposed, from day to day;

40. In 1827 "that" replaced "which," to avoid the misunderstanding "which ever." Compare with the idea of this ode the sonnet "Nuns fret not," and the poem on "The Pass of Kirkstone."

TO A SKY-LARK ("Up with me!").

Written in 1805; published in 1807. Wordsworth, after Miss Fenwick's "Rydal Mount," added a MS. note: "Where there are no skylarks; but the poet is everywhere." The poem reached its final form in 1832. In 1807, after l. 25 came the following close:

> Hearing thee, or else some other,
> As merry a Brother,
> I on the earth will go plodding on,
> By myself, chearfully, till the day is done.

These lines in 1820 were replaced by the following:

> What though my course be rugged and uneven,
> To prickly moors and dusty ways confined,

> Yet hearing thee, or others of thy kind,
> As full of gladness and as free of heaven,
> I on the earth will go plodding on,
> By myself chearfully, till the day is done.

In 1827 the last six lines of the present text were substituted; but they followed immediately l. 7, " The spot which seems so to thy mind," the intermediate lines, 8–25, being omitted. Finally in 1832 these were restored.

5. Before 1827 this line was " With all the heav'ns about thee ringing." Altered, perhaps, because " all the heavens " suggests a cloudless sky.

10. Wings in 1815 replaced " soul." Has a fairy a soul? It is certainly with wings that it flies.

12. There is madness about thee. Compare the last stanza of Shelley's " Skylark " :

> Teach me half the gladness
> That thy brain must know,
> Such harmonious madness
> From my lips would flow,
> The world should listen then, as I am listening now.

14. Before 1832 : " Up with me, up with me, high and high."
Wordsworth told Barron Field that having succeeded so well in the second " Skylark " (p. 280), and in the stanzas of " A Morning Exercise," which notice the bird (p. 281), he became indifferent to this poem, which Coleridge used severely to condemn and to treat contemptuously : " I like, however, the beginning of it so well, that for the sake of that I tacked to it the respectably-tame conclusion." Coleridge in " Biographia Literaria " notes the two noble lines

> With a soul as strong as a mountain river
> Pouring out praise to the Almighty giver

as placed amid incongruous surroundings.

FIDELITY.

Written in 1805 and published in 1807. In the spring of 1805 a young man named Charles Gough came to Patterdale for the sake of angling. While attempting, early in April, to cross over Helvellyn to Grasmere, he slipped from a rock on which the ice had not thawed, and he perished. The body was found July 22, still watched by his terrier. Scott and Wordsworth climbed Helvellyn together in that year, and each, without knowing that the other had taken up the subject, wrote a poem on the dog's fidelity. Scott's poem named "Helvellyn" is that beginning with the line "I climbed the dark brow of the mighty Helvellyn." Wordsworth said to Crabb Robinson that he "purposely made the narrative as prosaic as possible, in order that no discredit might be thrown on the truth of the incident."

7, 8. Less prosaic than in 1807, which edition read :

> From which immediately leaps out
> A Dog, and yelping runs about.

The change was made in 1815, with "from" for "through" in l. 8 ; "through," 1820.

20. A silent tarn, the Red Tarn (*tarn*, a small mountain lake), which lies at a great height between Striding Edge and Catchedecam.

25. Doth in 1820 replaced "does," probably to avoid the repeated final "s" in "sometimes does."

26. Cheer, enlivenment or solace.

33. Holds : before 1837, "binds," less appropriate to a barrier than "holds."

34. In 1807 (only) : "Not knowing what to think, a while."

36. Before 1837 : "Towards the Dog, o'er rocks and stones " ; altered to avoid the dissyllabic "towards."

40. In 1807 (only) : "Sad sight ! the shepherd with a sigh." "Sad sight ! " was a feeble exclamation.

50, 51. In 1807 (only), with a clumsy division of "for sake of which " :

> But hear a wonder now, for sake
> Of which this mournful Tale I tell!

59. Before 1827 : "On which the Traveller thus had died " ; altered to avoid repeating from ll. 48, 49.

61. His master's side. Scott, more exact to the fact in this particular, makes the faithful dog female.

ELEGIAC STANZAS, SUGGESTED BY A PICTURE OF PEELE CASTLE.

Written in 1805 and published in 1807. The poet's brother, Capt. John Wordsworth, went down with his ship, an East Indiaman, off the Bill of Portland, Feb. 5, 1805. This poem should be read in connection with "To the Daisy" ("Sweet Flower ! belike one day to have "),

" Elegiac Verses in Memory of my Brother," " When to the attractions of the busy world," " The Brothers," and " The Happy Warrior." The Wordsworth Society in 1881 erected a small memorial to John Wordsworth at the spot close to Grisedale Tarn, where he last parted from William Wordsworth on Michaelmas Day, 1800.

Wordsworth's friend Sir George H. Beaumont, the landscape painter, painted two pictures of Peele Castle, one of which was intended for Mrs. Wordsworth. An engraving is given in Wordsworth's Poems, ed. 1815, vol. II, and again in 1820, vol. IV. There are two Peele Castles, — one in the Isle of Man, the other, the subject of Sir G. Beaumont's picture, in Lancashire, just south of Barrow-in-Furness. The opening lines of the poem refer to a visit of four weeks paid during a college summer vacation by Wordsworth to his cousin Mrs. Barker, who lived at Rampside, the nearest village on the mainland to Peele Castle. There is no evidence to connect picture or poem with the castle in the Isle of Man.

14-16. In an unhappy moment Wordsworth altered this — the original reading, to which he reverted in 1832 — for the 1820 edition, which has

> . . . and add a gleam
> Of lustre, known to neither sea nor land,
> But borrowed from the youthful Poet's dream,

which was retained in 1827 with the change, " the gleam," " The lustre." The reader should not overlook the comma after " was " in l. 15; the ideal light never existed, except as conferred by the imagination.

21, 22. In 1807 and 1815 the reading was " a treasure-house, a mine Of peaceful years." It seems as if Wordsworth thought it forced to call the castle "a mine of peaceful years," for he omitted the stanza (ll. 21-24) from the ed. of 1820, and only restored it, with the present altered reading, in 1845.

29. Illusion: in 1807, " delusion."

32. Before 1837 : " A faith, a trust that could not be betray'd."

33-36. Compare this stanza with the close of the " Ode : Intimations of Immortality."

54. **The Kind,** our human species.

THE HAPPY WARRIOR.

Written early in 1806 and published in 1807. Some of the features of " The Happy Warrior" were derived from the character of Nelson, and with Nelson the poem was connected in a note of 1807; but Nelson's relations with Lady Hamilton prevented Wordsworth from "thinking of him with satisfaction in reference to the idea of what a warrior ought to be." Other features were taken from Wordsworth's brother John, who in 1805 was drowned when the ship which he commanded, an East Indiaman, sank off the Bill of Portland.

Observe the evolution of the idea. The poem begins with boyhood, and that continuity of life, from childhood unto maturity, on which Wordsworth so often dwells; it closes with perseverance and progress to the end, and a death of faith, — faith in good and in heaven. The characteristics insisted on are high aims, cultivation of the intellect, moral rectitude, the power to educe good from evil, tenderness, placability, purity, fortitude, obedience to the law of reason, the choice of right means as well as right ends, fidelity, joy in domestic pleasures, heroism in great crises of life. "This short poem," says Myers, "is in itself a manual of greatness; there is a Roman majesty in its simple and weighty speech."

When Harriet Martineau told Wordsworth that it was Channing's favourite among his poems, he replied: " Ay, that was not on account of the *poetic conditions* being best fulfilled in that poem, but because it is (solemnly) a chain of extremely *valooable* thoughts."

5. Boyish thought in 1845 replaced "childish thought," "childish" having an ambiguous meaning.

33. Until 1837 : " He fixes good on good alone, and owes." To fix good on good alone may not always be possible, Wordsworth felt, still the effort should be made.

75, 76. In 1807 Wordsworth quoted as Chaucer's lines from *The Flowre and the Leafe :*

> For Knightes ever should be persevering
> To seek honour without feintise or slouth
> Fro wele to better in all manner thing.

79. In 1807 : " Or he must go to dust without his fame "; in 1837 : " Or he must fall and sleep without his fame." The present reading dates from 1840.

A COMPLAINT.

Written at Town-end, Grasmere, in 1806; published in 1807. The text is unchanged, except l. 9 where "that" in 1836 replaced "this." " Suggested," Wordsworth says, " by a change in the manner of a friend." Perhaps the friend was S. T. Coleridge.

STRAY PLEASURES.

Dated by Wordsworth 1806; first published in 1807. In the *Fenwick note* Wordsworth says: "Suggested on the Thames by the sight of one of those floating mills that used to be seen there. This I noticed on the Surrey side between Somerset House and Blackfriars' Bridge. Charles Lamb was with me at the time; and I thought it remarkable that I should have to point out to *him*, an idolatrous Londoner, a sight so interesting as the happy group dancing on the platform." The changes of text are so unimportant as not to need recording.

The London surroundings are excluded from the poem, or are reduced to the one particular of "the spires," illumined by the setting sun; the imagination is concentrated on the three dancing figures. The idea of freedom in a voluntary captivity (ll. 3, 17) is a favourite one with Wordsworth; compare the sonnet "Nuns fret not" (p. 322).

De Quincey ("On Wordsworth's Poetry") says he had heard a complaint that in this poem, which has for its very subject the universal and gratuitous diffusion of joy, occurs a picture of overpowering melancholy — "In sight of the spires," etc. "Undoubtedly," he writes, "there is (and without ground for complaint there is) even here, where the spirit of gaiety is professedly invoked, an oblique though evanescent image flashed upon us of a sadness that lies deep behind the laughing figures, and of a solitude that is the real possessor in fee of all things, but is waiting an hour or so for the dispossession of the dancing men and maidens who for that transitory hour are the true, but alas! the fugitive tenants."

The kissing leaves of l. 34 were perhaps suggested by lines in Drayton's "The Muse's Elysium."

POWER OF MUSIC.

Written in 1806 and published in 1807. "Taken from life," says Wordsworth. In April, 1806, he went to London, and there spent two months.

3. The stately Pantheon, a building in Oxford Street, formerly a concert hall, theatre, bazaar.

15. Dusky-browed replaced in 1815 "dusky-faced," "face" also occurring in the line.

37. Mark that Cripple: before 1827, "There's a Cripple," and, **at** the same time, in l. 39, "That Mother" replaced "A Mother."

It may be noted that Wordsworth, though his ear was most finely organised for apprehending the sounds of nature, was himself deficient in a feeling for music.   See notes on " Star-Gazers."

STAR–GAZERS.

Written in 1806 and published in 1807.   " Observed by me in Leicester Square [London] as here described," says Wordsworth.   This poem may be viewed as a companion piece to " Power of Music "; both poems are derived from London street-gatherings ; one, a poem of the art of the people, and inspired by joy; the other, of popular science, and touched with the sadness of knowledge.   Both poems, as well as " Stray Pleasures," doubtless belong to Wordsworth's visit to London in the spring of 1806.   A MS. copy of " Star-Gazers," sent by Dorothy Wordsworth to Lady Beaumont, Nov. 14, 1806, is printed in " Memorials of Coleorton," vol. I, pp. 178–180.   The variations shown by this MS. copy are unimportant, except that the sixth and seventh stanzas, as printed in the text, appear in a reverse order in the MS., and that l. 21 runs " Or is it — last unwelcome thought ! — that these spectators rude," and l. 24, " Not to be lifted up at once to power and majesty ? "

8.   And envies him that's looking.   In 1840 this reading was restored from editions before 1827.   From 1827–36 : "Impatient till his moment comes " ["come," 1836].

16.   Before 1827 : "Do they betray us when they're seen ? and are they but a dream ? "   The moon, being personified, rightly becomes the betrayer.

" YES, IT WAS THE MOUNTAIN ECHO."

Written at Town-end, Grasmere, in 1806; published in 1807.   "The echo came from Nab-Scar," says Wordsworth, "when I was walking on the opposite side of Rydal Mere. . . .   On my return from my walk I recited these verses to Mrs. Wordsworth."

1–4.   Before 1827 :

> Yes ! full surely 't was the Echo
> Solitary, clear, profound,
> Answering to Thee, shouting Cuckoo,
> Giving to thee Sound for Sound.

5, 6.   A stanza, judiciously omitted in all editions after 1807, originally followed stanza 1, and the present ll. 5, 6 stood differently :

> Whence the Voice? from air or earth?
> This the Cuckoo cannot tell;
> But a startling sound had birth,
> As the Bird must know full well.
>
> Like the voice through earth and sky
> By the restless Cuckoo sent;

The change was made in 1815.

17–19.   This stanza attained its present form in 1836.   In 1807 :

> Such within ourselves we hear
> Oft-times, ours though sent from far ;
> Listen, ponder, hold them dear ;

In 1827 the idea that the echoes are heard within us was dropped, and
the lines became :

> Such rebounds our inward ear
> Often catches from afar ; —
> Giddy Mortals ! hold them dear ;

In 1832 " Listen, ponder, hold them dear " was happily restored, and
the two other lines were changed from a statement to a warning :

> Often as thy inward ear
> Catches such rebounds, beware —

" The word *rebounds*," Wordsworth wrote to Barron Field, " I wish
much to introduce here ; for the imaginative warning turns upon the
echo, which ought to be revived as near the conclusion as possible."

The word " too " in l. 13 occurring after " two " in l. 12 is a fault
which it is strange that Wordsworth did not remove; to the ear it comes
with a momentary ambiguity.

PERSONAL TALK.

The date of this poem is uncertain ; it lies between 1802 and 1807,
the date of publication.   The stanzas are in fact sonnets, and from
1820 to 1843 " Personal Talk " was placed among the " Miscellaneous
Sonnets "; afterwards, as in 1815, among " Poems of Sentiment and
Reflection."

3. Of friends: in 1807 (only), "About friends," which was metrically a fault.

7. Forms with chalk, *i.e.,* to guide the dancers.

12. Wordsworth says (*Fenwick note*) : " The last line but two stood, at first [*i.e.,* in 1807, only], better and more characteristically thus : ' By my half-kitchen my half-parlour fire.' My Sister and I were in the habit of having the tea-kettle in our little sitting-room [*i.e.,* in Dove Cottage, Grasmere where this poem was written], and we toasted the bread ourselves."

37–40. Before 1827 :

> There do I find a never-failing store
> Of personal themes, and such as I love best ;
> Matter wherein right voluble I am :
> Two will I mention, dearer than the rest ;

41. Wordsworth pronounced " Othello," Plato's record of the last scenes of the career of Socrates (the " Apology "), and Walton's " Life of George Herbert " the most pathetic of human compositions.

42. Spenser's " Faerie Queene," Bk. i.

51–54. These lines were inscribed, at the suggestion of Principal Shairp to Dean Stanley, under the statue of Wordsworth in Westminster Abbey.

LINES, etc. (" Loud is the Vale ! ").

Written in 1806 and published in 1807. Fox, the eminent statesman, died on Sept. 13, 1806. The text is unchanged except l. 19, which before 1837 was " But when the Mighty pass away."

Wordsworth ardently admired Fox, though at a later date (1812), in conversation, he denied to Fox the higher qualities of mind, — philosophy and religion (H. Crabb Robinson's " Diary "). In January, 1801, Wordsworth sent Fox a copy of " Lyrical Ballads," calling his attention in particular to " Michael" and " The Brothers." " In common with the whole of the English people," he wrote, " I have observed in your public character a constant predominance of sensibility of heart." Fox's habit of regarding men not merely in classes but as individuals made him, says Wordsworth, dear to poets ; " and I am sure that if, since your first entrance into public life, there has been a single true poet living in England, he must have loved you." Fox's reply is not very discriminating as regards the " Lyrical Ballads." He did not care for " Michael " or " The Brothers " because he was " no great friend to

blank verse for subjects which are to be treated of with simplicity."
The poems which gave him greatest pleasure were " Harry Gill," " We
are Seven," " The Mad Mother," and " The Idiot Boy." Compare
Scott's eulogy of Fox in the poetical Introduction to the first Canto of
" Marmion."

ODE : INTIMATIONS OF IMMORTALITY.

Composed at Town-end, Grasmere, and dated by Wordsworth
1803-6; published in 1807. Perhaps the date should be 1802-6.
Dorothy Wordsworth writes in her Journal, Mar. 27, 1802 : " A divine
morning. At breakfast William wrote part of an Ode " ; on the preceding day he had written " The Rainbow " (" My heart leaps up "), and
worked at " The Cuckoo," which are in idea so closely connected with
the " Ode." On June 17, 1802 : " William added a little to the Ode he
is writing." In arranging his poems (1815) Wordsworth placed " My
heart leaps up " first and the " Ode " last, thus rounding his work with
the thought of the " celestial light " present in childhood, and the hope
of immortality. In 1815 he replaced the earlier motto of the " Ode,"
" Paulo majora canamus," by words of his own from " My heart leaps
up." " Two years at least," Wordsworth says, " passed between the
writing of the four first stanzas and the remaining part." Before the
poem was complete he had lost his brother John. " Nothing," he
says, " was more difficult for me in childhood than to admit the notion
of death as a state applicable to my own being. . . . It was not so
much from feelings of animal vivacity that *my* difficulty came as
from a sense of the indomitableness of the Spirit within me. I used
to brood over the stories of Enoch and Elijah, and almost to persuade
myself that, whatever might become of others, I should be translated,
in something of the same way, to heaven. With a feeling congenial to
this I was often unable to think of external things as having external
existence, and I communed with all that I saw as something not apart
from, but inherent in, my own immaterial nature. Many times when
going to school have I grasped at a wall or tree to recall myself from
this abyss of idealism to the reality. In later periods of life I have
deplored, as we have all reason to do, a subjugation of an opposite
character, and have rejoiced over the remembrances, as is expressed in
the lines —

> Obstinate questionings
> Of sense and outward things,
> Fallings from us, vanishings."

As to the doctrine of a prenatal state, Wordsworth protests against it being supposed that he would inculcate such a belief : " It is far too shadowy a notion to be recommended to faith, as more than an element in our instincts of immortality." He maintains, however, that the notion has sufficient ground in humanity to authorise a poet to make use of it for his own purpose.

The " Essay on Epitaphs," given in Wordsworth's notes to " The Excursion," should be compared with this " Ode." " Forlorn, " he there writes, " and cut off from communication with the best part of his nature, must that man be, who should derive the sense of immortality, as it exists in the mind of a child, from the same unthinking gaiety or liveliness of animal spirits with which the lamb in the meadow, or any other irrational creature, is endowed. . . . We may be justified in asserting that the sense of immortality, if not a coexistent and twin birth with Reason, is among the earliest of her offspring ; and we may further assert that from these conjoined, and under their countenance, the human affections are gradually formed and opened out."

Compare also " The Excursion," Bk. ix :

> Ah ! why in age
> Do we revert so fondly to the walks
> Of childhood — but that there the soul discerns
> The dear memorial footsteps unimpaired
> Of her own native vigours — thence can hear
> Reverberations ; and a choral song
> Commingling with the incense that ascends
> Undaunted toward the imperishable heavens
> From her own lonely altar ?

And " The Prelude," Bk. v :

> Our childhood sits,
> Our simple childhood, sits upon a throne
> That hath more power than all the elements.
> I guess not what this tells of Being past,
> Nor what it augurs of the life to come.

An interesting parallel to the " Ode " will be found in " The Retreat," by Henry Vaughan, a religious poet of the 17th century. Wordsworth refers to the fact that a doctrine of preëxistence was " an ingredient in Platonic philosophy."

Wordsworth's poem should be regarded not as an argument for immortality, but as a record of feelings which support the belief. His line, " We feel that we are greater than we know," expresses part of the drift of this poem. It asserts our essential detachment from what is merely material; it declares the dignity of the spirit of man from early childhood onward, until years bring " a faith that looks through death." And at the same time it expresses the deep regard of a spirit for the material universe, which has cultivated its affections and called forth its powers.

" Alone in his time," says Emerson, " Wordsworth treated the human mind well, and with an absolute trust. His adherence to his poetic creed rested on real inspirations. The *Ode on Immortality* is the high-water mark which the intellect has reached in this age." See on this poem Ruskin's " Modern Painters," part III, chap. v, " Of Typical Beauty."

6. Hath in 1820 replaced " had."

28. The fields of sleep, Professor Hales explains : " The yet reposeful slumbering country side." But perhaps it merely means that a west wind blows ; the west, where the sun sets, being emblematic of sleep. Or are " the fields of sleep " those deep and shadowy parts of our own souls which lie out of the view of consciousness ?

43. Before 1837 : " While the Earth."

45. Culling : before 1837, "pulling."

66. This line is not rhymed.

86. An interesting alteration : " Six years' Darling " in 1815 replaced " four years' Darling " of 1807.

103. Wordsworth had in his mind the speech of Jacques in " As You Like It," II, 7, beginning " All the world 's a stage."

117. This line was introduced in 1820.

120, 121. In connection with the change last noted, another, the most important in the " Ode," was made (in deference to Coleridge's opinion) in 1820. The following lines occurring between 120 and 121 were omitted :

> To whom the grave
> Is but a lonely bed without the sense or sight
> Of day or the warm light,
> A place of thought where we in waiting lie ;

122. In 1815 this reading replaced that of 1807 : " Of untam'd pleasures, on thy Being's height."

134. Before 1827 : "benedictions."

137, 138. In 1815 the text replaced the reading of 1807 :

> Of Childhood, whether fluttering or at rest,
> With new-born hope for ever in his breast : —

143. See Wordsworth's words quoted in the opening of the notes on this poem.

153. In 1815 this line replaced that of 1807 : " Uphold us, cherish us, and make."

188. Perhaps to avoid the repeated " of," the words " Forebode not " in 1837 replaced " Think not of."

192. Compare Keats's " In a drear-nighted December," of the bubblings of a frozen stream, " They stay their crystal *fretting*."

199. A sunset reflection. The sun, " like a strong man going forth to his race," has now reached the goal and won the palm ; and so with the life of a man when death comes.

202, 203. These lines have been often quoted as an illustration of Wordsworth's sensibility to external nature ; in reality, they testify to his enriching the sentiment of nature with feeling derived from the heart of man and from the experience of human life. The words " The meanest flower that blows " are appropriated by Scott in the Introduction to the first Canto of " Marmion."

"O NIGHTINGALE! THOU SURELY ART."

Wordsworth dated this poem 1806 and said that it was written at Town-end, Grasmere, where no nightingales sing; it was first published in 1807. Mrs. Wordsworth corrected her husband's note, and stated, probably correctly, that it was written at Coleorton, Sir George Beaumont's place in Leicestershire. It may have been written (from memory of the bird's song) in November or December, 1806. The text is unaltered, but in 1815 (only) a lamentable variation, " ebullient heart " for a " fiery heart " in l. 2, appeared. In his modernisation of " The Cuckoo and the Nightingale," Wordsworth speaks of the " loud rioting " of the nightingale's voice; nothing corresponding is found in his original. In " The Excursion," Bk. iv, l. 1167, he speaks of the " solemn nightingale." In the Evening Voluntary " By the side of Rydal Mere," he refers to the fact that the bird does not visit Westmoreland. In the sonnet " June, 1820 " (" Fame tells of groves ") he writes :

> For I have heard the quire of Richmond hill
> Chanting with indefatigable bill
> Strains that recalled to mind a distant day.

To follow the poetry of the nightingale outside of Wordsworth would take us far. Most lovers of literature will remember what has

been written by Milton, by Coleridge, and by Keats. The latest con-
tribution to this part of the poetry of birds is Mr. Robert Bridges's
beautiful lyric, " Nightingales."

As to the stock-dove, Mr. Wintringham, in "The Birds of Wordsworth," maintains that the poet here and in " Resolution and Independence (" Over his own sweet voice the stock-dove broods ") confused the
wood-pigeon or ring-dove with the stock-dove. The stock-dove's voice
has been compared, he says, to a grunt; the wood-pigeon's is the sweet
coo roo, coo coo. On l. 13 Wordsworth himself comments in his Preface
to the ed. of 1815: " His voice was buried among trees," a metaphor
expressing the love of *seclusion* by which this bird is marked, and charac-
terising its note as not partaking of the shrill and the piercing, and
therefore more easily deadened by the intervening shade, yet a note so
peculiar and withal so pleasing that the breeze, gifted with that love of
the sound which the poet feels, penetrates the shades in which it is
entombed and conveys it to the ear of the listener."

SONG AT THE FEAST OF BROUGHAM CASTLE.

Composed in 1807 at Coleorton, while Wordsworth walked to and
fro along the path from Sir George Beaumont's farmhouse, then occupied by the Wordsworth household, to the Hall, which at that time
was building; published in the same year. The following is Wordsworth's note :

" Henry Lord Clifford, etc., who is the subject of this Poem, was the
son of John Lord Clifford, who was slain at Towton Field, which John
Lord Clifford, as is known to the reader of English History, was the
person who after the battle of Wakefield slew, in the pursuit, the young
Earl of Rutland, son of the Duke of York, who had fallen in the battle,
' in part of revenge ' (say the Authors of the History of Cumberland and
Westmoreland) ; ' for the Earl's Father had slain his.' A deed which
worthily blemished the author (saith Speed) ; but who, as he adds,
' dare promise anything temperate of himself in the heat of martial fury?
chiefly when it was resolved not to leave any branch of the York line
standing ; for so one maketh this Lord to speak.' This, no doubt, I
would observe by the by, was an action sufficiently in the vindictive
spirit of the times, and yet not altogether so bad as represented; ' for
the Earl was no child, as some writers would have him, but able to bear
arms, being sixteen or seventeen years of age, as is evident from this
(say the Memoirs of the Countess of Pembroke, who was laudably

anxious to wipe away, as far as could be, this stigma from the illustrious name to which she was born), that he was the next Child to King Edward the Fourth, which his mother had by Richard Duke of York, and that king was then eighteen years of age : and for the small distance betwixt her children, see Austin Vincent, in his Book of Nobility, p. 622, where he writes of them all.' It may further be observed, that Lord Clifford, who was then himself only twenty-five years of age, had been a leading man and commander two or three years together in the army of Lancaster, before this time ; and, therefore, would be less likely to think that the Earl of Rutland might be entitled to mercy from his youth. — But, independent of this act, at best a cruel and savage one, the Family of Clifford had done enough to draw upon them the vehement hatred of the House of York; so that after the Battle of Towton there was no hope for them but in flight and concealment. Henry, the subject of the Poem, was deprived of his estate and honours during the space of twenty-four years ; all which time he lived as a shepherd in Yorkshire, or in Cumberland, where the estate of his Father-in-law (Sir Lancelot Threlkeld) lay. He was restored to his estate and honours in the first year of Henry the Seventh. It is recorded that, ' when called to Parliament, he behaved nobly and wisely; but otherwise came seldom to London or the Court ; and rather delighted to live in the country, where he repaired several of his Castles, which had gone to decay during the late troubles.' Thus far is chiefly collected from Nicholson and Burn; and I can add, from my own knowledge, that there is a tradition current in the village of Threlkeld and its neighbourhood, his principal retreat, that in the course of his shepherd-life he had acquired great astronomical knowledge. I cannot conclude this note without adding a word upon the subject of those numerous and noble feudal Edifices, spoken of in the Poem, the ruins of some of which are, at this day, so great an ornament to that interesting country. The Cliffords had always been distinguished for an honourable pride in these Castles ; and we have seen that, after the wars of York and Lancaster, they were rebuilt; in the civil wars of Charles the First they were again laid waste, and again restored almost to their former magnificence by the celebrated Lady Anne Clifford, Countess of Pembroke, etc. Not more than twenty-five years after this was done, when the estates of Clifford had passed into the Family of Tufton, three of these Castles, namely, Brough, Brougham, and Pendragon, were demolished, and the timber and other materials sold by Thomas Earl of Thanet. We will hope that, when this order was issued, the Earl had not consulted the text of Isaiah, 58th chap. 12th verse, to which the inscription placed over the gate of Pendragon Castle by the Countess of Pembroke (I believe his Grandmother), at the time she repaired that structure, refers the reader: '*And they that shall be of thee shall build the old waste places: thou shalt raise up the foundations of many generations; and thou shalt be called, The repairer of the breach, The restorer of paths to dwell in.*' The Earl of Thanet, the present possessor of the Estates, with a due respect for the memory of his ancestors, and a proper sense of the value and beauty of these remains of antiquity, has (I am told) given orders that they shall be preserved from all depredations."

1. The ruins of Brougham Castle stand on a hill near the junction of the rivers Esmont and Lowther, a mile and a half from Penrith.

7. Thirty years, *i.e.,* of the Wars of the Roses, 1455–85.

11. Alludes to the marriage of Henry VII to Elizabeth of York.

27. "This line is from 'The Battle of Bosworth Field' by Sir John Beaumont (brother of the dramatist), whose poems are written with much spirit, elegance, and harmony, and have deservedly been reprinted lately in Chalmers's Collection of English Poets." — Wordsworth's note.

At Bosworth battle Richard III was slain.

36. Skipton, a market town in the West Riding of Yorkshire. Its castle was "deserted" while the shepherd-lord was in concealment.

37. Before 1845: "Though she is but a lonely Tower"; altered, probably, to vary from l. 49. Before 1827 two lines followed:

> Silent, deserted of her best,
> Without an Inmate or a Guest —

Altered in 1827 to the following:

> To vacancy and silence left;
> Of all her guardian sons bereft —

and omitted in 1845.

40. Pendragon, a border fortress in the hands of the Cliffords, situated on the river Eden, ten miles southeast of Appleby. It took its name from Uther Pendragon, the father of King Arthur, its fabled founder.

44. Brough, the castle of Brough or Burgh-under-Stainmore, County Westmoreland, eight miles southeast of Appleby, also belonging to the Cliffords.

46. Appleby Castle is meant; the river Eden runs by Appleby.

51. One fair house, Brougham Castle.

54. The "shepherd-lord" and his mother.

73. Carrock's side. "Carrock-fell is three miles southwest from Castle Sowerby in Cumberland." — Knight.

89.   Mosedale's groves, to the north of Blencathara, or Saddleback.

92.   Glenderamakin's lofty springs : this river "rises in the lofty ground to the north of Blencathara."

95.   Sir Lancelot Threlkeld. See Wordsworth's note, and compare "The Waggoner," canto iv, ll. 42–56, where the shepherd-lord is spoken of.

116, 117.   Before 1845 four lines :

> Yet lacks not friends for solemn ["simple," 1845] glee,
> And a cheerful [" A spirit-soothing," 1836] company,
> That learn'd of him submissive ways ;
> And comforted his private days.

122, 123.   "It is imagined by the people of the country that there are two immortal fish, inhabitants of this tarn, which lies in the mountains not far from Threlkeld. Blencathara, mentioned before, is the old and proper name of the mountain vulgarly called Saddle-back." — Wordsworth's note.

126–137.   Several lines here were made more syllabically regular in 1836, perhaps with a loss of metrical beauty.   The earlier readings are :

126, 127 :

> They moved about in open sight
> To and fro, for his delight.

129.   "On the mountains visitant."

131.   "And the caves where Faeries sing."

135.   "Face of thing that is to be."

136, 137.   From 1807 to 1820 :

> And, if ["if that," 1836] Men report him right,
> He can ["could," 1827–36] whisper words of might

The present text dates from 1840.

142, 143.   "The martial character of the Cliffords is well known to the readers of English history; but it may not be improper here to say, by way of comment on these lines and what follows, that besides several others who perished in the same manner, the four immediate progenitors of the person in whose hearing this is supposed to be spoken all died in the field." — Wordsworth's note.

157–159.   Before 1845 :

> Alas ! the fervent Harper did not know
> That for a tranquil Soul the Lay was framed,
> Who, long compelled in humble walks to go,

The religious spirit is characteristic of other changes made in the revision of 1845.

171. When nearly sixty years old the good Lord Clifford fought at Flodden. He died in 1523, and was buried in the choir of Bolton Priory.

The feudal and chivalric spirit of this poem is remarkable, but it would hardly be characteristic of Wordsworth if this were the predominant note. Its peculiar virtue resides especially in the stanza which tells of the love of humanity gained in the cottage and the teaching of nature among the lonely hills, — that beginning "Love had he found in huts where poor men lie."

THE FORCE OF PRAYER.

In its first form the poem was written in 1807 ; it was recast in 1808, and was published with "The White Doe of Rylstone" in 1815. On Oct. 18, 1807, Dorothy Wordsworth writes that "about a month ago" her brother composed a poem on "the story of young Romelli and the Strid." This earliest form remained in MS. until it was printed by Professor Knight ("Poet. Works," IV, 205, 206). The opening stanzas differ more than the others from the text of Wordsworth, and may here be given :

> " *What is good for a bootless bene?* "
> The Lady answered, "*endless sorrow*."
> *Her* words are plain ; but the Falconer's words
> Are a path that is dark to travel thorough.
>
> These words I bring from the Banks of Wharf,
> Dark words to front an ancient tale :
> And their meaning is, whence can comfort spring
> When prayer is of no avail?
>
> " What is good for a bootless bene ? "
> The Falconer to the Lady said,
> And she made answer as ye have heard,
> For she knew that her Son was dead.

Wordsworth calls the poem "an appendage to ' The White Doe.'" It is so in idea — that of pious dealing with personal grief ; it is so also through its connection with Bolton Abbey. He found the story in Whitaker's "History of Craven." Bolton Abbey, Yorkshire, stands upon a beautiful bend of the Wharfe. Not far from the Abbey the Wharfe rushes through a deep rift in the rock, called the Strid. Here

" the boy of Egremond " was drowned.   The Priory, originally founded at Embsay, a village about four miles distant, by William de Meschines and his wife in 1121, was removed to Bolton a little after 1150 by their daughter Adeliza, mother of young Romilly.   Rogers has written a poem, " The Boy of Egremond," on the same subject, beginning :

> " Say, what remains when Hope is fled ? "
> She answered, " Endless weeping ! "
> For, in the herds-man's eye she read
> Who in his shroud lay sleeping.

1.   Bootless bene, profitless prayer.   Old English *bén*, perhaps from root *ba*, cry.

40.   Yarrow.   See notes on " Yarrow Unvisited," p. 433.

The variations of text are trivial; they include certain differences between two texts of 1815, — that in " The White Doe " volume and in " Poems."

The spirit of this poem is expressed in the following lines of " The Excursion " :

> The darts of anguish *fix* not where the seat
> Of suffering hath been thoroughly fortified
> By acquiescence in the Will supreme
> For time and for eternity.

Lamb in 1815 wrote to Wordsworth with a generous extravagance : " I never saw parental love carried up so high, towering above the other loves.   Shakespeare had done something for the filial in Cordelia, and, by implication, for the fatherly, too, in Lear's resentment ; he left it for you to explore the depths of the maternal heart."   " Letters of Lamb," ed. Ainger, vol. I, p. 288.

CHARACTERISTICS OF A CHILD THREE YEARS OLD.

Written at Allanbank, Grasmere, in 1811 ; published in 1815.   The text is unchanged.   The child was Wordsworth's daughter Catherine, who died the year after.   See the sonnet " Surprised with joy."

SOURCES OF SPIRITUAL STRENGTH.

[From " The Excursion," Bk. iv.]

It is not possible to fix precisely the date at which the fourth book of " The Excursion " was written.   Much of the poem belongs to Wordsworth's residence at Allanbank, 1808–11.

GREEK DIVINITIES.

[From " The Excursion," Bk. iv.]

See note on preceding extract.

THE SEA–SHELL.

[From " The Excursion," Bk. iv.]

Wordsworth was supposed by some — with no foundation, in fact — to have taken the suggestion of the sea-shell from Landor's " Gebir," Bk. i. Landor's lines deserve to be quoted, not as a source, but as a parallel. The sea-nymph speaks :

> But I have sinuous shells of pearly hue
> Within, and they that lustre have imbibed
> In the sun's palace-porch, where when unyoked
> His chariot-wheel stands midway in the wave :
> Shake one and it awakens, then apply
> Its polisht lips to your attentive ear,
> And it remembers its august abodes,
> And murmurs as the ocean murmurs there.

Majestic lines, but not designed as an illustration of spiritual truth.

LAODAMIA.

Written at Rydal Mount in 1814; published in 1815. About this time, 1814–16, Wordsworth's attention was given to the education of his elder son, and he read again the principal Latin poets. " The incident of the trees growing and withering," he says, " put the subject into my thoughts, and I wrote with the hope of giving it a loftier tone than, so far as I know, has been given to it by any of the Ancients who have treated of it. It cost me more trouble than almost anything of equal length I have ever written." Crabb Robinson says (1815) it was not much esteemed by Wordsworth, as being rather a poem "founded on the affections " than one of the imagination. But the author afterwards placed it among " Poems of the Imagination," and he is said to have named " Lycidas " and " Laodamia " as " twin-immortals." For Landor's criticism of the poem, see the " Imaginary Conversations " (Southey and Porson).

As noted by Wordsworth, some of the features of the character of
Protesilaus are derived from the "Iphigenia in Aulis" of Euripides;
this acknowledgment was made in ed. 1815 in special connection with
ll. 110–113.   The thirteenth epistle in Ovid's " Heroïdes " is from
Laodamia to Protesilaus; she cautions him against excess of intre-
pidity.   Something of the conception of Laodamia as erring through
excess of passion may have been suggested by Ovid, and something by
the passage in the poem of Catullus " Ad Manlium," which treats of
Wordsworth's heroine :

> . . . tanto te absorbens vortice amoris
> Æstus in abruptum detulerat barathrum.

The trees growing and withering, as Wordsworth tells us, put the subject in his thoughts, and in accordance with the suggestion the first
conclusion to the poem was inspired with pity for Laodamia.   She
receives no punishment in this form of the poem.   Lines 158–163 stood
as follows in 1815 and 1820 :

> Ah, judge her gently who so deeply loved !
> Her, who, in reason's spite, yet without crime,
> Was in a trance of passion thus removed;
> Delivered from the galling yoke of time
> And these frail elements — to gather flowers
> Of blissful quiet 'mid unfading bowers.

The ethics of the poem, however, as Wordsworth reconsidered it,
seemed to require a different ending, and in 1827 he substituted the
following :

> By no weak pity might the Gods be moved ;
> She who thus perished, not without the crime
> Of Lovers that in Reason's spite have loved,
> Was doomed to wander in a grosser clime,
> Apart from happy Ghosts — that gather flowers, etc.

In 1831, in a letter to his nephew John Wordsworth, he defends the
alteration : " As first written the heroine was dismissed to happiness in
Elysium.   To what purpose then the mission of Protesilaus?   He
exhorts her to moderate her passion; the exhortation is fruitless and
no punishment follows.   So it stood : at present she is placed among
unhappy ghosts for disregard of the exhortation.   Virgil also places her
there, but compare the two passages and give me *your* opinion."   Next
year, 1832, appeared a new edition in which the line " Was doomed to

wander in a grosser clime" became "Was doomed to wear out her appointed time." In 1840 the stanza opened thus :

> She — who, though warned, exhorted, and reproved,
> Thus died, from passion desperate to a crime —

then proceeding as in the final text. In 1845 the entire stanza assumed its ultimate form. Thus, while Wordsworth softened the harshness of his second text, he never reverted to the first, and maintained to the end that the justice of the gods required the punishment of his heroine, while yet man and mortal things may rightly mourn for her. Laodamia was "exhorted" as well as "reproved"; her error was not merely that she clung passionately to earthly love, which was now forbidden by divine decree, but that she failed to lift up her heart to "a higher object." Wordsworth justifies excess of passion (ll. 145–150), but as a means of education, — "that self may be annulled," and that man may ascend to a higher object by means of a "mortal yearning." Laodamia's affections were not to be crushed out, but to be "raised and solemnized"; she was to seek reunion with her husband, but a blest reunion, to be won only through fortitude; and she fails in the test. The words "to wear out her appointed time" suggest that her separation from Protesilaus is not for ever, that her state is, in truth, purgatorial.

For a discussion of the ethics of the poem and an unfavourable criticism of the alteration of the close, see "Guesses at Truth."

1–4. Date from 1827. In 1815 and 1820 they stood thus :

> With sacrifice before the rising morn
> Performed, my slaughtered Lord have I required;
> And in thick darkness, amid shades forlorn,
> Him of the infernal Gods have I desired.

Landor objected to the rhyme "required," "desired," and Wordsworth admitted that the rhyme was unsatisfactory.

Sacrifices to the infernal deities were made between midnight and sunrise. See Virgil's Æneid, VI, 242–258.

11. Compare the description of Virgil's Sibyl, Æneid, VI, 46 ff. :

> . . . her heart with frenzy heaves,
> And, larger grown, dilating to the eye, etc.

12. A MS. copy of the poem gives two stanzas intended originally to follow this line:

> That rapture failing, the distracted Queen
> Knelt and embraced the Statue of the God:
> " Mighty the boon I ask, but Earth has seen
> Effects as awful from thy gracious nod;
> All-ruling Jove, unbind the mortal chain,
> Nor let the force of prayer be spent in vain!"
>
> Round the high-seated Temple a soft breeze
> Along the columns sighed — all else was still —
> Mute, vacant as the face of summer seas,
> No sign accorded of a favouring will,
> Dejected she withdraws — her palace-gate
> Enters — and, traversing a room of state,
>
> O terror, etc.

18, 19. Mercury (Hermes, the Greek name) is the conductor of souls; the wand with which he summons and dismisses souls is mentioned in the Æneid, IV, 242.

27. Compare the Æneid, II, 794, and VI, 699.

58. **Thou should'st elude** replaced in 1845 the less dignified " That thou should'st cheat."

65. **Parcæ,** the Fates.

68. Replaced in 1836 the earlier " Know, virtue were not virtue if the joys."

71. **Erebus,** a region of the lower world.

76. In 1815: " The fervor — not the impotence of love."

79–81. This is the subject of the " Alcestis " of Euripides, rendered by R. Browning in " Balaustion's Adventure." Compare Milton's sonnet " On his deceased Wife."

82. **Vernal** in 1827 replaced " beauty's."

83, 84. See Ovid's Metamorphoses, VII, 159–293. Æson, father of Jason, was restored to youth by Medea's art. Compare " Merchant of Venice," V, i, 12.

90. This line and also l. 157 are alexandrines.

101, 102. Replaced in 1827 the following:

> Spake, as a witness, of a second birth
> For all that is most perfect upon earth.

Landor had objected to " witness " and " second birth " as savouring of the conventicle. Wordsworth would not admit the objection, but in the next edition he altered the lines. Compare Virgil's Æneid, VI, 637–665.

105. Compare Æneid, VI, 639 :

> Largior hic campos æther et lumine vestit
> Purpureo, solemque suum, sua sidera novunt.

115–120. This stanza was added while the poem was going through the press.

Aulis was a port in Bœotia where the Greek fleet was detained until Artemis was appeased by the sacrifice of Iphigenia.

146. Until 1836 the reading was " Towards a higher object." In his earlier texts Wordsworth treats " towards " as a dissyllable, from 1836 onward as a monosyllable. See *The Academy*, Dec. 2, 1893, p. 487.

147. That end replaced in 1827 " this end," probably because " this " occurs in the next line.

160. " We think of Virgil's tender line in a similar passage about Orpheus and Eurydice, Georg. IV, 488 :

> Quum subita incautum dementia cepit amantem,
> *Ignoscenda quidem, scirent si ignoscere Manes.*

' To be pardoned indeed, if the fates knew how to pardon.' " — W. A. Heard (quoted in Knight's " Wordsworth ").

164–174. The metre changes to distinguish the reflection and the narration of the sequel from the main narrative.

YARROW VISITED (" And is this," etc.).

Written in 1814 and published in 1815. " As mentioned in my verses on the death of the Ettrick Shepherd " (see p. 304), said Wordsworth, " my first visit to Yarrow was in his company. We had lodged the night before at Traquhair, where Hogg had joined us, and also Dr. Anderson, the Editor of the British Poets, who was on a visit to the Manse. Dr. A. walked with us till we came in view of the vale of Yarrow, and, being advanced in life, he then turned back." Wordsworth's wife and her sister Sara Hutchinson were his travelling companions. " I seldom read or think of this poem," he said, " without regretting that my dear sister was not of the party, as she would have had so much delight in recalling the time when, travelling together in Scotland, we declined going in search of this celebrated stream, not altogether, I will frankly confess, for the reasons assigned in the poem on the occasion."

13. St. Mary's Lake. See notes on " Yarrow Unvisited."

25. The famous Flower. Principal Shairp in his "Aspects of Poetry" ("The Three Yarrows") says that here Wordsworth fell into an inaccuracy; for Mary Scott of Dryhope, the real "Flower of Yarrow," never did lie bleeding on Yarrow, but became the wife of Wat of Harden and the mother of a wide-branching race. Yet Wordsworth speaks of *his* bed, evidently confounding the lady "Flower of Yarrow" with that "slaughtered youth" for whom so many ballads have sung lament. But doubtless Wordsworth had Logan's "Braes of Yarrow" in his mind, where the lady laments her lover and names him "the flower of Yarrow."

31. The Water-wraith ascended thrice, from Logan's "Braes of Yarrow":

> Thrice did the water-wraith ascend,
> And gave a doleful groan through Yarrow.

55. Newark's Tower, on the banks of Yarrow, about three miles from Selkirk. Here Scott's "Last Minstrel" sang his "Lay":

> He pass'd where Newark's stately tower
> Looks out from Yarrow's birchen bower.

62–64. These lines date from 1827; in 1815:

> It promises protection
> To studious ease and generous cares,
> And every chaste affection!

In 1820:

> To all the nestling brood of thoughts
> Sustained by chaste affection!

Of this poem Professor Veitch says ("History and Poetry of the Scottish Border," II, 316): "We have there the true Yarrow, the truest Yarrow that ever was pictured; real yet not literal — Yarrow as it is for the spiritual sense made keen, quick, sensitive, and deep through the brooding over the stories of the years and living communion with the heart of things."

DION.

"Dion" is dated by Wordsworth 1816; it was first published in 1820.

Dion was a disciple of Plato when the philosopher visited Syracuse; he seems to have been naturally austere of character. When banished from Syracuse by political intrigue he retired to Athens, and lived in close intercourse with Plato. He subsequently became master of Syracuse, and put to death his chief opponent Heracleides. One of his followers, Callippus, conspired against Dion, and caused him to be assassinated, B.C. 353.

We print, immediately after the poem, in accordance with a suggestion of Wordsworth's, a stanza rejected in 1837, which originally opened " Dion." It was rejected, Wordsworth says, because it detained the reader too long from the subject, and rather precluded than prepared for the due effect of the allusion to the genius of Plato.

1, 2. Following until 1837 the rejected stanza, the lines ran thus :

> So pure, so bright, so fitted to embrace,
> Where'er he turned, a natural grace

and until the same date ll. 7, 8 were :

> Nor less the homage that was seen to wait
> On Dion's virtues, when the lunar beam

Mr. Heard contributed to Knight's edition of Wordsworth notes illustrating Wordsworth's obligations to Plutarch, from which some extracts are here given.

10. Grove of Academe. The Academus was the grove in the suburbs of Athens in which Plato taught, so called after a hero Academus, to whom it was said to have belonged.

11. Plutarch writes : " Plato being anxious that Dion's disposition should be sweetened by mingling with society of a pleasant kind, and not aloof on proper occasions from well-bred raillery." — Heard.

12, 13. " Arrogance," said Plato, " is the house-mate of solitude." — Heard.

19. " Seeing Dion wearing a garland," says Plutarch, " on account of the sacrifice, those that were present with one impulse put on garlands one and all." — Heard.

20. " Poorly armed," says Plutarch, " as chance enabled them." — Heard.

24, 25. " Now they could discern," says Plutarch, " Dion himself advancing at their head, clad in gleaming armour and wearing a garland." — Heard.

28–30. " The Syracusans," says Plutarch, " receiving them as a holy procession beseeming the Gods, escorting freedom and democracy back to the city after an exile of forty-seven years." — Heard.

32, 33. Derived from Plutarch.

35-37. In 1820 (only) these lines stood:

> And, wheresoe'er the great Deliverer passed,
> Fruits were strewn before his eye,
> And flowers upon his person cast.

At the same time in l. 39 " doth " replaced " did."

42. Ilissus, one of the principal rivers of Attica.

50, 51. In a celebrated utterance Kant, in like manner, brings together the sublimities of the starry heavens without and the moral law within.

52. Sublime delight. The word " sublime " was added in 1837.

65-70. " He happened," writes Plutarch, " to be sitting late in the evening in a corridor of the house in solitary meditation : suddenly a sound was heard in the further end of the portico, and, looking up, he saw in the lingering light the form of a majestic woman, in dress and face like the Fury as she appears in tragedy — sweeping the house with a brush." Mr. Heard notes that in Plutarch the apparition is simply ominous of coming evil; the moral significance is Wordsworth's interpretation.

71. Auster, the south wind; **Boreas,** in l. 73, the north wind.

75. Mænalus, a mountain in Arcadia.

82. Exclaimed the Chieftain in 1827 replaced the earlier " Intrusive Presence ! "

106. Matchless perfidy. Callippus, the friend of Dion, had taken a solemn oath that he had no thought of treason.

110. Marble city. A marble quarry, near Syracuse, added to the magnificence of the city.

115-117. Dion declared " that he was willing to die a thousand deaths . . . if life were only to be had by guarding against friends as well as foes." — Plutarch, quoted by Heard.

The moral of " Dion," that our means should be as spotless as our ends, is enforced also in " The Happy Warrior ":

> He labours good on good to fix, and owes
> To virtue every triumph that he knows.

Lamb wrote to Mrs. Wordsworth (May 25, 1820): "The story of Dion is divine — the genius of Plato falling on him like moonlight — the finest thing ever expressed."

ODE TO LYCORIS.

Composed in front of Rydal Mount in May, 1817 ; published in 1820. The poem originated, Wordsworth says, in the last four lines of stanza 1 : " Those specks of snow, reflected in the lake [the lake was Ullswater] and so transferred, as it were, to the subaqueous sky, reminded me of the swans which the fancy of the ancient classic poets yoked to the car of Venus." Wordsworth's note goes on to tell of his youthful delight in Greek and Roman poetry. In deference, he says, to the disgust of the general reader caused by the hackneyed and lifeless use into which mythology fell towards the close of the 17th and during the 18th century, he abstained in his earliest writings from all introduction of pagan fable ; but " surely, even in its humble form, it may ally itself with real sentiment, as I can truly affirm it did in the present case."

The quantity of the second vowel is long — Lycŏ´ris. This was the name under which C. Cornelius Gallus celebrated in his lost poems his mistress Cytharis. See Virgil, Eclogue x, 42. In Wordsworth's "Poetical Works," the "Ode" is followed by a poem in blank verse "To the Same," of which the closing lines seem to show that by Lycoris he meant either his sister or his wife :

> Dearest Friend !
> We too have known such happy hours together
> That, were power granted to replace them (fetched
> From out the pensive shadows where they lie)
> In the first warmth of their original sunshine,
> Loth should I be to use it : passing sweet
> Are the domains of tender memory !

" Thee, thee my life's celestial sign " (l. 28) seems to belong of right to Mary Wordsworth.

14. **Halcyon,** the kingfisher. The plumage of the bird is blue, white, and purple ; it darts along the water " like a meteor." In the next line Wordsworth in 1827 changed " its " to " her."

31, 32. In 1827 Wordsworth made these lines more special to early autumn. Previously :

> Pleased with the soil's requited cares ;
> Pleased with the blue that ether wears ;

37. On the art of growing old, compare Emerson's admirable poem " Terminus."

45-48. Before 1837 :

> Frank greeting, then, to that blithe Guest
> Diffusing smiles o'er land and sea
> To aid the vernal Deity
> Whose home is in the breast !

In the later text Wordsworth admits that the " Deity of youth " is no longer in the breast.

The reader should complete the impression made by this poem by reading in the " Poetical Works " its companion piece, " To the Same "; he will find in this selection two poems placed near " Lycoris " by Wordsworth, " September, 1819," in which the poet does honour to the autumn of the year and of human life.

THE LONGEST DAY.

Written in 1817 ; published in 1820. It was suggested by the sight of Wordsworth's daughter Dora playing in front of Rydal Mount, and in great part was composed on the same afternoon. Wordsworth often thought of writing a companion poem on the *shortest* day. After his daughter's death her name was given in l. 13, displacing the " Laura " of edd. previous to 1849. (So also in " The Kitten and the Fallen Leaves.")

3. In 1843 this line happily replaced the earlier " Sol has dropped into his harbour."

The idea of the poem has much in common with that of the " Ode to Duty." The sportive child, in her thoughtless joy, is one of the " glad hearts, without reproach " of the second stanza of the " Ode "; but it is well that she should learn, even already, the deeper lesson of life. This poem is elevated by its imaginative power into something higher than mere didactic verse.

COMPOSED UPON AN EVENING OF EXTRAORDINARY SPLENDOUR AND BEAUTY.

Written in 1818 and published in 1820. " Felt, and in a great meas-ure composed," Wordsworth says, " upon the little mount in front of our abode at Rydal." A copy in MS. was sent to the American painter, Washington Allston, of whose picture Wordsworth speaks in the note on l. 49 (see *The Athenæum*, July 7, 1894). It is evident that the earlier lines of stanza 3 are also connected with Allston's "Jacob's Dream."

13. Before 1832 : "Or ranged like stars along some sovereign height."

49. Before 1837 : "shoulder." Wordsworth writes : "In these lines I am under obligation to the exquisite picture of ' Jacob's Dream ' by Mr. Alstone [Allston], now in America. It is pleasant to make this public acknowledgment to men of genius, whom I have the honour to rank among my friends."

52. Practicable way, a ladder that may be scaled.

62. In 1837 "mine eye" replaced "my eye," to avoid the clash of sound.

Wordsworth's footnote directs the reader to compare with stanza 4 the opening of the "Ode : Intimations of Immortality."

SEPTEMBER, 1819 (" The sylvan slopes ").

Written 1819; published 1820. Text unaltered.

With this poem, imbued with the autumnal tranquillity, might be read the " Ode to Lycoris," which maintains that we should balance the calm of declining years with something of youth and springtime maintained within the soul.

UPON THE SAME OCCASION.

Composed in front of Rydal Mount and during walks in the neighbourhood in 1819 ; published in 1820. The only change made after 1820 was in l. 47, happily altered in 1827 from the earlier " With passion's finest finger swayed." In the River Duddon volume of 1820, in l. 58 we find " Horace boasted " ; the better word "gloried " is found in " Miscellaneous Poems " of the same year.

In his " Description of the English Lakes," Wordsworth speaks of the peculiarly favoured days — worth whole months — which occur sometimes in springtime, more often in autumn : " But it is in autumn that days of such affecting influence most frequently intervene ; — the atmosphere seems refined, and the sky rendered more crystalline, as the vivifying heat of the year abates ; the lights and shadows are more delicate ; the colouring is richer and more finely harmonised ; and in this season of stillness, the ear being unoccupied, the sense of vision becomes more susceptible of its appropriate enjoyments."

31-36. Wordsworth imagines the Druids as the earliest British bards.

38. Alcæus, of Mytilene, in the island of Lesbos, the earliest of the Æolian lyric poets. " He thought that his lyre was best employed in animating his friends to warlike deeds, and his house is described by himself as furnished with the weapons of war rather than with the instruments of his art." — Smith's Dictionary of Greek and Roman Biography and Mythology.

46. The Lesbian Maid, Sappho. "There are passages in her poems referring to her love for a beautiful youth whom she endeavoured to conciliate by her poetry " — perhaps the foundation of the legend of her passion for Phaon. — Smith's Dictionary.

50. In excavating Herculaneum, a number of papyrus rolls were found containing treatises on the Epicurean philosophy.

52. Theban fragment, some lines of Pindar, the Theban poet, whose poems have come down to us, with the exception of his " Epinicia," or triumphal odes, in fragments.

54. Simonides, the poet of the island of Ceos, born B.C. 556. " Belonging to a people eminent for their orderly and virtuous character, Simonides himself became proverbial for that virtue which the Greeks call σωφροσύνη, temperance, order, and self-command in one's own conduct, and moderation in one's opinions and desires and views of human life ; and this spirit breathes through all his poetry." — Smith's Dictionary.

59. Maro, Virgil.

TO THE REV. DR. WORDSWORTH.

(*With the Sonnets to the River Duddon, etc.*)

Written and published in 1820, when Wordsworth's brother Christopher, afterwards Master of Trinity College, Cambridge, was Rector of Lambeth. The text was never altered.

51. Cytherea's zone, Cytherea, a name for Venus, who was said to have sprung from the foam of the sea near Cythera, now Cerigo, an island on the southeast of the Morea. On her zone, or cestus, were represented all things tending to excite love.

65. Lambeth's venerable towers, Lambeth Palace on the banks of the Thames, the official residence of the Archbishops of Canterbury since 1197.

TO THE LADY FLEMING, etc.

Written in 1823; begun in December, 1822; a copy, with inferior readings (recorded by Knight) was sent to Lady Beaumont, February 5, 1823; published in 1827.

"The Fleming family," writes Professor Knight, "is descended from Sir Michael le Fleming, a relative of Baldwin, Earl of Flanders, a brother-in-law of William the Conqueror." In the *Fenwick note* Wordsworth expressed regret that the architect of the chapel did not furnish an elevation better suited to the site in a narrow mountain pass, and that the interior was not better constructed for purposes of worship. Improvements were effected in 1884.

21. Stanzas 3 and 4 appeared in 1827 in a reverse order. The sequence of ideas in 4 and 5 is closer than between 3 and 5.

21–23. These lines were admirably altered in 1832; in 1827:

> Even Strangers slackening here their pace,
> Shall bless this work of pious care
> Lifting its

35. Wild wandering: before 1837 a hyphen connected these adjectives.

41–46. These lines in 1832 replaced the following of 1827:

> Not yet the corner stone is laid
> With solemn rite; but Fancy sees
> The tower time-stricken, and in shade
> Embosomed of coeval trees;
> Hears, o'er the lake, the warning clock
> As it shall sound with gentle shock.

69, 70. In 1845 Wordsworth wisely restored this, the text of 1827. From 1832 to 1843:

> Yea, strives for others to bedim
> The glorious Light too pure for him.

81. From Spenser's description of Archimago, "Faerie Queene," Bk. i, canto i, st. 37, "a bold, bad man."

83. Dark opprobrious den, from "Paradise Lost," Bk. ii, l. 58, "this dark opprobrious den of shame."

86. This line in 1832 replaced that of 1827: "Through Mosedale-Cove from Carrock's side." Fairfield is a mountain at Rydal Head, four miles northwest of Ambleside.

TO ———.

Written at Rydal Mount in 1824 and published in 1827. Addressed, as Wordsworth told Miss Fenwick, to Mary Wordsworth.

8. Sober certainties, from Milton's "Comus," ll. 263–265:

> But such a sacred and home-felt delight,
> Such sober certainty of waking bliss,
> I never heard till now.

9–12. This stanza was altered in 1836; previously, " If a faint sigh . . . tell . . . cherish me still . . . uphold me to the end." The appeal is rather for strength than for tenderness, and so " cherish me still " gave place to " yet bear me up."

WRITTEN ON A BLANK LEAF OF MACPHERSON'S OSSIAN.

Written in 1824; published in 1827. The text is unchanged except l. 1 which in 1827 was " Oft have I caught from fitful breeze."

Wordsworth mentioned to Miss Fenwick that the verses

> . . . or strayed
> From hope and promise, self-betrayed,

were suggested by apprehensions of the fate of Hartley Coleridge.

Compare with this poem "Glen Almain; or the Narrow Glen," p. 176. Wordsworth's complaint here against Macpherson is for having tricked out and dressed up the Ossianic poetry, and for having manufactured continuous epic poems out of fragments. And this censure justly applies to his " Fingal," " Temora," and other poems ; but in a far less degree to Macpherson's first little volume, " Fragments of Ancient poetry collected in the Highlands of Scotland " (Edinburgh, 1760). In Wordsworth's " Essay, Supplementary to the Preface to the second edition of Lyrical Ballads," he declaims vigorously against the pretensions of Macpherson's " Ossian." " Having had the good fortune," he writes, " to be born and reared in a mountainous country, from my very childhood I have felt the falsehood that pervades the volumes imposed upon the world under the name of Ossian. From what I saw with my own eyes, I knew that the imagery was spurious. In nature everything is distinct, yet nothing defined into absolute independent singleness. In Macpherson's work, it is exactly the reverse; everything (that is not stolen) is in this manner defined, insulated, dislocated, deadened — yet nothing distinct. It will always be so when words are substituted for things." For a sympathetic criticism of Macpherson's "Ossian," see Matthew Arnold "On the Study of Celtic Literature."

39. Of the semi-mythical poet Musæus referred to here we possess a few fragments of doubtful authenticity. The later Musæus, of the 5th century, is the author of the Greek poem "Hero and Leander," Englished by Marlowe and Chapman.

77. Morven's lonely shore. In the "Supplementary Essay," Wordsworth speaks more disrespectfully of Ossianic topography; with the steeps of Morven before his eyes, Macpherson, he says, could talk familiarly of car-borne heroes; "of Morven, which, if one may judge from its appearance at the distance of a few miles, contains scarcely an acre of ground sufficient for a sledge to be trailed along its surface."

79. Son of Fingal, *i.e.,* Ossian.

80. Mæonides, Homer, reputed the son of Mæon.

82. Referring to Milton's invocation of the muse in "Paradise Lost," VII, 1, "Descend from Heaven, Urania," and 30, 31 :

> Still govern thou my song,
> Urania, and fit audience find, though few.

TO A SKY–LARK ("Ethereal Minstrel!").

Written at Rydal Mount in 1825 and published in 1827, then consisting of three stanzas. One of these stanzas — the second — beginning "To the last point of vision" was transferred in 1845 to the poem "A Morning Exercise." Wordsworth desired that the last five stanzas of this latter poem should be read with "To a Sky-lark"; accordingly we place them in our text after the "Skylark."

8. Compare Shelley's "Sky-lark," "Like a Poet hidden In the light of thought."

10. The 1827 text (only) read "rapture" for "instinct."

The idea of this poem may be found in "The Prelude," Bk. xiv, ll. 382–387 :

> . . . and hence this Song, which like a lark
> I have protracted, in the unwearied heavens
> Singing, and often with more plaintive voice
> To earth attempered and her deep-drawn sighs,
> Yet centring all in love.

Compare Hogg's "The Lark," "Thy lay is in heaven — thy love is on earth."

"THE DAISY SLEEPS."

(A FRAGMENT.)

Written at Rydal Mount in 1828 and first printed in 1832, being the last six stanzas of "A Morning Exercise." See note to the preceding poem, "To a Sky-lark."

TO MAY.

This poem is dated by Wordsworth 1826–34; it was published in 1835. The text is unchanged. It is connected with "Ode composed on May Morning," which Wordsworth placed next to it. Both poems originated in ll. 81–88, "How delicate the leafy vale," etc. "My daughter and I," said Wordsworth (*Fenwick note*), "left Rydal Mount upon a tour through our mountains with Mr. and Mrs. Carr in the month of May, 1826, and as we were going up the vale of Newlands, I was struck with the appearance of the little chapel gleaming through the veil of half-opened leaves ; and the feeling that was then conveyed to my mind was expressed in the stanza referred to above. As in the case of 'Liberty' and 'Humanity' my first intention was to write only one poem, but subsequently I broke it into two, making additions to each part so as to produce a consistent and appropriate whole." Some of these additions were probably made in "the tame and manufacture-disfigured county of Lancashire" in the late autumn of 1830, when the faded leaves reminded Wordsworth (as he mentions in a letter to W. Rowan Hamilton) of spring.

59. Rathe primrose, early primrose, from Milton's "Lycidas."

> Bring the rathe primrose that forsaken dies.

THE WISHING–GATE.

Written at Rydal Mount in 1828; published in an annual, "The Keepsake," 1829, and again in Wordsworth's "Poetical Works" in 1832. A second poem, "The Wishing-Gate Destroyed," was written probably between 1837 and 1842, on a rumour, happily false, that the gate had been removed and the walls closed up. In this later poem Wordsworth mourns over the gate of happy superstition, but finds consolation in the thought that man is not Fortune's slave, and that a sense of the true law of life will suffice to glorify mountain and vale.

The text of "The Wishing-Gate" is unaltered, except that in l. 31 "Yea" replaced "Yes" of the "Keepsake" version, and that in l. 64, "thirst" in 1836 replaced "yearn."

40. Local Genius, the tutelar spirit of the place.

"IN THESE FAIR VALES HATH MANY A TREE."

Wordsworth dates this "Inscription" 1830; it was published in 1835. Possibly the date is 1831, for on September 9 of that year Wordsworth sent a copy (differing slightly in ll. 6, 7) to John Kenyon. The inscription, he says, was intended for "a field [named 'Dora's field'] adjoining our garden which I purchased two or three years ago. Under the shade of some pollard oaks, and on a green terrace in that field, we have lived no small part of the long bright days of the summers gone by; and in a hazel nook of this favourite piece of ground is a Stone, for which I wrote one day the following serious Inscription." The lines were engraved, during Wordsworth's absence in Italy, 1837, upon a brass plate inserted in the Stone.

1, 2. Compare, as regards Wordsworth's desire to preserve trees, the sonnet beginning "Degenerate Douglas!" and "The Pine of Monte Mario." In his "Description of the Scenery of the Lakes" he writes: "The want most felt, however, is that of timber trees. There are few *magnificent* ones to be found near any of the lakes; and unless greater care be taken, there will, in a short time, scarcely be left an ancient oak that would repay the cost of felling. The neighbourhood of Rydal, notwithstanding the havoc which has been made, is yet nobly distinguished."

6, 7. In the text of 1835 the following appears:

> To let it rest in peace; and here
> (Heaven knows how soon) the tender-hearted

But this is cancelled in errata, and the present reading is substituted.

THE PRIMROSE OF THE ROCK.

Written at Rydal Mount in 1831; published in 1835. The text is unchanged.

"The rock," said Wordsworth, "stands on the right hand a little way leading up the middle road from Rydal to Grasmere. We have been in the habit of calling it the Glow-worm Rock from the number of glow-worms we have often seen hanging on it as described." The name must have been given early, for in Dorothy Wordsworth's Journal, Apr. 24, 1802, we find : " We walked in the evening to Rydal. Coleridge and I lingered behind. . . . We all stood to look at Glow-worm Rock — a primrose that grew there and just looked out on the road from its own sheltered bower." In 1878 Professor Knight wrote (" The English Lake District," p. 76) : " The primrose has disappeared, and the glow-worms have almost deserted the place, but the rock is unmistakable."

Mr. Hutton, in illustrating the difference between Wordsworth's earlier and later styles, contrasts the poem " Daffodils," so wonderful for buoyancy, with this poem, in which there is less exultant buoyancy " and yet a grander and more stately movement." The style " is altogether more ideal — reality counts for less, symbol for more." Aubrey de Vere says of this poem that it is " as distinctly Wordsworthian in its inspiration as it is Christian in its doctrine." A poem by Tennyson, which may not be " Christian in its doctrine," expresses at least part of the idea of " The Primrose of the Rock," — that the humblest fragment of nature is inseparably connected with the Highest :

> Flower in the crannied wall,
> I pluck you out of the crannies,
> I hold you here, root and all, in my hand,
> Little flower — but *if* I could understand
> What you are, root and all, and all in all,
> I should know what God and man is.

But Tennyson emphasises *if* with italics ; his mood is one of awed inquisition; Wordsworth's is one of faith.

YARROW REVISITED.

Written in 1831 and published in 1835. The changes of text are too slight to deserve notice. In the autumn of 1831 Wordsworth with his daughter visited Scott at Abbotsford, before Scott's departure, in shattered health, to Italy. They found him grievously changed in body and mind. On the morning after their arrival Scott accompanied them to Newark Castle on the Yarrow. " When we alighted from the carriages," wrote Wordsworth, " he walked pretty stoutly, and had great pleasure in revisiting those his favourite haunts. Of that excursion the verses ' Yarrow Revisited ' are a memorial. Notwithstanding the romance that pervades Sir Walter's works and attaches to many of his habits, there is too much pressure of fact for these verses to harmonise as much as I could wish with other poems [*i.e.*, in the volume of 1835]. On our return in the afternoon we had to cross the Tweed directly opposite Abbotsford. The wheels of our carriage grated upon the pebbles in the bed of the stream, that flows somewhat rapidly; a rich but sad light of rather a purple than a golden hue was spread over the Eildon hills at that moment; and thinking it probable that it might be the last time Sir Walter would cross the stream, I was not a little moved, and expressed some of my feelings in the sonnet beginning ' A trouble not of clouds or weeping rain.' " Two days later the Wordsworths left Abbotsford. Both the verses " Yarrow Revisited " and the sonnet were sent to Scott before his departure from England.

Before leaving, Wordsworth expressed a hope that Scott's health would be benefited by the climate of Italy. Scott's reply is recorded in Wordsworth's " Musings at Aquapendente " :

> Still, in more than ear-deep seats,
> Survives for me, and cannot but survive,
> The tone of voice which wedded borrowed words
> To sadness not their own, when with faint smile
> Forced by intent to take from speech its edge,
> He said " When I am there, although 't is fair,
> 'T will be another Yarrow."

102, 103. Scott's minstrel of the " Lay " passes the " embattled portal arch " with " hesitating step " (Introduction to the " Lay of the Last Minstrel," ll. 31, 32).

On the Yarrow poems, see Shairp's " Aspects of Poetry," chap. xi, " The Three Yarrows," and Veitch's " History and Poetry of the Scottish Border."

DEVOTIONAL INCITEMENTS.

Written at Rydal Mount in 1832 and published in 1835. The motto is from " Paradise Lost," Bk. v, 78–80.

47. By art to unsensualise the mind. Wordsworth probably had in his memory some lines of Coleridge's early poem " Religious Musings " (ll. 208–212) :

> All the inventive arts, that nursed the soul
> To forms of beauty, and by sensual wants
> Unsensualized the mind, which in the means
> Learnt to forget the grossness of the end,
> Best pleasured with its own activity.

50-54. The two pairs of lines before 1836 appeared in a reverse order.

69. Eternal Will: before 1836, "almighty Will."

71. In 1835: " Her admonitions Nature yields." In 1836, "Divine admonishment She yields." Altered to present text in 1845.

"CALM IS THE FRAGRANT AIR."

(An Evening Voluntary.)

Written 1832; published 1835.

22. The busy dor-hawk: before 1837, " Far-heard the dor-hawk." The night-jar or European goat-sucker, called dor-hawk from the sound it makes, would not be " far-heard."

25, 26. These lines were happily added in 1837.

"IF THIS GREAT WORLD OF JOY AND PAIN."

Written in 1833 ; published in 1835. The text is unchanged. The lines may have been suggested by the Reform Bill of 1832, to which Wordsworth had been opposed.

ON A HIGH PART OF THE COAST OF CUMBERLAND.

(An Evening Voluntary.)

Written in 1833 ; published in 1835. The text is unchanged. " The lines," said Wordsworth (*Fenwick note*), " were composed on the road between Moresby [County Cumberland] and Whitehaven, while I was on a visit to my son, then rector of the former place. This and some other Voluntaries originated in the concluding lines of the last paragraph of the poem." Wordsworth had been familiar from earliest childhood with this coast.

24. Psalms cxi. 10, " The fear of the Lord is the beginning of wisdom."

" NOT IN THE LUCID INTERVALS OF LIFE."

(An Evening Voluntary.)

Written in 1834 and published in 1835. The only change of text is the alteration in 1837 of " dares " to " dare " after " if," a change made in several instances in the ed. of 1836-37. Wordsworth notes that ll.

7–15 "were written with Lord Byron's character, as a poet, before me, and that of others, his contemporaries, who wrote under like influences."

6. Mammon's cave. Perhaps Wordsworth thought of the " Faerie Queene," Bk. ii, canto vii, where Guyon finds Mammon "in a delve, sunning his threasure hore."

The poem expresses Wordsworth's feeling for nature in its latest phase :

> By grace divine
> Not otherwise, O Nature! we are thine.

TO A CHILD.

WRITTEN IN HER ALBUM.

Written in 1834 and published in 1835. "This quatrain," said Wordsworth (*Fenwick note*), "was extempore on observing this image, as I had often done, on the lawn of Rydal Mount. It was first written down in the Album of my god-daughter, Rotha Quillinan."

2. Before 1845 : "Of friends, however humble, scorn not one."

Another poem of Wordsworth's, that beginning "So fair, so sweet, withal so sensitive," was suggested by the shadow of a daisy, seen in July, 1844, near Loughrigg Tarn, whither Wordsworth walked in company with Archer Butler, Julius C. Hare, Sir W. Rowan Hamilton, and R. Perceval Graves. The poet wishes

> That to this mountain-daisy's self were known
> The beauty of its star-shaped shadow, thrown
> On the smooth surface of this naked stone!

WRITTEN AFTER THE DEATH OF CHARLES LAMB.

Lamb died Dec. 27, 1834; this poem was written in November, 1835, and was privately printed; in 1837 it appeared in Wordsworth's " Poetical Works," but without a title; the title was given in 1845. The text of 1837 remained unaltered, but several variations found in the rare private impression are recorded in the Aldine ed. of Wordsworth's " Poetical Works." At first an epitaph (ll. 40–43) was designed for inscription on the stone, but the poem grew too long for this purpose. The epitaphs of Chiabrera (some of which had been translated by Wordsworth in earlier years) served as the model.

It may suffice to note here with respect to the private impression that it opened with the line, " To the dear memory of a frail good Man," and closed thus :

> The sacred tie
> Is broken, to become more sacred still.

Lamb's place of burial is Edmonton church-yard. His sister, who survived him nearly thirteen years, was buried by his side.

Elegiac poems in memory of the dead may either aim at perpetuating the memory of the dead by a monumental portrait or by an impassioned lament in which there is little of portraiture. To the latter class belong Milton's " Lycidas," Shelley's " Adonais," and Matthew Arnold's " Thyrsis "; to the former Daniel's " Memorial of the Earl of Devonshire," Henry Taylor's admirable lines in remembrance of Edward Villiers, and the present poem. Lamb's birth in London, his love of the great city, his service in the India House, his delight in books, his literary work, his gentleness of nature, his wit and pathos, his devotion to his sister and her devotion to him, are here recorded; and with becoming reserve reference is made to the great affliction of Mary Lamb's life, her tendency to insanity, which brought out the heroism of Charles Lamb's character. The reader should consult Ainger's " Charles Lamb " in the series of " English Men of Letters."

In illustration of the lines

> Thou wert a scorner of the fields, my Friend,
> But more in show than truth,

see a letter from Lamb to Wordsworth of Jan. 30, 1801 : " Separate from the pleasure of your company, I don't much care if I never see a mountain in my life. I have passed all my days in London, until I have formed as many and as intense local attachments as any of you mountaineers can have done with dead Nature." What follows, on the delights of London, is in Lamb's most characteristic manner, but is too long to quote.

EXTEMPORE EFFUSION UPON THE DEATH OF JAMES HOGG.

Hogg, the Ettrick Shepherd, died on Nov. 21, 1835, and these verses were, Wordsworth says, written extempore immediately after reading a notice of his death in a Newcastle paper. To the editor of that paper he sent a copy for publication, and the poem may have been printed first there. It appeared on Dec. 12, 1835, in *The Athenæum*. The only change of text in the "Poetical Works" is in l. 25, where " slumber " before 1845 was "slumbers."

Wordsworth added the following note :

"Walter Scott	. . . .	died 21st Sept., 1832.
S. T. Coleridge	. . . . .	" 25th July, 1834.
Charles Lamb	. . . . .	" 27th Dec., 1834.
Geo. Crabbe	. . . . .	" 3rd Feb., 1832.
Felicia Hemans	. . . . .	" 16th May. 1835."

In the *Fenwick note* is much interesting gossip about Crabbe and Mrs. Hemans, but to Mrs. Hemans Wordsworth is unjust.

1–4. Refers to the tour in Scotland, 1814. See "Yarrow Visited," p. 251.

5–8. Refers to the visit to Abbotsford in 1831. See "Yarrow Revisited," p. 290, and the sonnet "A trouble not of clouds," p. 341.

17, 18. Hazlitt, in describing S. T. Coleridge ("My First Acquaintance with Poets "), writes : "His forehead was broad and high, light as if built of ivory, with large projecting eyebrows, and his eyes rolling beneath them like a sea with darkened lustre."

32. Wordsworth frequently met Crabbe at Mr. Hoare's upon Hampstead Heath, where Crabbe was accustomed to pay a visit of some length in the spring.

35. Crabbe died in his 78th year.

39. Felicia Hemans died in Dublin in her 42d year.

41, 42. Referring to the ballads of Yarrow. See notes on " Yarrow Unvisited," p. 433.

SONNETS.

COMPOSED BY THE SEASIDE, NEAR CALAIS, AUGUST, 1802.

(" Fair Star," etc.).

Taking advantage of the Peace of Amiens, Wordsworth and his sister visited Calais in the summer of 1802. This sonnet, written in August of that year, was first published in 1807. The text is unchanged except in l. 10, where "that" was substituted in 1837 for the earlier "it." Dorothy Wordsworth writes in her Journal : "We arrived at

Calais at four o'clock on Sunday morning (Aug. 1). . . . We had
delightful walks after the heat of the day was past — seeing far off in
the west the coast of England, like a cloud, crested with Dover Castle,
which was but like the summit of the cloud — the evening Star, and the
glory of the sky ; the reflections in the water were more beautiful than
the sky itself ; purple waves brighter than precious stones for ever melt-
ing away upon the sands."

The war of England against the French Republic had for a time
alienated Wordsworth from his own country ; but he had lost his faith
in France and was now restored in heart to England.   Yet he had fears
that England was fallen in moral temper from her ancient simplicity
and strength.   This invocation of the evening star as his country's
emblem serves as an appropriate introduction to the political sonnets.
The Poet looks away from France, which had once been the source of
his hopes and faith, to England and her glorious crest.

CALAIS, AUGUST, 1802 (" Is it a reed ").

This sonnet first appeared in *The Morning Post*, in January, 1803;
it was first included among Wordsworth's poems in 1807.   On Aug. 2,
1802, Napoleon was appointed First Consul for life.

1, 2.   From St. Matthew xl. 7.

1801 (" I grieved," etc.).

This sonnet was written on May 21, 1802; it was first published on
Sept. 16, 1802, in *The Morning Post*, and again in the same paper in
January, 1803 ; first included among Wordsworth's poems in 1807.   In
Dorothy Wordsworth's Journal, May 21, 1802, we read: " William
wrote two sonnets on Buonaparte, after I had read Milton's sonnets
for him."   Napoleon had been chosen First Consul for ten years to
come on May 8.   Wordsworth's date " 1801 " is perhaps an error, or
perhaps it refers to the treaties of peace of that year viewed as prelimi-
naries to Napoleon's supreme power.

As the text stood in 1807 " vital blood " appeared in l. 2 where
" tenderest mood " (1837) appears in the present text.   In edd. 1815–32
ll. 2–4 were as follows :

> . . . for who aspires
> To genuine greatness but from just desires
> And knowledge such as *He* could never gain ?

Happily Wordsworth reverted to his original text, with the alteration of "vital blood" just noted. The alteration of rhymes in 1815 removed the sonnet farther from the Italian model than it originally was or is now.

ON THE EXTINCTION OF THE VENETIAN REPUBLIC.

Written, probably, in August, 1802 ; first published in 1807. The text has never been altered.

" The Venetians were called on to recognize the French Republic ; they refused, but did not join the coalition against it. When Bonaparte was at the gates of Mantua, they at length decided to treat with him ; but it was too late. . . . On 8th May [1797] the great council decided to offer no resistance to the French ; the doge abdicated on the 12th ; and Napoleon entered the city on the 16th, and proclaimed the end of the Republic. On 17th October following, Bonaparte, by the treaty of Campo Formio, abandoned the territory of Venice to Austria. Venice was buffeted to and fro between France and Austria from 1798 to 1814, when the new coalition assigned her to Austria." — Encyc. Brit., article "Venice."

1. "The crusading expeditions of the Doge Faliero, followed up by his successor Doge Michele, riveted the power of Venice in Syria by the reduction of Tyre. . . . Enrico Dandalo reduced Trieste, reconquered Zara, and headed the fourth crusade, nominally for Palestine, really against Constantinople, which he stormed." — Chambers's Encyc., article "Venice."

2. The latter half of the 15th century was partly occupied with hostilities against the Turks.

7, 8. From the Bucentaur on every Ascension Day the doge solemnly espoused the Adriatic.

13, 14. Compare Burke on the fall of greatness in the French Revolution : "Why do I feel so differently from the Rev. Dr. Price, and those of his lay flock, who will choose to adopt the sentiments of his discourse ? For this plain reason — because it is *natural* I should ; because we are so made as to be affected at such spectacles with melancholy sentiments upon the unstable condition of mortal prosperity and the tremendous uncertainty of human greatness ; because in those natural feelings we learn great lessons ; because in events like these our passions instruct our reason."

TO TOUSSAINT L'OUVERTURE.

Written in 1802 ; first published, with an inferior text, in *The Morning Post*, Feb. 2, 1803 ; first included among Wordsworth's poems in 1807.

Toussaint (surnamed L'Ouverture in 1793, because he broke through the entrenched quarters of the Spaniards), one of the liberators of Hayti, was born in slavery 1743, joined the negro insurgents in 1791, was made a general by the French Convention for his services against the Spaniards, and became chief of the army of St. Domingo. About 1800 he " began to aim at independence of France. Bonaparte having, after the peace of Amiens, proclaimed the reëstablishment of slavery in San Domingo, Toussaint declined to obey, whereupon General Le Clerc was sent with a strong fleet to compel him. The liberator soon submitted, but was treacherously arrested, sent to France, and flung into a damp, dark dungeon at Fort de Joux, near Besançon, where he sank after ten months, Apr. 27, 1803." — Chambers's Encyc.

2-4. Date from 1827. The earlier readings were :

> Whether the rural milk-maid by her Cow
> Sing in thy hearing, or thou liest now
> Alone in some deep dungeon's earless den ;   (1807.)

> Whether the all-cheering Sun be free to shed
> His beams around thee, or thou rest thy head
> Pillowed in some dark dungeon's noisome den.   (1815.)

> Whether the whistling Rustic tend his plough
> Within thy hearing, or thou liest now
> Buried in some deep dungeon's earless den.   (1820.)

The reading of 1815 was probably rejected because the powers of nature, of which the sun is one, should not be introduced until the sextet, where they appear as taking up and carrying on Toussaint's work of liberation. There was also in 1815 a loss to the regular rhyme-system of the sonnet.

Observe how the powers of external nature and of human passion are presented as conjoint workers on behalf of freedom.

SEPTEMBER, 1802, NEAR DOVER.

First published 1807 ; the text was never altered. The thought that material powers will not avail for the defence of freedom unless supported by moral powers is of frequent recurrence in Wordsworth, especially in these political sonnets and in the pamphlet on the Convention of Cintra. In Dorothy Wordsworth's Journal we read : " On Sunday, the 29th of August, we left Calais at twelve o'clock in the morning and landed at Dover at one on Monday the 30th. . . . The next day was very hot. We . . . bathed, and sate upon the Dover Cliffs, and looked upon France with many a melancholy and tender thought. We could see the shores almost as plain as if it were but an English lake."

THOUGHT OF A BRITON ON THE SUBJUGATION OF SWITZERLAND.

This sonnet, which was composed while Wordsworth was pacing to and fro between the Hall of Coleorton (Sir George Beaumont's residence), then rebuilding, and the principal farmhouse on the estate, occupied by the Wordsworth family for several months, belongs to the close of 1806 or opening of 1807 ; it was first published in 1807 ; the text was never altered. In September, 1808, Wordsworth called it his best sonnet.

The invasion of Switzerland by France in 1797 completely alienated Coleridge's sympathies from the French, and he expressed his feelings in his great poem " France : an Ode." Carnot, one of the founders of the French Republic, gives expression to a like indignation in his " Réponse . . . au Rapport fait sur la conjuration du 18 fructidor . . . par J.-Ch. Bailleul . . ." But Wordsworth's sonnet probably has special reference to Bonaparte's " Act of Mediation," 1803, by which the Swiss Confederation was reinstituted. While it was an improvement in many respects on the Helvetic Republic, the new arrangement guaranteed by Bonaparte made French influence predominant in Switzerland.

WRITTEN IN LONDON September, 1802 (" O Friend!" etc.).

" This was written immediately after my return from France to London, when I could not but be struck, as here described, with the vanity and parade of our own country, especially in great towns and cities, as contrasted with the quiet, and I may say the desolation, that the revolution had produced in France. This must be borne in mind, or else the reader may think that in this and the succeeding sonnets I have exaggerated the mischief engendered and fostered among us by undisturbed wealth." — Wordsworth's note.

The sonnet was first published in 1807 ; the text was unaltered except that in the collected volume of "Sonnets," 1838, — and here alone, — the first line stands "O thou proud City! which way shall I look."

The recoil from city luxury had been often expressed by Cowper; see, for example, "The Task," Bk. i, ll. 678–749.

The "Friend" of l. 1 was Coleridge.

LONDON, 1802 ("Milton!" etc.).

Written in 1802 ; first published 1807. The only textual change is the word "herself" in the last line, substituted in 1820 for "itself." On the personification of Milton's heart as feminine, compare "The Excursion," Bk. iii, l. 738 : "My *soul* diffused *herself*," etc., and "The Old Cumberland Beggar," l. 104 (note). The mood in which this sonnet was written is akin to that which gave birth to the sonnet "Written in London, September, 1802."

In the third book of "The Prelude," Wordsworth tells how he imagined Milton as one of his predecessors at the University of Cambridge :

> Yea, our blind Poet, who in his later day,
> Stood almost single ; uttering odious truth —
> Darkness before, and danger's voice behind,
> Soul awful — if the earth has ever lodged
> An awful soul — I seemed to see him here
> Familiarly, and in his scholar's dress
> Bounding before me, yet a stripling youth —
> A boy, no better, with his rosy cheeks
> Angelical, keen eye, courageous look,
> And conscious step of purity and pride.

He goes on to tell how the only time his brain was ever excited by wine was when drinking to Milton's memory in the room once occupied by the poet.

10. Tennyson, thinking of Milton as an "inventor of harmonies," calls him the "organ-voice of England." Wordsworth has Milton's art less in his mind than Milton's native power. Swinburne, in his "Inscriptions for the Four Sides of a Pedestal," ascribes the first sea-like sound in English song to Marlowe :

> . . . he
> First gave our song a sound that matched our sea.

"IT IS NOT TO BE THOUGHT OF," etc.

Written in 1802 or 1803; first published in *The Morning Post* in 1803; first included in Wordsworth's poems 1807.

5, 6. Date from 1827, when they replaced lines entirely different in meaning :

> Road by which all might come and go that would,
> And bear out freights of worth to foreign lands.

The opposition between "British freedom" and what he deemed its "salutary bonds" would naturally occur to Wordsworth in days not long before Catholic Emancipation and the Reform Bill.

The words quoted, l. 4, are from Daniel, "Civil War," Bk. ii, stanza 7.

"WHEN I HAVE BORNE IN MEMORY," etc.

This sonnet was probably written in 1802 or 1803 ; it was first published in *The Morning Post*, Sept. 17, 1803, and first included among Wordsworth's poems in 1807.

The alterations of text were few and slight; the only one that need be noted illustrates Wordsworth's vigilant superintendence of detail : in l. 6 "Now" replaced in 1845 the earlier "But"; in l. 9 "But" also stood until 1845 (except in the Sonnet volume of 1838 where "Most" is found). It might seem that the logic here is injured by the idea of "unfilial fears" (l. 8) ; for the last line of the sonnet — designed to express the same mood and moment — justifies such fears on the ground that they are filial, those which an anxious child might feel for a mother. Wordsworth doubtless means that the fears, filial as offspring of love, are unfilial as lacking faith.

OCTOBER, 1803 ("These times strike monied worldlings," etc.).

First published in 1807. The only change of text is the substitution in l. 1 of the word "strike" in 1837 for the earlier "touch." There were expectations of an invasion of England by the French in 1803 ; see the sonnets "In the Pass of Killikranky" and "To the Men of Kent."

10, 11. In a sonnet of 1811 (that beginning "Here pause") Wordsworth speaks of hope as "the paramount *duty* that Heaven lays

> For its own honour on man's suffering heart."

And in the pamphlet on the Convention of Cintra he writes : "But, from the moment of the rising of the people of the Pyrenean peninsula, there was a mighty change; we were instantaneously animated; and, from that moment the contest assumed the dignity, which it is not in the power of anything but hope to bestow."

This sonnet applies to the individual man the doctrine which Wordsworth so often urges with respect to national life, — that the source of strength is from within, a moral power, not an accumulation of external resources.

IN THE PASS OF KILLIKRANKY.

First published 1807. The text was never altered. Dorothy Wordsworth writes in her Journal, Sept. 8, 1803: "When we were travelling in Scotland an invasion was hourly looked for, and one could not but think with some regret of the times when from the now depopulated Highlands forty or fifty thousand men might have been poured down for the defence of the country, under such leaders as the Marquis of Montrose or the brave man who had so distinguished himself upon the ground where we were standing. I will transcribe a sonnet suggested to William by this place, and written in October, 1803."

Killiekrankie is "a beautiful wooded pass in Perthshire, on the Garry River, 15 miles N.N.W. of Dunkeld." Here in 1689 John Graham, Viscount Dundee ("Bonnie Dundee," "Bloody Claverhouse"), met the government forces under General Mackay: "Two minutes decided the contest; before the wild rush of the clansmen the redcoats wavered, broke, and ran like sheep"; but Dundee fell mortally wounded.

8–10. Compare the following from Wordsworth's pamphlet on the Convention of Cintra: "The discipline of the army was well known; and as a machine, or a vital organized body, the Nation was assured that it could not but be formidable; but thus to the standing excellence of mechanic or organic power seemed to be superadded, at this time and for this service, the force of *inspiration:* could anything therefore be looked for but a glorious result?"

TO THE MEN OF KENT, October, 1803.

First published 1807. The personification in ll. 2, 3 was incomplete until 1827, when "Her" was substituted for the earlier "Its."

2. Advance is here probably used in the sense *lift up*, as in Shakespeare's "Tempest," I, ii, 408: "The fringed curtains of thine eyes advance," and in Wordsworth's "White Doe of Rylstone," III, 158:

> At need he stood, advancing high
> The glittering, floating Pageantry.

F. W. Robertson writes in a lecture on Wordsworth ("Lectures and Addresses," 1861, p. 255) : "There is a difference between the Kentish men and the men of Kent. The Kentish men are simply the inhabitants of the County of Kent. The 'Men of Kent' is a technical expression applied to the inhabitants of that part of Kent who were never subdued in the Norman invasion, and who obtained glorious terms for themselves, on capitulation, receiving the confirmation of their own charters. . . . It was to the 'Men of Kent,' the inhabitants of that part of the county nearest to the neighbouring land of France, that Wordsworth addressed this sonnet."

NOVEMBER, 1806 ("Another year!" etc.).

First published 1807. Suggested by the events of October and November, 1806, the battle of Jena, October 14, battle of Auerstadt, flight of King Frederich William of Prussia, and the occupation of Berlin by the French, October 25, and perhaps the decree of Napoleon at Berlin, November 20, declaring Great Britain in a state of blockade.

12. The word "servile" in this line replaced in 1820 the earlier "venal."

TO THOMAS CLARKSON.

First published 1807.

5. The words "that enterprise" in 1837 replaced the earlier "this pilgrimage." The earlier reading connects itself with l. 1, "an obstinate hill to climb."

9. Duty's intrepid liegeman in 1837 replaced the earlier "With unabating effort." In the same year "blood-stained" (l. 11) was substituted for "bloody," and "wilt" for "shalt" in l. 12.

Thomas Clarkson (1760–1846) was of Wordsworth's college, St. John's, Cambridge, but by some years his predecessor. "The subject for the Latin essay of 1785 was the question 'Anne liceat invitos in servitutem dare?' and the contest for this prize determined the whole course of Clarkson's life. The bill for the abolition of the slave trade was introduced by Lord Grenville in the House of Lords on 2 Jan., 1807, and received the royal assent on 25 March. Wordsworth was personally acquainted with Clarkson. In an unpublished letter of

Hartley Coleridge's of the year 1836 he speaks of Clarkson's special labour as that of collecting evidence ' by toil, by patience, at the sacrifice of health, at the frequent risk of life.' Wilberforce, he says, ' undertook the easier task of bringing the evidence into the court, corroborating it by his acuteness and illuminating it by his eloquence.' "

COMPOSED BY THE SIDE OF GRASMERE LAKE, 1807.

In August, 1807, Wordsworth returned to Grasmere from Coleorton. The sonnet was not published until 1819.

1. Until 1827 the opening line was "Eve's lingering Clouds extend in solid bars."

9-11. In 1827 the present text appears except that the personification was not completed; "it" and "Its" stood for "she" and "Her" until 1837. Before 1827 an inferior reading stood here:

> . . . the nether Sphere
> Opening its vast abyss, while fancy feeds
> On the rich show! But list!

There is a self-consciousness implied in the return of the poet on his own state of mind ("While fancy feeds on the rich show!") which Wordsworth doubtless felt to be out of place.

COMPOSED WHILE THE AUTHOR, etc.

Written in November or December, 1808; first published 1815. Wordsworth fears that in society our view of public affairs may be obscured by transitory objects, by self-interest or the interest of a party, and finds that the soul best communes with itself and with truth in solitude or among the permanent, passionate, and free presence of nature.

"ALAS! WHAT BOOTS THE LONG LABORIOUS QUEST."

This sonnet was first published in *The Friend*, Nov. 16, 1809, the year of composition. The text is unchanged. The title in *The Friend* is " Sonnet suggested by the Efforts of the Tyrolese, contrasted with the Present State of Germany."

1811 ("The Power of Armies," etc.).

First published in 1815. In 1811 the French were much harassed by the Spanish guerillas. In the tract on the Convention of Cintra Wordsworth had written : "It was never dreamt by any thinking man that the Spaniards were to succeed by their army ; if by their *army* be meant anything but the people. The whole people is their army, and their true army is the people, and nothing else. . . . A military spirit should be there, and a military action, not confined like an ordinary river in one channel, but spreading like the Nile over the whole face of the land. . . . In the moral virtues and qualities of passion which belong to a people must the ultimate salvation of a people be sought for. . . . They must now be taught that their strength *chiefly* lies in moral qualities, more silent in their operation, more permanent in their nature; in the virtues of perseverance, constancy, fortitude, and watchfulness, in a long memory and a quick feeling, to rise upon a favourable summons, a texture of life which, though cut through (as hath been feigned of the bodies of the Angels) unites again — these are the virtues and qualities on which the Spanish People must be taught *mainly* to depend."

2. **Space** in 1827 was substituted for the earlier "place."

1811 ("Here pause," etc.).

First published in 1815. Text unchanged.

7-9. Compare S. T. Coleridge in his Sixth Letter to the editor of the *Courier*, 1809 ("Essays on his own Times," p. 645, ed. 1850) : "The error, which of all others most besets the public mind, and which yet of all others is the most degrading in its nature, the most tremendous in its consequences, is an inward prostration of the soul before enormous POWER, and a readiness to palliate and forget all iniquities to which prosperity has wedded itself ; as if man were only a puppet without reason and free will, and without the conscience which is the offspring of their union, a puppet played off by some unknown power ! as if success were the broad seal of the divine approbation, and tyranny itself the Almighty's inauguration of a Tyrant ! . . . The main strength of Bonaparte, Sir, is in the imaginations of men, which are dazzled and blinded by the splendid robes and gaudy trappings which have been purchased by guilt for its own disguise."

COMPOSED UPON WESTMINSTER BRIDGE, Sept. 3, 1802.

" Written," says Wordsworth, " on the roof of a coach on my way to France." Dorothy Wordsworth writes in her Journal of 1802 : " We left London on Saturday morning at half past five or six, the 30th [an error, the 31st] of July. We mounted the Dover coach at Charing Cross. It was a beautiful morning. The city, St. Paul's, with the river, and a multitude of little boats, made a most beautiful sight as we crossed Westminster Bridge. The houses were not over-hung by their cloud of smoke, and they were spread out endlessly, yet the sun shone so brightly, with such a fierce light, that there was something like the purity of one of nature's own grand spectacles."

Wordsworth in edd. 1807–37 dates the sonnet " Sept. 3, 1803," a mistake as to the year; in later editions " Sept. 3, 1802," correct as to the year, but not giving the actual month, July. On his return from France in 1802, he arrived in London on the evening of August 30, and remained there till September 22. He could hardly have forgotten that it was in July he travelled to France, not long before his marriage. Possibly he thought July with its " fierce light " less in harmony with the sonnet than September, which he was accustomed to associate with those rare days of affecting influence described in his " Guide to the Lakes." See the poem " September, 1819," and notes. The text is unchanged.

Bagehot, in his article on " Pure, Ornate, and Grotesque Art in Poetry," selected this sonnet of Wordsworth and that on " The Trossachs " as " luminous examples " of pure art : " The compactness of the sonnet and the gravity of the sentiment hedging in the thoughts, restraining the fancy, and helping to maintain a singleness of expression. Instances of barer style than this may easily be found, instances of colder style, — few better instances of purer style. Not a single expression (the invocation in the concluding couplet perhaps excepted) can be spared, yet not a single expression rivets the attention." The great subject, he adds, the religious aspect of a city about to awaken and be alive, is the only idea left in our mind. " To Wordsworth has been vouchsafed the last grace of the self-denying artist — you think neither of him nor his style, but you cannot help thinking of — you *must* recall — the exact phrase, the *very* sentiment he wished."

"IT IS A BEAUTEOUS EVENING," etc.

"Composed," Wordsworth says, "on the beach near Calais," in August, 1802; published in 1807. Dorothy Wordsworth writes in her Journal: "We found Annette and Caroline chez Madame Avril. . . . We walked by the seashore almost every evening with Annette and Caroline, or William and I alone." Who Annette and Caroline were I do not know, but one of them may have been the "Dear Child! dear Girl!" of the sonnet. Attempted improvements were made in the sonnet in 1837 and 1840, from some of which Wordsworth reverted to the earlier text.

1. This line returned in 1845 to the original reading. In 1837, "Air sleeps, — from strife or stir the clouds are free"; in 1840, "A fairer face of evening cannot be."

5. Broods o'er: before 1837, "is on."

6. Listen! a return in 1840 to the original text; in 1837, "But list!" — as if there were an opposition between the sound of the sea and the quietude of the evening.

9, 10. In 1840 Wordsworth returned to the earliest text, which was as now except that "appear'st" stood for "appear"; altered in 1845. In 1837:

> Dear Child! dear happy Girl! if thou appear
> Heedless — untouch'd with awe or serious thought,

In 1838 l. 10 became "Heedless — unawed, untouch'd with serious thought." For another contrast between the reflective and the child-like nature, each justified after its kind, see "Ode to Duty," and compare the last line of the sonnet "Sole listener, Duddon."

COMPOSED AFTER A JOURNEY ACROSS THE HAMBLE-TON HILLS, YORKSHIRE.

"Composed," says Wordsworth, "October 4th, 1802, after a journey on a day memorable to me — the day of my marriage. The horizon commanded by those hills is most magnificent." The sonnet, with that which follows, was published in 1807. Dorothy Wordsworth in her Journal describes the sky-prospect, and it is not possible to say whether her Journal is derived from the sonnet or the sonnet from the Journal. "Far off from us," she writes, "in the western sky we saw shapes of castles, ruins among groves, a great spreading wood, rocks and single trees, a minster with its tower unusually distinct, minarets in another quarter, and a round Grecian Temple also; the colours of the sky of a bright gray, and the forms of a sober gray, with a dome."

Compare with this sonnet "Sky-Prospect — From the Plain of France" in "Memorials of a Tour on the Continent, 1820," and also the magnificent description in "The Excursion," Bk. ii, ll. 830–869.

1–3. The present text is of 1837. In 1807 :

> Ere we had reach'd the wish'd for place, night fell:
> We were too late at least by one dark hour,
> And nothing could we see of all that power

"Night" was a word inappropriate for an hour just after sunset. In 1815 :

> Dark and more dark the shades of Evening fell;
> The wish'd for point was reach'd; but late the hour,
> And little could we see of all that power

In 1827: "And little could be gained from all that dower," leaving only a touch to be added in 1837.

5–12. The text here was also reached in 1827, except that in l. 5 the reading was "in all its power." In 1807 :

> The western sky did recompense us well
> With Grecian Temple, Minaret, and Bower;
> And, in one part, a Minster with its Tower
> Substantially distinct; a place for Bell
> Or clock to toll from. Many a glorious pile
> Did we behold, sight that might well repay
> All disappointment! and, as such, the eye
> Delighted in them;

Observe that to improve the sonnet Wordsworth did not hesitate to depart from the regular arrangement of rhymes in the octave. This reading of 1807 remained little altered until 1827; in 1815 l. 10 became "Did we behold, fair sights that might repay," and in l. 8 "expressed" replaced "distinct."

"THOSE WORDS WERE UTTERED," etc.

The date is uncertain; published with the preceding sonnet in 1807.

1, 2. In 1807 :

> These words were uttered in a pensive mood
> Even while mine eyes were on that solemn sight;

In 1815 : "Mine eyes yet lingering on that solemn sight."

The opening word in all editions (except 1838) previous to 1845 was "these."

6.   Before 1827 : "It is unstable, and deserts me quite."

9.   Before 1827 : "The Grove, the sky-built Temple, and the Dome."

COMPOSED AT [NEIDPATH] CASTLE.

Written on Sept. 18, 1803 ; published in 1807. The text is unchanged. Neidpath Castle is near Peebles, overlooking the Tweed. Scott had told Wordsworth on September 17 of the fact that the Duke of Queensberry was felling the trees.

2.   Despite, malice.

12.   Bosoms, curvatures of the river banks.   Compare Fairfax, "Tasso," XIX, 8 :

> Where into creeks and bosoms blind
> A winding hill his corners turn'd and cast.

R. Burton speaks of "a bosom of the South Cape of Massachusetts Bay."

"NUNS FRET NOT," etc.

Of uncertain date ; published in 1807. The idea of liberty within a voluntary limitation is frequent in Wordsworth's poems. See "Ode to Duty," and "In the Pass of Kirkstone" the following lines, in which constraint, even without choice, is justified :

> Be thankful, even though tired and faint,
> For the rich bounties of constraint ;
> Whence oft invigorating transports flow
> That choice lacked courage to bestow.

6.   Furness-fells. "The hills east of the Duddon, south of the Brathay, and west of Windermere." — Knight.

9.   For me : one of Wordsworth's latest corrections ; before 1849, "to me."

14.   Brief solace : before 1827, "short solace." Perhaps changed to avoid the repeated "s" in the line.

For a commentary on the idea of this sonnet, see Sir Henry Taylor's article on "Wordsworth's Sonnets."

ADMONITION.

Written not earlier than 1802 nor later than 1807, the date of publication. In his "Guide to the Lakes," Wordsworth writes of the cottages : " These humble dwellings remind the contemplative spectator of a production of Nature [see l. 7], and may (using a strong expression) rather be said to have grown than to have been erected, — to have risen by an instinct of their own out of the native rock, — so little is there in them of formality, such is their wildness and beauty."

1. Before 1837 : " Yes, there is holy pleasure in thine eye ! " Perhaps Wordsworth thought the " holy pleasure " would, without admonition, preclude all danger of coveting the abode.

5. Forbear to sigh : before 1827, " O do not sigh." The " do " was too nearly followed by " As many do."

7. Before 1827 : " Sighing a wish to tear from Nature's book."

8. Precious leaf : before 1827, " blissful leaf." " Harsh impiety " in 1815 replaced " worst impiety."

9. Must be : before 1827, " would be " ; the change strengthens the poet's plea.

14. Before 1838 this closing line was a needless alexandrine, " would melt and melt away ! "

"THE WORLD IS TOO MUCH WITH US," etc.

The date of this sonnet is uncertain ; it was first published in 1807, and the only change in the text is the word " rising " in l. 13, which was substituted in 1827 for the earlier " coming." Lines 13, 14 seem to be written with a memory of Spenser's " Colin Clout's come Home Again," ll. 244–248 :

> Of them the shepheard which hath charge in chief
> Is Triton, blowing loud his wreathed horne :
> . . . .
> And Proteus eke with him does drive his heard.

" Pleasant lea " is found in the same poem.

In the "Excursion," Bk. iv, Wordsworth expresses the thought that superstition is better than apathy, — even the vulgar superstitions of a village, and much more the noble mythology of Greece, which he describes later in the same book :

> Rather would I instantly decline
> To the traditionary sympathies
> Of a most rustic ignorance, and take

> A fearful apprehension from the owl
> Or death-watch : and as readily rejoice
> If two auspicious magpies crossed my way;—
> To this would rather bend than see and hear
> The repetitions wearisome of sense,
> Where soul is dead, and feeling hath no place.

TO SLEEP.

One of three sonnets "To Sleep," written at some time between 1802 and the date of publication, 1807.

5. This line caused Wordsworth much consideration. It dates from 1845. From 1807 to 1820: "I 've thought of all by turns; and still I lie." The contraction "I 've " was disapproved, and edd. 1827 and 1832 read : "By turns have all been thought of; yet I lie." From 1837 to 1843 (except "Sonnets," 1838) : "I thought of all by turns, and yet I lie." In 1838 (only) : "I have thought of all by turns and yet I lie." The jingle "I lie " following "I " at the opening of the line offended Wordsworth's ear, and the present reading was substituted.

13. Between : before 1832, "betwixt."

"WHERE LIES THE LAND," etc.

The composition cannot be earlier than 1802 nor later than 1807, the date of publication.

2, 3. Before 1837 :

> Festively she puts forth in trim array ;
> As vigorous as a lark at break of day.

TO THE MEMORY OF RAISLEY CALVERT.

Date uncertain, but between 1802 and 1807, when this sonnet was published. The text is unchanged. Raisley, brother of Wordsworth's friend William Calvert, died of consumption at Penrith in 1795 ; during his last illness Wordsworth remained with him. In his will it was found that he had left Wordsworth £900, not merely as a token of friendship, "but because he believed that, if Wordsworth were only free from the pressure of monetary cares, he would write something in verse or prose that would benefit the world " (Knight). See "The Prelude," Bk. xiv, ll. 354–369.

"METHOUGHT I SAW THE FOOTSTEPS," etc.

The date is uncertain, but between 1802 and 1807, when it was published. Wordsworth connected with this sonnet another written many years after, with a recollection of the appearance in death of his wife's sister, Sarah Hutchinson, who died in June, 1836. The latter part of the present sonnet had been a great favourite with her.

3. **Who might sit:** before 1815, "him who sate."

9. Before 1837: "I seem'd to mount those steps; the vapours gave"; in 1837: "Those steps I mounted, as ['while,' 1838] the vapours gave"; in 1840: "Those steps I clomb; the opening vapours gave." The present text is of 1845. "I seem'd" detracted from the authentic character of the vision.

"BROOK! WHOSE SOCIETY THE POET SEEKS."

Of uncertain date, perhaps after 1807; first published, 1815.

6. Before 1827: "If I some type of thee did wish to view"; altered to avoid the feeble "did wish."

13. **Safer:** before 1845, "better." "Better" went ill with "good" as a noun, being itself the comparative of the adjective "good."

TO LADY BEAUMONT.

Written early in 1807 and published in the same year. Dorothy Wordsworth refers to the sonnet in a letter of February, 1807. The Wordsworths were residing at the farmhouse, Coleorton, and Mrs. Wordsworth, Dorothy, and the poet superintended the formation of a winter garden for Lady Beaumont.

2. In 1807: "framing beds of"; in 1815: "framing beds for." The present text is of 1827. The word "frame" had been frequently and somewhat inaccurately used by Wordsworth in early editions, and he found substitutes in a large number of passages in the later editions. See *The Academy*, Dec. 2, 1893, for Mr. T. Hutchinson's full discussion of Wordsworth's use of this word.

UPON THE SIGHT OF A BEAUTIFUL PICTURE.

Written in 1811 at the Parsonage, Grasmere; published in 1815. The picture is one of Bredon Hill and Cloud Hill near Coleorton; the images of the smoke and the travellers are taken from it. "The rest," Wordsworth wrote to Sir G. Beaumont, "were added in order to place the thought in a clear point of view, and for the sake of variety." During the later part of Wordsworth's residence at the Parsonage he lost two children. "Our sorrow," he says, "upon these events often brought the sonnet to my mind, and cast me upon the support to which the last line of it gives expression, — 'The appropriate calm of blest eternity.'"

9. Before 1838 "Art" was not personified, "which," not "whom," occurring in the line.

14. Appropriate calm, etc., the calm belonging, as an attribute, to Eternity.

"SURPRISED BY JOY," etc.

"This sonnet was," says Wordsworth, "suggested by my daughter Catherine long after her death. Catherine Wordsworth died on June 4, 1812, in her fourth year. The sonnet was published in 1815. The poem "Characteristics of a Child Three Years Old" was suggested by Catherine in 1811. Dorothy Wordsworth describes her as "comical in every look and motion."

2. Turned: an improvement — like the next — of 1820. In 1815, "wished."

3. Deep buried: in 1815, "long buried."

11, 12. Wordsworth was away from home when Catherine died.

"HAIL, TWILIGHT," etc.

This sonnet is of uncertain date; first published, 1815. It is probably later than 1807. The text is unchanged, except that "flood" in l. 13 replaced in 1837 "floods."

"I WATCH AND LONG HAVE WATCHED," etc.

Written probably between 1815 and the date of publication, 1819. This sonnet was omitted from one edition — that of 1827 — possibly because Wordsworth then believed that its desponding close was alien from the higher spirit of poetry; but he knew that it was the true expression of a mood of his mind and restored it in 1832. " Suggested," he says, "in front of Rydal Mount, the rocky parapet being the summit of Longhrigg Fell opposite. Not once only, but a hundred times, have the feelings of the sonnet been awakened by the same objects seen from the same place."

7–9. Before 1837 :

> He burns, transmuted to a sullen fire
> That droops and dwindles ; and, the appointed debt
> To the flying moments paid, is seen no more.

The words "sullen fire" are of interest to the student of Wordsworth in connection with another sonnet, — that beginning "Even as a dragon's eye," — where a cottage taper amid the mountains is compared to a sepulchral lamp "sullenly glaring " ; in all editions (except 1838) from 1827 to 1849 this is printed "suddenly glaring," and so in posthumous editions except that in the Aldine Series ; but "sullenly " is right and may be compared with a "sullen star " in "The Excursion," Bk. iv, and the expression "sullen light," of a blown-out candle with smouldering wick, which is found in Wordsworth's prose.

11. Before 1837 : " glory, pitiably decline."

See the sonnet "After-Thought," p. 332, as showing one of Wordsworth's thoughts of resistance to such despondency as is expressed here.

TO B. R. HAYDON.

This sonnet was written in December, 1815, and was published by Haydon (with two other sonnets) in Leigh Hunt's Journal, _The Examiner_, March 31, 1816; again published by Wordsworth in the same year. The text is unchanged. Benjamin Robert Haydon, the painter, born in 1786, painted the portrait of Wordsworth on Helvellyn, and introduced his portrait among the figures of "Christ's Entry into Jerusalem." His want of success caused Haydon's mind to give way, and on June 20, 1846, he shot himself in his studio before an unfinished picture. In a letter to Wordsworth of Nov. 27, 1815, he expressed the "highest enthusiasm " for Wordsworth's genius, and wrote of himself : "I will bear want, pain, misery, and blindness, but I will never yield one step I have gained on the road I am determined to travel over."

NOVEMBER 1.

Written in December, 1815; published, 1816. "Suggested," says Wordsworth, "on the banks of the Brathay by the sight of Langdale Pikes."

3. In 1816: "Which, strewn with snow as pure as Heaven can shed"; in 1832: "snow smooth as the heaven can shed." The final text is that of 1837.

A characteristic of the snow-clad mountains, not brought out in this sonnet, is dealt with in Wordsworth's "Guide to the Lakes,"—the varieties of colour in various lights and shadows, which takes away from the monotony of snow.

"SOLE LISTENER, DUDDON!" etc.

No. V of "The River Duddon" sonnets. This series was written at intervals during many years and was published in 1820. The text is unchanged. "The Duddon rises on Wrynose Fell, near to the 'Three-Shire Stone,' where Westmoreland, Cumberland, and Lancashire meet" (H. Rix, in Knight's "Wordsworth"). This sonnet is "generally taken to be descriptive of Cockley Beck. Here, as we emerge from Wrynose Bottom, the first trees meet the eye, after a full two miles of monotony and stones, and here, too, is the first cottage." The cottage is not now surrounded by "sheltering pines," but Mr. Rix, from whom I quote, ascertained (*The Athenæum*, July 18, 1891, p. 98) from natives of the valley that the pines had been there within living memory.

On the Duddon sonnets, see "Wordsworth and the Duddon," in "Holiday Studies of Wordsworth," by Rev. F. A. Malleson (Cassell & Co., 1890).

THE PLAIN OF DONNERDALE.

This is No. XX of "The River Duddon" series. The text is unchanged. Donnerdale, says Mr. Rix (in Knight's "Wordsworth") is strictly "the district on the east bank of the Duddon from Broughton up to Ulpha Bridge, and extending thence parallel by Seathwaite, from which it is divided by fells."

14. **Thyrsus:** Gr. θύρσος, a staff or spear wrapped with ivy and vine branches. The Bacchanals bore thyrsi when celebrating the orgies of Bacchus.

"RETURN, CONTENT!" etc.

No. XXVI of "The River Duddon" series. See note on "Sole Listener, Duddon!" The only variation of text is in l. 7, where the "Sonnets" volume of 1838 — and this alone — reads, " Sparkling like salt-sea billows."

8. Choral multitude. This expression, applied to streams, is of interest to the student of Wordsworth as helping to fix the text in a line of the poem, "To —— on her First Ascent to the Summit of Helvellyn":

> Thine are all the choral fountains
> Warbling in each sparry vault
> Of the untrodden lunar mountains;

" Choral " appears in 1820 and 1827 ; " coral " in all later editions (except that in the Aldine series). I cannot doubt that " choral " is the true reading.

AFTER–THOUGHT.

The concluding sonnet of " The River Duddon " series.

5. Happily, Wordsworth in this line returned in 1840 to the text as found in the first form of 1820 (" The River Duddon " volume). In " Miscellaneous Poems," 1820, and all other editions before 1840: " Still glides the stream and shall not cease to glide."

14. Wordsworth quotes as a parallel Milton's " And feel that I am happier than I know " (" Paradise Lost," VIII, 282), and he adds : " The allusion to the Greek poet will be obvious to the classical reader." He refers here to l. 103 in the " Lament of Bion ":

> ἄμμες δ' οἱ μεγάλοι καὶ καρτεροὶ ἢ σοφοὶ ἄνδρες

of which the line of the sonnet, " While we, the brave, the mighty, and the wise," is a reminiscence.

BETWEEN NAMUR AND LIEGE.

No. VI of " Memorials of a Tour on the Continent, 1820 "; probably written in 1821 ; published in 1822. The text is unchanged. In the *Fenwick note* Wordsworth says : " The scenery on the Meuse pleases me more, upon the whole, than that of the Rhine, though the river itself is much inferior in grandeur. The rocks, both in form and colour, especially between Namur and Liege, surpass any upon the Rhine, though they are in many places disfigured by quarries, whence stones were taken for the new fortifications." Professor Knight, in Wordsworth's "Poetical Works," vol. VI, gives extracts from Mary Wordsworth's Journal of this tour, and in the "Life of Wordsworth," vol. III, extracts from Dorothy's Journal.

THE MONUMENT COMMONLY CALLED LONG MEG AND HER DAUGHTERS.

First published in "A Description of the Scenery of the Lakes," 1822; probably written in 1821. In a letter to Sir G. Beaumont, Jan. 6, 1821, Wordsworth tells how his road suddenly brought him into presence of Long Meg and her Daughters : "Next to Stonehenge it is, beyond dispute, the most noble relic of the kind that this or probably any other country contains." It is situated six miles northeast of Penrith, in the lake district. Wordsworth's note on the sonnet is the following : "The daughters of Long Meg, placed in a perfect circle eighty yards in diameter, are seventy-two in number above ground ; a little way out of the circle stands Long Meg herself, a single stone, eighteen feet high. When I first saw this monument, as I came upon it by surprise, I might overrate its importance as an object; but though it will not bear a comparison with Stonehenge, I must say I have not seen any other relique of those dark ages which can pretend to rival it in singularity and dignity of appearance."

4. Before 1837 : "When first I saw that Sisterhood forlorn."

5. In 1822 : "And Her, whose strength and stature seem to scorn." "Seem" is feeble, and ed. 1827 reads, "And Her, whose massy strength and stature scorn." The present text is of 1837.

12. In 1827 : "Thy progeny, in hieroglyphic round." The present text is of 1837. In 1822, ll. 11–13 were less imaginative :

> When, how, and wherefore, rose on British ground
> That wondrous Monument, whose mystic round
> Forth shadows, some have deemed, to mortal sight.

SECLUSION.

This and the following sonnet are XXI and XXII, part I, of "Ecclesiastical Sonnets "; probably written in 1821 ; published in 1822.

12. **Strictures serpentine,** serpentine compressions. It is curious

to note how Wordsworth's diction became Latinized in describing a somewhat similar phenomenon in " Yew-Trees," ll. 17, 18 :

> Of intertwisted fibres serpentine
> Up-coiling, and inveterately convolved;

13. Before 1837 : " Yet, while they strangle without mercy, bring." There was a certain paradox in mercilessness and bringing recompense, which the later text removed.

CONTINUED.

7. Sylvan : before 1837, " forest."
9. Before 1827 : " Perchance would throng my dreams."
13. Thorp, village or hamlet. **Vill,** a manor or a farm.

RURAL CEREMONY.

This is sonnet XXXII, part III, of " Ecclesiastical Sonnets." It was published in 1822 and probably was written in 1821. The ceremony, as Wordsworth's note informs the reader, " is still continued in many churches in Westmoreland. It takes place in the month of July, when the floor of the stalls is strewn with fresh rushes, and hence it is called the ' Rush-bearing.' "

We print the sonnet from the text of 1827, which detaches itself better than the earlier or later forms from the sequence of sonnets. Originally it followed " Catechizing," and the opening was :

> With smiles each happy face was overspread,
> That trial ended. Give we to a day

In 1845 it followed a number of sonnets suggested by portions of the Church Service, and the opening was :

> Closing the sacred Book which long has fed
> Our meditations, give we to a day

In 1827 it followed " Sacrament."
3. Annual : in 1822, " festal."
13, 14. Hooker and Laud are named on account of their respect for rites and ceremony.

MUTABILITY.

This is No. XXXIV of part III of "Ecclesiastical Sonnets"; it was probably written in 1821 and was published in 1822. A preceding sonnet of the series expresses regret for the decay of graceful rites and usages connected with the Church, and one which follows treats gently of the fall of the old Abbeys.

The only textual change deserving notice is that "his" in 1837 replaced "its" in l. 12.

14. The touch of Time so imperceptibly fine that it cannot even be brought before the imagination.

INSIDE OF KING'S COLLEGE CHAPEL.

In December, 1820, Wordsworth visited Cambridge, and certainly wrote one sonnet on that occasion; perhaps the three suggested by King's College Chapel belong to that date; they were published among the "Ecclesiastical Sonnets" in 1822. The text is unchanged. King's College was founded by King Henry VI, and there is good ground for believing that he laid in person the first stone of the Chapel. Fuller writes: "The Chapel is one of the rarest fabrics in Christendom, wherein the stonework, woodwork, and glasswork contend which most deserve admiration. Yet the first generally carries away the credit (as being a Stonehenge indeed), so geometrically contrived that voluminous stones mutually support themselves in the arched roof, as if Art had made them to forget Nature, and weaned them from their fondness to descend to their centre." Mr. Ruskin is far from being so enthusiastic.

THE SAME.

2-4. In 1822 (only):

> Their portraiture the lateral windows hide,
> Glimmers their corresponding stone-work, dyed
> With the soft

CONTINUED.

The text is unchanged.

8. That younger Pile, St. Paul's Cathedral, London.

12-14. St. Paul's is less crowded with illustrious dead than Westminster Abbey.

A PARSONAGE IN OXFORDSHIRE.

Written in 1820 and published in a note in " Ecclesiastical Sketches,"
1822. Wordsworth was engaged upon this sonnet at Bruges in July,
1820. The Parsonage was that of his friend the Rev. R. Jones, to
whom he dedicated " Descriptive Sketches."

11, 12. In 1822 (only):

> Meanwhile between these Poplars, as they wave
> Their lofty summits, comes and goes a sky

"A VOLANT TRIBE OF BARDS," etc.

Probably written between 1820 and 1823; first published in 1823 in
Joanna Baillie's " A Collection of Poems chiefly MS. and from living
Authors."

1. **Volant,** flying, light and nimble, here with a touch of irony.

3. **" Coignes of vantage "** from " Macbeth," I, 6, 7, a corner that
may be taken advantage of.

In Joanna Baillie's " Collection " (only) ll. 4–10 run thus:

> Work cunningly devised, and seeming sound;
> But quickly from its airy hold unbound
> By its own weight, or washed or blown away
> With silent, imperceptible decay.
> If man must build admit him to thy ground,
> O Truth! to work within the eternal ring,
> When the stars shine,

In l. 12 also " when " is found in 1823.

"NOT LOVE, NOT WAR," etc.

The date is uncertain; first published in 1823 in Joanna Baillie's
" A Collection of Poems chiefly MS. and from living Authors." The
only changes of text which require notice are the following.

7, 8. Before 1837:

> Watching the blue smoke of the elmy grange
> Skyward ascending from the twilight dell.

In 1838 (only) " hut " stood in place of " cot."

12. **Diaphanous:** Gr. διαφανής, transparent, translucent.

13. Charm: in 1823, "please." "Charm" (Lat., *carmen*, a song) has a special appropriateness to music.

Observe the succession of double rhymes in the sextet.

TO [LADY FITZGERALD], IN HER SEVENTIETH YEAR.

The date is probably 1824; published in 1827. The text is unchanged (except "toward," in l. 11, substituted for "towards " in 1832). The "Lady bright " was Lady Fitzgerald, as described to Wordsworth by Lady Beaumont. Professor Knight prints an earlier version, sent by Mary Wordsworth to Lady Beaumont, Dec. 9, 1824 :

> Lady, what delicate graces may unite
> In age — so often comfortless and bleak !
> Though from thy unenfeebled eye-balls break
> Those saintly emanations of delight,
> A snow-drop let me name thee; pure, chaste, white,
> Too pure for flesh and blood ; with smooth, blanch'd cheek,
> And head that droops because the soul is meek,
> And not that Time presses with weary weight.
> Hope, Love, and Joy are with thee fresh as fair ;
> A Child of Winter prompting thoughts that climb
> From desolation towards the genial prime :
> Or, like the moon, conquering the misty air
> And filling more and more with chrystal light,
> As pensive evening deepens into night.

The gain in the sonnet as printed in 1827 is remarkable.

"SCORN NOT THE SONNET," etc.

This sonnet, composed almost extempore in a short walk on the western side of Rydal Lake, is of uncertain date ; probably, however, after 1820, and certainly not later than 1827, when it was published.

The only textual change is a transposition of words in l. 6 ; before 1837, " Camoëns soothed with it."

1, 2. Through the earlier part of the 18th century the sonnet was not in favour. Johnson, who carried on this feeling, wrote that the fabric of a sonnet has never succeeded in our language; of the best of Milton's sonnets "it can only be said that they are not bad." " Milton, Madam," he said to Hannah More, " was a genius that could carve a Colossus from a rock, but could not carve heads upon cherry stones."

Wordsworth in l. 12 refers more especially to Milton's political sonnets, which first inspired his own.

2, 3. Shakspeare. In Wordsworth's " Essay, Supplementary to the Preface " to " Lyrical Ballads," he speaks of the sonnets of Shakspeare as expressing " his own feelings in his own person." Robert Browning, in the poem " House," writes :

> ' *With this same key,*
> *Shakespeare unlocked his heart,*' once more!
> Did Shakespeare ? If so, the less Shakespeare he !

4. Petrarch's wound. The sonnets suggested by Laura are meant, especially those written after her death.

5. Tasso. Tasso's sonnets are not of the highest order. Some were inspired by his love of Leonora, some by the sufferings of his life.

6. Camoëns was banished from Lisbon partly on the ground of his passion for the golden-haired Donna Caterina. At Goa he heard of her death, and laments her in his " Rimas."

8. Dante. Many of Dante's sonnets will be found in the " Vita Nuova," translated by Dante Rossetti.

10. Spenser. Spenser's sonnets tell the story of his love for Elizabeth Boyle, who became his wife.

TO ROTHA QUILLINAN.

The date of the sonnet is unknown; it probably lies between 1820 and 1827, when it was published. The text is unchanged. Rotha was the daughter of Edward Quillinan (afterwards married to Wordsworth's daughter) by his first wife. Southey's beautiful lines written in Rotha Quillinan's album may be compared.

"IN MY MIND'S EYE," etc.

The date is uncertain ; probably between 1820 and 1827, when it was published. The text is unchanged.

2. Invidious, envious, malignant, hostile.

ON THE DEPARTURE OF SIR WALTER SCOTT FROM ABBOTSFORD FOR NAPLES.

Written in 1831, a day or two after Wordsworth left Abbotsford, and published in the " Literary Souvenir " for 1833; and again in

"Yarrow Revisited and other Poems," 1835. The text remains unchanged.

For the occasion which suggested this sonnet, see note to "Yarrow Revisited."

13.   **The midland sea,** the Mediterranean.

14.   **Parthenope,** the classical name for Naples, from the siren Parthenope. Her tomb was there shown, and a torch-race was held every year in her honour.

THE TROSSACHS.

This is No. VI of the "Yarrow Revisited" series, 1831; published in 1835. "The sentiment that runs through this sonnet," Wordsworth says, "was natural to the season in which I again saw this beautiful spot; but this and some other sonnets that follow were coloured by the remembrance of my recent visit to Sir Walter Scott, and the melancholy errand on which he was going [*i.e.*, to Italy in broken health]."

The text is unchanged, except that "which" in l. 5 in 1837 replaced "that," and in l. 13 "That" at the same time replaced "This."

"THE PIBROCH'S NOTE," etc.

No. VII of the "Yarrow Revisited" series, composed during a tour in the autumn of 1831; published in 1835. The only textual changes are the substitution in 1845 of "And of" in l. 9 for the earlier "And some," and the personifying of imagination at the same date by "she" in l. 13 replacing "it."

1.   **Pibroch,** either the series of variations played on the bagpipe, or used, as by Byron in "Lachin Gair," for the bagpipe itself.

EAGLES.

No. IX of the "Yarrow Revisited" series; written in 1831, published in 1835. In the autumn of 1829 Wordsworth visited Ireland; this sonnet contains a reminiscence in his verse of the Irish tour, in its reference to the eagle which he saw on the wing (l. 5) off the promontory of Fairhead, County Antrim. He travelled through Ireland in October, when the days were short, and with speed, in a carriage and four, to which circumstances, he says, "may be ascribed this want of notices, in my verse, of a country so interesting." His spirits and imagination also were depressed by the sight of Irish misery.

12.   Before 1845: "In spirit for a moment he resumes."

HIGHLAND HUT.

Written in 1831, the year of Wordsworth's visit to Abbotsford and of "Yarrow Revisited"; published in 1835. The text is unchanged.

TO THE PLANET VENUS, AN EVENING STAR.

No. XVII of the "Yarrow Revisited" series; written in 1831, published in 1835. The text is unchanged.

1. **Orient,** rising.
12. **This seat of care,** the earth.

ROMAN ANTIQUITIES.

No. XXV of the "Yarrow Revisited" series; written in 1831, published in 1835. The text was not altered, except one word, "tenacious" in l. 10, which in 1837 replaced "insatiate."

12. **Fibulæ** (Lat.), buckles, clasps.
14. **Lacrymals,** vessels intended to contain tears.

TO THE AUTHOR'S PORTRAIT.

The portrait was painted in 1832 and now hangs in the Hall of St. John's College; an autograph copy of the sonnet is in the Library. The sonnet was probably then written; it was published in 1835. Pickersgill's portrait, which fails to give the strength of Wordsworth's countenance, has been frequently engraved. "The last six lines," Wordsworth said, "are not written for poetical effect, but as a matter of fact, which, in more than one instance, could not escape my notice in the servants of the house." The text is unchanged except that "And," l. 8, replaced in 1837 "To."

2. Wordsworth's College, St. John's, Cambridge, was founded by the Lady Margaret, Countess of Richmond and Derby, mother of King Henry VII. She died June 29, 1509; the College was begun in or about 1511 and was formally opened by Bishop Fisher in 1516.

IN SIGHT OF THE TOWN OF COCKERMOUTH.

This is one of the poems composed or suggested during a tour in the summer of 1833; it was published in 1835. The text is unchanged.

MARY QUEEN OF SCOTS.

One of the poems composed or suggested during a tour in the summer of 1833 ; published in 1835. Mary escaped from her imprisonment at Lochleven May 2, 1568. On May 16 she crossed the Solway in a fishing boat to Workington in Cumberland ; thence she was conducted with many marks of respect to Carlisle.

3, 4. In 1835 :

> And to the throng how touchingly she bowed
> That hailed her landing on the Cumbrian shore;

Altered in 1837 to bring "throng" and "that" into closer connection.

5. Before 1840 : "Bright as a Star (that, from a sombre cloud," except "Sonnets," 1838, which reads, "And like a Star (that, from a sombre cloud." In four instances where he had used the word "sombre" or "sombrous" in early texts, Wordsworth found substitutes, apparently reserving it for the meaning "affording shade" and not using it in the sense of "dark" or "dusky." Over and over again, Wordsworth, as he mentions in the *Fenwick note*, paused at the sight of what he here describes, seen among the Scotch firs near Ambleside, and particularly those near Green Bank.

9. Saturnian. Saturn is generally identified with the Greek Kronos (Time), and is often represented as an old man bent through age, holding in his right hand a scythe.

"DESIRE WE PAST ILLUSIONS TO RECALL?"

No. XIV of poems composed or suggested during a tour in the summer of 1833. It sets forth more clearly, perhaps, than anything else that Wordsworth has written his view of modern science and its limitations.

12. In 1835 (only) : "Of Power, whose ministering Spirits records keep"; altered, perhaps, on account of the excess of elision in "power," "ministering," and "spirits."

BY THE SEASHORE, ISLE OF MAN.

No. XVI of the poems composed or suggested during a tour in the summer of 1833. The text is unchanged.

"'THERE!' SAID A STRIPLING,", etc.

One of the poems composed or suggested during a tour in the summer of 1833; published in 1835. The text is unchanged. Wordsworth's *Fenwick note* is interesting in its criticism of Burns and may be given in full: "Mossgiel was thus pointed out to me by a young man on the top of the coach on my way from Glasgow to Kilmarnock. It is remarkable that, though Burns lived some time here, and during much the most productive period of his poetical life, he nowhere adverts to the splendid prospects stretching towards the sea and bounded by the peaks of Arran on one part, which in clear weather he must have had daily before his eyes. In one of his poetical effusions he speaks of describing 'fair Nature's face' as a privilege on which he sets a high value; nevertheless, natural appearances rarely take a lead in his poetry. It is as a human being, eminently sensitive and intelligent, and not as a poet, clad in his priestly robes and carrying the ensigns of sacerdotal office, that he interests and affects us. Whether he speaks of rivers, hills, and woods, it is not so much on account of the properties with which they are absolutely endowed, as relatively to local patriotic remembrances and associations, or as they ministered to personal feelings, especially those of love, whether happy or otherwise; — yet it is not always so. Soon after we had passed Mossgiel Farm we crossed the Ayr, murmuring and winding through a narrow woody hollow. His line — 'Auld hermit Ayr strays through his woods' — came at once to my mind with Irwin, Lugar, Ayr, and Doon, — Ayrshire streams over which he breathes a sigh as being unnamed in song; and surely his own attempts to make them known were as successful as his heart could desire."

4. **The Daisy.** See Burns's "To a Mountain Daisy," written "on turning one up with the plough."

6. **Arran,** a mountainous island, off the coast of Ayrshire.

9. **Bield,** shelter. The quotation is from Burns's "To a Mountain Daisy."

"TRANQUILLITY! THE SOVEREIGN AIM," etc.

One of the poems composed or suggested during a tour in the summer of 1833; published in 1835. It was suggested by a sonnet (which precedes it in the series) on the monument of Mrs. Howard by Nollekens in Wetheral Church, near Corby, on the banks of the Eden,

County Cumberland. The monument, which Wordsworth had previously seen in the sculptor's studio, represents the mother dying, her dead infant upon her lap; the mother's head is raised heavenward, and one hand touches tenderly the child.

1, 2. "ἀταραξία was the aim of Stoic, Epicurean, and Sceptic alike." — Knight.

12. That Idea, the idea of the Infinite.

"MOST SWEET IT IS," etc.

One of the poems composed or suggested during a tour in the summer of 1833; published in 1835. The text is unchanged.

10. Commerce, intercourse or converse, as in "The Prelude," Bk. xiv. 354:

> We sank
> Each into commerce with his private thoughts.

COMPOSED ON A MAY MORNING.

This sonnet was written in 1838 and was published in the volume of "Sonnets" of the same year. The text is unchanged.

"A POET!—HE HATH PUT," etc.

It is unknown when this sonnet was written; perhaps between 1838, when a collected volume of "Sonnets" appeared, and 1842 when it was first published. Wordsworth says that he was impelled to write it by "the disgusting frequency with which the word 'artistical,' imported with other impertinances from the Germans, is employed by writers of the present day; for artistical let them substitute artificial, and the poetry written on this system, both at home and abroad, will be for the most part much better characterized." The text is unchanged. The converse truth to Wordsworth is expressed by Burke when he writes, "Art is man's Nature," and by Shakespeare in "The Winter's Tale," IV, 4:

> ... this is an art
> Which does mend nature, change it rather, but
> The art itself is nature.

THE PINE OF MONTE MARIO AT ROME.

One of the " Memorials of a Tour in Italy, 1837 "; probably written in 1840 or 1841 ; published in 1842. The text is unchanged. When the sun had just set on Apr. 26, 1837, two hours after entering Rome, Wordsworth and Crabb Robinson walked to the Pincian Hill. The sculptor Theed informed them that the pine-tree had been rescued by the artist Sir George Beaumont, Wordsworth's dead friend, who paid a sum of money on the condition that the proprietor would not cut it down. Later Wordsworth ascended the Monte Mario and could not resist embracing the tree-trunk. " I could almost have kissed it," he wrote home, " out of love for his memory."

TO A PAINTER AND ON THE SAME SUBJECT.

Written in 1840, when Miss Margaret Gillies, staying at Rydal Mount, painted portraits of Mary Wordsworth and of her husband the poet; published in 1842. The text is unchanged. Wordsworth wrote to his daughter, Apr. 7, 1840 : " Dearest Dora, your mother tells me she shrinks from copies being spread of those sonnets ; she does not wish one, at any rate, to be given to Miss Gillies, for that, without blame to Miss Gillies, would be like advertising them. I assure you her modesty and humble-mindedness were so much shocked, that I doubt if she had more pleasure than pain from these compositions, though I never poured out anything more truly from the heart."

" WANSFELL! THIS HOUSEHOLD," etc.

Dated by Wordsworth Dec. 24, 1842; first published in 1845. Text unchanged.

INDEX OF FIRST LINES.